E184.54674 2001
E449.F772008
F152.F8652004

"Rememb'ring our Time
and Work is the Lords"

The Pennsylvania History and Culture Series
Susquehanna University Press

The Pennsylvania History and Culture Series is dedicated to publishing books that explore the state's rich heritage. From social, literary, economic, political, environmental, and religious perspectives, the series seeks to piece together Pennsylvania's past and delve into its future. From cookbooks to cultural analyses of Pennsylvania's legal history, we welcome all submissions.

Titles in This Series

M. Ruth Kelly, *The Olmsted Case: Privateers, Property, and Politics in Pennsylvania, 1778–1810*

Karen Guenther, *"Rememb'ring our Time and Work is the Lords": The Experiences of Quakers on the Eighteenth-Century Pennsylvania Frontier*

"Rememb'ring our Time and Work is the Lords"

The Experiences of Quakers on the Eighteenth-Century Pennsylvania Frontier

Karen Guenther

SUP

Selinsgrove: Susquehanna University Press

Associated Unviersity Presses
2010 Eastpark Boulevard
Cranbury, NJ 08512

The paper used in this publication meets the requirements of the American National Standard for Permanence of Paper for Printed Library Materials Z39.48–1984.

Library of Congress Cataloging-in-Publication Data

Guenther, Karen, 1959–
   "Rememb'ring our time and work is the Lords" : the experiences of Quakers on the eighteeenth-century Pennsylvania frontier / Karen Guenther.
      p. cm. — (The Pennsylvania history and culture series)
   Includes bibliographical references and index.
   ISBN 1-57591-093-4 (alk. paper)
1. Quakers—Pennsylvania—Berks County—History—18th century. 2. Pioneers—Pennsylvania—Berks County—History—18th century. 3. Quakers—Pennsylvania—Berks County—Social conditions—18th century. 4. Frontier and pioneer life—Pennsylvania—Berks County. 5. Berks County (Pa.)—History—18th century. 6. Pennsylvania—History—Colonial period, ca. 1600–1775. 7. Exeter Monthly Meeting (Society of Friends : 1742–1829) 8. Berks County (Pa.)—Church history—18th century. 9. Berks County (Pa.)—Religious life and customs. I. Title: Remembering our time and work is the Lords. II. Title. III. Series.

F157.B3G84   2005
974.8′1602—dc22

                                                                                    2005010854

Contents

List of Maps and Tables

Maps

Tables

Acknowledgments

No WORK OF HISTORY IS WRITTEN WITHOUT ANY OUTSIDE ASSISTANCE, and this is especially true for this book. First and foremost, I would like to acknowledge the contributions of the clerks of Exeter Monthly Meeting during the eighteenth century, who kept detailed minutes of the meeting, certificates of removal, and other records that made this study possible. The staffs of the Friends Historical Library at Swarthmore College, Quaker Collection at Haverford College, Historical Society of Berks County in Reading, Recorder of Deeds and Register of Wills offices at the Berks County Court House in Reading, General Manuscript Division of the Historical Society of Pennsylvania in Philadelphia, Pennsylvania State Archives at the Pennsylvania Historical and Museum Commission in Harrisburg, Archives of the Moravian Church in Bethlehem, Evangelical and Reformed Historical Society at Lancaster Theological Seminary, Lutheran Archives Center at Philadelphia, Schwenkfelder Library in Pennsburg, Clayton Library for Genealogical Research in Houston, and Balch Institute for Ethnic Studies in Philadelphia all graciously permitted me to use their resources while preparing this study. The Houston, Texas East Stake branch of the Genealogical Library of the Church of Jesus Christ of Latter-day Saints assisted me in the acquisition of microfilm copies of the minutes and records of Exeter Monthly Meeting, along with tax lists, wills, deeds, and other sundry genealogical materials. In addition, the interlibrary loan staffs of Pattee Library at The Pennsylvania State University, Houston Public Library, M. D. Anderson Library at the University of Houston, and Mansfield University all provided me with the necessary secondary literature to complete this book.

Several individuals merit special recognition for the assistance they have provided me. Christopher Fritsch provided insight into the legal culture of colonial Pennsylvania. Dr. Kenneth L. Cook, current recording clerk of Exeter Monthly Meeting, served as a sounding board and helped me understand the inner workings of Quaker society. James A. Lewars, site manager at Daniel Boone Homestead, hired me to work one summer as an intern and allowed me to understand, experience, and research the lifestyle

9

of Berks County's early pioneers. Research assistance was provided by Barbara Gill, Librarian and Archivist at the Historical Society of Berks County, and by Dr. Kenneth L. Cook of Exeter Monthly Meeting. Dr. J. William Frost, Director of the Friends Historical Library, made suggestions on the methodology of writing about Quakers. Dr. John B. Frantz made occasional suggestions on how to improve the final product, even though it was no longer his job. Emma Lapsansky of Haverford College and Robert Sayre of Millersville University made recommendations while reviewing the manuscript for Susquehanna University Press. Dr. Roland M. Baumann of Oberlin College, Dr. Rachana Sachdev, Director of the Susquehanna University Press, and Sarah Bailey, Managing Editor of Susquehanna University Press, assisted in seeing this book through the proposal and review process. Christine A. Retz and the staff at Associated University Presses oversaw the project through the publication process. Finally, preliminary versions of chapters 2, 4, 5, 8, 9, and 10 were presented as class assignments for research seminars at the University of Houston; the graduate students in these classes deserve mention for their recommendations to improve the final product.

Academic assistance is yet another matter. Professor Harry S. Stout, formerly of The University of Connecticut and currently at Yale University, and Professor Gerald J. Goodwin at the University of Houston provided exceptional training in American religious history. Professor Cheryll Cody at the University of Houston helped in the understanding and application of quantitative methods. Professors Karen Ordahl Kupperman, A. William Hoglund, and R. Kent Newmyer at The University of Connecticut made suggestions during the project's infant stages. At the University of Houston, Professors Gerald J. Goodwin and Steven Mintz of the Department of History and Professor E. Lynn Mitchell, Jr., Coordinator of Religious Studies, graciously served on my dissertation committee and commented on the earliest version of this manuscript. Professors John W. Dahmus and Allen Richman at Stephen F. Austin State University and John B. Frantz at The Pennsylvania State University deserve special thanks for encouraging me to complete my degree in the face of adversity.

Previous versions of chapters 2, 3, 4, 5, 7, and 9 were presented at annual meetings of the Pennsylvania Historical Association (2), of the Southwestern Historical Association (3, 7) and at a Phi Alpha Theta Regional Meeting (9) and an International Convention (4, 5). In addition, preliminary drafts of chapter 3 appeared in the April 1990 issue of *Pennsylvania History,* of chapter 5 in the Fall 2001 issue of *Quaker History,* and of chapter 7 in the Fall 2003 issue of *Pennsylvania History.* Financial assistance for dissertation research came from Phi Alpha Theta in the form of a Donald B. Hoffman Graduate Scholarship Award and from the University of Houston through a Murry Miller Scholarship.

Finally, I would be remiss in not acknowledging the assistance of three people without whose help the dissertation—and thus this book—would never have been written. My parents, Donald Guenther of Houston, Texas, and Faye Guenther of Mansfield, Pennsylvania, provided me with a home to live in and a room to clutter while completing the PhD. On the academic front, Professor James Kirby Martin at the University of Houston proved to be an invaluable dissertation advisor. Not many faculty members would be as willing as he was to assist on a topic that was not close to their own research interests, yet he has continued to amaze me with his insight into Quaker history. Although I did have considerable training as an historian prior to my arrival at the University of Houston, through his time, guidance, criticism, and concern, I developed into a more polished scholar, and I will be eternally grateful for his assistance.

"Rememb'ring our Time
and Work is the Lords"

1

Introduction:
The Origins of Exeter Monthly Meeting

PENNSYLVANIA'S ROLE IN THE DEVELOPMENT OF AMERICAN CULTURE and society has received an increasing amount of attention throughout the past quarter century, as the tercentenary celebrations of the founding of the province led to a reexamination of the colony and state's contributions to the ethnic and religious diversity of modern America. With increasing pluralism, however, the religious group that was most prominent in the establishment of the province—the Society of Friends, or Quakers—declined in its impact and importance. This book, by focusing on the activities of Exeter Monthly Meeting of Friends, based in Berks County, Pennsylvania, will examine how changes in the world around them affected backcountry Quakers.

❧

Religion was the primary motive in the establishment of Pennsylvania. William Penn made sure that freedom of worship was not only a religious principle, but he guaranteed this right in the various frames of government drafted and adopted during the early years of the province. Owing to the appeal of religious freedom, Penn's colony attracted a broader diversity of settlers than any other. With this promise, too, Penn intended to prove that a multiplicity of religious groups could coexist, relatively peacefully, with the result that the province of Pennsylvania itself indeed became a model for the pluralistic future of the American nation.[1]

Key to the growth of Penn's colony were the beliefs of the Society of Friends. William Penn had converted to Quakerism while a student at Oxford, despite the opposition of his father, Admiral Sir William Penn. Preferring unstructured worship to ritual, the Quakers believed that God inspired all people directly through the "inner light." No minister or priest was necessary for a person to accept God's grace; religious faith was something that was personal and individual. Evolving from this rejection of religious authority was an emphasis on pacifism, a refusal to swear oaths, and a desire to live simple, uncomplicated lives. In addition, through

15

gainful employment Quakers would glorify and honor God; all occupations were useful and equal, regardless of wealth. Finally, unlike other religious faiths practiced in England (and on the continent) during the mid-seventeenth century, Quakers believed that both men and women were equal in the sight of God, and the only distinction in the meeting was over degree of piety, not gender or wealth.[2]

Shortly after arriving in Pennsylvania, members of the Society of Friends began to recreate the hierarchical organization that they had formed in England. Meetings for worship, also known as indulged or particular meetings, began in 1681 at Shackamaxon in Philadelphia County; during the next decade settlers formed at least twenty meetings in Bucks, Philadelphia, and Chester Counties. Preparative meetings, held each month by leaders of one or more indulged meetings prior to the monthly meeting to discuss business that would be presented for consideration at the monthly meeting, began in the same year, as did the first monthly meeting.[3]

Monthly meetings served as the local Quaker organization. According to Quaker practice, the primary purpose of the monthly meeting was to serve as a business meeting for all of the Quakers in a specific geographical area. Among the duties conducted by the business meeting were receiving new members, issuing certificates of marriage and removal, managing the financial affairs of the local meeting, ensuring the enforcement of Quaker discipline, promoting social control among its members, and maintaining correspondence with the regional organization (quarterly meeting) concerning the activity of the members of the various indulged meetings under its care. The correspondence usually involved responding to a series of queries posed by the quarterly meeting that enabled Friends an opportunity to consider and reflect upon individuals' conduct and the meetings' activities. Every three months each monthly meeting selected members to attend the quarterly meeting, and once a year representatives from the quarterly meetings (located in each of the three original counties) gathered in Philadelphia with Friends from Delaware and New Jersey at Philadelphia Yearly Meeting.[4]

Within the monthly meeting structure there were four categories of leadership positions. Ministers were men and women whom the monthly meeting had recognized for their ability "to speak of the mercies and goodness" of God. They often traveled to other monthly meetings, encouraging Friends' piety and "proclaim[ing] the blessed doctrine of life and salvation." Elders were responsible for ensuring that Friends conducted the meetings for worship properly and assisted and supervised ministers with the spiritual guidance of members. Entrusted to the overseers was the welfare and behavior of the members of the preparative meetings; they informed the monthly meeting of violations of the discipline and of members' requests for assistance. Overseers also served on committees formed to investigate Friends' religious condition before preparing a certificate of removal (a document similar to a letter of transfer that attested to a member's status within the meeting). The final position, the clerk, "conduct[ed] all business sessions of the meeting" and prepared a complete and impartial record of the proceedings.[5]

In general, Quaker settlement was concentrated in the original three counties of Pennsylvania. Fewer than ten percent of the indulged meetings established by 1776 could be found outside this region. One of the monthly meetings along the Pennsylvania frontier was Exeter Monthly Meeting, located approximately fifty miles northwest of Philadelphia in present-day Berks County.

The first European inhabitants of the Pennsylvania backcountry were from the continent, in particular the Palatinate in southwest Germany, rather than the British Isles. Those British subjects who did venture into the interior were generally either late arrivals to the colony (i.e., post-1700) or younger sons who had little hope for advancement in the already crowded city of Philadelphia and the surrounding region. Unlike the founders of the province, those Quakers who settled in rural Pennsylvania experienced different pressures in trying to maintain their faith because of a greater opportunity and perhaps necessity to deviate from established discipline in order to adapt to the frontier environment.[6]

The European immigrants who settled in Berks County represented nearly every part of northern and western Europe and the British Isles and practiced almost every religious faith known to the Europeans. Among these early settlers were German, Danish, and Swedish Lutherans; French, Swiss, and German Reformed; Scots, Welsh, and English Anglicans; English, Welsh, and Irish Quakers; German and Irish Roman Catholics; English and Welsh Baptists; German Dunkards, Mennonites, Amish, New Born, Schwenkfelders, and Seventh-Day Baptists; English Methodists; and Moravians and Jews. By the end of the colonial period, these settlers had established at least seventy-eight distinct congregations.[7]

It was in this setting as an ethnic and religious minority that Exeter Monthly Meeting operated during the eighteenth century. Philadelphia Quarterly Meeting, the regional organization for Berks County Quakers, established Exeter out of Gwynedd Monthly Meeting in northwestern Philadelphia County to serve the needs of Friends along the northwestern frontier of Pennsylvania. From 1737 until 1789, when Philadelphia Quarterly Meeting created Robeson Monthly Meeting for the members of Exeter Monthly Meeting who resided south and west of the Schuylkill River, indulged meetings conducted at Exeter (1725), Maiden Creek (1735),

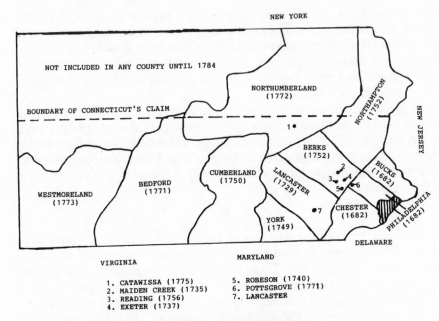

Map 1. Pennsylvania in 1780

Robeson (1741), Tulpehocken (1749–1758), Reading (by 1756), Potts-town (by 1771), Catawissa (1775), and Muncy (1788) were under the supervision of Exeter Monthly Meeting (See Map 1). In addition to these formally established meetings for worship, in the 1750s and 1760s the homes of Anthony Lee and Jacob Thomas served as locations for first-day meetings during the winter months for Friends residing in the outlying areas of Oley and near Pottstown.[8]

Exeter Monthly Meeting serves as an ideal case study to determine the impact of life in the backcountry on members of the Society of Friends. From 1737 until 1789 it was the only organization for Quakers who had settled in the Berks County area and beyond; by 1775 it included meetings for worship in the upper Susquehanna Valley, over one hundred miles away. Friends within the realm of Exeter Monthly Meeting had to confront matters the Quaker founders of the province could hardly have anticipated, such as surviving as a religious and ethnic minority and reconciling their pacifist beliefs with constant threats of Native American attacks. One response was an increasing rigidity in discipline that resulted in the expulsion of wayward members in the hopes of maintaining a more stable society. Some Quakers moved to other areas, either back east or to the south. In addition, members of the monthly meeting had to interact with neighbors of varied faiths and linguistic backgrounds. By studying the reaction of Exeter Friends to crises, whether they were an internal problem concerning exogamy (marriage outside the faith) or members "endeavouring to learn the art of war," this book will demonstrate that the demise of the Quaker oligarchy as social, economic, and political leaders as a result of political change in 1776 merely confirmed what had been occurring in the backcountry for over fifty years. At the same time, the story of Exeter Monthly Meeting will both reinforce and contradict traditional perceptions of the activities of members of the Society of Friends in William Penn's province.[9]

❧

The thrust of much of the earlier literature on the "rebirth" of colonial Pennsylvania history involved the concept that life in Pennsylvania and the other middle colonies most closely resembled the pluralistic conditions that would develop later in the United States. In particular, the economic, religious, and ethnic diversity of the region became characteristic of the new American nation. Economically, the country was not one of large plantations as in the southern colonies, but rather one of smaller landholdings with either subsistence or small-scale commercial agriculture. Industry also flourished in Pennsylvania, primarily shipbuilding in the Delaware Valley and ironmaking in the Schuylkill Valley of southeastern Pennsylvania. Furthermore, Philadelphia served as the cultural, economic, and political center of the new republic.[10]

The religious diversity characteristic of the Middle Colonies particularly served as a blueprint for the new nation. By permitting a wide variety of religious groups to settle in the region, the proprietors and, out of necessity, the British Crown proved that an established church was not necessary to maintain political stability. Accompanying this religious pluralism was a multiplicity of ethnic groups from continental Europe, the British Isles, and Africa who worked and lived together in a degree of harmony that became unique to America. Consequently, the assertion that the Middle Colonies, especially Pennsylvania, deserve greater emphasis in the history of colonial America is a valid one, for the region served as a model for what could be done—i.e., economic, religious, and ethnic diversity could occur without the warfare and strife that had been prevalent in Europe.[11]

Although the recent thrust of the historiography of colonial Pennsylvania has emphasized how the province represented a microcosm of modern America, the vast majority of the literature does not reflect this theme. The earliest histories of the colony concentrated on only one aspect of the religious diversity of the province, specifically the dominant role played by Quakers in its early history. Consistent with the emphasis on the importance of politics in the evolution of colonial society, the first specialized studies examined the history of Quaker political activity. By the 1960s, the social sciences contributed a new methodology to these political histories. According to one historian, private interests and personal goals affected the evolution of politics during the early years of the province; lofty ideals were largely rhetoric. Other studies employed the techniques of anthropologists to address the effect that role conflict played on the political milieu of colonial Pennsylvania and explored the impact of ethnicity on provincial politics.[12]

The "new social history" that saw the explosion of New England community studies in the early 1970s also affected the historiography of colonial Pennsylvania. James Lemon focused "on the interplay of society and land in early Pennsylvania" and "on the Pennsylvanians' attachment to the land," using Chester and Lancaster counties as his region of analysis. Over the course of the next two decades, historians wrote and published studies of life in at least six communities in colonial Pennsylvania—Carlisle (1994), Germantown (1976), Lancaster (1979, 1990), Paxton (1989), Reading (1978), and York (1985).[13]

Towns, however, were not the only local units examined; dissertations also appeared on New Garden Monthly Meeting in Chester County (1972) and on Middletown Monthly Meeting in Bucks County (1990). These two histories of Quaker meetings, however, were provincial in their efforts, as neither attempted to place the Quaker experience within the framework of the local society in which they lived. That these two meetings operated in areas of the province in which members of the Society of Friends were a sizable minority, if not a majority, of the population further demonstrated their irrelevance to the current themes of colonial Pennsylvania historiography.[14]

The existing monographs on Pennsylvania towns also have some deficiencies. In some instances, the authors attempted to provide demographic analysis to examine the ethnic and religious diversity of the province. These community studies, however, often neglected to address the impact that variety had on minority groups within the population.[15]

Surprisingly, the most recent works on the social history of colonial Pennsylvania have returned to the original three counties and consequently do not contribute significantly to the understanding of Pennsylvania's pluralism. A study of farm women between 1750 and 1850 used Chester County, Pennsylvania, and New Castle County, Delaware as the microcosm, a region in which the Society of Friends supplied the dominant culture. Philadelphia and Chester Counties served as the comparative regions in recent monographs on Quakers and slavery, marital unrest, and the experiences of widows. The most recent work on the Quaker family employed sophisticated quantitative methods, yet concentrated on Friends in Bucks and Chester Counties. As a result, the existing works neglected to examine conditions in the hinterland, where ethnic and religious diversity created an environment in which Friends faced constant threats to their faith.[16]

Recent works on colonial Pennsylvania have focused on the frontier experience, yet they concentrate on other groups besides the Society of Friends. In particular, the encounters between backcountry settlers and Native Americans have received particular attention, but these works only include mention of the Quakers as political leaders in the colony, not as pioneers confronting the same challenges as German and Scots-Irish immigrants. The main contribution of these books is that they all increase awareness of the tumultuous nature of frontier life during the eighteenth century, and they all clearly include Native Americans as actors rather than reactors as colonial settlements expanded into the interior.[17] This examination of a Quaker meeting in a backcountry county whose population was at least eighty percent German-speaking in origin will not only enhance the understanding of life along the early American frontier but also will demonstrate that, unlike most other minority religious groups in early America, the Quakers could adapt to and flourish in an unfamiliar and perhaps hostile environment.

The location of rivers, creeks, and mountains affected the settlement of Berks County and the development of Exeter Monthly Meeting. The most prominent feature is the Schuylkill River, which flows through the central and eastern sections of the county. Tributaries of the Schuylkill, most importantly Manatawny, Ontelaunee, and Tulpehocken Creeks, provide water and transportation routes for the eastern, northern, and western parts of the county, respectively. The Blue Mountains currently form the northern boundary of the county; during the eighteenth century these hills were a natural barrier between the European settlers and the Native Americans, as the county's boundaries extended northward toward the New York border.[18]

Morton L. Montgomery, a nineteenth-century historian of Berks County and author of the most complete one-volume history of the county, divided it into five geographic regions (see map 2). In the first region, which he called the "Manatawny Section," settlements sprang up along Manatawny Creek and spread throughout eastern Berks County. The following townships comprised the Manatawny Section: Amity (1719), Douglass (1736), Oley (1740), Exeter (1741), Colebrookdale (1741), Alsace (1744), Hereford (1753), Rockland (1758), District (1759), and Ruscombmanor (1759). Swedes were the earliest residents of this region, establishing a small settlement along the Schuylkill River in present-day Amity Township and organizing a church. Next came German and French settlers, who built homesteads farther north in the Oley Valley. English immigrants also migrated to this area; they were particularly active in the development of the iron industry in the region.[19]

The second section, "Ontelaunee," took its name from Ontelaunee or Maiden Creek, which drained the area. Located in northern Berks County, this section included Maxatawny (1742), Maiden Creek (1746), Albany (1752), Windsor (1752), Richmond (1755), Greenwich (1755), and Long-swamp (1761) townships. The earliest settlers in this region were members of the Society of Friends; the Germans who later entered this area migrated there from the Oley Hills. Unlike the Manatawny section, this region was predominantly agricultural in nature.[20]

Montgomery called southern Berks County the "Schuylkill Section" because all of the townships were south of that river. Predominantly settled by English and Welsh, this section included Robeson (1720), Caernarvon (1729), Cumru (1737), Brecknock (1741), and Union (1753) townships. Similar to the Manatawny section, this region included several iron planta-tions, in addition to family farms.[21]

German immigrants dominated western Berks County, the region called the "Tulpehocken Section," because Tulpehocken Creek flowed through the area. It included Tulpehocken (1729), Heidelberg (1734), Bern (1738), and Bethel (1739) townships. The earliest settlers in this section were predominantly German. Iron furnaces and forges flourished in this area, as did scattered family farms. During the 1750s, this region was especially susceptible to Native American raids because of its proximity to the Blue Mountains.[22]

Montgomery's final geographic division consisted solely of the town of Reading, county seat of Berks County. As early as 1733, agents of the Penn family sold parcels of land in the area. Several associates of the proprietor purchased additional property there in the early 1740s, but no significant settlement occurred until after the Penns reacquired the land and founded the town in 1748. At that time, approximately 1,000 people lived within the present county limits, although no towns or villages had yet been established. Within two years, Reading had increased in size from one to sixty houses; this rapid growth, along with other factors, encouraged the Assembly to create a new county in the region.[23]

Surprisingly, the first Europeans to settle in present-day Berks County were not from the persecuted regions of central Europe, but from a nation in which their church received government support. In 1701, several Swedes, led by the Reverend Andreas Rudman, petitioned William Penn for over 10,000 acres along the Schuylkill River near the mouth of Mana-

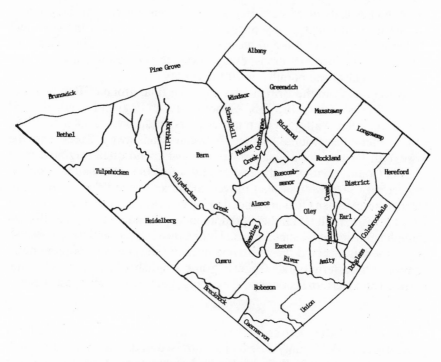

Map 2. Berks County in 1780

tawny Creek. Approximately fifty in number, these settlers soon made permanent settlements and started to farm the fertile soil of the region. By 1720, the community had become stable enough to build a church and obtain the services of a clergyman.[24]

Immigrants from central Europe were the second group to settle in the county. This group did not simply include German speakers; among these seekers of religious freedom were one Pole and several French Huguenots who had fled from their homeland to the Palatinate following the revocation of the Edict of Nantes in 1685. These settlers had arrived in the province through the port of Philadelphia, and from there they proceeded up the Schuylkill River. By 1720, enough immigrants had settled in the Oley Valley in eastern Berks County for the settlers to petition the court in Philadelphia for the establishment of a township in the region.[25]

Perhaps more significant to the history of German settlement in the county, however, were the later waves of German immigration that entered Pennsylvania between 1727 and 1754. These Germans came to Berks County from both Europe and the Schoharie Valley in western New York. Unlike their European counterparts, the settlers from New York established homesteads in western Berks County near the present borough of Womelsdorf, although many of the later immigrants from the continent also moved into northern and western Berks County. By 1790, Germans comprised a majority in almost every township and accounted for at least eighty percent of the population of the county.[26]

Immigrants from the British Isles were the final group of Europeans to settle in Berks County. In 1718, Anthony Lee, an English Friend, claimed land in the Oley Valley. Within a few years, additional Quaker families, among them the Boones, settled between Manatawny Creek and the Schuylkill River. Welsh Quakers and Baptists, who often migrated from Chester County, settled in the eastern and southern sections of the county, respectively. A few Irish also moved to Berks County during the eighteenth century; Irish Quakers tended to locate near Maiden Creek in central Berks, while Irish Catholics predominantly resided near the Roman Catholic mission at Goshenhoppen. Unlike the German settlers, the British generally concentrated their settlements along the southern border and in central and eastern Berks County. Some English did own land in the northern and western sections of the county, but few lived in those areas.[27]

Anthony and Mary Lee and their family were the first Quakers to settle in present-day Berks County. Lee had been raised in the Church of England, but upon his arrival in Philadelphia he became apprenticed to a Quaker living in Darby and converted. They moved from Darby to Gwynedd in 1714 and resided near members of the John Hughes family. Four years later, Lee purchased a tract of 440 acres in northwestern Philadelphia County on which to build his home and farm. After a few more families from Gwynedd settled in the Oley Valley, Friends began to meet around 1720 in the Lee home for first-day meetings.[28]

Within a few years of the Lee migration to present-day Berks County, other English Quakers settled in the Oley Valley. In 1713, George Boone, Sr. sent his three eldest children to Pennsylvania to locate favorable land. Four years later, Boone and the remainder of his family left Bradninch, England, for America. They first settled in Abington north of Philadelphia, and by 1720 had moved west to the Oley Valley.[29]

In 1725, George Boone approached the leaders of Gwynedd Monthly Meeting concerning the possibility of holding a preparative meeting in Oley. After three months' deliberation, Gwynedd Monthly Meeting approved his request that September. Anthony Lee began serving as overseer for the meeting in October 1730. Six months later, George Boone, Sr. and Ellis Hughes visited the families belonging to this meeting.[30]

Ellis Hughes came to Pennsylvania from Merionethshire, Wales, in 1698 with his parents and settled at Gwynedd. During the early years of their residence, Quakers conducted meetings for worship in the family home, and his father John Hughes served as a leader of the meeting. His piety led Friends to acknowledge him as a minister in October 1722, and he often visited the families residing within the limits of Gwynedd Monthly Meeting. In February 1725/6 and February 1728/9, he represented Gwynedd at Philadelphia Quarterly Meeting. Around 1735, Hughes "felt his mind drawn to remove with his family to the new settlement of Friends at Exeter," and he moved to the Oley Valley.[31]

Thomas Ellis also migrated to Pennsylvania from Merionethshire, arriving in Philadelphia in 1707 and settling near Gwynedd. Five years later, he married Ellis Hughes's sister Jane. They moved to Exeter by 1734, when Oley Friends appointed him overseer of their meeting. Ellis served as an elder for Exeter Preparative Meeting for over thirty years; his wife was a minister for almost fifty years.[32]

For the Maiden Creek Friends, settlement occurred at a slower pace. Among the first Quakers to move to this area were transfers from New Garden Monthly Meeting in Chester County. Isaac Starr, Joseph Wily, and Nehemiah Hutton, who had migrated from Ireland in the 1710s, arrived in Maiden Creek in 1731. A year later, Isaac Starr's brother Moses and John Wily moved there with their families. Enough Friends had settled in the Maiden Creek area by early 1734 that they had begun construction on a meetinghouse in the vicinity. By the end of 1735, Francis Parvin, Robert Penrose, Siesmer Wright, and their families had migrated north from Chester County, and Gwynedd Monthly Meeting had authorized the establishment of a preparative meeting in Maiden Creek. Richard Lundy, who had come from Buckingham Monthly Meeting in Bucks County, and Wright served as the first overseers of Maiden Creek Preparative Meeting.[33]

Unlike at Exeter, whose members were predominantly English and Welsh, Friends who attended meetings for worship at Maiden Creek during the eighteenth century had migrated from Ireland. Isaac and Moses Starr moved with their parents from County Meath to New Garden Preparative Meeting in 1712. At the same time, John Wily brought with him a certificate from his previous monthly meeting in County West Meath when he settled near Kennett Monthly Meeting. Nehemiah Hutton came from County Carlow in 1716 and also settled within the confines of Kennett Monthly Meeting. Robert Penrose arrived in Philadelphia from County Wicklow in October, 1717, with his wife and two daughters. Upon arriving in Pennsylvania in 1725, Siesmer Wright presented a certificate for himself and his wife from Ballycane Monthly Meeting in County Wicklow to New Garden Monthly Meeting. Francis Parvin settled at New Garden in 1728 after leaving Moate Monthly Meeting in County West Meath shortly after the death of his wife. Although these Irish Friends did not all emigrate from the same area of Ireland, they all did live in Chester County prior to migrating to Berks and settled near each other in the central part of the county within two decades of arriving in Pennsylvania.[34]

In March 1737, representatives of Oley and Maiden Creek Preparative Meetings indicated to members of Gwynedd Monthly Meeting that they desired a separate monthly meeting. The next month, Gwynedd appointed Ellis Hughes, Thomas Ellis, and Anthony Lee, along with three other male Friends, to attend the next quarterly meeting held in Philadelphia. The regional organization consented to the establishment of another monthly meeting, to convene alternately at the meetinghouses at Oley and Maiden Creek. In 1742, upon a division of Oley Township, the congregation became known as Exeter Monthly Meeting.[35]

For the next decade, the activities of Exeter Monthly Meeting probably did not differ from those of similar groups throughout Pennsylvania. Quakers continued to settle in the interior; enough English and Welsh Friends had moved to Robeson Township by 1741 to warrant the creation of an additional meeting for worship and preparative meeting for Friends residing south of the Schuylkill River. The size of the meeting further increased through the acceptance of converts whose "Life and Conversation [were] agreeable with the Principles of Truth." Members of the meeting performed religious visits among the families of the meeting and traveled to other Friends' meetings throughout the colonies in a "Labour of Love." Until 1754, overseers of Exeter Preparative Meeting, with one exception, came from the Boone, Ellis, Hughes, and Lee families who had played a prominent role in the organization of the meeting; all elders were Lees. At Maiden Creek, the early overseers included members of the Hutton, Lundy, Penrose, Starr, and Wright families, in addition to newer settlers from New Garden and Goshen. All of the overseers of Robeson Preparative Meeting came from other monthly meetings in Pennsylvania; John Scarlet, a native of Chester Monthly Meeting, served as overseer for fifteen years and as an elder for over thirty, succeeded in the latter post by his son John, Jr. In addition, some Friends left Exeter for other monthly meetings in Pennsylvania and New Jersey during this era.[36]

The distinctiveness of Exeter Monthly Meeting's experiences provides a common theme throughout this book. Life in the Pennsylvania backcountry brought challenges to these Friends that William Penn could hardly have anticipated when he promoted his colony in 1681. As this study will show, not all Quakers were alike—yet at times Exeter Friends probably wished that they were not the vanguards of Quaker settlement along the frontier. For approximately the first fifty years of Exeter's existence as an independent monthly meeting, its members dealt with the impact of ethnic and religious diversity, warfare, political unrest, economic growth, social change, and spiritual reform—all while clearing land, building houses and farms, practicing trades, and raising families. The physical environment influenced their daily lives, and their faith shaped their spiritual lives.

The story of Exeter Monthly Meeting during the eighteenth century will be told in a chronological and topical fashion. Chapter 2 will explore the religious diversity of eighteenth-century Berks County, including the establishment of churches by denomination, instances of interdenominational cooperation and discrimination, and problems with obtaining suitable religious leaders. Chapter 3 examines how successfully Exeter Friends enforced the discipline and why the Society of Friends tightened the rules in the 1750s. In chapter 4, Exeter Friends confronted the first real threat to their pacifism, the Seven Years' War, and experienced the terror of life along the frontier amid Native American raids. The War for Independence presented another crisis for Berks County Quakers; in chapter 5 Friends not only dealt with an allegiance dilemma over supporting the revolution or following the tenets of their faith, but they also had to cope with the consequences of their decision. In chapter 6, the economic life of Exeter Friends receives attention, including an analysis of their economic status within the townships, business interaction with non-Quakers, and the disposition of property after death. Geographic mobility, both within the meeting and to other locations, is the topic for chapter 7. Chapter 8 explores the attitudes of members of Exeter Monthly Meeting toward education, comparing them with those of other Pennsylvania Quakers and other residents of Berks County. Chapter 9 focuses on the impact of slavery and abolitionism on this Quaker community, as the responses of members of Exeter Monthly Meeting more strongly resembled those of their fellow backcountry residents instead of those of their religious organization. Chapter 10 addresses the relationship between Exeter Friends and the outside world, specifically as it relates to politics, religious visits to other monthly meetings, and participation in the affairs of Philadelphia Quarterly Meeting. In chapter 11, Exeter Monthly Meeting will begin to contract following the formation of Robeson Monthly Meeting in 1789 and, in central Pennsylvania, Catawissa Monthly Meeting in 1796.

2

A Land of Diversity and Contention: The Religious Environment of Eighteenth-Century Berks County, Pennsylvania

WHEN THE PENNSYLVANIA HISTORICAL COMMISSION DEDICATED THE Daniel Boone Homestead as a "Museum of the Pennsylvania Pioneer" in 1938, the agency recognized that this historic site in eastern Berks County honored not only the noted American pioneer but also the variety of settlers who had lived in the region. Boone's parents, Squire and Sarah Boone, were overseers of Oley Preparative Meeting and were instrumental in the establishment of Exeter Monthly Meeting of the Religious Society of Friends in 1737. During the next decade, however, Squire Boone found it increasingly difficult to follow the Quaker discipline while living along the frontier. As a result, when the family moved to North Carolina in 1750, only Sarah Boone requested a certificate of removal from Exeter Monthly Meeting. After the departure of the Boones, two families owned the property for the remainder of the eighteenth century—the English Anglican Maugridges and the French/German Reformed DeTürks. In essence, the Pennsylvania Historical Commission not only enabled future generations to visit the birthplace of one of America's most famous pioneers, but it also made it possible for them to interpret the ethnic and religious diversity of early Berks County.[1]

Although historians have only recently begun to devote attention to Pennsylvania's diversity, settlers and visitors to the province almost immediately recognized the colony's heterogeneity. As early as 1684, Francis Daniel Pastorius, one of the founders of Germantown, wrote "in my household I have those who hold to the Roman, to the Lutheran, to the Calvinist, to the Anabaptist, and to the Anglican church, and only one Quaker." The contemporary recorder of the history of the Moravian Church at Oley in the 1740s identified Dunkards, Mennonites, Seventh-Day Baptists, Lutherans, Reformed (Calvinists), Catholics, Separatists, and Inspirationists among the religious groups of the region. The Reverend Henry Melchior Muhlenberg, patriarch of the Lutheran Church in America, commented that, upon his arrival in Philadelphia, several Englishmen "asked me whether I was a *Moravian,* a *Lutheran,* a *Calvinist,* or a *Churchman.*" He appeared to be shocked at this inquiry, for he "gave them a reprimand and said they must learn better manners and not welcome strangers with such questions." Gottlieb Mittelberger, a German schoolmaster and organist who briefly resided in Pennsylvania during the 1750s, noted that "one can encounter Lutherans, members of the Reformed Church, Catholics, Quakers, Mennonites or Anabaptists, Herrenhütter or Moravian Brothers, Pietists, Seventh-Day Adventists, Dunkers, Presbyterians, New-born, Freemasons, Separatists, Freethinkers, Jews, Mohammedans, Pagans, Negroes, and Indians" in the province. He further remarked that "it is possible to meet in one house, among one family, members of four or five or six different sects." This diversity, however, so appalled Mittelberger that he returned to Germany in 1754 rather than continue employment in Pennsylvania.[2]

Not surprisingly, then, secular and religious leaders in Pennsylvania did not always look favorably on the diversity that resulted from the waves of German immigration. Governor George Thomas noted in a letter to the Anglican Bishop of Exeter in 1748 that "the Germans imported with them all the religious whimsies of their country, and . . . have sub-divided since their arrival." Leaders of the German religious groups accustomed to established churches frowned upon the ecclesiastical chaos they faced. The Reverend John Philip Boehm, organizer of the German Reformed Church in Pennsylvania, found it "astonishing to hear about the many sects" among the German settlers in the Oley Valley. He noted that "the number of those who since that time have gone over to the 'Tumplers' [Dunkers], Seventh-day people, Mennonites and others is so large that it cannot be stated without tears in one's eyes, and who knows how many there are yet in this widely-extended country, who are unknown to us." Muhlenberg noted upon his arrival in 1742 the "wretched and slovenly" conditions of the churches that resulted in a situation where "many believed nothing and some had been drawn into the numerous sects, etc." If the plurality of religious faiths caused this much distress among the Germans, certainly English colonists who settled in regions dominated by German immigrants wondered about William Penn's wisdom in permitting religious freedom.[3]

Settlement patterns of early residents of Berks County are especially evident in the religious life of the county during the eighteenth century. In fact, it is possible that Berks was more diverse in the number of religious groups than any other county in colonial America. Adherents of at least sixteen distinct denominations resided there during this period, and most of these groups established congregations and built churches or meeting-houses where their followers could worship.[4] (See table 2.1 for a list of these congregations.) The European immigrants who settled Berks County represented nearly every part of northern and western Europe and prac-ticed almost every religious faith known to the Europeans. By the end of the colonial period, these settlers had established at least eighty distinct congregations.

Swedes, the first national group to settle in the county, were the first to organize a congregation. A Swedish Lutheran minister, the Reverend An-dreas Rudman, assisted several Swedish settlers in petitioning William Penn for over 10,000 acres along the Schuylkill River near the mouth of Manatawny Creek in 1701. Approximately fifty in number, these settlers soon made permanent settlements near present-day Douglassville and started to farm the fertile soil of the region. By 1720, the community had become stable enough to build a church and obtain the services of the Reverend Samuel Hesselius "to dwell among them, and exercise there his office for their spiritual edification." Hesselius, who also preached at a Dutch Reformed church in Bucks County during his pastorate, gave up his charge in Pennsylvania in 1723 and moved to Wilmington, Delaware.[5]

Pastoral instability characterized the Swedish Lutherans after Hes-selius's departure. Supply pastors from Wicacoa (present-day Gloria Dei Church) served the congregation, known as Morlatton. Between 1745 and 1753, the Reverend Henry Melchior Muhlenberg, a German Lutheran, preached occasionally in German and English, trying to provide some regular religious services to the people of Morlatton. By the mid 1750s, however, the pulpit had become vacant once again. Rather than continue in ecclesiastical disarray, the Swedes at Morlatton, like several other Swedish Lutheran congregations in Pennsylvania, chose to come under the supervi-sion and control of the Church of England. The small size of the community at Morlatton, the lack of a resident pastor, and the ease with which the Swedes assimilated into English society all contributed to the demise of the Swedish Lutheran denomination as a separate entity in the province.[6]

For German Lutherans, however, the story was quite different from that of their Swedish counterparts. Soon after their arrival, German immigrants began to dominate the religious life of the county. In 1723 settlers in the Tulpehocken area established the first German Lutheran church in present-day Berks County. At first, laymen conducted the worship services and read printed sermons, because no ordained Lutheran clergy had settled in the province. During the early 1730s Conrad Weiser, one of the early settlers who became known for his skill at improving relations with the Native Americans, assisted the congregation in submitting a call for a minister to the court preacher in London. In the meantime, some members invited the Reverend John Casper Stoever, who ministered throughout

Table 2.1
Churches in Eighteenth-Century Berks County

Name of Congregation	Location	Establishment Date
New Born	Oley	1719–1730s
Morlatton Swedish Lutheran	Amity	1720–53
Zion (Reed's) Lutheran	Tulpehocken	1723–42, 1747
Oley Dunkard	Oley	1724
Oley/Exeter Indulged Meeting	Exeter	1725
St. John's (Host) Reformed	Tulpehocken	1727
Christ (Little Tulpehocken) Lutheran	Tulpehocken	1729
Hereford Mennonite	Hereford	1731
St. John's (Maxatawny) Reformed	Maxatawny	1734
Washington Meeting (Schwenkfelder)	Hereford	1735
Maiden Creek Indulged Meeting	Maiden Creek	1735
Alsace Lutheran*	Alsace	1735
Alsace Reformed*	Alsace	1735
Salem (Oley) Reformed	Oley	1735
St. John's (Hain's, Cacusi) Reformed	Heidelberg	1736
Tulpehocken Baptist	Cumru	1738
Zion (Blue Mountain) Lutheran*	Tulpehocken	1739
Zion (Blue Mountain) Reformed*	Tulpehocken	1739
Bern Reformed	Bern	1739
St. Thomas Anglican	Caernarvon	1740
Robeson Indulged Meeting	Robeson	1740
Northkill Amish	Bern	1740–57
Zion (Richmond) Lutheran	Richmond	1741
St. Paul's (Goshenhoppen) Roman Catholic	Hereford	1741
Oley Moravian	Oley	1742
Zion (Reed's) Moravian	Tulpehocken	1742–47
Christ (Tulpehocken) Lutheran	Tulpehocken	1743
New Jerusalem (Dunkel's) Reformed	Greenwich	1744
North Heidelberg Moravian	Heidelberg	1744
Universalist	Oley	1745–55
Northkill Lutheran	Bern	1745
Altalaha Lutheran	Tulpehocken	1746
St. Joseph's (Hill) Lutheran*	Oley	1747
St. Joseph's (Hill) Reformed*	Oley	1747
Christ (Mertz) Lutheran	Rockland	1747
Mohrsville Dunkard	Windsor	1748
Northkill Dunkard	Bern	1748–70
Longswamp (Little Lehigh) Reformed	Longswamp	1748
Tulpehocken Indulged Meeting	Tulpehocken	1749–58
Schwartzwald Lutheran*	Exeter	1740s
Schwartzwald Reformed*	Exeter	1740s

continued

Table 2.1—*Continued*

Name of Congregation	*Location*	*Establishment Date*
Jerusalem (Allemangel) Lutheran*	Albany	1740s
St. Daniel (Corner) Lutheran	Heidelberg	1750
Trinity (Reading) Lutheran	Reading	1751
Reading Reformed	Reading	1752
St. John's (Maxatawny) Lutheran*	Maxatawny	1752
St. Paul's (Amity) Lutheran	Amity	1753
St. Paul's (Amity) Reformed	Amity	1753
St. Gabriel's (Morlatton) Anglican	Amity	1753
St. Peter's (Reading) Roman Catholic	Reading	1755
St. Paul's (Smoke, Lebanon) Lutheran	Windsor	1756
Reading Indulged Meeting	Reading	1756
Zion (Windsor Castle) Lutheran*	Windsor	1758
Zion (Windsor Castle) Reformed*	Windsor	1758
Christ (DeLong's) Reformed	Maxatawny	1759
Huff's (Hereford) Lutheran*	Hereford	1760
Huff's (Hereford) Reformed*	Hereford	1760
Allegheny Mennonite*	Brecknock	1760
Gehman Mennonite	Brecknock	1760
New Bethel (Eck) Reformed*	Albany	1761
New Bethel (Eck) Lutheran*	Albany	1761
New Bethel-Zion Lutheran	Greenwich	1761
St. Peter's Reformed	Richmond	1762
St. Mary's (Reading) Anglican	Reading	1763
Epler Reformed	Bern	1765
Allegheny Lutheran*	Brecknock	1767
Allegheny Reformed*	Brecknock	1767
Jerusalem (Allemangel) Reformed*	Albany	1768
Zion (Spies) Lutheran*	Alsace	1769
Zion (Spies) Reformed*	Alsace	1769
St. Michael's Lutheran*	Bern	1769
St. Michael's Reformed*	Bern	1769
Maidencreek Amish	Maiden Creek	1760s
Salem (Belleman's) Lutheran*	Bern	1760s
Salem (Belleman's) Reformed	Bern	1760s
Frieden's (White) Lutheran*	Albany	1770
Frieden's (White) Reformed*	Albany	1770
Robeson (Forest, Plow) Lutheran	Robeson	1770
St. Paul's (Old Forest) Methodist	Robeson	1770
Pricetown Dunkard	Ruscombmanor	1777

*union churches
Lutheran and Reformed are German unless otherwise noted.
Indulged meetings are local Quaker meetings for worship affiliated with Exeter Monthly Meeting.

western Berks County from the 1730s through the 1770s, to serve as their pastor. The establishment of this congregation, known as Zion or Reed's Lutheran, located at Stouchsburg, began a movement that eventually saw the organization of twenty-seven German Lutheran congregations in the county by 1789.[7]

Technically, all of the German Lutheran congregations of Berks County came under the administration of the Evangelical Lutheran Ministerium of Pennsylvania, established in 1748 as the denominational organization for Lutherans in the province. According to the records of the Ministerium, the majority of Lutheran congregations in the county did not affiliate with this body. The settlement at Tulpehocken, however, did remain under the control of the Ministerium for most of this period. In addition, the congregations at Reading and in the Oley Valley (St. Joseph's or Hill) often sent representatives to the meeting, even when the churches did not have a pastor. By the 1770s, eleven congregations, scattered throughout the county, regularly dealt with this organization. The remaining Lutheran congregations relied upon irregular or unordained clergy to conduct worship services; the Ministerium had no control over these parishes, which often chose schoolmasters to perform ministerial duties.[8]

German settlers who professed the tenets of Reformed theology influenced by the Swiss reformer Ulrich Zwingli and Luther's associate Philip Melanchthon faced similar problems. Again, members of the Tulpehocken settlement established the first congregation, known as St. John's or Host. From 1727 until the 1740s, the Reverend John Philip Boehm visited the community approximately twice a year to administer communion. In the mid-1730s, French Huguenots and German Reformed settlers in the Oley Valley in present-day eastern Berks County formed Salem (Oley) Reformed Church to meet the needs of residents of this region. By 1789, adherents of the German Reformed Church had established twenty-five congregations throughout the county.[9]

The German Reformed Church also set up a supervisory organization in the colony. Unlike the Lutherans, who dealt with officials in Halle, Germany, the German Reformed Coetus (Synod) received its authority from the Classis of Amsterdam in the Netherlands. In addition, a higher percentage of Reformed congregations in the county belonged to the Coetus, as the minutes of this organization include statistics for at least thirteen of the twenty-five German Reformed congregations. Consequently, the Reformed churches in the county appeared more stable than the Lutheran congregations, yet their members too caused problems for the Coetus throughout the eighteenth century.[10]

Unlike the Lutherans and Reformed, Roman Catholics who settled in Berks County did not have a denominational organization in the colony, as the region lacked a resident bishop until the nineteenth century. German

Jesuit priests conducted services and performed ministerial duties at the two parishes in the county, Reading and Goshenhoppen. The Reverend Theodore Schneider founded the mission at Goshenhoppen (present-day Bally) and supervised the erection of a church building shortly after his arrival in 1741. During the 1740s and 1750s, Schneider traveled throughout the Berks County area baptizing parishioners at their homes, whether they lived in Morlatton, Maxatawny, Oley, or Allemangel (Albany). Although baptisms commonly occurred in the home, marriages usually took place in the chapel. In addition, as early as 1755, priests from Goshenhoppen conducted Mass once a month at Reading where Catholics had built a wooden chapel for holding services. After Schneider's death in 1764, German Jesuits continued to minister to the Roman Catholics in the county until the 1780s.[11]

Settlers from the British Isles emigrating to Berks County followed other religious faiths besides Quakerism. Unlike other religious groups in Pennsylvania, the Church of England was the only denomination specifically mentioned in King Charles II's royal grant to William Penn. In Berks County, missionaries of the Society for the Propagation of the Gospel in Foreign Parts (SPG) assisted in the establishment of three congregations—at Morgantown in Caernarvon Township (1740), at Morlatton (1753), and in Reading (1763). SPG missionaries from Lancaster provided services for St. Thomas Church in Morgantown, usually on every other Sunday. This congregation began to request a full-time minister in 1749 but did not succeed in obtaining regular visits until 1758, when the Reverend Thomas Barton settled in Lancaster. In 1764, after the congregation had constructed a new stone building, Barton described the group as "between 50 and 60 [families], all of Welch extraction." Communicants declined from forty in 1764 to thirty in 1770, mainly because of death or removal of families.[12]

The other two Anglican parishes, at Morlatton and Reading, had a different experience during this period. Anglicans from both communities petitioned the Archbishop of Canterbury in 1760 for a minister, and the SPG responded two years later by sending the Reverend Alexander Murray of Scotland. British church officials apparently did not warn Murray about the location and religious condition of the area, as almost all of his letters to the SPG reflected both surprise and disgust at the actions of the German congregations, especially those in Reading. He once remarked that "the Lutherans of this town are just suing & execrating one another on the occasion of electing a Minister & this satisfaction they frequently indulge themselves being fonder of new Clergy than new Cloths. . . ." He also delighted in noting in early 1764 that "some Presbyterians, some Baptists, [and] some Quakers" had joined the church at Reading.[13]

Because Murray was eager to baptize Anglicans and to convert believers of other faiths to Anglicanism, he particularly enjoyed describing the growth of his two congregations to his superiors in London. The two parishes had included only 280 people and forty-three families upon his arrival in 1762; three years later they had increased to fifty-two families and 331 members. The promise of growth, however, soon subsided, as the lack of a bishop in the colonies to confirm church membership and further migration into the interior contributed to a slight decline to 297 members in 1774. Coincidentally, even though Reading Anglicans had raised funds for the construction of a church building (the Anglicans at Morlatton, some of whom were former Swedish Lutherans, continued to use the old Swedish Lutheran church), they did not erect an edifice until the 1820s.[14]

The failure to build a house of worship in Reading might have resulted from the small size of the congregation, but the coming of the American Revolution certainly was a factor. Anglicans in Reading were among the local leaders in the movement for independence—one was even speaker of the assembly when the war began and served in the Second Continental Congress. The Reverends Murray and Barton, however, were loyalists. Their vows professed loyalty to the king, and they depended on stipends from Britain for their survival. In 1778, after the rebels had torched and looted Murray's property, he fled to England. Because of poor health, Barton could only make it to New York, where he died in 1780. As a result of the departure of the ministers, the Anglican churches effectively became dormant in the 1780s; the Reverend Traugott Frederick Illing, who had been ordained by the Bishop of London but also preached at Lutheran churches in Pennsylvania, did occasionally serve the church at Morgantown.[15]

Other religions of British origin established congregations in early Berks County. Welsh Baptists in Cumru Township built a meetinghouse in 1738 and joined the Philadelphia Baptist Association that year. The congregation never was large; it included twenty-one members in 1738 and peaked at twenty-nine in 1763. Members represented the group at the annual meetings of the Philadelphia Baptist Association between 1761 and 1770. By 1774, however, the congregation had ceased to exist, because its minister had moved to Chester County.[16]

Methodists, who were an offshoot of the Church of England, also established a congregation during this period. Characteristically a movement led by itinerant clergy, the first activity by a Methodist minister consisted of a sermon preached by the Reverend Joseph Pilmore in 1772 at the county courthouse in Reading. A year later, settlers in Robeson and Union Townships erected the first Methodist chapel on the Pennsylvania frontier. Known as "Old Forest" or "The Church in the Forest" because of its location in the region of the county known by that name, the log building, according to tradition, served as a fort for protection in the event of Native American uprisings. Methodist circuit riders, often from neighboring Chester County, supplied the congregation during its early years.[17]

Although the traditional churches of Berks County prospered during the eighteenth century, they constantly confronted the problem of sectarians. One of the most notorious sects, a peculiar group called the New Born, was the first to establish itself in the county. Adherents of this faith believed that through the "new birth" they became God and Christ Himself and could no longer sin. They subscribed only to those Biblical passages that appeared to favor their unusual tenets, and they considered the holy sacraments laughable. Matthias Baumann, a Palatine immigrant who founded the sect, promulgated these unusual religious beliefs in his treatise *Ein Ruf an die Nicht Wiedergebornen* (1730), or "A Call to the Unregenerate." To demonstrate the authenticity of his beliefs and to show that he was in God's favor, he even offered to wade across the Delaware River.[18]

After Baumann's death in 1727, opposition developed to the New Born and their beliefs. The Reverend John Philip Boehm remarked that Baumann's successor spoke "such blasphemous words against our Saviour . . . that the ears of a true Christian tingle and his heart must weep, when hearing them." The Reverend George Michael Weiss, another Reformed minister, published a pamphlet to refute the heresies of the sect. In this work, written as a dialogue between a minister and a representative member of the group, Weiss called the advocate of the "new birth" "a miserable earthly worm." Even though the New Born never became a major religious body, leaders of the established churches apparently feared the influence the sect might have on the settlers in the region, particularly those without regular religious services.[19]

Members of the Church of the Brethren, or Dunkards, who believed in baptism by immersion, also settled in central and eastern Berks County. In the early 1730s, they began to hold services in Oley under the direction of Elder Peter Becker of Germantown. Shortly thereafter, they erected a church. The group flourished for about ten years before many of its members departed to other settlements. One problem they faced was that the region "was at this time a hotbed of sectarianism and also an exposed frontier," which inhibited their growth. Their pacifism prevented them from bearing arms against possible attack by Native Americans along the frontier, so relocation in some instances was indeed a matter of life and death. In addition, the small congregation was unsuccessful in its attempts to attract a preacher to reside among them. By 1770, the group at Oley included about twenty members, while the Northkill congregation in central Berks only had eleven.[20]

Mennonites and Amish also settled in Berks County during the colonial period. Mennonites had settled in the Oley Valley as early as 1714, and two representatives of their congregation attended the conference of Mennonites held in 1727. Primarily farmers, they were one of the first to realize the need for interdenominational cooperation. When the congregation built a meetinghouse in 1732, the elders neglected to purchase the land. In 1747, the owner of the land sold the property, not to the congregation but to the local Catholic priest. Finally, in 1755, the Hereford congregation bought the land from Father Schneider. Another Mennonite congregation, in Brecknock Township near the border with Lancaster County, erected a meetinghouse in 1767 in which Mennonites, Lutherans, and Reformed worshiped on alternate Sundays.[21]

One of the most important Amish communities in colonial Pennsylvania began in the late 1730s along Northkill Creek. Between 150 and 200 Amish settled in Bern Township. This community, however, was short-lived. Native American raids along the frontier in 1757 resulted in the death of several members and the abduction of their children. A few years later, members from the Northkill settlement organized the other Amish settlement in Berks County, located in Maiden Creek Township. This group was not as large as the one at Northkill, mainly because most of the early settlers had moved on to Lancaster County.[22]

The final German sect to establish a church in eighteenth-century Berks County was the Schwenkfelders. Members of this religious group settled in Hereford Township in eastern Berks County in the 1730s, near the other Schwenkfelder communities in northern Philadelphia County. Christopher Schultz, a leader of the sect, served as spiritual adviser for the group and as a liaison to the Quakers and other pacifist groups. During the Revolution, Schultz also was a member of the county's Committee of Observation, representing the pacifist viewpoint at this organization's meetings.[23]

One of the more significant religious groups to settle in Berks County was the Moravians. Perhaps the most controversial church organization in colonial Pennsylvania, the Moravian Church, or *Unitas Fratrum,* advocated missionary work among the Native Americans and supported a union of all German religious groups. During the 1740s, Moravians established congregations in Tulpehocken, Heidelberg, and Oley Townships. Each of these displayed some of the features of Moravian activity in Pennsylvania—to provide religious services in communities that did not have ordained clergy and to foster interdenominational unity.[24]

The church in Tulpehocken Township, in particular, represented a direct threat to Lutheranism in the county and colony. Between 1723 and 1742, disputes had arisen between church members concerning which of the Lutheran pastors would minister to the congregation. Part of the group favored the preachings of Casper Leutbecker, a tailor by trade who had assumed the duties of a minister. Most of them, however, preferred to have the Reverend John Casper Stoever as their pastor. These quarrels became so intense that on several occasions the church leaders requested intervention by civil authorities to resolve the disagreements. When Count Nicholas Ludwig von Zinzendorf, leader of the Moravian Church in Pennsylvania, decided to mediate, it caused great confusion for the community. Those members of Reed's Lutheran Church who supported Stoever withdrew and formed Christ Lutheran in 1742; the followers of Leutbecker supported the Moravian minister. The Moravian influence at Reed's, however, did not last long, as by 1745 many of the Moravians had withdrawn and united with the congregation at North Heidelberg.[25]

More significant, however, were the Moravian congregations at North Heidelberg and Oley. The settlement in Heidelberg Township differed from the group at Reed's in that the residents of the region were predominantly Reformed. But, unlike the Reformed Church, the Moravians were able to supply the community with ministers to preach the word of God. For instance, between 1744 and 1830, when the congregation at North Heidelberg resumed its affiliation with the Lutheran and Reformed denominations, six men served as pastors for the Moravian church. In contrast, the nearest Reformed church, St. John's (Hain's) Reformed, had at least eight Reformed ministers between 1738 and 1789.[26]

Although the Moravian church in Heidelberg Township lasted the longest, the one at Oley was more important. In December 1741, Henry Antes, a pious Reformed layman from Philadelphia County who had become an ordained Moravian minister, appealed to religious leaders of all denominations and sects to unite into one Protestant movement, to be known as "The Pennsylvania Congregation of God in the Spirit." Count Zinzendorf, who supported this proposal, planned a series of synods to achieve such an organization. The crucial synod met in February 1742, on the farm of John DeTürck in Oley. Moravian leaders, Native Americans, and representatives from other Protestant denominations attended the meeting. In addition to ordaining ministers and missionaries, the Moravians at this meeting baptized their first Native American converts by sprinkling. This action, however, proved to be a fatal blow to the Moravians' hopes of uniting all of the varied German religious groups. The Dunkards immediately departed because this form of baptism contradicted their beliefs. Others also left shortly thereafter. Consequently, the Moravians failed to achieve their goal on a large scale, although they did manage to create a nondenominational congregation at Oley.[27]

In effect, instead of forming a union of Protestants in Pennsylvania, Zinzendorf's synods contributed to the emergence of a stubborn denominational consciousness. German Lutheran and Reformed officials in Europe soon realized the necessity for a colonial church organization. By the end of 1742 the Reverend Henry Melchior Muhlenberg had arrived from Germany to create some order out of the ecclesiastical chaos. The Reverend Michael Schlatter settled in Philadelphia County in 1746 to provide the same for the Reformed. By the end of the decade, the Lutheran and German Reformed churches in Pennsylvania had established formal organizations to oversee clergy and congregations.[28]

While the Moravians were experiencing and creating problems in Oley, Dr. George DeBenneville, a Huguenot physician and an independent preacher, settled in the area. A highly educated and effective speaker, DeBenneville became a pioneer of the Universalist faith in America. Preaching a doctrine of universal salvation, DeBenneville contended that any punishment that God decreed would happen on earth, and all souls would be saved. At first, DeBenneville preached in the Moravian schoolhouse, but his interpretation so offended them that by the mid-1740s he had established a chapel in his home in which to preach.[29]

Settlers of the Jewish faith also moved to Berks County during the eighteenth century. Arriving in the county by the early 1750s, Jews comprised a minuscule fraction of the population of Reading, the county seat. Among the Jewish residents of the town were two merchants and a tavern keeper. As Reading lacked a sufficient number to form a synagogue, Jews requested visitors for holy days or visited other Jews to maintain a community for themselves while confronting the hardships of isolation and distance.[30]

In a region with such a degree of diversity, religious prejudice occasionally became evident. Tax assessors identified pacifist Quakers, Mennonites, Amish, Dunkards, and Schwenkfelders as Tories for choosing not to pay taxes in 1779. During the 1780s, the taxpayer's religion was identified for only one man—a Jew who lived in Reading. Perhaps the most extreme case of discrimination, however, occurred in the family of Conrad Weiser. Even though Weiser was a Lutheran (and Muhlenberg's father-in-law), he had supported the Moravian faction at Reed's Church, joined the Seventh-Day Baptist Community at Ephrata in Lancaster County, and served as a trustee for the German Reformed Church in Reading. Nevertheless, Weiser's open mind concerning religious matters had its limits, as he disowned his one daughter for marrying a Roman Catholic. When he died in 1760, he did not leave her anything; instead, her children received her share of the inheritance.[31]

Indeed, Roman Catholics were one of the few religious groups who confronted discrimination in colonial Pennsylvania. As early as 1689, Lieutenant Governor John Blackwell notified the Provincial Council of "Rumours of danger from ye french & Indians, in conjunction with ye Papists, for ye Ruine of the Protestants in these parts. . . ." By 1705, the provincial assembly required Catholics to take an oath before they could hold office that, in effect, denounced the basic tenets of Catholicism. During the Seven Years' War, anti-Catholicism reached a peak. Many colonists incorrectly assumed that the Catholics would support the objectives of France in the war. This concern led Berks County magistrates (including Conrad Weiser) to request permission from Governor Robert Morris "to enable Us by some legal Authority to disarm or otherwise to disable the Papists from doing any injury to other People who are not of their vile Principles." They also expressed fears that the Catholics would ally themselves with the Native Americans and contended that the priests conferred with the French at Fort Duquesne when not conducting Mass.[32]

One result of this petition was a census of the Catholics in Pennsylvania. Father Theodore Schneider noted that 117 Catholics were under his care at Goshenhoppen, and Father Ferdinand Farmer, who served German parishes in Lancaster and Philadelphia and who preached once every four weeks at Reading, reported that eighty-eight Catholics lived in the town. Over 100 of the Catholics in the county were women, who obviously would not arm themselves against the British. The assessment of Catholics demonstrated the paranoia of the local officials, as it was extremely unlikely that Germans of any religious affiliation would ally themselves with the French, who had been their enemies for years.[33]

Although some discrimination existed, interdenominational cooperation was more common. Marriages occurred frequently between members of religious groups, especially between Lutheran and Reformed. The Reverend Henry Melchior Muhlenberg wrote in 1747, "the members of both faiths are so intermarried in this country, that here you will find a Lutheran husband with a Reformed wife and there a Reformed husband with a Lutheran wife." In addition, members of the Reformed Church in the Oley Valley assisted the Lutherans in building a church. In return, the Reformed received the right to bury their dead in the Lutheran cemetery and to send their children to the Lutheran school at the same tuition rate. Quakers served as witnesses or executors for at least fifty wills written by non-Quakers. Non-Catholics were sponsors for at least eight baptisms recorded by Father Jean Baptiste de Ritter between 1765 and 1785. Furthermore, a Jew contributed toward the construction of the first Lutheran church building in Reading. Interdenominational and interfaith cooperation, however, did have its limits, as it rarely crossed ethnic boundaries.[34]

The development of the union church was the best physical evidence of interdenominational cooperation. In Berks County, as in the Palatinate, the union church represented a building shared by more than one denomination, usually Lutheran and Reformed. Early settlers found it difficult to raise enough funds to build a church and to pay a pastor, so two or more denominations joined economic resources to establish a religious community along the frontier. Each denomination contributed to the upkeep of the church building, with the groups maintaining separate denominational identities. At least thirty-one congregations participated in this type of arrangement. In Brecknock Township in southern Berks County, a Mennonite donated the land on which Lutherans, Reformed, and Mennonites erected a union church. The various denominations alternately conducted worship services, usually every other week. This arrangement enabled them to conserve resources as well as to accommodate the scarcity of clergy along the frontier.[35]

Because the Quakers and other sectarians did not rely upon an ordained clergyman to conduct their worship services, they did not experience some of the problems faced by the German churches. For instance, the Lutheran and Reformed churches, which dominated the religious life of the county during the eighteenth century, persistently had to deal with the scarcity of educated ministers. The Reverend John Philip Boehm commented in a letter to the Classis of Amsterdam in 1730 that he had received less than £40 in salary from his congregations after serving over four-and-a-half years, "yet I dare not say anything, because of the many sects which revile a minister most shamefully for receiving a salary." A few years later, Boehm noted in a letter to the Coetus that when he attempted to collect a salary in Philadelphia, "the ridicule and derision, to which I had to listen from outsiders, hurt me very much." In 1768, one of the Reverend Henry Melchior Muhlenberg's relatives, a Berks County Justice of the Peace, noted that settlers north of the Blue Mountains "hunger and thirst after the pure Word of God," especially "because of the godless vagabonds (Land-Laüfer), who represent themselves as preachers."[36]

One reason why these comments provide such valuable insights into the religious conditions of the German settlers is that the average Lutheran or Reformed clergyman ministered to at least three parishes at a time. In 1748, approximately thirty German Lutheran and Reformed pastors served 110 congregations in the colonies. By 1776, the ratio of pastors to congregations had increased, as eighty-two ministers conducted worship services at 348 congregations. No wonder Muhlenberg would note in his journal in 1747 that "the poor sheep are really hungering for the pure milk and sweet food of the Gospel!"[37]

The difficulty in obtaining suitable clergy resulted from several factors. The fact that the churches were not state-supported in Pennsylvania left ministers at the mercy of their congregations. In the early 1750s, Gottlieb Mittelberger remarked, "throughout Pennsylvania the preachers do not have the power to punish anyone, or to force anyone to go to church. Most preachers are engaged for the year, like cowherds in Germany, and when any one fails to please his congregation, he is given notice and must put up with it." Mittelberger further noted that he "would therefore rather be the humblest cowherd at home than be a preacher in Pennsylvania." As a result, congregations occasionally selected someone who did not have proper ordination to serve as pastor, as that person at least had a trade by which he could earn a livelihood.[38]

Another factor explaining the difficulty in obtaining full-time ministers was the denominations' reliance upon European-trained clergy. Not surprisingly, the colonies generally were not the first choice of graduates from seminaries. Young pastors who came from Germany were reluctant to settle in rural areas where they often had to minister to several congregations. In 1768, the German Reformed Coetus reported to its superiors in Holland that "in the country, where a minister has four or more congregations, and where, on Sundays, he has to hold services in two churches which are seven, ten, and even twelve miles apart, the riding horses and the clothing (of which latter not enough can be provided on account of the narrow and overgrown roads), take away the greater part of the salary."[39] The situation was so deplorable, in fact, that the Reverend Tobias Wagner, who preached at many of these outlying congregations, chose to return to Germany in 1759 rather than remain in Pennsylvania and face these conditions.[40]

An additional cause of poor clerical leadership was the abundance of men who assumed the role of minister if they had a modicum of education. Muhlenberg wrote in 1762 that some men had "set themselves up as preachers and exercise the office without any ordination or examination whatsoever, if they have some gift of speech." This problem was especially evident in Berks County. Of the sixty-five men who performed ministerial duties at Berks County's Lutheran or Reformed congregations during the eighteenth century, only forty-two had been ordained either in Germany, London, or the colonies. At least seven were schoolmasters who assumed the duties of pastor because of the scarcity of clergy. Other "irregular" or unordained preachers were tailors, masons, or weavers.[41]

One of these "vagabond" ministers was Philip Jacob Michael, a weaver by trade. Born in 1716, Michael married Sarah Webb, a cousin of Daniel Boone. After the marriage, Michael purchased land in Rockland Township and established a farm. From this homestead he began to minister to the vacant Reformed congregations in the region, leaving behind his loom to spread the faith. From 1750 until his death in 1786, Michael served at least twenty-four Reformed congregations without the approval of the Coetus (Synod). He did apply for ordination by this organization in 1764. The Coetus noted that his theology was sound and that his work conformed to their policies. The Coetus then ardently recommended that the church authorities in Holland allow it to approve Michael as a Reformed minister: "We would not put our pen to this were we not convinced that it would be of advantage to us, and of greater profit to his congregations." In reply, the

Holland fathers demanded that Michael travel to Holland for ordination, which of course was impossible, so Michael continued to preach without ordination. He faithfully served his scattered congregations until his death, leaving them only to become an army chaplain during the Revolution. In spite of his lack of ordination, his parishioners' support of his preaching was so unique that when settlers in Bern Township built a new log church in 1769, they named it St. Michael's Church in honor of their beloved pastor.[42]

Despite Michael's contributions and the works of other unordained preachers who ensured the growth and stability of Lutheran and German Reformed congregations throughout Berks County during the eighteenth century, the Lutheran Ministerium and German Reformed Coetus frowned upon their activities. Their reluctance to support these men stemmed primarily from the problems these organizations faced in dealing with the moral quality of the ordained clergy. The provincial and city court of Lancaster convicted the Reverend Casper Schnorr, an early Reformed minister at Tulpehocken, of rape. The Reverend Lewis Voigt, who served the Lutheran church in Amity Township, "maintain[ed] a household with young wenches." The Reverend John Casper Stoever once "in anger drank himself drunk in an inn and vomited in the presence of all sorts of sectarian people." In 1753, Reading Lutherans dismissed the Reverend Henry Borchard Gabriel Wordman because of allegations that he had mistreated his wife and family. Fifteen years later, the Coetus suspended Reading pastor Frederick Berger because "there was not a tavern in or near the city [in] which he did not dishonor his name with excessive drinking, swearing, scolding, and making debts to the disgrace of his brethren and the members of his congregation." The Reverend Henry Müller departed Reading in 1776 amid accusations that his wife had attempted to poison him with verdigris. A decade later, members of the consistory (church council) of Reading's Reformed Church found it necessary to forbid the Reverend Bernhard Willy from preaching in the town anymore after they found him guilty of lying, forgery, and bigamy. Lutheran and Reformed pastors, however, were not the only religious leaders to experience problems in providing a moral example for their parishioners. Between 1737 and 1789, more than one-sixth of the leaders of Exeter Monthly Meeting committed a violation of Quaker discipline.[43]

In spite of the ordained clergy's disdain for the actions of the irregular ministers, both groups were essential to the survival of the German Lutheran and Reformed churches in the colony. Only five of the sixty-five men who performed the duties of a minister served more than twenty years at one congregation; two of them provided stability for the Lutherans in Tulpehocken between 1746 and 1809. Over the course of his career, Daniel Schumacher performed clerical duties for at least a dozen separate Lutheran congregations in Berks County; Schumacher's baptismal register is one of the most complete surviving records of any ministerial activity in colonial Pennsylvania. The Reverend Tobias Wagner, an ordained minister who worked outside the auspices of the Lutheran Ministerium, preached at ten congregations between 1743 and 1759 and was the only minister who resided in Berks County during the eighteenth century known to have published a sermon. In addition, the Reverend John Waldschmidt of the Reformed Church served eight parishes between 1756 and 1786, in spite of being considered "lazy and negligent in the ministry" by his peers. Finally, the Reverend Christopher Emanuel Schultze, son-in- law of the Reverend Henry Melchior Muhlenberg, provided a stable religious home for Lutherans in western Berks County, serving five churches in the Tulpehocken region between 1771 and 1809. During this same period, the Reformed churches in the area had at least six different ministers.[44]

An examination of the status of the religious denominations in Pennsylvania in 1776 shows the degree that English settlers in Berks County, especially Quakers, were clearly in the minority (see table 2.2). Every other county in colonial Pennsylvania with a monthly meeting had at least twenty other churches whose membership was predominantly British in origin. In Chester County, almost three-fourths of the sixty congregations were Anglican, Presbyterian, Methodist, Baptist, or Quaker. Even in Lancaster County, the only other county with just one monthly meeting, British residents could worship at three Anglican or twenty-one Presbyterian churches if they suffered a lapse in discipline. Furthermore, the major German religious groups (Lutheran, Reformed, and Roman Catholic) totaled over ninety percent of the births and baptisms recorded in Berks County church records between 1705 and 1780. Quakers in Berks County such as Squire Boone did not have the ethnic reinforcement that was available to Quakers in other Pennsylvania counties, perhaps explaining his lapse in adhering to the Quaker discipline.[45]

When William Penn promoted his colony in Europe and throughout the British Isles, he hardly could have anticipated the multiplicity of faiths that would find a haven in Pennsylvania. Settlers in the region had a choice of more than one dozen separate and distinct religious beliefs to follow. If they became dissatisfied with their church or denomination, there usually was another one nearby. Not only might subsequent owners of property adhere to other faiths; within one family members might belong to different denominations—Daniel Boone's uncle Benjamin joined the Anglican Church after his disownment from Exeter Monthly Meeting for exogamy, and his cousin Sarah Webb married a German Reformed preacher. Surprisingly, though, the religious conflict that characterized Europe during

Table 2.2
Denominations by County in 1776

	Bedford	Berks	Bucks	Chester	Cumberland	Lancaster	Northampton	Northumberland	Philadelphia	Westmoreland	York	Total
Amish	0	3	0	1	0	0	0	0	0	0	0	4
Anglican	0	3	2	9	1	3	1	0	7	0	2	28
Baptist	0	2	8	5	2	1	0	0	3	3	0	24
Congregational	0	0	0	0	0	0	1	0	0	0	0	1
Dutch Reformed	0	0	2	2	0	0	4	1	0	0	0	9
Dunkard	1	6	0	2	5	5	1	0	4	0	4	28
German Reformed	0	25	8	6	5	35	30	0	10	2	18	139
German Lutheran	0	29	9	1	5	30	24	0	24	0	18	140
Keithian Baptist	0	0	1	3	0	0	0	0	1	0	0	5
Mennonite	0	3	8	4	0	26	8	1	8	0	3	61
Methodist	0	1	0	4	0	0	0	0	2	0	1	8
Moravian	0	5	1	0	0	8	10	2	9	3	4	42
New Born	0	1	0	0	0	0	0	0	0	0	0	1
Presbyterian	2	0	12	14	17	21	4	4	7	7	17	105
Roman Catholic	0	2	1	0	0	2	2	0	3	0	3	13
Schwenkfelder	0	1	0	0	0	0	0	0	1	0	0	2
Seventh-Day Baptist	0	0	0	2	0	1	0	0	1	0	0	4
Society of Friends*	0	5	15	24	0	5	1	1	22	1	7	81
Swedish Lutheran	0	1	1	1	0	0	0	0	3	0	0	6
Totals	3	87	68	78	35	137	86	9	105	16	77	701

*includes preparative and indulged meetings

Sources: Charles H. Glatfelter, *Pastors and People: German Lutheran and Reformed Churches in the Pennsylvania Field, 1717–1783*, vol. 1: *Pastors and Congregations* (Breinigsville, PA: Pennsylvania German Society, 1980), 223–482; Jeffrey J. Howell, comp., *Genealogical Guide to Berks County Churches* (Reading, PA: 1984); *Inventory of Church Archives, Society of Friends in Pennsylvania* (Philadelphia: Friends Historical Association, 1941); and Frederick Lewis Weis, *The Colonial Churches and the Colonial Clergy of the Middle and Southern Colonies, 1607–1776* (Lancaster, MA: Society of the Descendants of the Colonial Clergy, 1938), 19–107.

the seventeenth and early eighteenth centuries was rare in Berks County. Contrary to the beliefs of European rulers ever since Constantine, English monarchs gradually realized that religious uniformity was not necessary to hold society together. William Penn astutely used this notion in promoting the settlement of his colony throughout Europe, and the migrants to Berks County demonstrated the wisdom of this philosophy. Consequently, the ethnic and religious diversity that led historians to consider the mid-Atlantic region "a model for the nation" was especially evident in Berks County, leading to a unique religious environment for these frontier Friends. As the ownership of Daniel Boone's birthplace transferred from his Quaker father to an English Anglican and then to a French/German Reformed (whose father had hosted the Moravian synod at Oley), the site demonstrated on a small scale the changing ethnic and religious composition of the Pennsylvania backcountry.[46]

3

Maintaining "Ye Establish'd Order Amongst Us": Religious Discipline and Exeter Monthly Meeting

BY THE MIDDLE OF THE EIGHTEENTH CENTURY, MEMBERS OF THE Society of Friends had resided in Pennsylvania for almost seventy years. During that period, the religious group had faced few challenges. The only significant threat to their organization was the Keithian controversy in the early 1690s, in which George Keith, a Quaker minister, caused havoc for the Society by arguing that Friends should withdraw from politics, adopt a creed, and celebrate communion—in other words, become more like a conventional church. These actions led to Keith's expulsion from the Society; within a decade the Church of England ordained him, and he had become a SPG missionary in New Jersey.[1]

Part of Keith's goal was to create some order within the Society. Although Philadelphia Yearly Meeting disapproved of his methods, it did consider some of his suggestions. Beginning in 1703, Friends in Pennsylvania gathered the advices of the yearly meeting into a formal "discipline." Ministers and elders would read these guidelines quarterly in the meetings for worship to make certain that all members were aware of them. By 1709, the quarterly meetings had begun to require monthly meetings under their supervision to provide written responses to these "queries." At first, these questions dealt in general terms with ensuring proper marriages between Friends, enforcing moral conduct, and resolving disputes without violence or legal action. In 1725, the yearly meeting devised a set of uniform subjects on which the monthly meetings would report; these standards officially became formalized in 1743. The primary purpose of these queries was to ascertain a "state of the Society" each year, along with reinforcing the necessity for order among the scattered monthly meetings.[2]

For Exeter Friends, these queries provided leaders with an opportunity to assess the success or failure of their activities along the frontier. Every three months, the monthly meeting requested responses from the leaders of the assorted preparative meetings to each of the queries and appointed members to present the report at Philadelphia Quarterly Meeting. Because of Exeter Monthly Meeting's location, the responses indicated that its leaders tried their best to maintain religious discipline in the Pennsylvania backcountry. Because of their location and the ethnic and religious diversity present in the region, these leaders often faced challenges that could have caused Friends to abandon the notion of establishing settlements in the hinterland.[3]

Although members of the Society of Friends did not participate in the revival or awakening of religion occurring in Britain's North American colonies in the 1730s and 1740s, the spirit of reform accompanying the movement affected Quakers. A few years after Gilbert Tennent warned colonial Presbyterians of "The Danger of an Unconverted Ministry," effectively causing colonists to question the piety of their religious leaders, Friends began to reform the discipline. These changes essentially prepared Pennsylvania Quakers for life in a society in which they did not possess political control. When Philadelphia Yearly Meeting revised the queries in 1756, it provided the monthly meetings with "the Oppertunity of making such observations as may tend to excite to vigilance & care in the diligent exercise of our Christian discipline, & promote a united Labour for the good of the Church; . . ." These questions addressed such issues as attendance at meetings for worship, maintenance of proper dress and speech, excessive drinking, care for the poor and for slaves, indebtedness, military service, improper marriages, and the rapid resolution of investigation into violations of the discipline.[4]

According to the responses to these queries, the most common spiritual weakness of members of Exeter Monthly Meeting between 1756 and 1788 was that "some for want of a proper Exercise, are at Times overcome with Drowsiness." In addition, although members of the monthly meeting feared that "reading the Holy Scriptures is too much neglected," at least "many Friends discourage[d] the Use of pernicious Books." Furthermore, economic circumstances in the region occasionally caused leaders to excuse violations; in 1784 the monthly meeting noted that "on Account of the scarcity of Money, [Friends] are not as punctual in paying their Debts, as they could wish to be."[5]

Occasionally, the leaders of Exeter Monthly Meeting decided to solve a problem by trying to set an example for other Friends in Berks County. Since the inception of the monthly meeting, members had to be admonished to attend the first-day meetings more regularly. The dilemma of nonattendance, in fact, spurred the leaders of Exeter Monthly Meeting to hold higher standards for themselves. Starting in 1756, representatives from the preparative meetings had to supply an acceptable explanation for their failure to attend the monthly meeting. For Robeson Friends, the Schuylkill River provided a natural obstacle, as high waters or ice occasionally prevented residents from crossing it. Illness, either of the representative or of a family member, also hindered attendance.[6]

In one instance, however, the monthly meeting did not consider the reason given to be an acceptable one. Thomas Thomas of Robeson did not attend the monthly meetings held at Maiden Creek in November and at Exeter in December of 1760. At the gathering at Maiden Creek meeting-house in January 1761, he explained that he had not come because "it looked likely for bad Weather until he thought it was too late." Leaders of the monthly meeting viewed this occurrence as an opportunity to remind Quakers of their duty: "this Meeting can do no less than Press it upon all Friends when appointed to Service that they endeavour to perform the same, and not let trifling Excuses prevent; rememb'ring our Time, and the Work is the Lords."[7]

Along with formalizing the queries, by the 1750s Philadelphia Quarterly Meeting had also begun to take a more active role in recommending proper behavior to Friends. In 1758, the quarterly meeting informed Exeter Monthly Meeting that "the Practice of Serving Drams or other strong Liquors at Burials," which the meeting had acknowledged in its response to the queries, "[was] Inconsistent with such Awful seasons." The report from Philadelphia Quarterly Meeting continued, "And when Friends, in the Course of their Temporal Concerns, attend Publick Houses or such like Places, it is much desired by this Meeting, that Friends would dispatch their Businesses as soon as Possible, and retire from them, as Snares attend such Places, and true Moderation not always regarded."[8]

Taverns, however, were not the only temptations that Friends were supposed to avoid. In October 1764, Philadelphia Women's Quarterly Meeting expressed a wish "that Friends be careful to restrain themselves and those under their Care from attending Fairs." The women of Exeter Monthly Meeting advised, "altho' our remote Situation may not at present expose us to this one particular evil, yet there are other Places of Diversion equally as hurtful." Throughout the eighteenth century, too, the provincial assembly passed a series of laws designed to prohibit "riotous sports, plays, and games" and levied fines for noncompliance. Finally, although the queries did not specifically address this issue, the yearly meeting fully expected Friends "to remember the sabbath day, to keep it holy" and refrain from "any kind of Play whatsoever, or boisterous Sports on Sundays."[9]

●

When examining the disciplinary activity of Exeter Monthly Meeting, it is evident that its leaders were familiar with the rules and regulations of the Society of Friends. Christian discipline served as a way to hold the Society together, especially along the frontier. By the end of the eighteenth century, Philadelphia Yearly Meeting had published the formal summary of Quaker belief, the *Rules of Discipline*. In this volume, Friends included a series of topically arranged extracts from major doctrinal writings and indicated the year of adoption for the specific policy or consequence. The yearly meetings fully expected leaders of monthly meetings such as Exeter to be familiar with these regulations and to enforce them as necessary.[10]

Whenever the overseers of a preparative meeting complained against the actions of a Friend who had violated one or several of the regulations in the *Rules of Discipline,* there were usually two options available to resolve the situation. If a Friend admitted his or her guilt, he or she needed to write a few lines condemning the misconduct. In this confession, the accused admitted his or her guilt, apologized for bringing shame to family and Friends, and requested divine assistance in preventing a recurrence of the offense. This letter, if accepted, would then be approved by the meeting and read publicly, usually at the next first-day meeting. Other locations for reading the confession were possible; for example, in 1757 the meeting ordered Samuel Wilkinson to read his condemnation at the tavern in Reading in which he had become drunk.[11]

If the Friend chose not to condemn his or her misbehavior, the meeting had no recourse but to prepare a letter of testimony against the offender. In over three-fifths of the cases, the accused were unwilling to condemn their actions, and the meeting produced a testimony against the offender (see table 3.1). The testimony restated the charges and passed sentence on the offender.[12]

Quakers whom the monthly meeting had disowned for their misconduct were not shunned like the Amish, for they were still welcome to attend the meetings for worship. Once a meeting disowned a person, however, in most instances the punishment applied to the entire family. A notable exception occurred in 1747 when Exeter Monthly Meeting disowned Squire Boone, father of the famous Daniel, for approving the improper marriage of one of his children; his wife Sarah remained an active member until the family's departure to Virginia in 1750.[13]

During the 1780s, however, Philadelphia Yearly Meeting began to urge the monthly meetings to inspect the religious condition of the children of fallen brethren. Exeter Monthly Meeting formed a committee in 1783 whose purpose was to visit the children of disowned Friends and inform them that they were welcome to attend first-day meetings. David Hopkins, whose father Matthew had been disowned in 1758 for making a false affirmation in court against John Wells and then denying it, welcomed the opportunity to become part of the Society and requested that a certificate of removal be sent to Fairfax Monthly Meeting in Virginia, where he had moved. Most of the children, however, had joined other denominations and did not wish to switch. David's sister, Hannah Hopkins Galleher, informed the committee that she preferred to continue worshiping with the Methodists, so Exeter Monthly Meeting disowned her for exogamy and for joining

Table 3.1
Exeter Monthly Meeting
1737–1789
Disposition of Cases
[N=320]

Type	Number	Percentage
Testimony/Disowned	135	42.2
Paper of Condemnation	89	27.8
Testimony	39	12.2
Resolved	20	6.3
Disowned, then Paper of Condemnation	19	5.9
Repentant	12	3.8
Dismissed	2	.6
Ordered to Pay Debt	2	.6
Disownment Reversed by Quarterly Meeting	2	.6

another church. Although expulsion applied to the entire family, then, the monthly meeting could reinstate the children if they proved to be faithful followers of the discipline and could disown those who continued to stray from the Quaker way.[14]

Prior to 1737, when Philadelphia Quarterly Meeting established Exeter, Gwynedd Monthly Meeting made only six charges (involving five people) against members of Oley Preparative Meeting (the original name of Exeter meeting). Surprisingly, all of the offenders were members of the Boone family, perhaps anticipating the difficulties that the descendants of George Boone would have in following the discipline. In fact, George himself was the first violator, as in 1720 he "openly acknowledg[e]d his forwardness in giving his Consent to John Webb to keep Company with his Daughter in order to Marry Contrary to ye Establish'd order amongst us." A decade later, John and Mary Webb submitted papers "Condemning their Faults and Ill Conduct . . ." to Gwynedd Monthly Meeting. Joseph and Benjamin Boone faced retribution for marrying non-Quakers in 1733 and 1736, respectively; Joseph had also committed fornication with his fiancée.[15]

Once Exeter Monthly Meeting was on its own, however, the number of violations began to increase. Between 1737 and 1744, eighteen cases, involving twenty-one charges, came before the meeting (see tables 3.2 and 3.3). Of these, the women's meeting handled five; Exeter Women's Monthly Meeting considered infractions involving female members of the meeting, with the advice of the men's meeting. The total decreased slightly to fifteen cases between 1745 and 1749, but during the next decade the total increased dramatically to reach a peak of sixty cases and eighty-nine charges between 1755 and 1759. Forty-seven of these cases came from the

Table 3.2
Disciplinary Activity
Exeter Monthly Meeting
1737–1789

Years	Number of Cases		Total
	Men	Women	
1737–1739	2	0	2
1740–1744	11	5	16
1745–1749	12	3	15
1750–1754	23	9	32
1755–1759	47	13	60
1760–1764	20	9	29
1765–1769	18	14	32
1770–1774	5	10	15
1775–1779	35	14	49
1780–1784	20	11	31
1785–1789	19	20	39
TOTALS	**212**	**108**	**320**

Table 3.3
Disciplinary Activity
Exeter Monthly Meeting
1737–1789

Years	Number of Charges		Total
	Men	Women	
1737–1739	2	0	2
1740–1744	13	6	19
1745–1749	16	4	20
1750–1754	27	19	46
1755–1759	61	20	81
1760–1764	35	10	45
1765–1769	33	21	54
1770–1774	8	18	26
1775–1779	56	25	81
1780–1784	34	19	53
1785–1789	32	37	69
TOTALS	**317**	**179**	**497**

men's meeting. Very likely the Seven Years' War had a tremendous impact on discipline during this period. This pattern fits what was occurring in the Quaker meetings throughout colonial Pennsylvania.[16]

As is evident by examining tables 3.2 and 3.3, there often were differences between the number of cases (i.e., the number of people accused) and the number of violations. In fact, 40.6 percent of the cases involved more than one violation, with the most common combination exogamy (marriage with a non-Quaker) along with another offense. In addition, in twenty-eight cases (eighteen for men, ten for women), Exeter Monthly Meeting accused Quakers of three violations, and in nine cases (six for men, three for women), of four.[17]

When examining the "complaints" made against Exeter Friends for wayward behavior, several patterns are evident. Recidivism accounted for 19.1 percent of the total number of cases, with fifty-four cases for the men and seven for women involving repeat offenders. In two of these sixty-one cases, members of the monthly meeting testified against and/or disowned the accused for their actions. This penalty, however, was not always sudden. Members of Exeter Preparative Meeting accused William Hughes of excessive drinking three times and of indebtedness once between 1744 and 1754 before they finally disowned him for drunkenness in 1755. In another instance, the monthly meeting disowned Thomas Hughes, William's brother, in 1765 after Maiden Creek Preparative Meeting accused him of "bearing Arms with an Intent to Defend himself (if attacked) where there was Danger of an Indian Enemy" and later of being "Joined in Marriage by a Priest." Thomas Hughes rejoined the Quaker fold in 1777 after the monthly meeting accepted a written condemnation of his actions, but he did not remain in good standing for long. In 1781, Exeter Monthly Meeting disowned him again, this time for complying with the Test Act and for excessive drinking. This particular example is an exception, as the meeting eventually readmitted nineteen of the 156 Friends disowned for assorted indiscretions after they had condemned their actions. Only Thomas Hughes ever erred again.[18]

When the monthly meeting appointed a committee of at least two Friends to inquire into the circumstances of a complaint, in over ninety percent of the cases leaders of the meeting investigated the violation and questioned the offender. Being a leader might have been a prerequisite most of the time for investigating a case, but it did not exempt someone from being prosecuted. Five of the men's twenty-one cases in 1779 involved a leader or former leader of the men's meeting, and the monthly meeting disowned three of them. Overall, 15.9 percent of the cases (17 percent for men, 13 percent for women) involved leaders of the men's and women's meetings. Exeter Monthly Meeting expelled 21 of the 37 leaders of the men's meeting for improper conduct, although 4 did later condemn their actions. No category of leadership was immune, either, because those disowned included three of the clerks, in addition to overseers and elders.[19]

Moreover, Quaker discipline seldom was speedy. Occasionally the situation could be resolved by the subsequent monthly meeting, but in thirty-six cases over a year passed between the original complaint and disposition. According to table 3.4, Exeter Monthly Meeting usually spent ap-

Table 3.4
Exeter Monthly Meeting
1737–1789
Average Duration of Investigation
(in months)

Year	Men	Women
1737–1739	1.00	0.00
1740–1744	2.27	4.25
1745–1749	5.67	5.00
1750–1754	2.29	8.75
1755–1759	5.19	10.46
1760–1764	7.60	4.22
1764–1769	4.20	2.25
1770–1774	3.00	4.20
1775–1779	7.30	4.25
1780–1784	3.40	5.20
1785–1789	3.94	2.35

proximately four and one-half months investigating an accusation before reading a verdict, either by accepting a paper of condemnation or by drafting a testimony. Not surprisingly, the longest duration between complaint and disposition occurred in the 1755–1764 period and the 1775–1779 period, both times in which external events undermined Quaker order.[20]

One recent historian of Quakerism has suggested four major categories of Quaker violations: Marriage Delinquency, Sectarian Delinquency, Sexual Delinquency, and Delinquency with Victims, occurring in that order. The unstable nature of life along the Pennsylvania frontier, combined with the constant threat of Native American attacks in the 1750s and 1760s and the turmoil surrounding the War for Independence during the 1770s and 1780s, contributed to a different pattern for Exeter Friends and forced them to choose between survival and their faith. Sectarian delinquency was the largest category of offenses for Exeter Monthly Meeting, consisting of 190 of 496 (38.3 percent) of all violations (See table 3.5). Sectarian delinquency included behavior that only Quakers considered inappropriate, such as nonattendance at worship, attending or approving of an irregular marriage, supporting the war effort, or keeping undesirable company. In addition, such behaviors as drunkenness, gambling, and profanity that were prohibited by the laws of Pennsylvania have been included in this category. The two largest offenses within this group related to excessive drinking (33) and military activity (24). In many ways, Exeter Monthly

Table 3.5
Exeter Monthly Meeting
1737–1789
Varieties of Charges
[N=496]

Offense	Number	Percentage
SECTARIAN DELINQUENCY	**190**	**38.3**
Excessive drinking	33	6.6
Military activity	24	4.8
Complying with Test Act	23	4.6
Profanity	18	3.6
Inattendance	16	3.2
Attending/Approving Irregular Marriage	12	2.4
Quarreling	11	2.2
Lewdness	6	1.2
Disapproved Company	4	.8
"Difference"	4	.8
Signing Association Paper	4	.8
Lying	3	.6
Gambling	3	.6
Attending Shooting Match	3	.6
Paying Substitute Fine	3	.6
Dress	2	.4
Disobeying Parents	2	.4
Changing Denominations	2	.4
Dancing	2	.4
Administering Oath	1	.2
Attending Horse Race	1	.2
Hiring Musician	1	.2
Children Baptized by Priest	1	.2
"Dressing a Wedding Dinner"	1	.2
False Affirmation in Court	1	.2
Fortune Telling	1	.2
Holding Office	1	.2
Keeping House for Non-Quaker	1	.2
Tavernkeeping	1	.2
Riding Horse in Race	1	.2
Singing in Tavern	1	.2
Use of Law	1	.2
Visiting Indians	1	.2
Taking Oath	1	.2
Disorderly Conduct	1	.2
MARRIAGE DELINQUENCY	**166**	**33.5**
Exogamy	82	16.5
Married by Priest or Minister	60	12.1

continued

Table 3.5—*Continued*

Offense	Number	Percentage
Married by Justice or Magistrate	17	3.4
Married Cousin	7	1.4
SEXUAL DELINQUENCY	**81**	**16.3**
Fornication	53	10.7
Fathering or Bearing Illegitimate Child	26	5.2
Adultery	2	.4
DELINQUENCY WITH VICTIMS	**59**	**11.9**
Debt	17	3.4
Removal without Requesting Certificate	12	2.4
Fighting	6	1.2
Slander	5	1.0
Theft	4	.8
Assault	3	.6
False Accusations	3	.6
Breach of Contract	2	.4
Deceit	2	.4
Bribery	1	.2
Jumping Bail	1	.2
Murder	1	.2
Refusing to Pay Rent	1	.2

Meeting's location along the Pennsylvania frontier impacted the ability of its members to remain in good standing.[21]

Excessive drinking particularly plagued some members of Exeter Monthly Meeting. Between 1737 and 1789, representatives of the three preparative meetings accused thirty-three men and women of this violation. In addition, several reports to Philadelphia Quarterly Meeting referred to "the unnecessary Frequenting of Taverns & places of Diversion"; there also was "an Excess of spirituous Liquors amongst [them] especially in Harvest Time."[22]

The monthly meeting disowned approximately half of the Friends guilty of this offense. Some of them had previously submitted papers of condemnation and were repeat offenders. Papers condemning misbehavior often went into detail with respect to how the violation had occurred. In 1741, Joseph Gibson described the circumstances surrounding his drunkenness:

> having occasion to go one morning to a mill in Tulpehoccon, but my corn not being Ground as I expected, was obliged to stay all Night; and next Morning as I went home it was so very Cold that I called at a Dutch Man's House to warm myself and my Lad at the stove; and the Man seeing me very Cold went and

brought me some Bread and a Dram, and was Urgent for me to Eat; but notwithstanding I had not eaten anything from the Morning before, I could not eat then. Then he persuaded me to take two or three Drams, and that was the most; but however, it proved too much; which I am very sorry for. . . .[23]

Two years later, Gibson again condemned his actions after he had been "overcome by Liquor at Maxatawny." Samuel Wilkinson apologized in 1757 because he "was Drunk with French Brandy at Reading"; five months later, Exeter Monthly Meeting disowned him because he had not obeyed "the dictates of that Divine Principle which teacheth Sobriety and Moderation in all things, [and] hath been Guilty of the Notorious Sin of Drunkenness."[24] In other instances, the investigating committee uncovered other problems and added these offenses to the testimony that pronounced disownment. The women of Exeter Monthly Meeting charged Gobitha Woolaston, Jr., in August 1752 with "Drinking to Excess," "having Stolen a Lace from a Shopkeeper in Reading; and also of . . . being Guilty of very indecent and bad Language." When the monthly meeting disowned her fifteen months later, the men recommended that the testimony be read "in Reading at such Places where she hath been charged with Misbehaviour." In 1756, Exeter Monthly Meeting expelled Samuel Woolaston, Jr., Gobitha's brother, because he "hath walked Disorderly, particular in that Notorious Sin of Drinking to Excess . . . and Notwithstanding he hath been repeatedly Admonished, he is still subject to be overcome with strong Liquor." In that same testimony, the men also noted that Woolaston had used profanity and had "Accomplish[ed] his Marriage before a Justice Contrary to the good Order practised by Friends as well as the known Rules of our Discipline." Members of the Woolaston family, however, were not the only Exeter Friends to commit another violation along with excessive drinking; in other cases, the monthly meeting also accused the violator of fighting, fornication, or joining the militia.[25]

The increased percentage of military activity and compliance with the Test Act, which combined for 9.4 percent of the total percentage of all offenses, are the primary reasons why Sectarian Delinquency surpassed the other categories for Exeter. The *Rules of Discipline* opposed any support for warlike activity, not only bearing arms but also furnishing wagons or paying a substitute fine. During the American Revolution, this opposition to war included complying with the Test Act, which required an oath of allegiance to support the state constitution of 1776. In the rest of Pennsylvania, in contrast, fewer than four percent of all Friends disciplined during the eighteenth century had decided to bear arms.[26]

The frontier location of Berks County contributed to the increased amount of military-related problems among Exeter Friends. During the Seven Years' War era (1755–1764), fourteen of the seventy-eight cases

(18 percent) handled by the men's monthly meeting dealt with violations of pacifist principles, while between 1775 and 1784, eleven of fifty-five cases (20 percent) related to participation in the war effort. The only conviction for murder occurred in 1763, as the meeting disowned Hezekiah Boone for killing Native Americans in self-defense.[27]

The second most common deviance from the Quaker order by Exeter Friends was in the realm of marriage, as 33.5 percent of the violations fell into this category. Friends who wished to marry would attend a monthly meeting and publish their intentions, and the men's and women's meetings would separately appoint a committee of two or three members to inquire into the moral character of the couple and to check into prior commitments. Any couple who did not follow this procedure, or any Quaker who chose a nonmember as a spouse, was subject to disciplinary action. In addition, any Quaker who attended or assisted in a marriage contrary to the rules suffered the same penalty as those participating in the ceremony. For Quakers, violations of the marriage regulations were serious, because Friends believed that the faith was transferred most successfully from one generation to the next through the parents, and both spouses must be in good standing in order for this to occur. The devotion of the parents was especially suspect if they assisted in a marriage ceremony contrary to the discipline, and Exeter Monthly Meeting disowned many others besides Squire Boone for this offense.[28]

The third most common category of violations for Exeter Friends was Sexual Delinquency. Sexual delinquency, which involved fornication, fathering, or bearing an illegitimate child, and adultery, accounted for 16.3 percent of the offenses committed by Exeter Friends. This classification was undoubtedly the most difficult to prove, because it often relied upon hearsay or upon a confession by the offender.[29]

In some cases, the monthly meeting discovered the misbehavior when a couple published their intentions to marry and the investigating committee found evidence of improper conduct. Ellis Hughes and Thomas Ellis, appointed to inquire into Joseph Boone, Jr.'s "Clearness in relation to Marriage," reported to Exeter Monthly Meeting in September 1749, that Boone's fiancée, Elizabeth Warren, "is with Child by the said Joseph." Two months later, Boone indicated, "he is Sorry for the Trouble he has brought on Friends & Disgrace he has been to Truth." The case continued unresolved, however, until June 1751, when the monthly meeting finally disowned Boone for fornication and for fathering an illegitimate child. While it took the men's meeting almost two years to resolve the matter, the women acted more speedily. Elizabeth Warren expressed remorse over her actions in December 1749, and the women's monthly meeting accepted her repentance.[30]

Women who were found to be with child out of wedlock also seldom let the father go unpunished. In 1756, for example, Rebecca Coleston accused John Ellis of being the father of her bastard child, and the men's meeting investigated the complaint. As the drama developed, John Ellis's father Morris, a former overseer of Exeter Preparative Meeting, confessed that he, and not his son, had committed "the hainous Sin of Adultery" and had been responsible for the young woman's pregnancy. The monthly meeting, however, disowned both men, because it could not be proven that John was innocent of "unchast[e] Familiarity" with Rebecca Coleston.[31]

Sometimes the offending parties did not think their misbehavior was something Friends had a right to investigate. In May 1757, representatives from Exeter Preparative Meeting reported to the monthly meeting "that Joseph Millard is Accused of keeping unseemly, or unbecoming Company with Mary Pratt." That September, after being visited by several leaders of the meeting, Millard admitted that "he had been Guilty of some Indecent Behavior towards John Pratt's Wife; but said it was only done with Design to know whether she was an Honest Woman or not; and that as the Offence was Private, he would not Condemn it Publickly."[32] In December, with the matter still unresolved, the monthly meeting appointed another investigating committee. Their report, presented at the Maiden Creek meetinghouse in January 1758, indicated that Millard had indeed wandered from the "Dictates of Truth":

> his Behaviour toward the said Woman, according to his own Confession, is very Shameful, Vile and Scandalous; that his Bitterness against Friends in general for their Dealing with him in this Occasion, together with his almost entire Neglect of attending our Religious Meetings . . . are strong Indications of a Mind deeply corrupted, and a Heart widely strayed from the Path of Peace and Salvation . . .

That same month, the women's monthly meeting formally charged Mary Pratt with indecent behavior, lying, and adultery, and they disowned her two months later.[33]

Finally, the least frequent category of Quaker violations was Delinquency with Victims. This group, which accounted for 11.9 percent of the total number of offenses, included such criminal offenses as indebtedness, assault, deceit, slander, and theft. Within this category, debt and removal without a certificate were by far the most frequent offenses, and occasionally they occurred simultaneously if a Friend left the geographical confines of the meeting without satisfying his creditors.[34]

In the case of Richard Moore, however, obtaining a certificate of removal led to the resolution of the indebtedness charge. Moore informed Exeter Monthly Meeting in September 1756 of his desire to move to North

Carolina. The monthly meeting contributed 25s. toward his expenses, with another 25s. raised to cover some outstanding debts in Berks County. Moore, however, still had not paid off all his obligations prior to his departure, so Exeter Monthly Meeting appointed three men to write to Cane Creek Monthly Meeting in North Carolina to inform them of his neglect. Part of the concern for notifying this meeting might have been because this was not the first time that Moore had been accused of indebtedness, and, in fact, Exeter Monthly Meeting had even supported another member's efforts to recover money through legal action when resolving a previous complaint. Other members who attempted to flee the control of the meeting as did Moore were caught and reprimanded as necessary.[35]

Throughout the eighteenth century, Exeter Monthly Meeting disowned 80 percent of the members testified against, although 9.7 percent later condemned their misbehavior. Condemnation at a later date, however, was not the only way that a Quaker could reverse the decision of the monthly meeting. Within the structure of the Quaker organization, a procedure existed for appealing cases. For example, in March 1749, John Wily, an overseer for Maiden Creek Preparative Meeting, charged "that there are many Friends belonging to this Meeting that have opened a Door, and have gone, and are going on in the way to lay waste and Destroy the Order & Discipline of the law and the Gospel." That October, the monthly meeting produced a testimony against him for these accusations. Wily appeared at the next monthly meeting and indicated that he intended to appeal the decision to the next quarterly meeting at Philadelphia. In May 1750, the monthly meeting received the news that the quarterly meeting had overturned their verdict and had reinstated Wily as a member of the Society. Few appeals had the same result as did Wily's, for in 1780 the quarterly meeting upheld Exeter's decision to disown members who had complied with the provisions of the Test Act.[36]

Whenever Friends moved to another region, they would request a certificate of removal from the monthly meeting that supervised the indulged meeting they attended to take with them to the new location. These documents, which served as letters of transfer, indicated the Quaker's standing in the community and any outstanding disciplinary violations or other problems. For three women who came to Exeter Monthly Meeting, these certificates reflected "outgoings in Marriage," as they had married non-Quakers; the husbands of Gobitha Woolaston and Hannah Nuzum joined the Society shortly after settling in Berks County. The monthly meeting at Brighouse in Yorkshire, England, informed Exeter Monthly Meeting that William Horshall "being naturally of a free & affable Disposition was liable to be drawn into Company tending to his Hurt, as, drinking to Excess." Furthermore, several Exeter Friends attended Chester Monthly

Meeting in February 1777 to provide "concuring Testimony" of the reformed behavior of Jonathan Worrall and Hannah Nuzum, who wished to settle in Robeson Township.[37]

As a Friends Meeting along the frontier, Exeter Monthly Meeting did not merely serve as a magnet for spiritually challenged Quakers; it also saw some of its less dutiful members move away. According to the remarks in these certificates, five Friends had either married a non-Quaker or had consented to the marriage of their child to a non-Quaker. Two members had recently condemned their actions for "drinking too much strong Drink"; Jesse Faulkner's certificate remarked that his wife Martha "has been so unguarded as to drink Spirituous Liquors to some degree of Excess, which, tho' her Conduct herein doth not fully appear to have deserv'd public Censure, yet we thought a private Hint to You incumbent upon us, for her Good." In two other cases, "residing remote from Meeting" and illness resulted in irregular attendance at first-day meetings. In general, Exeter Friends tended to be in good standing when they left Berks County; only thirteen of the 291 certificates sent between 1737 and 1789 included comments about Friends' spiritual and temporal weaknesses.[38]

Exeter Monthly Meeting included only 1.8 percent of all offenders among Quaker meetings in Pennsylvania prior to the Revolution. Only Richland Monthly Meeting in Bucks County, established five years after Exeter, had fewer offenders during this period. The types of violations committed by Exeter Friends did not differ appreciably from those at other monthly meetings. New Garden Monthly Meeting in Chester County, for instance, where many Exeter Friends had resided prior to moving to Berks County, also disowned members for drunkenness, fornication, fighting, profanity, gambling, joining the militia, and selling rum to the Native Americans. Over forty-three percent of their cases involved marriage violations; New Garden Monthly Meeting disowned almost half of these offenders.[39]

At Middletown Monthly Meeting in Bucks County, marriage offenses also dominated the statistics. The types of violations reflected the Quaker dominance of that county. Charges made against Middletown Friends included family irresponsibility, loose conversation, violating the Sabbath, disregarding the discipline, and "schismatic" behavior. Other offenses included participating in the slave trade, receiving stolen goods, counterfeiting, unsanctioned printing, political activity, soliciting entertainment, military activity, slander, excessive drinking, fighting, fornication, fraud, quarreling, adultery, gambling, larceny, and smuggling. Unlike at Exeter or New Garden, the women of Middletown Monthly Meeting did not actively participate in the "impulse to tighten up all the particular aspects of outward behavior" until the 1770s.[40]

The violations committed by members of Philadelphia Monthly Meeting reflected the urban and commercial nature of the city. In the 1740s, the monthly meeting testified against Quakers for refusing to pay debts or rent, joining other denominations, "going on a Privateering Voyage," being "Owner of a private Ship of War fitted out in this City," "unbecoming behavior," and "contributing to & promoting of Warlike preparations, &c.." Philadelphia Friends also committed the usual marriage offenses of marrying non-Quakers and having their wedding ceremony performed contrary to discipline; one woman faced disownment because she had remarried despite "not having a certain account of the decease of her said first husband." Women were not the only ones guilty of premature marriages, as Philadelphia Monthly Meeting disowned one man in 1748 for "marrying a woman whose husband at that time supposed to be living."[41]

In some ways, the experiences faced by the leaders of Exeter Monthly Meeting as they attempted to enforce the discipline were typical of those of other meetings. Exeter Friends committed essentially the same types of offenses, although the frequency occasionally varied. The leaders did their best to maintain stability within the Society by prosecuting known violators of the rules, and they dealt with the accused as speedily as possible under the circumstances. After all, Exeter Friends were in a sense attempting to maintain the faith in what could be perceived as an unfriendly environment, explaining the need to require total support for the discipline.

Unlike most other religious groups in colonial America, leaders of the Society of Friends preferred to disown rather than to reclaim fallen brethren, believing that it was better to have a few "good" members than to have many whose devotion was suspect. Although lapsed Quakers were always welcome to attend meetings for worship, and, while they could at any time rejoin the Society if they were willing to condemn their actions to the satisfaction of the leaders, the Quakers never sought to proselytize or gain converts like most other religious organizations.[42]

Men and women whose beliefs were compatible with the tenets of Quakers were welcome to worship among Friends and, if they chose, to declare themselves in unity with them. Generally, those Berks Countians who joined Exeter Monthly Meeting through this process proved to be faithful additions to the Society. Some, in fact, including Hannah Iddings and Jonathan Stephens, even became overseers of preparative meetings. Not all of these men and women, however, remained within the Quaker fold until their death. Of the 123 men and women who indicated to the satisfaction of the leaders of the monthly meeting that "their Lives and Conversations [would] Correspond with the Principles of Friends," almost two dozen committed violations of the discipline. Thirteen had chosen to marry someone who was not a Quaker or did so in a manner contrary to Quaker practice. The monthly meeting charged two men with complying with the provisions of the Test Act. Another two men failed to attend worship services on a regular basis. Finally, four converts—three women and a man—faced disciplinary action for fornication.[43]

In general, the disciplinary problems faced by Exeter Monthly Meeting in the eighteenth century were typical of yet distinctive from those experienced by other Quaker meetings in Pennsylvania.[44] The frontier location undoubtedly contributed to the unrest, especially when war came to the province. The leaders of the meeting did their best to maintain order, but it must have been difficult to set a good example when almost one-sixth of the leaders were guilty of assorted violations of the *Rules of Discipline.* Nevertheless, perhaps the most remarkable aspect of the enforcement of the discipline was that it indeed strengthened rather than weakened the Society as a whole. Not only did Exeter Monthly Meeting manage to maintain the most stable religious organization in Berks County during many years of turmoil; it also served as a social control model for other Quaker meetings along the advancing frontier.

4

War and the Frontier Friends:
Exeter Monthly Meeting and the Seven Years' War

THE SOCIETY OF FRIENDS HAS BEEN WELL KNOWN FOR ITS ORIGINAL commitment to pacifism. In colonial Pennsylvania, political control of the province by members of this religious group resulted in a reluctance to support the British Crown in its conflicts with France over North America. This political dominance rested in the hands of the Quaker elite of Philadelphia, Chester, and Bucks counties in southeastern Pennsylvania, far from the Native American raids and turmoil of the frontier. With the onset of war with the French and the Native Americans in the mid-1750s, members of the Society of Friends throughout the province began to confront obstacles to their pacifism, hindrances that in some ways did not disappear for another thirty years. These trying times for Pennsylvania Quakers were especially difficult for Friends along the frontier, who not only had little political experience but also had been an ethnic and religious minority for almost fifty years. In spite of these difficulties, backcountry Quakers managed to survive and expand along the Pennsylvania frontier.[1]

By the middle of the eighteenth century, members of the Society of Friends had resided in Pennsylvania for almost seventy years. Throughout that time, they controlled the province politically and economically, with the center of both located in Philadelphia, William Penn's "greene country town." Over the years, the population of the province increased tremendously. By the time of the Revolution, Pennsylvania was one of the largest colonies in terms of population (approximately 270,000), even though it was one of the youngest in terms of existence.[2]

Although hundreds of thousands of Europeans migrated to the interior of the province in search of religious freedom and economic opportunity during the colonial period, they did not find a democratic society. Even though inhabitants in the interior of the province outnumbered the residents of the Delaware Valley by mid-century, political control continued to rest in Philadelphia. The only county that the legislature had even established in the interior was Lancaster County in 1729; not for another twenty years did the Assembly recognize the backcountry settlers' needs for local government. Part of this reluctance stemmed from fears that the frontiersmen would try to overturn Quaker political control and upset the economic stability of the colony. Even after the Assembly established new counties in the 1750s and 1770s, it limited them to one or two representatives each, compared with eight from each of the three original counties. This disparity prevented the backcountry Pennsylvanians from having much of a voice in the government, a situation that would have dire consequences for frontier residents during the 1750s.[3]

One of the newer counties established after mid-century was Berks County, home of Exeter Monthly Meeting. Residents of the area had been active in efforts to form a new county in the region since the late 1730s, mainly because of the difficulty in traveling over forty miles on the crude roads to Philadelphia, the county seat. In the settlers' requests for a new county, they claimed that distance prevented them from profitably marketing the crops grown on their farms. The petitioners particularly emphasized that the Schuylkill River, which cut through the proposed county, would provide an effective natural means of shipping goods to Philadelphia.[4]

The key factor that led to the establishment of Berks County was the foundation of the town of Reading in 1748. Thomas and Richard Penn, sons of the founder of the province, saw the potential of the region and laid out the seat for the proposed county, naming it after the ancestral home of their family. Government officials viewed the town, situated near several trading paths, as an ideal meeting place for conducting negotiations with the Native Americans. These advantages finally contributed to the establishment of the county in 1752, with its borders extending from approximately forty miles northwest of Philadelphia to the southern border of western New York, a distance of about two hundred miles. For the next twenty years, Berks County served as the northwestern frontier of Pennsylvania, and settlers in the county continued to cope with the problems of frontier life.[5]

Before the 1750s, members of Exeter Monthly Meeting had generally concentrated on establishing their homesteads and on serving God according to the Society's principles. With the outbreak of war in the province and the subsequent Native American raids, these frontier Quakers had to choose between following their pacifist consciences or defending their property. Members of Exeter Monthly Meeting did both, just like the other settlers in the region. Unlike the majority of frontiersmen, Friends faced a spiritual crisis when arming themselves against the Native Americans.[6]

When war came to Pennsylvania in 1754, residents of the province finally became involved in the conflict between the British and the French for the control of North America that had been brewing for over half a century. As early as 1750, Conrad Weiser, a prominent German settler of the Tulpehocken region of western Berks County who had achieved success in earlier negotiations with the Native Americans, indicated to Governor Andrew Hamilton that the French were gaining influence with the Iroquois Confederacy and the Delaware and Shawnee tribes of eastern Pennsylvania. Provincial officials failed to heed Weiser's warning. Following the defeat of British and colonial forces in western Pennsylvania at the Battle of the Monongahela in 1755, not only did settlers temporarily abandon western Pennsylvania, but natives proceeded to conduct raids along the undefended frontier. By 1756, they had crossed the Appalachian Mountains into southeastern Pennsylvania, attacking settlements and forcing the residents to flee.[7]

The immediate response of the Assembly to this crisis was to raise money to pay for the defense of the frontier. Beginning in 1755, Quakers confronted a particular concern over the propriety of war taxes. The first such levy had occurred in 1711, when the Assembly raised funds for the use of Queen Anne, who then could spend the money as the Crown chose. But with the arrival of war within the borders of Pennsylvania, the situation changed. Members of the Assembly soon realized that they would need to develop some method of defending the province, and funds must be raised. When the legislature voted to levy a tax on all land—including proprietary estates—specifically for the war effort in 1755, Friends began to question their role in the government. Of this Quaker-dominated body, five Friends, including Berks County's representative, Francis Parvin of Maiden Creek, voted against the tax.[8]

Friends outside the political arena quickly recognized the difficulty of the dilemma. Members of Philadelphia Yearly Meeting began to consider the issue of taxation in December 1755 and reached a consensus only after much debate. Those Friends who supported the payment of a war tax withdrew from the meeting, with the result that the Society began to divide over what some considered a sectarian issue. Friends who opposed the tax argued that it was "principally intended for purposes inconsistent with our peaceable testimony . . . as we cannot be concerned in wars and fightings, so neither ought we to contribute thereto by paying the tax." They did not begin a boycott of the tax or suggest the expulsion of members who paid it, but they merely explained their concerns about the precedent being set by the Assembly. After all, they feared, the step between assessing a war tax and forming a land force for defense was not a large one.[9]

In general, Quakers viewed the mistreatment of Native Americans by frontiersmen as the main cause of the conflict. Therefore, these Friends did not see the immediate need for military spending. Backcountry residents held a different view. The lack of defense caused them to request assistance from the Board of Trade in London. In this petition, the settlers contended that the Quakers in Pensilv[ani]a, are not one Fifth of the People there; . . . they are generally settled, in the South Part of the Province, most out of Danger, & are the P[er]sons that are *last* to be devoured; So that the Murder & Destruction of their Fellow Subjects, the more modern Settlers, who make their Frontier, is, to them, a light matter, being *themselves,* out of the present Danger, & They, most piously, Cant, that according to their religious Perswasions, *Self Defence,* is *unlawful.*[10]

The petitioners, of course, had neglected to consider the possibility that Quakers also lived in the area under attack.

By early 1756, it had become evident that the frontier was in turmoil, and more drastic measures needed to be taken. When the Governor of Pennsylvania and the Supreme Executive Council declared war against the Delaware that spring, Quaker Assemblymen again faced a problem. That June, six members of the Assembly, including Francis Parvin, realized that their mere presence as members of this legislative body implied support for the prosecution of the war and chose to relinquish their political power rather than consent to the increasing militarism. Several other Friends declined reelection that fall, resulting in an Assembly that for the first time did not have a Quaker majority. While some Quakers resumed their seats in the 1760s, never again did a Friend represent Berks County after the 1750s, nor did members of the Society control the Assembly.[11]

The Quaker response to the passage of the Militia Act of 1757 further raised the ire of colonial leaders. They ordered "all Quakers, Menonists, Moravians, and others conscientiously scrupulous of bearing Arms . . . [to] be ready to obey the Commands of the Officers in the following Particulars, that is to say, In extinguishing Fires in any City or Township, whether kindled by the Enemy from without, or by traiterous Inhabitants within." That Philadelphia Yearly Meeting in 1758 ordered Friends to refrain from "voluntarily assisting with their Ships, waggons or other carriages" when transporting "Implements of War or military Stores" did little to dispel concerns about the Quakers' lack of support for the war.[12]

The discord in the Pennsylvania Assembly that led to the partial withdrawal in 1756 also resulted from a renewed emphasis on Quaker ideals within the Society. New leaders were gaining control of Philadelphia Yearly Meeting, which contributed to a stricter enforcement of Quaker discipline. Gradually, presence in the Assembly implied complicity with prowar legislation; Quaker Assemblymen could thus be disowned for attendance at these meetings.[13]

While the Quaker politicians of Philadelphia, Bucks, and Chester counties were attempting to rationalize their opposition to defending the frontier, backcountry settlers continued to suffer at the hands of the Native Americans. Over 150 died and another thirty-five were taken prisoner or declared missing between June 1754 and November 1763. Conrad Weiser expressed a particular concern in 1755 about the state of the frontier. In a letter to William Allen, he remarked that "all our Indians are gone off with the French . . . what is worse I am afraid the French are about Fortifying themselves this side of the Allegheny Hills, . . . where they will find and have found plenty of Provisions, as the Country is deserted by its Inhabitants, leaving their Corn and Cattle behind them." The threat had become so severe, in fact, that a company formed in the area included "two or three long Beards . . . one a Menonist who declared he would live and die with his neighbours; he had a good gun with him."[14]

Berks County residents had for the most part sought peaceful asylum in Pennsylvania; consequently, they were not well-prepared to defend the county against native attacks. Political and cultural conditions had caused the settlers to ignore the pleas of local political leaders such as Weiser who encouraged preparedness, even after Native Americans were sighted in the vicinity of Reading in July 1755. The town's magistrates recognized the need for action. When the natives attacked the Tulpehocken settlement that November, they responded quickly. Five county officials, including Weiser, pleaded to Governor Robert Hunter Morris that they were "all in uproar, all in Disorder, all willing to do, and have little in our power." They continued, "We have no authority, no commissions, no officers practised in War, and without the commiseration of our Friends in Philadelphia, who think themselves vastly safer than they are." If provincial officials did not respond soon enough, they vowed to go to the capital and "Quarter ourselves on its Inhabitants and wait our Fate with them."[15]

To demonstrate further the immediacy of the crisis, farmers from western Berks County converged upon the city. Carrying the dead bodies of the mutilated victims of these raids, the frontiersmen traveled to Philadelphia. Within days, the Assembly responded to the pleas of the settlers and authorized the construction of a chain of forts between the Schuylkill and Susquehanna Rivers to protect the region.[16]

By early 1756, troops had begun to arrive in central and eastern Pennsylvania to defend the frontier from the combined French and Native American forces. Governor William Shirley of Massachusetts sent the first volunteer company to protect Berks County, which arrived in Reading that January. Governor Morris ordered the townspeople of Reading to provide quarters for the soldiers, along with food and beverage. While these troops were a welcome sight in early 1756, Reading's citizens gradually became weary of having to care for soldiers stationed in their town. In 1759, the news that three companies of Highland Soldiers would be quartered in Reading upset some of the residents. Weiser remarked in a letter to Richard Peters, "the Tavern Keepers [were] under the Greatest Consternation, having received nothing as yet for last years quartering of Soldiers."[17]

In spite of the erection of the forts and the arrival of troops to defend the county, native raids continued. Weiser informed Governor William Denny in 1756 that "the People are moving away, leaving their Barnes full of Grain behind them; and there is a lamentable cry among them." Between October 1755, and September 1757, the natives either murdered or took captive no fewer than sixty men, women, and children from Bern, Bethel, and Tulpehocken townships in western Berks County; hundreds of others fled their homesteads rather than face the attacks.[18]

News of the Native Americans' activities soon traveled throughout the colony. Beginning in November 1755, the *Pennsylvania Gazette*—partly owned by Benjamin Franklin—published accounts from Berks County settlers "advising us of a great deal of mischief done in Tulpehocken by the Indians." Undoubtedly printed to stir public sentiment for defense spending, these notices described the atrocities committed by the Native Americans and the soldiers' efforts to capture them.[19]

Political officials of Berks County were not the only local leaders concerned about the turmoil on the frontier. In a letter to the religious authorities of the German Reformed Church in Holland, Reformed minister Henry William Stoy wrote in 1757:

Our Indians, more savage than wild beasts, have either dragged away innumerable inhabitants of British America from our borders as captives, or slain them in a most wretched and indescribable manner. Cold horror shakes my body and an icy tremor runs through my very bones when I recall what I have seen myself and learned from hearsay. Neither would the tiger nor the most ferocious lion rage so fiercely when meeting a man, as these wild barbarians do. They scalp the living, and what is more even the dead. I myself have seen them slay them and mutilate their bodies with tomahawks. Like wolves they wander through the continuous forests of these regions. They go and return unimpeded. In this manner they have devastated our land far and wide. We have lost some of our congregations either entirely or in part.[20]

The environment for Quakers in Berks County, then, was undoubtedly more unstable than that of their fellow Friends in Bucks, Chester, and Philadelphia counties.

For Exeter Friends, the Seven Years' War had a special effect. Native American raids led to the destruction of property and the loss of life. In response to the ravages of the war, Philadelphia Yearly Meeting established the Meeting for Sufferings in 1756. Created to handle the emergency conditions arising during the conflict, the primary purpose of this organization was to assist Quakers and others who had fled their homes by providing financial assistance and clothing and by assisting children of refugees in locating apprenticeships in safe areas of the province. Friends in the eastern counties, even though they opposed war, did recognize the need to supply aid for the fellow colonists.[21]

During this conflict, at least five families affiliated with Exeter Monthly Meeting required assistance from the Meeting for Sufferings because of distressed circumstances. All of the heads of these families resided "over the mountains" in 1754, indicating that they lived in an area highly susceptible to attack.[22]

Thomas Ellis, Jr., a member of one of the more prominent families of the monthly meeting, was the first Exeter Friend to obtain aid. In December 1756, the monthly meeting gave Ellis £2.2.6 "in Consideration of his having lately met with Considerable Loss by being obliged to Remove from his Habitation on account of the Indians." That fall, he had "left a Plantation beyond the Mountains & hath lost his Crop by horses & breaking into the Field" when he returned to Exeter Township with his pregnant wife and four young daughters. Apparently his situation continued to be bleak, for he received additional assistance over the next few years. Because of the destruction and constant threat of attack, Ellis probably never returned to his home before he moved to Virginia in 1764.[23]

A few weeks after the monthly meeting had begun to assist Ellis, Benjamin Lightfoot, clerk of Exeter Monthly Meeting, attended the Monthly Meeting for Sufferings in Philadelphia. Lightfoot informed this organization that several members of Exeter Monthly Meeting had "left their Habitations from Apprehensions of Danger from the Indian Enemies." The Meeting for Sufferings responded by appointing a committee to investigate the situation. In the meantime, this relief organization recommended that Exeter Monthly Meeting provide assistance as necessary, with reimbursement to occur at a later date. Exeter Monthly Meeting proceeded to appoint its own committee "to Inquire into [the] Circumstances," and if relief was necessary "to hand it to them on this Meetings' account." At the next monthly meeting, the committee reported that "none seem to be in immediate want of Bread," so the situation remained stable for a few more months.[24]

By September 1757, an increase in native raids led to a renewed request for assistance. In a letter to the Meeting for Sufferings, Lightfoot identified five families who had fled their homes. None of the heads of these families could meet their debts after abandoning their property, further contributing to their financial distress. Thomas Ellis, Jr., received an additional £5 to cover expenses, as did Richard Stephens, Thomas Willits, Joseph Yarnall, and Jemima Green.[25]

Richard Stephens's situation was particularly unique. Both he and his wife had joined Exeter Monthly Meeting in the early 1750s through a profession of faith, finding the ideals of the Society of Friends closely aligned with their spiritual well-being. Identified in Lightfoot's correspondence as "a lame Man" with seven children, Stephens had begun to experience difficulty caring for his family by early 1757. When the natives attacked, he and his family "left a Plantation with about 30 Acres of Land Cleared." He had grown wheat and rye the previous summer, both to feed his family and "to pay some small Debts which he Owes." What the natives had not ruined "has been almost all destroyed with the Frost which . . . has reduced his circumstances to a very Low Ebb." The dire straits faced by his family, in fact, soon forced Stephens to consider relocating to another region of the province.[26]

The same month that Lightfoot asked for aid, Stephens requested a certificate of removal for his family to Chester Monthly Meeting. Members of Exeter Monthly Meeting noted in the certificate that "there are some small Debts unpaid, occasion'd (we believe) by his being drove from his Habitation by the Indians, and his removal with Consent of his Creditors." A month later, Lightfoot forwarded a certificate of removal to Philadelphia Monthly Meeting for Stephens's eldest son, Richard, Jr., who had become an apprentice in that city. Not until 1763, once the turmoil of the frontier had subsided, did the family return from Chester and resume the cultivation of crops at their homestead along the frontier. Except for a ten-month relocation to Haverford in the mid-1760s, Richard Stephens remained an active member of Exeter Monthly Meeting, albeit a poor one, until his death in 1784.[27]

The circumstances surrounding the poverty of Thomas Willits, another distressed Exeter Friend, were quite different from those of Richard Stephens. The children of Willits and his wife Rachel had all grown by the time of the Seven Years' War; Lightfoot identified them as "both Ancient" in his correspondence. Exeter Monthly Meeting had disciplined Willits in September 1756 for excessive drinking, an offense that he acknowledged in a Paper of Condemnation accepted in October 1757. His family continued to require assistance in 1759, with Lightfoot making an additional request to the Meeting for Sufferings on his behalf. This organization sent an additional £5 for Willits, who "being indisposed & almost helpless" had fled his home again. Exeter Friends assisted Willits with money and shoes when he returned home in the fall of 1759, and the Meeting for Sufferings continued to provide additional financial assistance until 1761. In the fall of that year, Willits and his wife decided to move to Westbury, New York, to reside among family and friends for a year, rather then face continued hardship.[28]

While Thomas Willits and his wife relied upon the contributions of fellow Friends for their survival, two of their sons left the Quaker fold by joining the militia, and one of their daughters experienced her own financial distresses because of the conflict. Exeter Monthly Meeting had disowned Jemima Green in early 1751 for exogamy; the meeting reinstated her after she acknowledged this offense in September 1757. Green had moved to North Wales Township in Philadelphia County two years earlier, being forced to flee with her husband because of Native American attacks. Lightfoot noted to the Meeting for Sufferings that although Green's husband was not a member of the Society of Friends, "she, and her three small children are Objects worthy of your Notice." Green received another £5 in 1760 at the request of Gwynedd Monthly Meeting, as she and her family continued to suffer because of the destruction of their property. She rejoined Exeter Monthly Meeting in 1761; five years later she transferred her membership to Fairfax Monthly Meeting in Virginia.[29]

The last family that received financial assistance also moved to Virginia in the 1760s, although under different circumstances. In 1757, Exeter Monthly Meeting requested aid for Joseph Yarnall, his wife Elizabeth, and three daughters, all of whom suffered along the frontier. Yarnall had already "left a small Improvement beyond the sd mountains" and moved to Reading. He had some difficulty providing for his family, and in fact he was "likely to be Sued for Rent due on a House in which he lived some time ago" in the town. Members of Maiden Creek Preparative Meeting who had visited Yarnall suggested that he bind out his children to ease the financial burden. A cousin of Yarnall's took the eldest daughter, but the other two girls could not be apprenticed because of illness and age. Apparently his property sustained some damage during this time, because in August 1758, the Friends appointed to inspect his situation reported that they were assisting him in obtaining another residence.[30]

That December, these Quakers noted in their report that Yarnall was in prison and his family was still in distress. The monthly meeting responded by informing Elizabeth Yarnall "that as they have hitherto declined to take Friends advice, which if they still persist in, and Refuse to put their Children out where they may be suitably Employ'd and Maintained, the Meeting must of necessity rid themselves of such disorderly and Refractory Persons." Two months later, the monthly meeting charged both Joseph and Elizabeth Yarnall with violations of the Quaker discipline (Joseph for enlisting as a soldier, Elizabeth for keeping house for a non-Quaker); the meeting also admonished the Yarnalls for failing to put out their other two children as apprentices.[31]

In March 1759, the women's meeting dismissed the charges against Elizabeth, while the men's meeting disowned Joseph for neglecting to attend religious meetings and for military activity. At this time, Elizabeth seemed more agreeable to allowing the two youngest children to be bound out, if two Women Friends would take them. The monthly meeting also agreed to assist her in finding another house, a task that had been completed by the following month. Elizabeth Yarnall continued to receive financial assistance from Exeter Monthly Meeting until July 1762, when the monthly meeting heeded her request and abolished the committee appointed to investigate her circumstances. The Yarnall family probably never returned to their farm; in 1766 Elizabeth moved with her middle daughter to Fairfax Monthly Meeting, where several children from a previous marriage had migrated, after Joseph had "died insolvent."[32]

When examining these cases of economic distress, several common features become evident. First, even though Exeter Monthly Meeting did occasionally request the assistance of the Meeting for Sufferings, more often it provided funds out of its own resources and solicited contributions from each of the three preparative meetings. All but one of the families experiencing hardship left Exeter Monthly Meeting at some point during the war, three of them with certificates of removal and the head of the other because of disownment. Members of three of the families had encountered problems in adhering to the strict rules of their faith, and two had even managed to regain full membership just in time to be eligible for financial assistance. In addition, none of these recipients of aid were among the "elite" of the meeting; only Thomas Ellis, Jr., even had a relative who had served the meeting as a leader. Finally, among the seven Quaker men who lived "over the mountains" in 1754, four received financial assistance, one was the highest taxpayer, one fought in the war and was subsequently disowned, and one was killed by the natives.[33]

Quaker historians have remarked that Native Americans viewed Quakers as friends and sympathizers, and thus "not a single Quaker is known to have lost his life at their hands on the Pennsylvania frontier during the French and Indian War." However, four members of John Fincher's family, living on the edge of European civilization, experienced this tragedy. Fincher and his family settled "over the mountains" in the mid-1750s, and they became members of the Society of Friends shortly after their arrival in Berks County. In November 1756, "a Party of Savages set Fire to his House, Barn and Barracks of Corn and Hay." Captain Jacob Morgan sent a party out from Fort Lebanon in northern Berks County to investigate, finding "Finchers Barn, &c. consumed" but no natives in the area.[34]

Fincher rebuilt his homestead, only to face the natives once again. In September 1763, "a party of Indians came to the house of one John Fincher . . . they killed Fincher, his Wife, & two of his Sons; his Daughter is missing." One of the children did manage to escape and notified the local militia. Two of the surviving adult children moved to southern Chester County before the end of the year, and several members of Maiden Creek Preparative Meeting served as guardians for the smaller children. Genealogical records of Exeter Monthly Meeting indicated that the missing daughter later married an Indian chief, although her name does appear among a list of prisoners returned to Colonel Henry Bouquet in November 1764. To these Quakers, then, the issue of defense spending, while it might have conflicted with the pacifist principles of the Society of Friends, was very much a matter of life and death along the Pennsylvania frontier.[35]

Inevitably, one of the responses of members of Exeter Monthly Meeting was to bear arms against the Native American enemy. The Quaker *Rules of Discipline,* the formal summary of Quaker belief, included prohibitions against bearing arms, in addition to privateering and purchasing prize goods and furnishing wagons for the conveyance of military supplies. These Friends demonstrated through their actions that they were willing to compromise their faith for the defense of their property.[36]

Members of the Society of Friends even refused to participate in the fast days proclaimed by the government in 1756, because this action implied support for the war effort. Recognizing that neglect of the fast days could be construed not merely as opposition to the war but as approval of the raids, Pennsylvania Quakers published a statement outlining the reasons for their actions. Leaders of Philadelphia Yearly Meeting perceived the war as God's punishment for mistreating the natives. They considered the colony filled with "Pride, Strife, Contention, unnatural Heats, Broils, Animosities, Blood; from Luxury, Wantoness, Revellings, Drunkenness, Profaness, Impiety, Covetousness, Deceit, Fraud, Infidelity, and all manner of Evil." These Friends also remarked that only when "the Scourge which hangs over us" disappeared would the province "again be favour'd with Days of Peace and Tranquility." Participating in fast days, then, condoned the ways in which "Blood has been spilt and the Land is polluted therewith."[37]

Obviously, Quakers who did choose to fight realized that they would no longer be considered within the Quaker fold. During the Seven Years' War era (1755–64), fourteen of the sixty-seven cases (twenty-one percent) investigated by Exeter Monthly Meeting concerned the rejection of pacifist principles. All but one of these members faced immediate disownment, although two later condemned their wayward actions. Nine of the fourteen had family connections with other offenders; in one family four brothers and their father fought in the war. In addition, four of the violators were related to a Friend who received assistance from the Meeting for Sufferings, perhaps choosing defense of the family property over pacifist beliefs. Exeter Monthly Meeting disowned John Willits, son of the "ancient" Thomas Willits, in 1756 because "he hath for some time past not only neglected attending our religious Meetings (which is a visible Mark of Declension) but for want of a faithful Adherence to the Dictates Of that Divine Principle . . . 'They shall beat their Swords into Plowshares &c.' Hath Enlisted himself as a Soldier." In 1764, Hezekiah Boone, nephew of Elizabeth Yarnall, faced expulsion because he had "in his own Defence, did Fire at, and Killed one or more of the Indians, as he saith himself." Mere attendance at training exercises ("Shooting-Match") without actual participation resulted in the disownment of four of these men. The Seven Years' War thus contributed toward the spirit of reform that was spreading throughout Philadelphia Yearly Meeting, combining with other problems to result in a decline in membership for Exeter Monthly Meeting.[38]

The Seven Years' War not only contributed to an increase in disciplinary problems, but it also affected migration patterns of Exeter Friends. From 1755 to 1764, removals outnumbered additions, as members along the frontier fled to safer ground. Those Friends who departed usually went to other Friends' meetings in southeastern Pennsylvania, although a few migrated to other colonies.[39]

Although Quakers were not spared the wrath of Native American attacks, other Berks County residents believed that the Friends merited the abuse. Edward Biddle, a new resident of Reading who later became active in the revolutionary movement in the community, remarked in a letter to his father in November 1755 that "the Drum is beating to Arms, and Bells ringing & all the people under Arms. . . . This night we expect an attack, truly alarming is our situation. The people exclaim against the Quakers, & some are scarce restrained from burning the Houses of those few who are in this Town." Especially affecting popular perception of the Quakers' attitudes toward the conflict was the fact that Mennonites were willing to bear arms, as Conrad Weiser had indicated in his letter to William Allen. In addition, members of other pacifist groups, such as the Schwenkfelders, contributed money to arm and equip other men who would do the actual bearing of arms. Quakers, then, became suspect for their lack of support for frontier defense.[40]

Members of the Society of Friends were not the only Berks County residents to attract suspicion. Shortly after the first native attacks in the county, Berks County's justices wrote to Governor Morris expressing their worry about the actions of the Roman Catholic settlers of the county. The officers argued that "we know that the People of the Roman Catholick Church are bound by their Principles to be the worst Subjects and the worst of Neighbours." Near the chapel at Goshenhoppen in eastern Berks County, "it is reported and generally believed that 30 Indians are now lurking, well armed with Guns and Swords or Cutlashes." The justices also noted that the Catholic priests at Reading and Goshenhoppen "gave Notice to their People that they cou'd not come to them again in less than 9 Weeks," when services normally had been held at least once a month. The priests, of course, had "gone to consult with our Enemies at Du Quesne." The greatest fear was "that the Papists shou'd keep Arms in their Houses, against which the Protestants are not prepared." County officials urged disarming the Catholics for protection to prevent "a Massacre whenever the Papists are ready!" Fellow residents, then, incited a greater fear in local officials than did pacifist opposition to the war—or perhaps even the

natives themselves. Although Conrad Weiser had no qualms about nego-
tiating with Native Americans during the war, he was reluctant to allow
non-Protestant frontiersmen to protect their own property.[41]

In conclusion, the Seven Years' War contributed to the first break in the
Quakers' control of the province. As early as 1739, military conflict and
political dissension had begun to affect Quaker political activity throughout the colony. Not until 1756 was the threat serious enough to force
Quaker Assemblymen to question their conflicting values in appropriating
funds for the defense of the province. The frontier turmoil that began in the
mid-1750s and continued relatively unabated for a decade forced members
of the Society of Friends in Berks County not only to question their faith
but also to defend it. Rather than fight against the natives, they chose
instead to withdraw from political life. By doing so, members of Exeter
Monthly Meeting decided to become a resistant minority, one that would
maintain the principles of the Society of Friends along the Pennsylvania
frontier.

5

A Crisis of Allegiance: Berks County Quakers and the War for Independence

BY 1775, THE GEOGRAPHIC BOUNDARIES OF EXETER MONTHLY MEETING had become quite extensive. The monthly meeting still met alternately at the meeting houses at Exeter and Maiden Creek, located less than fifteen miles east and north, respectively, of the county seat at Reading. Another preparative meeting gathered at Robeson, approximately ten miles south of Reading. Particular meetings also assembled on first days at Reading and at Pottstown in northwestern Philadelphia County. In addition, by the end of this year a sufficient number of Quakers had moved into the interior to warrant formation of an additional particular meeting at Catawissa in newly formed Northumberland County. Consequently, members of Exeter Monthly Meeting resided between forty and 150 miles away from Philadelphia by the time of the Revolution. This geographical dispersion provided a different revolutionary experience for these frontier Quakers than that of their metropolitan counterparts, because they also had to cope with the remnants of a civil war in northern Pennsylvania while facing the prospects of war with the British. The War for Independence caused county residents to interpret the Friends' failure to fight as disloyalty toward the patriot cause, rather than a matter of religious conviction.[1]

The passage of the Boston Port Bill, one of the "Intolerable Acts" approved by Parliament, began the protest in Berks County. In July 1774, community leaders considered the act "unjust and tyrannical in the extreme" and pledged support for the formation of what became the First Continental Congress. Seven men, including nominal Quaker Dr. Jonathan Potts, formed a Committee of Correspondence that discussed plans and procedures with similar groups from other counties in the province. Potts was an especially active participant on the pre-Revolutionary committees, as he also served on the county Committee of Observation and as a delegate to the Provincial Convention. Another Friend, innkeeper James Lewis, also represented the pacifist viewpoint on the Committee of Observation. The vast majority of the members of these committees, however, belonged to one of the mainstream churches of the county—Lutheran,

Reformed, and Anglican—and only Christopher Schultz, a Schwenk-felder, came from one of the numerous German sects in the county.[2]

For residents of Berks County, the coming of the War for Independence was quite momentous. Within a week of the Battle of Lexington in April 1775, two companies of soldiers, commanded by two members of Reading's German Reformed congregation, had been formed to aid the patriot cause. By July, Berks Countians had organized at least forty companies to resist British authority. Over the course of the war, local militia and Continental regulars from the county participated in campaigns at Cambridge and in Canada, New York, New Jersey, Pennsylvania, and along the frontier.[3]

Not all residents of the county, however, supported the rebellion. After the commencement of hostilities in 1775, a group of "divers Inhabitants of the County of Berks, being conscientiously scrupulous of bearing Arms," met in Reading. William Reeser, the chairman of the gathering and a member of the German Reformed congregation and of the County Committee of Observation, wrote to the Committee of Safety on September 11, 1775, and stated that although this group opposed taking up arms, they realized the "justice of the cause" and promised to contribute to its support. In the county, Mennonites, Moravians, Schwenkfelders, and Amish, in addition to the Quakers, held theological reservations concerning the war; the German sects implied that they would neither fight nor pay militia fines, but they would provide supplies for the war effort. Demonstrating the good intent of these pacifists, Reeser forwarded the sum of £152 collected at this meeting to the Committee of Safety. With the Germans, who constituted an overwhelming majority of the population of the county, and most of the Anglicans supporting independence, no significant sentiment contrary to the movement existed.[4]

For members of the Society of Friends, the arrival of the American Revolution caused much turmoil. At a meeting held at Philadelphia in January 1775, Quakers publicly declared "against every usurpation of power and authority, in opposition to the laws and government, and against all combinations, insurrections, conspiracies and illegal assemblies." The same year, in order to restrain military activity further, Philadelphia Yearly Meeting directed Friends not to be spectators at militia muster days.[5]

Further restrictions fell upon Quakers in 1776. Philadelphia Yearly Meeting ordered them to refrain from participating in government "during the present commotions and unsettled state of public affairs." Friends also should not pay substitute fines or taxes that the assembly had levied to purchase drums and colors. The following year Quakers restated their opposition to the Revolution, contending that the benefits of union with Great Britain demanded that they abhor all attempts "to break off the happy connection we have heretofore enjoyed." At the same time Pennsylvania Friends were protesting the war, Philadelphia Yearly Meeting continued to correspond with London Yearly Meeting. The latter organization provided moral support for their coreligionists, who often faced persecution for failing to support the war effort. With their open opposition to the Revolution and their continued relationship with British Quakers, the Pennsylvania Friends should not have been surprised if fellow colonists confused their pacifism with loyalism.[6]

Friends had, however, already begun to notice the inner turmoil faced by some of their members. Leaders of Philadelphia Yearly Meeting urged those who were suffering to maintain the peace testimony and refrain from "promot[ing] any work or preparation for war." Resting on the theological principle that one's primary loyalty belonged to God and not to country, the yearly meeting leaders further guided Friends to "refuse to submit to the arbitrary ordinances of men, who assume to themselves the power of compelling others . . . to join in carrying on war." These men also expressed concern "for the deviation of some, who have made profession with us, from our peaceable principles." They especially feared that if Friends strayed too far away from the guidance of the yearly meeting, they could become "backsliders and transgressors who, after being treated with in the spirit of meekness, cannot be reclaimed." In essence, the American Revolution provided perhaps the ultimate test for the Quaker Reformation begun in the late 1740s, as Friends viewed the war as possible punishment for "the Declension which hath spread in the Time of ease amongst us."[7]

In spite of their pacifist beliefs, some Berks County Quakers chose to participate in the War for Independence. The *Rules of Discipline,* the formal summary of Quaker beliefs, included prohibitions against bearing arms, privateering, purchasing prize goods, and furnishing wagons for the conveyance of military supplies. By 1779, Philadelphia Yearly Meeting had extended violation of the peace testimony to include grinding grain for the army, feeding cattle, or selling property to the army. Consequently, patriotic Quakers had to choose between supporting their country's War for Independence and facing expulsion, or maintaining their pacifism and thus suffering possible civil and economic distress.[8]

One Berks County Quaker who played an active role in the American Revolution was Dr. Jonathan Potts. Son of one of the most prominent ironmasters in colonial Pennsylvania and a birthright Quaker, Philadelphia Monthly Meeting had disowned Potts in 1767 for premarital relations. He did continue to consider himself a Quaker, since he identified himself as a follower of the Society of Friends whenever he witnessed a will. As a result, even though Potts ardently believed in many of the tenets of the Society of Friends, Exeter Monthly Meeting could not discipline him for his participation in the war effort.[9]

Potts had received medical training at the University of Edinburgh in Scotland and a medical degree from the College of Philadelphia (now the University of Pennsylvania). As a country doctor, he had promoted inoculation for smallpox, but he was unsuccessful in his attempts to convince the German settlers of Reading of the importance of immunization against this disease that killed one-third of the children who contracted it. In the 1770s, he became more active in the political affairs of the community, serving on several of the local committees formed in response to the crises of the times. Less than four years after opening his practice, the doctor closed his office in response to the Continental Congress's call to arms in June 1775, and he accompanied one of the first companies formed in Berks County to assist General George Washington at Cambridge.[10]

By early 1776, Potts had returned to Pennsylvania to provide medical care for prisoners of war stationed in Reading. In May of that year, Congress assigned him to the army of General Horatio Gates, where he would tend to soldiers wounded at the battles of Ticonderoga and Crown Point. Potts performed his duties effectively, and in June 1776, Congress appointed him Director of Hospitals in Canada. Because the Canadian campaign ended soon after the defeats at Quebec and Montreal, Potts's position changed to Deputy Director General of Hospitals in the Northern Department. His expertise in smallpox inoculation proved quite beneficial; an epidemic was sweeping through the Continental Army, and his efforts helped check the spread of the disease. The travel associated with his duties, however, began to affect his health, and by the end of 1777 he returned home to Reading.[11]

New appointments awaited Potts upon his return to Pennsylvania. In February 1778, Congress transferred him to the Middle Department, and later he served as Purveyor General of the Hospital Department of the Continental Army. Potts, however, was not as skilled an administrator as he was a physician. While the death rate of soldiers because of disease had declined remarkably partly as a result of his work, Congress began to question what some perceived as excessive expenditures. From 1778 to 1780, Congress appropriated to Potts over $2.25 million for his department; this amount accounted for over three-fourths of the funds spent on Continental Army hospitals. These administrative duties, however, sapped Potts's health even more, and he had to resign in late 1780 because of illness. He died in October 1781, shortly before the country he had served so devotedly as a surgeon and a patriot achieved its independence on the battlefield.[12]

If Jonathan Potts had recanted his actions for exogamy, he undoubtedly could have submitted a Paper of Condemnation if he had been questioned for his actions in supporting the war effort as a physician. Quakers who actively engaged in combat, unlike Potts, were subject to expulsion.

Disciplinary action against arms-bearing Friends began in late 1775. In December of that year, Maiden Creek representatives to Exeter Monthly Meeting complained that William Thomas had left the Quaker fold by "endeavouring to Learn the art of war." Eight months later, Jonathan Gibson faced disciplinary action because he not only had joined the militia, but he had committed a breach of contract for leaving his master's service. By 1783, Exeter Monthly Meeting had disciplined thirteen members (almost nine percent of the adult male membership) for choosing to support the war effort by actively aiding the Continental Army or local militia, either by fighting as a soldier or by providing supplies.[13]

In some ways, Gibson's case was more typical; while the details often varied from one instance to another, Friends accused of participating in the war generally had more than one charge included on their testimony for disownment. In two cases, Exeter Monthly Meeting also accused the wayward Friend of excessive drinking. William Boone assisted in a "clandestine marriage" in addition to joining the militia. Abner Williams not only served in the army; he also married a non-Quaker, complied with the provisions of the Test Act, and moved to Philadelphia without requesting a certificate of removal (similar to a letter of transfer). The monthly meeting disowned Abraham Wickersham for driving a team for the army and for disobeying his parents by committing this offense. Exeter Monthly Meeting disowned the remainder of the men who had been charged with participating in the war effort; none of them ever rejoined the monthly meeting. Four of these men were related to leaders of the meeting, which undoubtedly strained family relations after the war had ended.[14]

Exeter Friends were not alone in performing military service. Between 1775 and 1783, monthly meetings throughout southeastern Pennsylvania disowned 948 Quakers for participating in the patriot cause. Reasons for volunteering for military service included economic and social discontent, family ties, and a desire to improve one's status within the secular community by obtaining a political or military post. In Pennsylvania, almost 78 percent of the volunteers were only guilty of bearing arms and had no prior violations of the Quaker discipline; only 7.4 percent ever rejoined the Society of Friends.[15]

In addition to aiding the rebelling forces, three members faced disciplinary action for paying a substitute fine. Two of them, John Scarlet, Jr. (an elder for Robeson Preparative Meeting) and Martha Thomas, who paid the fine for her son, submitted written acknowledgment to the monthly meeting condemning their actions. Surprisingly, the name of only one of these three Friends, that of John Scarlet, Jr., appeared on the list identifying Berks County residents from whom Jacob Morgan, county lieutenant, had collected militia fines between March 1777 and March 1780. Martha Thomas, of course, confessed to paying a substitute fine in October 1780;

this fee might have been paid after March 1780, or credited to her husband Thomas.[16]

These three were not the only members of Exeter Monthly Meeting who paid militia/excise fines; between March 1777 and March 1780, Morgan's henchmen assessed these fees to at least fifty-six Berks County Quakers. Almost a dozen of these Friends refused to pay the militia fines; consequently, public officials chose to confiscate property and/or imprison delinquent taxpayers. The monthly meeting disowned another nine for also complying with the provisions of the Test Act. The majority of those Friends on Morgan's list, however, went unpunished. That two of those charged with this violation had submitted papers condemning their actions prior to Exeter Monthly Meeting formally charging them with this offense (and the third case involved someone who had sworn the oath of allegiance) indicates that perhaps the monthly meeting either did not consider the payment of a substitute fine a serious enough offense for prosecution, or realized that over thirty-seven percent of their adult male members appeared on Morgan's list, and this loss would have severely crippled the meeting.[17]

For those Friends who opted to keep the faith, opposition to the War for Independence occurred in a variety of forms. In January 1776, the Berks County Committee of Observation became aware of a plan "to depreciate the Continental Currency." One of those accused was Gaius Dickinson, an overseer for Robeson Preparative Meeting. In meeting with the committee, Dickinson condemned his actions. He admitted to them that "such a conduct is highly unbecoming the duty of an American" and "most sincerely acknowledge[d] the heinousness of such offence." He particularly expressed remorse that his actions were "inconsistent with the religious principles of the Society with which I profess." Apparently Dickinson's apology satisfied the committee members, for they did not press formal charges. Still, in spite of this implied support for the independence movement that the confession contained, Dickinson was one of fourteen Quakers identified as "tory" on the 1779 tax list for refusing to pay taxes that would be spent on military expenditures.[18]

Like Dickinson, the vast majority of Friends chose not to support the war effort. To punish this perceived "toryism," the Revolutionary leaders of Pennsylvania passed an Act of Allegiance (Test Act) in June 1777. This law required all white male inhabitants of the state to take the oath of allegiance to the Commonwealth of Pennsylvania. Anyone who did not comply with the law "could not vote or hold public office, serve on juries, sue for debts, buy, sell or transfer real estate," and "was liable to be disarmed by the county lieutenant." Quakers in the state immediately protested against the law, contending that they were "still justly & lawfully entitled to all the Rights of Citizenship, of which [the Assembly is] attempting to deprive us." They realized that the Assembly had passed the Test Act in part to punish them, a group whose pacifism had hindered prosecution of the Seven Years' War twenty years earlier. Friends, however, could not take the oath, partly because compliance would indicate support for the Revolutionary government and partly because of the Society's prohibition against swearing oaths.[19]

Leaders of Exeter Monthly Meeting proceeded cautiously with respect to this volatile issue. Beginning in February 1779, Exeter Monthly Meeting commenced disciplinary proceedings against Friends whom they knew had complied with the provisions of the Test Act. Twenty-three members faced charges of supporting the Revolutionary government. Only five of these men condemned their actions and remained in good standing. At least eleven Exeter Friends avoided "prosecution" by affirming their allegiance; still, four who affirmed rather than swore their loyalty suffered disciplinary action. Merely five of those disciplined were leaders of the meeting, indicating that the wayward members were generally not among the elite of the meeting (although they might have been related to a leader). Only one of the five leaders charged with this offense, James Boone, never condemned his actions, and the monthly meeting disowned him for this violation. Because of the sensitive nature of the issue, the committee of Quakers appointed to investigate only included members of the leadership group of the monthly meeting. Eventually, Exeter Monthly Meeting disowned nineteen Friends (one-sixth of the male membership) for complying with the provisions of the Test Act. Expulsion did not occur, however, until after the meeting had consulted with Philadelphia Quarterly Meeting for advice on the matter.[20]

Unlike the dilemma over military participation, which lasted until Jesse Tomlinson's disownment in 1787 for "having associated with the Militia at their Muster," leaders of the three preparative meetings made charges against Friends who complied with the provisions of the Test Act primarily in 1779 and 1780. John Eves, who condemned his improper actions upon his transfer to Exeter Monthly Meeting in 1782, not only acknowledged that he had deviated from the discipline by swearing to the oath of allegiance, but he also admitted that he had committed exogamy, been married by a magistrate, and neglected to present his certificate of removal from Ireland immediately upon his arrival in Pennsylvania. More commonly, the members of Exeter Monthly Meeting had just the one complaint made against them; only two Quakers during these years faced an additional charge—Samuel Willits for paying a substitute fine and Moses Boone for having his marriage ceremony performed by a "priest." Thus, the Test Act indeed had an adverse effect on the membership of Exeter Monthly Meeting. Through the rigorous enforcement of the prohibition against demonstrating loyalty to the Revolutionary government, the leaders of the

monthly meeting effectively eliminated the presence of one of their founding families, the Boones, as active members of the meeting.[21]

While those Friends who complied with the Test Act faced possible
excommunication, Berks County Quakers who kept their faith and refused
to swear their allegiance faced secular rather than religious problems.
Anglican Alexander Graydon remarked in his memoirs that Thomas Parvin of Maiden Creek became "an object of much wanton oppression"
because of high taxes and militia fines. The government took some of
Parvin's livestock and sold it, without returning the surplus revenue to him.
Graydon had become acquainted with the Quaker while Parvin sold his
farm products in town; he often discussed the impracticality of Friends'
pacifist principles in the modern world with the farmer. When Parvin sent
him a treatise on Quaker tenets, Graydon appeared surprised that he "was a
well-educated man and no means polemic." Thus Parvin did earn the
grudging respect of at least one patriot and apparent sympathy for his
economic punishment.[22]

The confiscation of livestock was only one of the methods used by
patriot civil officials to punish those who did not actively support the war
effort. Between August 1777 and December 1778, Berks County officials
took from an unidentified Quaker "a cow for the £3.10.0 fine" that they
sold for £10.10; thirty-six bushels of wheat to pay a tax of £20; "a great
coat" worth £10; a horse valued at £200 for a £30 tax; and "four cows for
forty pounds fine said cows would at that time have Sold for £20: each." In
July 1778, the Berks County sheriff imprisoned three Quakers and fined
them 16s. each for refusing to take the oath of allegiance. Undersheriff
Conrad Foos arrested George Rush for failing to pay a militia fine; Rush
stated that he refused to comply with the law because he did not believe it
was "Right for me to pay or contribute to the Sheding of human Blood."
The officials detained Rush in the jail until they had confiscated enough
property to cover the amount of his fine. Benjamin Wright not only "suffered three months' imprisonment," but also had two horses, a steer, seventeen bushels of wheat, and fifty-one bushels of rye (valued at over £1,064)
seized between 1777 and 1782 to pay class taxes and militia fines. Moses
Starr, Jr., of Maiden Creek Township witnessed county officials remove
from his property "2 Horses, a Wagon, Gun, Bellows & the tools of the
Smith Shop" and "2400 Sheaves of Wheat, 740 Sheaves of Rye" on two
different occasions in 1778. Mordecai Lee, an elder for Exeter Preparative
Meeting, saw agents of the local sheriff take almost £297 worth of paper
money, livestock, and grain for fines and taxes totaling £67.17.6. County
officials also confiscated cows, sheep, hogs, oxen, colts, furniture, pewter-
ware, blankets, and a three-day clock from other Friends who refused to
comply with the law.[23]

Table 5.1
Value of Losses Sustained by Berks Country Quakers

Name	Preparative Meeting	Dates of Confiscation	Number of Visits	Total Amount*
Gaius Dickinson	Robeson	5/1777–2/1782	7	242.19.6**
James Embree	Robeson	9/1777–3/1782	6	254.19.6**
Moses Embree	Robeson	9/1777–1/1788	7	195.04.6**
Samuel Hughes	Exeter	8/1781	2	5.09.8
David Jackson	Robeson	4/1778	1	35.12.0**
Mordecai Lee	Exeter	7/1777–8/1780	9	296.19.9**
Richard Nuzum	Robeson	8/1777–3/1783	6	179.09.0**
Francis Parvin	Maiden Creek	12/1778	1	**
John Parvin	Maiden Creek	8/1777–12/1778	4	**
Benjamin Scarlet	Robeson	8/1777–6/1778	4	101.02.0
William Scarlet	Robeson	3/1778	1	**
Merrick Starr	Maiden Creek	8/1777–11/1778	3	**
Moses Starr	Maiden Creek	6/1778–12/1778	2	**
Moses Starr, Jr.	Maiden Creek	8/1777–11/1778	3	**
Jonathan Stephens	Robeson	8/1777–1/1781	4	50.05.0**
Thomas Thomas	Robeson	10/1778	1	**
William Tomlinson†	Maiden Creek	8/1777	1	**
Benjamin Wright†	Maiden Creek	8/1777–5/1782	8	1064.16.11**
Joseph Wright	Maiden Creek	8/1777–2/1782	5	142.15.6**

*in pounds (paper and hard)
**losses include property (e.g., livestock, grain, household furnishings, tools, farm equipment) for which no value was recorded
†also imprisoned in July 1778 for failing to take the oath of allegiance

Similar to other monthly meetings, the losses sustained by members of Exeter Monthly Meeting usually exceeded the actual value of the fines to be paid. Members of Robeson Indulged Meeting south of the Schuylkill River experienced particular distresses as a result of the actions of government officials. Gaius Dickinson, a former overseer of the preparative meeting, had over £242 of money, livestock, and furniture confiscated on seven different occasions between 1777 and 1782 for fines and class taxes totaling £81.5.0. One confiscation occurred in 1778, when "Captain Mc-Clean's guard" detained his wife Mary when she was traveling to Philadelphia Quarterly Meeting, taking £25 from her and also her horse. James Embree suffered the loss of £254.19.6 worth of paper and hard money and livestock for fines and taxes of £94.12.6 on seven different occasions between 1777 and 1782. His brother Moses Embree was slightly more fortunate, as government officials seized only £195.4.6 in paper and hard money, livestock, and crops for fines and class taxes of £67.13.6 on eight separate visits to his farm between 1777 and 1788. The largest percentage of discrepancy between amount taken and taxes owed occurred in the case of Richard Nuzum, who joined Exeter Monthly Meeting through a profession of faith in August 1777, and received his first visit from local officials the day after he became a member. Over the next three years, Nuzum experienced a total of six confiscations of paper and hard money totaling £115.10.0 and of livestock and farm equipment valued at £38.19.0 for militia fines, substitute fines, and class taxes that amounted to £47.15.0. In each of the cases discussed above, the value of the goods and money taken was almost three times the amount of the fine; other Friends in Robeson Township experienced confiscation, but the totals were not as disproportionate.[24] No wonder Quaker leaders feared that some members might choose their property and livelihoods over their devotion to the Quaker pacifist ideal.

The case of two Exeter Friends reinforces the proposition that the punishment suffered was overly harsh for the crime committed. Moses Roberts and Job Hughes both lived along the frontier in Northumberland County (which the Assembly had formed out of Berks and other counties in 1772) and were active in the establishment of Catawissa Indulged Meeting in 1775 to serve the needs of Quakers along the advancing frontier. Both Roberts and Hughes had moved there from Oley Township in eastern Berks County, and they had married daughters of Thomas Lee, one of the leaders of Exeter Monthly Meeting. Roberts remarked in 1780 that he had decided to settle in that region after noticing "the loos and irreligious lives and conversations of the people." The Quakers who migrated to Catawissa did not experience the harsh effects of the War for Independence until 1778, when some of the Connecticut migrants who had settled in northeastern Pennsylvania fled west to avoid Native American raids in the Wyoming Valley. The situation remained tense between the "Yankees" and the Quakers until April 1780.[25]

On April 9, 1780, representatives of the Northumberland County sheriff imprisoned five residents, including the two Quakers. When they arrived at the county seat, a military officer ordered them to jail without pressing any official charges. A few days later, a judge finally questioned them about the suspected crimes of high treason and of cooperating with Native Americans. All of the prisoners denied passing messages along to the British or to the natives and contended that the only native they had even seen since the beginning of the war was "one Dead one, that went down the River in a Canoe." They also did not know anyone who had gone to aid the natives, although they had heard reports of such activity. After the questioning, the law enforcement officials told them that they all would be leaving the county for another jail unless they posted £10,000 bail each and promised not to appear in the county for the rest of the war. None of the prisoners could afford the bail, so the sheriff ordered their removal to the jail in Lancaster.[26]

The imprisonment of Moses Roberts and Job Hughes prompted requests for assistance. In July 1780, Jane Roberts and Eleanor Hughes appealed to Chief Justice Thomas McKean, pleading for the release of their husbands. They contended that county officials had unjustly arrested their spouses, and that they too had suffered since then. Armed men had forced the Roberts and Hughes families to leave their homes without warning, not even allowing them to prepare food to sustain themselves on their journey back to their father's home in Oley Township. Their property losses included livestock, crops, furniture, a sawmill, a gristmill, and "a Chest of Carpenters tools which we were just burying under ground when the men came upon us." The soldiers also confiscated four horses, leaving the women with only two mares to use to transport their families and personal effects. In October, Exeter Monthly Meeting appointed a committee to visit the two women to inquire into their circumstances and raised £5 for the families' support.[27]

A month later, Philadelphia Meeting for Sufferings joined the call for assistance. A committee appealed to the General Assembly of Pennsylvania to inquire into the "oppression" suffered by the two men. Moses Roberts described in a letter to the assembly how "when the Calamities of war Encreased in [Northumberland] County, my heart and houses ware always open to Receive and Entertain my Distressed Country people, as well as feilds and Meadows to pasture their Cattle, without pay or Reward, when they fled from their own Dwellings for fear of the Indians." But because he was a Quaker and not an active supporter of the war effort, he suffered imprisonment; consequently, he feared "whether 'the Noble cause of Liberty' is not in Danger of being turned into Cruel Slavery, tyrany, and oppression." Job Hughes also wrote to the assembly, describing the manner in which Northumberland County officials had captured them and hauled them to jail without being "so much as charged with the breach of any Law." Hughes further pointed out that the assembly should "weightily Consider whether the Government you are establishing, is not in danger of being more Corrupt then that from under which you are come if such work as this is allowed of and acknowledged." The appeals of the Meeting for Sufferings and of Roberts and Hughes had little impact, as the assembly refused to consider the cases of the two men, and Chief Justice McKean ignored the pleas for justice. Finally, in mid-1781, the Lancaster County sheriff released the two men, perhaps recognizing that they no longer posed a threat to the Commonwealth.[28]

The war interrupted the lives of Moses Roberts and Job Hughes, as their families had to flee their farms while the heads of household languished in a distant jail. For Abel Thomas of Exeter Indulged Meeting, however, the Revolution merely hindered his religious activity, but it did not deter his visits. In January 1775, Thomas and Samuel Hughes visited the meetings affiliated with Western Quarterly Meeting in Pennsylvania and Maryland. That August, he traveled southward to the Carolinas, returning a year later with certificates from the quarterly meetings at Third Haven, Maryland, Cane Creek, North Carolina, and Perquimans County, North Carolina, and from the yearly meeting at Black Water, Virginia, all testifying to his good works. In November 1776, Abel and his brother James Thomas toured the meetings of Chester Quarterly Meeting. Three months later, the two brothers performed a religious visit to New Jersey, a trip that they repeated the following year. On the latter excursion, soldiers arrested the Thomases for having crossed enemy lines and for suspicion of treason. Governor William Livingston met with them, and after he learned their purpose released them with a letter permitting their travel throughout New Jersey without molestation.[29]

The detainment did not discourage Thomas from continuing his work. In November 1779, Samuel Hughes again accompanied him on a religious visit to Warrington, Fairfax, and West River Monthly Meetings in Pennsylvania, Virginia, and Maryland, respectively. A year later, Thomas and Amos Lee decided to tour the various monthly meetings in Virginia and the Carolinas. When Thomas returned in July 1781, he remarked to Exeter Monthly Meeting that "he had performed his Visit thro' divers trying Circumstances much to his Satisfaction and Comfort." The situation indeed had been tense; in Camden, South Carolina, the Continental Army captured Thomas and Lee. After they convinced the officers of their intentions, General Nathanael Greene freed the two Friends and gave them a pass to continue their journey. This excursion proved to be the last one Thomas made during the military phase of the Revolution, but only because of the surrender of Cornwallis's troops in October. By December 1781, the Quaker minister joined Samuel Hughes once again on a religious visit, this time traveling to the meetings affiliated with Salem and Bucks Quarterly Meetings in New Jersey and Pennsylvania.[30]

Thus, members of Exeter Monthly Meeting faced economic and physical hardships during the American Revolution. The families of Job Hughes and Moses Roberts received financial aid while the heads of household spent time in the Lancaster jail. Two older members of the meeting, John Cadwalader and his wife Sophia, also began to need assistance in 1780 because of economic disruption caused by the war. That April, Robeson Friends agreed "to supply them with Necessaries" while the monthly meeting appointed a committee to investigate the situation. In July, the meeting purchased grain for them and provided some financial support. Each preparative meeting contributed £2.5 in 1780, and they raised an additional

£8.8.1 combined in 1781. Two years later, the committee members reported that they had expended an additional £15.0.8 toward the Cadwaladers' relief, and they had only received £8.10.7. The monthly meeting ordered that the three preparative meetings each contribute £3, to be paid to Richard Lewis, the chairman of the committee. Apparently Cadwalader, who was over sixty years old, continued to experience economic difficulties, for Exeter Monthly Meeting contributed toward his support throughout the 1780s.[31]

The American Revolution affected members of Exeter Monthly Meeting in other ways. Isaac Potts of Pottsgrove Indulged Meeting rented his country home at Valley Forge to General George Washington to serve as his winter headquarters in 1777–78. In November 1777, Exeter Men's Monthly Meeting representatives to Philadelphia Quarterly Meeting "being intercepted by the American Army were obliged to return home." A similar circumstance occurred in May 1778, when women Friends were "stop'd on the Road, & prevented coming into the City" when attempting to attend the gathering of Philadelphia Quarterly Meeting. Finally, the indulged meeting at Catawissa had to be suspended in the early 1780s because of the imprisonment of some members and "others drove from their Habitations by the White Inhabitants."[32]

The Revolutionary War also influenced migration patterns for Exeter Monthly Meeting. Between 1779 and 1781, removals from the meeting exceeded additions, and, with the increased number of disownments during this period because of the Test Act and military service, active membership declined. The impact is especially evident with the suspension of the indulged meeting along the frontier and a reduction in the frequency of services at Reading. Those Friends who did migrate mostly remained within the state, although a few did move south to Maryland and even to North Carolina.[33]

Aside from military issues, Exeter Monthly Meeting also experienced other disciplinary problems during this era. The decade of the American Revolution (1775–1784) saw the second highest number of violations of Quaker discipline, with only the Seven Years' War surpassing it. Of course, offenses unique to the times, including signing an association paper and complying with the provisions of the Test Act, contributed to the increase in charges. One of the wayward Friends, Job Webb, submitted a Paper of Condemnation in June 1783, apologizing for "taking the Test or Affirmation required by the Rulers of Pennsylvania" and for "going to the Indians at Wioming . . . to enquire whether they intended to let us remain in our Settlement or not." Apparently the Northumberland County authorities, then, had not erred in assuming that Quakers were guilty of associating with the natives; they merely had neglected to verify that they had arrested the offending Friends.[34]

Of course, Exeter Monthly Meeting was not the only Quaker meeting to experience distress on account of "the current unsettled state of public affairs." In 1775, members of the meeting contributed to the relief of Friends in New England who were experiencing the brunt of the war at that time. Abington Monthly Meeting in Philadelphia County disowned "a considerable list of members" in October 1775, for joining the militia. Birmingham Indulged Meeting in Chester County saw their meetinghouse used as a hospital by both British and American troops during the Battle of Brandywine. Additionally, during the winter of 1777, members of Gwynedd Monthly Meeting met in a private home because their meetinghouse had been converted to a hospital.[35]

Members of Middletown Monthly Meeting in southern Bucks County experienced similar distresses as had Exeter Friends and other Quakers. Local militia officers visited the farms of Quakers who had failed to pay militia fines and proceeded to confiscate livestock, grain, hay, household items, and tools. Middletown Friends also faced imprisonment for not accepting the depreciated Continental currency for payment of debts. Finally, by the end of the war this monthly meeting had expelled eighteen men for supporting the war effort.[36]

Nottingham Monthly Meeting in Cecil County, Maryland, which counted Pennsylvanians among its membership, literally saw the army in its own backyard. The American army forced the meeting off of its property in 1778, as a monthly meeting took place "in a Friend's barn" because they were using the meetinghouse as a hospital. In addition, the Continental regiment commanded by General Lafayette camped on the meetinghouse property in 1781 while marching to Yorktown. Members of this meeting also experienced problems in conforming to Quaker discipline, as they acknowledged their errors in making cartridge boxes and gun barrels for the army, in accepting reimbursement for a horse taken by the army, in selling blankets, and in washing clothes for the soldiers.[37]

Quakers in Philadelphia, however, faced the greatest dilemma. Local citizens vandalized their houses for failing to support the days of fast and thanksgiving. The victory at Yorktown in 1781 only intensified property damage, as ecstatic Philadelphians looted homes and physically assaulted Quakers during the jubilant celebration. That few Friends fled when the British occupied the city did not dispel suspicions of loyalism instead of pacifism. Continued correspondence with London Yearly Meeting further intensified distrust. Philadelphia Quakers also spent time in jail, but instead of questioning them within the Commonwealth, state officials exiled some to Winchester, Virginia. In addition, Friends who served in the Revolutionary government faced disownment for supporting the war effort. Some of these excommunicated Quakers, like Clement Biddle, Timothy

Matlack, Thomas Mifflin, and Thomas Wharton became important leaders of the Revolutionary movement in Pennsylvania.[38]

One response of Philadelphia Quakers to the Revolution was to separate from the Society of Friends and form a distinct organization. In 1781, Quakers who had openly supported the Revolutionary cause and been expelled established the Free Quakers. This group perpetuated the discipline of their coreligionists, with the major distinction that they had either fought in or aided the army during the war. Among the members of the Free Quaker Society was James Boone, disowned by Exeter Monthly Meeting in 1780 for complying with the provisions of the Test Act.[39]

The era of the American Revolution did indeed have an adverse effect on the lives of many members of Exeter Monthly Meeting. During the American Revolution, Quakers not only faced opposition from the British but also persecution from their fellow colonists, who passed laws specifically aimed at punishing them for their beliefs. While the response of Exeter Friends did not differ greatly from that of other monthly meetings during this era, the location of the meeting along the Pennsylvania frontier contributed to different causes for their actions. Not only were the British an enemy; so were fellow Pennsylvanians and Yankees who feared cooperation with Native Americans. Furthermore, members of Exeter Monthly Meeting confronted the same problems as other settlers along the frontier; their faith forced them to question whether they would go along with the majority and support the war, and thus face expulsion, or remain pacifist and fear for their lives and property.

With the end of the war in 1783, everyday life for members of Exeter Monthly Meeting returned to normal. Quakers continued to move into the interior, resulting in the establishment of a monthly meeting at Catawissa in 1796. The Society of Friends had survived during its most trying period of the eighteenth century, and in some ways the organization had strengthened because of the turmoil. Members realized that "to bear Injuries with Patience is a Christian Virtue,"[40] choosing to maintain their pacifist beliefs regardless of the cost. The crisis of allegiance that these Friends confronted during the 1770s had strengthened their faith, rather than disillusioning it. These frontier Quakers had indeed become a model for the survival of their sect in an unfriendly environment.

6

The Quaker Ethic:
The Economic Activity of Berks County Quakers

ALTHOUGH WILLIAM PENN FOUNDED THE PROVINCE OF PENNSYLVANIA primarily as a haven for those experiencing religious persecution throughout Europe, economic factors proved to be equally important in attracting settlers. In "Some Account of the Province of Pennsylvania" (1681), the first promotional tract written after acquiring the charter to the colony, Penn described the natural attributes of the region:

> The commodities that the country is thought to be *capable* of, are *silk, flax, hemp, wine, cider, wood, madder, licorice, tobacco, potashes,* and *iron,* and it does actually produce *hides, tallow, pipe-staves,* beef, pork, sheep, wool, corn, as *wheat, barley, rye,* and also *furs,* as your *peltry, minks, raccoons, martens,* and such like; store of *furs* which is to be found among the *Indians,* that are profitable commodities in *Europe.*[1]

Friends and others who migrated to the Quaker colony had ample opportunity to achieve economic success in the New World.

Frederick Tolles proposed in 1948 that a "Quaker ethic" existed similar to the "Puritan ethic" held by the settlers in Massachusetts Bay. "Business success," he argued, "could be regarded as a visible sign that one was indeed living 'in the Light.'" This idea that economic prosperity was a sign of God's favor particularly appealed to the Quaker merchants of Philadelphia. Throughout the colonial period, the success of these entrepreneurs contributed toward an increasingly inequitable distribution of wealth in the largest colonial city.[2] Along the frontier, however, where frugal Germans dominated, it is questionable whether Quaker settlers held the monopoly on providential approval. An examination of the tax lists for the Berks County townships in which Quakers conducted preparative meetings should then test whether Friends were able to perpetuate the Quaker ethic along the frontier by maintaining economic dominance.

A second question that needs to be addressed pertains to the distribution of wealth. A century ago, Frederick Jackson Turner described the mid-

Atlantic region as one that had "a varied economic life [and] many religious sects." He characterized the frontier as an area that "did indeed furnish a new field of opportunity," one that promoted economic growth and democracy. His implication, then, is that wealth would be distributed with greater equity along the frontier than in seaport cities such as Philadelphia.[3]

Another issue is whether economic status had any bearing on whether an individual would hold a leadership position within the monthly meeting. According to one historian, a deferential society existed in colonial America, one that encouraged settlers to elect their social and economic "betters" to positions of importance in the community and colony.[4] Because the Society of Friends had no ordained clergy, as did many of the German and English congregations throughout Berks County and Pennsylvania, it would be intriguing to examine the relative wealth of overseers, elders, ministers, and clerks of Exeter Monthly Meeting, both in comparison with the total taxpaying population of the townships and with the membership of the respective preparative meetings.

Nine sample county tax lists for Exeter, Maiden Creek, and Robeson townships have been consulted to determine the distribution of wealth in this region, the applicability of the Quaker ethic to the frontier environment, and the importance of economic standing in the selection of religious leaders. The reverse side of prosperity, patterns of indebtedness, also warrants examination. In addition, several of the tax lists indicated the occupation of the taxpayer; this data will determine the extent of economic diversity in these townships. The ledgers of Reading storekeeper Benjamin Lightfoot and of Exeter Township tanner Moses Boone reflect the degree of interaction between these Quaker entrepreneurs and non-Quakers. The final section of this chapter concentrates on the disposition of Friends' property after their death by reviewing the participation of non-Quakers in the probate process and by considering whether wealth was a factor in the preparation of a will.

Little sign of economic equality can be found among the population of frontier Exeter, Maiden Creek, and Robeson Townships. Indeed, the distribution of wealth appears to become increasingly skewed over the thirty-year period (see tables 6.1, 6.2, and 6.3). Four separated classifications have been established for this study: "Top 10%," "Upper 30%," "Middle 30%," and "Bottom 30%." With one exception, the top 10 percent of the taxpayers in these townships paid at least twenty percent of the taxes assessed. Perhaps even more remarkably, the bottom 30 percent of the taxpayers paid less than ten percent of the tax bill in each of these three townships after 1760.

Table 6.1
Distribution of Wealth in Exeter Township,
1754–1785

	N	Top 10%	Upper 30%	Middle 30%	Bottom 30%
1754	66	23.8	38.7	24.5	13.1
1758	90	31.5	43.5	18.7	6.3
1762	114	27.6	50.5	18.1	3.9
1767	97	26.7	49.2	19.2	4.9
1770	108	26.7	46.3	20.9	6.1
1775	109	37.5	47.7	16.5	3.4
1779	137	46.3	46.5	6.6	0.6
1781	129	37.3	43.6	13.2	6.0
1785	138	37.5	45.5	12.1	4.8

Table 6.2
Distribution of Wealth in Robeson Township,
1754–1785

	N	Top 10%	Upper 30%	Middle 30%	Bottom 30%
1754	67	18.7	41.8	24.4	15.0
1758	66	20.2	46.0	25.2	8.6
1762	90	27.9	43.9	20.1	8.0
1767	104	34.7	40.3	16.7	8.3
1770	102	30.6	42.9	17.7	8.8
1775	114	33.6	41.0	20.0	5.5
1779	135	43.4	40.3	15.1	1.2
1781	139	41.0	38.1	17.9	3.9
1785	169	54.5	30.1	12.9	2.5

Table 6.3
Distribution of Wealth in Maiden Creek Township,
1754–1785

	N	Top 10%	Upper 30%	Middle 30%	Bottom 30%
1754	37	20.9	39.8	26.4	12.8
1758	44	24.7	36.7	24.1	14.5
1762	60	32.3	44.3	18.6	4.8
1767	71	28.2	45.8	20.4	5.4
1770	67	32.6	41.4	18.8	7.4
1775	81	32.0	45.0	19.0	3.7
1779	81	34.0	48.6	16.8	0.4
1781	65	27.9	42.1	23.8	5.2
1785	101	33.4	46.5	16.3	3.6

The first county tax list that has survived, for 1754, provided the year in which the distribution of wealth appeared most equitable. The top 10 percent of the taxpayers in all three townships paid less than one-fourth of the tax collected. The bottom 30 percent, which characteristically bore a smaller share of the tax burden, contributed between thirteen and fifteen percent of the tax revenue, while the upper 30 percent (similar to the upper middle class) paid approximately forty percent of the taxes.[5]

For each of the townships, the distribution of wealth changed over time. The top 10 percent of the taxpayers in Exeter Township, for instance, never paid less than one-fourth of the taxes after 1754, and after 1775 they contributed more than three-eighths of the revenue. After 1754, the bottom 30 percent never paid more than 6.3 percent of the taxes; three-tenths of the taxpayers therefore paid less than one-sixth of the amount collected from the top 10%. Furthermore, the upper 30 percent bore a greater share, as they contributed over forty-three percent of the tax revenue after 1754.[6]

The tax collectors for Robeson Township were somewhat more equitable in their assessments during the 1750s, but after 1762 a greater proportion of the levy fell upon the upper levels of the economic spectrum. In fact, by 1762, the top two economic groups—the top 10% and the upper 30 percent—paid more than seventy percent of the taxes collected, and after 1775 this amount exceeded eighty percent. Until 1770, the bottom 30 percent contributed between eight and nine percent of the revenue; after 1775 this group paid less than four percent of the total collected. Over time, wealth became increasingly more concentrated in Robeson Township.[7]

The tax lists for Maiden Creek Township reflected the most equitable distribution of wealth among the three townships, but even this distinction has a dubious quality. The top 10 percent, for example, never paid more than one-third of the revenue collected. After 1758, the upper 30 percent contributed more than forty percent of the taxes raised. The top forty percent did combine for more than seventy percent of the tax revenue between 1762 and 1785, and the bottom 30 percent paid more than 5.5 percent of the taxes only once during that period. With slightly more than one-third of the taxpayers in all three of these townships paying approximately three-fourths of the tax revenue within a decade of the establishment of Berks County, it is evident that economic democracy—a moderately equal acquisition of property—did not apply to this frontier region.[8]

The inequitable distribution of wealth in these three townships mirrored that of the county seat of Reading, where Quakers were only a small proportion of the population. In 1779, five percent of the taxpayers in Reading were Quakers, compared with 10.9 percent in Exeter, 19.8 percent in Maiden Creek, and 20.7 percent in Robeson (see table 6.4). The bottom 30 percent of Reading's taxpayers contributed 1.5 percent of the taxes in

Table 6.4
Percentage of Quakers in Taxpaying Population
1754–1785

	Exeter		Maiden Creek	Robeson
1754	16.7	(66)*	40.5 (37)*	24.4 (67)*
1758	10.0	(90)	45.5 (44)	27.3 (66)
1762	10.5	(114)	25.0 (60)	20.0 (90)
1767	14.4	(97)	23.9 (71)	18.3 (104)
1770	12.6	(108)	25.4 (67)	21.6 (102)
1775	12.0	(109)	23.5 (81)	18.4 (114)
1779	10.9	(137)	19.8 (81)	20.7 (135)
1781	11.6	(129)	23.1 (65)	20.9 (139)
1785	8.0	(138)	21.8 (101)	16.6 (169)

*Total number of non-single taxpayers for this year

1779, the middle 30 percent paid 8.4 percent, the upper 30% paid 36 percent, and the top 10% paid 54.1 percent. For Reading, the bottom 30% bore a greater share of the tax burden than their counterparts in the neighboring townships; Maiden Creek's bottom 30% paid only 0.4 percent of the taxes in 1779. Of course, property values in the economically diverse county seat were higher than in the surrounding townships that relied mainly upon agricultural production, even though land parcels were smaller. Surprisingly, the combined percentages of upper 30 percent and top 10 percent for Reading and Exeter are similar, but the top 10% in Reading paid eighteen percent more in taxes than did the upper 30 percent. For Exeter Township, the top 10 percent actually paid less than the upper 30 percent, 46.3 percent to 46.5 percent. In both of these communities the bottom sixty percent contributed less than ten percent of the taxes raised in 1779, indicating either a moderate to strong unequal distribution of wealth or the implementation of a possible "soak the property-rich" tax code in 1779 to raise funds for the war. Because the actual tax rate is not known, the true cause of this unbalanced tax revenue cannot be accurately determined.[9]

This inequitable distribution of wealth after the first decade of the county's establishment paralleled the situation in other parts of Pennsylvania. In Chester County, west of Philadelphia and southeast of Berks, the gap between the upper 10 percent and the lower 30 percent widened over the course of the eighteenth century. In 1693, the lowest 30 percent owned over one-sixth of the wealth, while the upper 10 percent possessed less than one-fourth. By 1782, the bottom group contributed less than five percent of the tax revenue, while the top economic class paid more than one-third. Throughout the eighteenth century, the middle two groups—the upper 30 percent and the middle 30 percent—remained relatively stable. As in Berks County, the poorer taxpayers in Chester County were experiencing a decline in economic status by the time of the Revolution, and it did not appear that "economic democracy" was occurring in this region, either.[10]

If economic success, as demonstrated through taxable wealth, reflected God's favor toward members of the Society of Friends, the economic status of Berks County Quakers to a certain extent paralleled the difficulty members experienced in adhering to the tenets of the Quaker discipline (see table 6.5). For example, Friends never comprised even half of the top 10% of the taxpayers in Exeter Township. Quakers, however, did provide two-thirds of this subgroup in Robeson Township in 1758 and over seventy percent of the wealthiest men in Maiden Creek Township in 1767. Although the percentage of Quakers among the economic elite exceeded their proportion of the total population of these townships, only in these two instances did they dominate the category.[11]

More commonly, members of the Society of Friends appeared in all classifications. Admittedly, in almost half of the cases, fewer than three Quakers appeared among the bottom 30% of the taxpayers, although in 1779 more than one-third of the Quakers on Robeson Township tax lists fell into this category. This instance, however, was certainly an aberration, because seven of the Friends in Robeson Township did not pay any taxes that year. They refused to support a levy for the war effort.[12]

While Maiden Creek Township was the most equitable overall in terms of wealth distribution, the percentage of Quakers among the top 10 percent and the upper 30 percent of the taxpayers regularly exceeded their proportion within the township. This same distribution occurred in Exeter and Robeson Townships. In fact, only in 1781, when just one Quaker appeared among the top 10 percent of the taxpayers in Robeson Township, did members of the Society of Friends fail to comprise at least one-sixth of the taxpayers in the highest bracket. Although Quakers appeared among all economic groups, then, they did generally constitute a greater proportion of the "wealthier" classes. Consequently, the proportion of Quakers in the bottom 30 percent exceeded their relative strength to the total population only three times—for Exeter Township in 1754 and for Robeson Township in 1779 and 1781.[13]

Berks County Friends might have been overrepresented among the higher wealth classifications, but members of Exeter Monthly Meeting considered religious devotion rather than economic status in determining who would serve as leaders of the meeting. For Maiden Creek Preparative Meeting, not until the 1760s did an overseer come from the top 10% tax bracket. Mordecai Lee, who served as an overseer for the preparative

Table 6.5
Economic Distribution of Quakers, 1754–1785

Exeter Township

	Top 10%	Upper 30%	Middle 30%	Bottom 30%
1754	42.9	15.0	5.0	21.1
1758	22.2	14.8	7.4	3.7
1762	36.4	12.1	9.1	3.0
1767	30.0	32.1	13.8	6.9
1770	30.0	10.0	16.7	6.7
1775	20.0	29.0	3.2	3.2
1779	14.3	20.0	7.5	5.0
1781	23.1	17.9	5.1	7.7
1785	21.4	11.9	7.1	—

Maiden Creek Township

	Top 10%	Upper 30%	Middle 30%	Bottom 30%
1754	50.0	77.8	40.0	20.0
1758	50.0	66.7	50.0	33.3
1762	50.0	27.8	27.8	11.1
1767	71.4	14.3	14.3	28.6
1770	50.0	25.0	25.0	22.2
1775	25.0	33.3	20.8	16.7
1779	37.5	16.7	20.8	16.7
1781	33.3	36.8	15.8	15.8
1785	40.0	30.0	23.3	6.7

Robeson Township

	Top 10%	Upper 30%	Middle 30%	Bottom 30%
1754	16.7	44.4	27.8	11.1
1758	66.7	35.0	25.0	10.0
1762	33.3	22.2	22.2	11.1
1767	30.0	26.7	13.3	13.3
1770	40.0	26.7	16.1	16.1
1775	36.4	33.3	6.1	12.2
1779	23.1	20.0	7.5	35.0
1781	7.1	23.8	19.0	23.8
1785	23.5	17.6	17.6	11.8

meeting from 1764 until 1787, consistently was one of the wealthiest taxpayers in the township. The remaining overseers were men of middling means, falling into the upper 30 percent and middle 30 percent tax brackets. Richard Penrose, for example, was in this grouping when he served during the 1750s and early 1760s; he also fell into this category when he held that position for Exeter Preparative Meeting between 1764 and 1774.[14]

None of the overseers for Exeter Preparative Meeting came from the bottom 30 percent; a greater proportion was among the top 10 percent of the taxpayers. James Boone, who served during the 1740s and 1750s, and John Lee, who held this position during the 1770s and 1780s, were among the wealthiest men in Exeter Township. The majority, however, came from the upper 30%—Morris Ellis (1741–1742), Ellis Hughes (1737–1739, 1740–1749), Samuel Hughes (1753–1755, 1759–1764), Anthony Lee (1770–1773), and Samuel Lee (1774–1790s). Only George Hughes, Samuel's nephew and Ellis's grandson, joined Richard Penrose in the middle 30 percent during the eighteenth century.[15]

Robeson Preparative Meeting had more overseers rank among the wealthier taxpayers in the township, but this reflection of riches was not entirely accurate. Granted, John Scarlet and his eldest son John, Jr., were the elders for the preparative meeting from 1742 until the formation of Robeson Monthly Meeting in 1789 and were among the wealthiest men in the township throughout the eighteenth century. Two of the "poorer" overseers, Enos Ellis (1758–1763) and James Cadwalader (1763–1767), left Robeson at the end of their service and migrated to Virginia, perhaps seeking better economic opportunity.[16]

Upward mobility also characterized the leadership of Robeson Preparative Meeting. Gaius Dickinson rose from the upper 30% when he first became an overseer in 1767 to the top 10% in 1770 and 1775. Based on taxes paid, Jonathan Stephens apparently had a greater increase in economic status, from the bottom 30% in 1779 to the upper 30 percent in 1781 and 1785, but his standing in 1779 resulted from a refusal to pay taxes for the war and not any lack of wealth.[17]

The men and women whom the monthly meeting thought displayed the spiritual devotion necessary to serve the Society of Friends as ministers also tended to be upwardly mobile. Mary Dickinson, wife of Gaius, joined him in their rise from the upper 30 percent in 1767 to the top 10 percent in 1770 and 1775, with their bottom 30% ranking in 1779 resulting from Gaius's refusal to pay taxes to support the war. James Thomas rose from the bottom 30 percent in 1762 to the upper 30 percent in 1775. Finally, Abel Thomas, who traveled throughout the Revolutionary War era in the middle and southern states, gradually increased his economic position from paying a tax on the border between the middle 30 percent and the bottom 30 percent shortly after he moved to Exeter Township in 1767 to reaching the upper 30 percent status in 1775 and top 10 percent in 1785.[18]

Surprisingly, the one leadership category in which piety did not matter as much—clerk—tended to attract wealthier members of the meeting. James Boone (1746/7–1749) and John Hughes (1749–1756) consistently ranked among the top 10 percent of the taxpayers of Exeter Township. Benjamin Lightfoot (1756–1766) was a prominent merchant, surveyor, and justice who was the wealthiest Berks County Quaker during the eighteenth century. Francis Parvin, Jr., (1766–1771), while he ranked in the bottom 30 percent prior to his father's death, rose to the upper 30 percent status by the end of his term as clerk. Only the last Exeter clerk during the period under examination, Thomas Lightfoot of Maiden Creek Township (1780–1790s), remained in the bottom 30 percent and middle 30 percent brackets after acceding to this office.[19]

In a fluid frontier region such as Berks County, members of the Society of Friends occasionally overextended themselves and became debtors. Of the seventeen members of Exeter Monthly Meeting who faced disciplinary action between 1737 and 1789 for indebtedness, the meeting charged almost one-half of them during the 1750s, when the Seven Years' War adversely affected the fortunes of several Berks County Friends (see table 6.6). The first case of indebtedness occurred in November 1745, when Samuel Woolaston and Rebecca Harbut separately "made Complaint" to Exeter Monthly Meeting "against Richard Moore for keeping [them] out of some Money which he oweth [them] too long." The next month, the committee appointed to visit with Moore remarked that the debtor had indicated that he could not pay either Woolaston or Harbut until the following March; three other Friends agreed to speak with Moore, "and let him Understand that if he does not pay Samuel [Woolaston] before next Month by Meeting he will be at liberty to recover it by Law." Rebecca Harbut, however, did not possess the same legal recourse as did Woolaston, as the same Friends merely reminded Moore "that he should Pay the Woman without delay." Richard Moore continued to face trouble in meeting his financial obligations; in spite of paying a tax that placed him in the middle 30 percent bracket of Robeson Township in 1754, the meeting discovered when Moore applied for a certificate of removal to Cane Creek, North Carolina, in 1756 that he was "indebted to sundry Persons," and money collected to assist in his travel expenses instead went to pay outstanding debts in Berks County.[20]

During the 1750s, other Exeter Friends decided to leave Berks County in search of better economic opportunity. In at least one instance, the Quaker involved left his financial affairs in disarray. In June, 1755, representatives from Maiden Creek Preparative Meeting charged Thomas Embree, brother of an overseer, with "departing the Province Considerably in Debt and Defrauding of his Creditors." The following month, the monthly meeting disowned him for failing to fulfill his financial obligations.[21]

Two members of the Jordan family also faced disciplinary action on multiple occasions, and the monthly meeting disowned one for this offense. In February 1754, Exeter Monthly Meeting acknowledged that Joseph Jordan had neglected to pay a debt owed to John Smith, which Jordan had satisfied by the next monthly meeting. Eight months later,

Table 6.6
Indebtedness Among Exeter Friends, 1737–1789

Offender	Date Charged	Disposition
Richard Moore	31/8/1745	Ordered to pay
Richard Moore	31/8/1745	Ordered to pay
William Hughes	28/9/1751	Resolved/Satisfied
Joseph Jordan	28/2/1754	Resolved/Satisfied
Derrick Cleaver	29/8/1754	Resolved/Satisfied
Joseph Jordan	31/10/1754	Resolved/Satisfied
James Jordan	29/5/1755	Resolved/Satisfied
Thomas Embree	26/6/1755	Testimony/Disowned[a]
John Willits	25/9/1755	Resolved/Satisfied
Richard Moore	28/10/1756	Resolved/Satisfied
Joseph Wily	26/1/1764	Resolved/Satisfied
Josiah Boone	23/2/1764	Resolved/Satisfied
James Jordan	28/1/1767	Testimony/Disowned[b]
Gideon Vore	28/8/1771	Resolved/Satisfied
Isaac John	28/2/1776	Testimony/Disowned[c]
Gideon Vore	28/4/1784	Resolved/Satisfied
Lewis Walker	24/9/1788	Paper of Condemnation

Resolved/Satisfied indicates that the debt was paid by the next monthly meeting
[a]Disowned for leaving Pennsylvania without settling debts
[b]Disowned for indebtedness and jumping bail
[c]Disowned for indebtedness and for assisting in an irregular marriage

William Hughes charged Jordan with failing to remit a payment for a bill; this time it took him two months to resolve the problem. Joseph's younger brother, James, also experienced difficulties in satisfying his financial obligations. In May 1755, the monthly meeting charged him with failing to pay a debt due to Evan Evans. James Jordan, who was one of the poorest Quakers residing in Maiden Creek Township in 1758, confronted similar accusations in 1767, but in the latter instance the monthly meeting disowned him for "plunging himself into Debt, beyond what he could honestly Answer or Discharge," a decision that Philadelphia Quarterly Meeting upheld.[22]

Of those Friends who had difficulty paying their debts on time, the majority fell into the bottom 30 percent of the wealth holders, suggesting that poorer Friends, and not wealthy ones who had overextended their credit, were more liable to face these problems. Not all indigent Quakers, however, had problems with indebtedness. Instead, some would request financial assistance from the monthly meeting, often merely to purchase the basic necessities. In 1762, Maiden Creek representatives informed the monthly meeting that Mary Kirby, a disabled young woman, needed assistance in obtaining constant care and medicine, and for the next fourteen months the meeting paid for her care. Former Robeson overseer Frances Dowdle received aid in early 1765, certainly not unexpected given her bottom 30 percent standing in 1758. Finally, John Cadwalader did not even appear on a Robeson Township tax list after 1762 because of his dire economic situation, and throughout the 1780s Exeter Monthly Meeting periodically supplied money for him and his wife. In fact, when Philadelphia Quarterly Meeting agreed to the creation of Robeson Monthly Meeting in 1789, both Exeter and Robeson agreed to contribute equally toward Cadwalader's support.[23]

All but one of the Berks County Quakers who faced disciplinary action for indebtedness during the eighteenth century were farmers, an occupation that could render their economic situation untenable if the weather or market were uncooperative. This, of course, was not an unusual career choice, given that Berks County was the heart of the province's breadbasket during this era. An examination of the Berks County tax lists for 1767 and 1779, in fact, revealed that almost three-fourths of the Quakers residing in the county were farmers. In 1767, other occupations identified for members of Exeter Monthly Meeting included weaver, carpenter, miller, shopkeeper, brewer, blacksmith, tailor, cutler, hatter, joiner, goaler (jailer), innkeeper, surveyor, and tanner. Almost all Friends pursuing these vocations lived in Reading or one of the adjacent townships; only the innkeeper, Thomas Paine, resided more than twenty miles from the county seat. Twelve years later, members of the Society of Friends held fewer occupations, and only the blacksmith, William Boone, did not practice his craft in a township adjacent to Reading. Not surprisingly, for both years, those taxpayers who were not farmers generally fell into the lower two-thirds of the economic spectrum, as they tended to own less property and therefore paid lower taxes than did their fellow Quakers who held sizable parcels of land.[24]

This apparent occupational diversity declined considerably once Reading taxpayers are withdrawn from the analysis. For example, Exeter Township Quakers in 1779 included farmers (81 percent), millers (13 percent), and tanners (6 percent). Two years later, farmers comprised 67 percent of the Quakers, followed by millers (17 percent), tanners (11 percent), and cooper and distiller (each 5 percent). In Exeter Township for these two years, fourteen and eighteen occupations, respectively, appeared on the tax lists. Consequently, Friends really did not reflect the economic diversity of this township.[25]

In contrast, Robeson Township taxpayers held a variety of occupations in 1779, but this diversity had virtually disappeared by 1781. In 1779, for instance, only 56 percent of the taxpayers were farmers; almost 20 percent were weavers or laborers. Overall in that year, Quakers held eight different occupations, while non-Quakers pursued ten distinct vocations. By 1781, however, Friends were farmers (94 percent) or millers (6 percent). Non-Quakers, meanwhile, held seven different occupations in this year. It is not clear why the innkeeper, cordwainers, fullers, and cooper who appeared on the 1779 list either became farmers in 1781 or left the township.[26]

Unfortunately, it is not possible to describe completely many business relationships that existed between Exeter Friends and their non-Quaker neighbors. Few ledgers, account books, or business journals for Berks County Friends have survived, and they are relatively incomplete. Judging from the known occupations of these Quakers (outside of farming), they undoubtedly had to deal with non-Quakers in order to operate a profitable business. Certainly, Quakers would patronize fellow Friends if logistically possible, but in all probability the farmer in Maiden Creek Township who needed to get new horseshoes would probably go to a local farrier rather than travel over thirty miles to William Boone's blacksmith shop in Amity Township near the Philadelphia County border.

The business relationships of Benjamin Lightfoot shed some light on the interaction of Berks County Quakers and their non-Quaker neighbors. Lightfoot, along with fellow Friend James Starr, operated a land speculation enterprise with Reading Anglican Edward Biddle. Lightfoot also hired two Germans to help him survey a road from Reading to Shamokin in 1759, but because of the war they refused to perform this duty unless they had a military escort. He then replaced them with three friendly Native Americans and ten Quaker associates, who accompanied him on this journey.[27]

Lightfoot's primary occupation while residing in Reading was operating a store on Penn Street. His daybook, which is a detailed record of his business transactions, reflected the diversity of his contacts. Less than one-fifth of the entries for 1754, for example, identified Berks County Quakers as customers. Occasionally, these Friends repaid a debt through labor; Joseph Barger received £6.4.0 credit in that year "for Work done" on Lightfoot's house in Maiden Creek Township. More often, these men purchased "Sundrys" from Lightfoot or borrowed money. The account for Jacob Lightfoot, Benjamin's uncle, indicated that the storekeeper had debited the account in 1755 "To Cash paid An Indian." Benjamin Lightfoot also continued to work as a surveyor; the store accounts indicated that John Fincher paid him £2 cash for surveying his land in Windsor Township in November of that year.[28]

The number of transactions recorded by Lightfoot in his daybook decreased throughout the 1750s, from 281 in 1754 to 160 in 1755 and 134 in 1756. Surprisingly, the percentage of Quakers among his customers increased to almost thirty percent during these two years, and four Friends—

Francis Parvin, who was serving as the county's assemblyman; his brother Thomas Lightfoot; Benjamin Pearson, a Reading carpenter; and William Iddings, a Robeson Township farmer—appeared more then ten times each during these two years. Again, the majority of these entries appeared to involve loaning cash to these men, suggesting that Lightfoot not only operated a store but also extended credit to local residents in a growing community.[29]

In spite of Lightfoot's status within the meeting—by mid-1756 he had become clerk—one interesting feature of this volume is that at the beginning he recorded dates in the English tradition, such as "Reading, May 13th 1754." But by the end of that year, Lightfoot had begun to identify entries in late December under "Reading the 12mo. . . 1754," using the Quaker method of recording dates. Lightfoot's daybook also recorded the resolution of civil suits, as he noted attorney's fees and his charges as surveyor in litigation relating to property disputes.[30]

Although the transactions recorded in the daybook ceased in early 1757, Benjamin Lightfoot continued to operate a store in Reading into the 1770s. By this time, he had begun to correspond regularly with Samuel Coates and John Reynell, two prominent Philadelphia merchants, to obtain stock for his store and to finance loans. Occasionally, he pondered on his life as a country merchant and expressed misgivings about his career choice. In a letter to Reynell in April 1770, Lightfoot remarked, "I have long wanted to be employ'd in Business which would not subject me to Trust People as is the Case in the Business I am now concerned in." Later that year, Lightfoot escaped from the hustle and bustle of Reading and returned to surveying, traveling to Tunkannock in northeastern Pennsylvania to lay out some proprietary lands. Even then, he realized the necessity of dealing with non-Quakers. On this excursion, he hired horses from two non-Quakers and bought supplies from several others.[31]

More than merely a country shopkeeper, Benjamin Lightfoot made his store into a backcountry outlet for the purchase of foreign and domestic goods available in Philadelphia. For Moses Boone, an Exeter Township tanner, life was quite different in the 1770s and 1780s. Moses was the youngest surviving son of James Boone, a former overseer of Exeter Preparative Meeting and former clerk of the monthly meeting. Unlike Lightfoot, Boone regularly fell into the middle 30% tax bracket, which made him one of the poorer Friends in the township. Residents of Alsace, Amity, District, Douglass, Earl, Hereford, Oley, Reading, Robeson, and Rockland Townships, in addition to Exeter, had business relationships with Boone during the 1770s and 1780s.[32]

Slightly more than one-sixth of Boone's customers were Quakers, and a few others were distant relatives. Over one-fourth of the entries in his ledger, which covered Boone's business activity from the late 1770s until the early 1820s, indicated that the debtor repaid Boone for tanning by hauling, reaping, or mowing his fields, "by shingling the house," or "by Mason Work." Daniel Thomas fulfilled his obligations "by Schooling" Moses's two eldest children. George Hughes, Richard Penrose, Sr., and Judah Boone had servants perform chores for him in order to repay their debts. Boone also noted in 1789 that Oley Township farmer Isaac Levan had settled his account after he had agreed to "the Run of his Waggon to Philad[elphi]a (with my Body)." In addition, some of the customers probably exchanged services with the tanner, as they included tailors, shoemakers, weavers, coopers, carpenters, and saddlers.[33]

Moses Boone's ledger differed from Benjamin Lightfoot's daybook not only in arrangement (the ledger being organized by debtor/creditor, not by date) but also by including records for another person. The accounts of Eve Knabb in 1786 and of Exeter Township blacksmith Henry Hine in 1784 and 1787 indicated that they had paid Moses's eldest brother, James Boone, Jr., "for Schooling" their children.[34]

The records of Benjamin Lightfoot, Reading merchant and surveyor, and Moses Boone, Exeter Township tanner, do reflect the necessity Quakers faced in maintaining economic relations with non-Quakers. Land records, wills, and inventories indicate another type of relationship between these two groups. For instance, when Exeter Friends purchased property during the eighteenth century, between one-third and one-half of the grantors were not Quakers. In addition, of the 135 individual Quakers listed in the Grantee Index for Berks County, only sixty-nine bought land from other Friends. Perhaps a better indicator of the necessity of dealing with members of other religious groups is that only four of the 119 Quakers whose property holdings appear on warrantee township maps had Quaker landholders adjoining all sides of their property. Consequently, members of Exeter Monthly Meeting realized that they needed to get along with their non-Quaker neighbors. Failure to do so, after all, could result in legal action that would violate the *Rules of Discipline*.[35]

In spite of this inclination, Exeter Friends tended to be more restrictive in their relationships when it came time to prepare wills and administer estates. None of the twenty-three administrations filed between 1752 and 1789 identified a non-Quaker as the administrator for the estate, and only Quakers served as executors for the forty wills written by Friends during this period. One reason for this constraint is that the quarterly and yearly meeting strongly encouraged Friends to write wills, and leaders might have perceived the process as another way to enforce the "Quaker way" and limit outside influence on Friends' daily lives.[36]

Non-Quakers, however, did participate in the process of probating the estate. Twenty-three non-Quakers witnessed the writing or dictation of wills, while Quakers were present at the drafting of fifty-two wills prepared by members of other religious groups. Interestingly, one Exeter Friend, William Boone, witnessed nine wills prepared between 1755 and 1769; that he was county coroner during part of this period could explain his timely presence at the drafting of these documents. He was merely doing his job, without reference to the faith of the decedent.[37]

According to the inventories of deceased Quakers, non-Quakers served as appraisers for sixteen of the forty-nine estates. The inventories of the estates of twelve Quakers indicated that non-Quakers owed them money at the time of their death. In three of the cases, the notations "doubtful" or "absconded" were made beside the names of these debtors, possibly suggesting the risk of loaning money to non-Friends. Consequently, Exeter Friends might have considered it necessary to deal with non-Quakers during their lifetimes, but they did not always find it important to include them when distributing their estates.[38]

Friends who did prepare wills often had real and personal property that they wished to control after their deaths. Anthony Lee, an elder for Exeter Preparative Meeting for twenty years, specified how much land each of his sons would receive and the amount of money to be given to each of his daughters. Douglass Township yeoman Derrick Cleaver provided legacies for his grandchildren in addition to specific bequests to his son John and unmarried daughter Mary, who apparently received her dowry through the will. Not all testators went into great detail; Benjamin Lightfoot left £500 for his young daughter Elizabeth when she reached age eighteen and bequeathed the remainder of his £2,646.16.3 estate to his widow.[39]

The monthly meeting strongly encouraged members of Exeter Monthly Meeting to prepare wills, repeating the concerns of the quarterly and yearly meeting about this obligation. Similar to other religious and ethnic groups in Berks County, economic success and marital status did not necessarily indicate whether Exeter Friends would prepare a will or die intestate. John Hughes, who died in 1763, consistently ranked among the top 10 percent of the taxpayers in Exeter Township during the 1750s, but he did not leave instructions on how his estate of £1,095.14.11 would be divided between his widow and four minor children. John Boone, older brother of Moses, passed away in 1773 without determining how relatives would distribute £1,125.1.2 of his belongings. Yet when drafting a will in 1769, Joseph Barger specified that his small parcel of land in Maiden Creek Township would be sold to support his family and requested that his six children be apprenticed to Quakers, even though appraisers valued his estate at only £18.15.6. Richard Stephens left most of his worldly possessions to his widow Dorothy in 1784, with eldest son George receiving the land. He then ordered the remainder of the estate to be sold, with the proceeds to be divided among the five children in varying increments of £50. This latter requirement must have proven difficult for the executors, as the estate was

Table 6.7
Values of Estates
Members of Exeter Monthly Meeting

Name	Date Recorded	Amount*	W/A**
Barger, John	28 Mar 1758	101.07.00	A
Barger, Joseph	17 Aug 1772	18.15.06	W
Boone, James, Sr.	17 Sep 1785	230.13.02	W
Boone, Jeremiah	30 Mar 1787	1918.18.04	W
Boone, John	24 Apr 1773	1215.01.02	A
Boone, Joseph	4 Jun 1776	265.08.03	A
Boone, John	5 Nov 1785	916.05.02¾	W
Boone, Judah	30 Jun 1787	373.09.10	A
Boone, William	10 Mar 1772	87.06.00	W
Clendennon, Elizabeth	2 Feb 1775	43.15.09	W
Clendennon, Isaac	15 May 1772	126.12.01	W
Clever, Derrick	30 Mar 1768	886.03.03	W
Clews, Mary	4 Apr 1782	216.16.11	A
Davis, Thomas	6 Nov 1786	60.16.04	A
Ellis, Rowland	5 Nov 1771	180.02.11½	W
Embree, Samuel	31 Jan 1786	131.07.03	W
Evans, Penal	16 Nov 1773	316.19.08	A
Fincher, John	30 Sep 1763	27.06.03	A
Fincher, Jonathan	11 Nov 1795	416.19.02	W
Harrison, John	12 Jun 1786	97.03.03	W
Hughes, John	13 Aug 1766	1095.14.11	A
Hughes, Jonathan	20 Jan 1769	77.06.06	W
Hughes, Owen	31 Oct 1774	79.07.11	A
Hutton, James	19 Mar 1782	557.16.10½	W
Hutton, Sarah	21 May 1767	225.00.11	W
Jackson, Ephraim	9 Mar 1768	108.03.09	A
Jackson, Mary	24 Nov 1767	170.11.04	A
Lee, Anthony	11 Mar 1763	828.02.10	W
Lightfoot, Benjamin	21 Dec 1778	2646.16.3	W
Lightfoot, Jacob	23 Oct 1784	348.13.01½	W
Lightfoot, Joseph	21 Dec 1784	211.06.11	A
Parvin, Eleanor	16 Jan 1776	497.17.06	W
Parvin, Francis	13 Apr 1768	491.00.10½	W
Parvin, William	15 Jun 1772	249.03.08	W
Pearson, Lawrence	4 Mar 1754	101.02.00	A
Penrose, Joseph, Jr.	12 Aug 1784	139.05.06	A
Roberts, Moses	6 Dec 1788	274.16.02½	A
Stephens, Richard	22 Apr 1784	27.03.00	W
Thomas, Evan	4 Feb 1757	102.03.00	A
Tomlinson, William, Jr.	23 Nov 1784	47.10.09	A
Webb, Joseph	21 Mar 1781	67.07.09	A

continued

Table 6.7—Continued

Name	Date Recorded	Amount*	W/A**
Willits, Henry	11 Feb 1755	613.05.07¼	W
Willits, Jesse	5 Apr 1782	125.13.04	A
Wily, John, Jr.	30 Sep 1755	701.11.00	W
Wily, John	29 Nov 1756	911.03.05	W
Woolaston, Samuel	3 Aug 1768	180.18.11	W
Woolaston, Rebecca	9 Jan 1776	32.08.07	A
Woolaston, Samuel, Jr.	11 Oct 1768	89.16.05	A
Wright, Mary	14 May 1771	231.14.00	W

*Amount listed as pounds, shilling, pence (£.s.d.)
**W/A*: W—Will; A—Letter of Administration

valued at only £27. More often, extended illness or age would determine whether a person would prepare a will, although Joseph Boone was almost seventy-two years old when he died intestate in 1776.[40]

When the husband died intestate and left minor children, occasionally the widow requested the assistance of the monthly meeting. Evan Thomas died in late 1756 and had his estate probated in early 1757. Valued at only £102.3.0, it was scarcely enough to provide for his widow Rachel and their two children, much less Evan's three sons from a previous marriage. As a result, in December 1756, Rachel Thomas asked Exeter Monthly Meeting for help in placing the children out to trades. This assignment proved to be a difficult one, as five years later the clerk noted that the Orphans' Court had chosen William Iddings and James Starr to be guardians for the youngest son, for whom they had not yet found a master.[41]

Women members of Exeter Monthly Meeting participated in the will-making process as well as men. Between 1752 and 1789, 125 Berks County women had their personal estates probated, either through a will (in forty-three percent of the cases) or letters of administration (fifty-seven percent). Ten of these women were Quakers, a percentage approximating their relationship to the total populace of the county. Of these ten women, seven wrote wills, and three died intestate. Surprisingly, only three of the other women were Anglicans; the overwhelming majority belonged to one of the assorted German congregations throughout the county or worshiped outside Berks County. Because it was consistent with Germanic legal tradition for women to write wills, it is conceivable that Exeter women adopted a part of the continental culture, rather than the German immigrants totally assimilating into English traditions.[42]

Although the women of Exeter Monthly Meeting were not unique in that they prepared wills, the documents they developed were not necessarily typical of those written by other women in the county. Unmarried women, in fact, wrote two of these testaments. Mary Wright, who died in 1771 shortly before her twenty-third birthday, left her estate to her mother, sister, and sister's children. In a will written weeks before her death in early 1770, Jane Wily (whose brother John had married Mary Wright's mother in 1751) bequeathed items to three Quaker women who were not members of her family, in addition to leaving money and property to relatives.[43]

Married women occasionally included intriguing provisions in their wills. Sarah Hutton bequeathed 20s. to each of her sons, £10 to her daughter Sarah, £20 to her youngest daughter Tamar, and then divided the remainder of her estate equally among her six surviving daughters and the children of her eldest daughter. Elizabeth Clendennon, whose husband Isaac had predeceased her by two years, made provisions in her 1774 will empowering the executor "to bring up or place out to Trades or Business my two Children as he may think best." Clendennon also bequeathed. specific items to her daughter and stepdaughter, with the remainder of her £43 estate to be divided between her two children. Eleanor Parvin split her wealth among male and female family members, but she also gave £5 to the overseers of Maiden Creek Preparative Meeting "to be applyed to such uses as the said Meeting shall Direct." This certainly was an unusual stipulation, as of the thirty-nine wills written by members of Exeter Monthly Meeting between 1752 and 1789, only three left legacies to the local Quaker organization—Parvin, William Boone (1771), and Jeremiah Boone (1787).[44]

Members of Exeter Monthly Meeting played an active role in the economic life of Berks County during the eighteenth century. Quakers pursued the same occupations as other county residents, although an overwhelming majority of them were farmers rather than artisans or merchants. Benjamin Lightfoot achieved renown throughout the province as a surveyor and locally as a trusted merchant. Moses Boone, of course, must have performed skillfully as a tanner, as evidenced by his clientele from eleven townships in Berks County.

Friends, however, did not dominate the economic elite of Exeter or Robeson Townships. In Maiden Creek, where Quakers comprised at least one-fifth of the taxpayers between 1754 and 1785, at least one-half of the top 10 percent were members of the Society of Friends until 1775, and from 1779 until 1785 they comprised more than one-third. Robeson Township Friends skewed the numbers in 1779 and 1781, as they were between one-fourth and one-third of the bottom 30%. Overall, Quakers did tend to possess greater wealth than non-Quakers, but they did not dominate local economic activity as they did in Philadelphia.

Although economic success—or more accurately, fear of economic failure—helped inspire New England Puritans to revolt against the British during the mid-1770s,[45] a similar Quaker ethic, fostered by pacifism and an opposition to revolt, did not lead to massive support for the war effort among members of the Society of Friends. Instead, Berks County Quakers were more inclined to suffer a decline in economic status (and in wealth) during the Revolution rather than pay taxes for what they perceived as an unnecessary and immoral conflict. Furthermore, while members of Exeter Monthly Meeting who were active in local politics during the 1750s did tend to come from the wealthier economic groups of the townships, representatives from each of the three preparative meetings did not invariably consider economic standing when selecting elders, overseers, and ministers. The fact that Friends comprised a greater proportion of the top 10 percent of the taxpayers in each of these townships than their actual numbers, while the majority of leaders did not fall into this category, indicated that the Quakers were more equitable in this process and did not consider it necessary to perpetuate the ideal of the deferential society in the selection of religious officials.

The unstable nature of the frontier economy, as shown by the inequitable distribution of wealth in Exeter, Maiden Creek, and Robeson Townships, also resulted in instances of indebtedness among members of the monthly meeting. Generally, Quakers accused of being negligent in the timely payment of their financial obligations settled the matter within a month or two, but in three instances the monthly meeting disowned the delinquent. In addition, several Friends left Exeter Monthly Meeting after experiencing problems in paying their debts, suggesting that even the fertile soil of Berks County had become exhausted or difficult to obtain by the 1750s.[46]

Although Berks County Quakers found it essential to cooperate with non-Quakers to maintain successful businesses during the eighteenth century, they never arranged for non-Quakers to serve as the executor or administrator of their estates and only on rare occasions did non-Quakers witness wills written by Friends. Family members generally received the bulk of the estates, although on occasion the decedent would bequeath personal items to Quaker friends. Marital status, wealth, or property holdings did not determine whether a person would prepare a will, although the monthly meeting strongly encouraged Friends to write wills (and the quarterly and yearly meetings constantly reminded Exeter Friends of this duty).[47] Of course, there was little that the monthly meeting could do if a Friend died intestate.

While parts of the colonial Pennsylvania frontier might have provided economic opportunity to new settlers, by the 1760s and 1770s the "age of equality" had already passed by these residents of Berks County. Quakers who had moved into the interior hoping to find as good a life as their forefathers had achieved in Philadelphia and its vicinity instead faced the reality that they were an ethnic and religious minority, and consequently had fewer coreligionists or even other English speakers to offer assistance. The illusion of equality fostered by the Revolution had failed to reach fruition along the Berks County frontier; instead, these residents continued to experience the economic equivalent of "status quo antebellum." Economic discontent, combined with other factors, ultimately contributed immensely to the fluidity of Exeter Monthly Meeting's membership throughout the eighteenth century.

7

"A Restless Desire":
Geographic Mobility and Exeter Friends

American social development has been continually beginning over
again on the frontier. This perennial rebirth, this fluidity of American
life, this expansion westward with its new opportunities, its continuous
touch with the simplicity of primitive society, furnish the forces
dominating American character. . . . In this advance, the frontier is the
outer edge of the wave—the meeting point between savagery and
civilization.[1]

THE FRONTIER THAT FREDERICK JACKSON TURNER DESCRIBED IN HIS
landmark address, "The Significance of the Frontier in American History"
(1893), was not southeastern Pennsylvania, but the American West. Immigrants to colonial Pennsylvania, however, whether they came from the
British Isles or central Europe, found the province to be the type of wilderness that Turner described. Members of the Society of Friends initially
concentrated their settlements close to the Atlantic coast and the Delaware
River valley, only advancing into the interior after land purchases had
satisfactorily enabled the acquisition of additional territory from the natives. When Quakers moved into the interior of the province, they con-
sciously maintained familiar institutions to ease the process of adapting to
new environs. Unlike the experiences of Friends in the original three
counties, members of Exeter Monthly Meeting experienced the fluidity
described by Turner as they sought to provide a stable religious environment for British settlers in the backcountry.[2]

The Quakers who settled in colonial Pennsylvania predominantly resided in the original three counties of Bucks, Chester, and Philadelphia.
Within weeks of their arrival, Quakers had begun to form monthly meetings. By 1684, eleven monthly meetings had been established in these
counties, almost one-third of the total number that would be formed in
Pennsylvania by the end of the colonial period. Over the next hundred
years, Quaker activity expanded farther into the interior, and by 1776
meetings for worship (similar to individual congregations) had been created west of the Susquehanna River and north of the Blue Mountains.[3]

The dispersion of Quakers throughout the province paralleled the process of settlement. Throughout the remainder of the seventeenth century, settlement concentrated in the Delaware Valley, with little migration into the interior. The massive numbers of immigrants arriving in the early eighteenth century forced people to move into the Pennsylvania backcountry to seek available land and to establish homesteads. The vast majority of settlers along the frontier were from central Europe and from the northern regions of the British Isles. Those English and Welsh who ventured into the interior were either late arrivals to the province or younger sons who had little hope for advancement in the already crowded city of Philadelphia.[4]

Beginning in the 1710s, members of the Society of Friends settled along the outer limits of European civilization, in the area that became Berks County. In 1713, the three eldest children of George Boone sailed from Bristol, England, to Pennsylvania to determine whether conditions in the New World would be better than in their homeland. The young Boones found the colony to be everything that William Penn had described, and they sent favorable reports back to their father. The rest of the family arrived in 1717, and within the year George Boone had purchased some land in the Oley Valley, along the northwestern border of settlement in Philadelphia County. Neighbors of the Boones were Anthony Lee, who had also purchased land in the region in 1718, and his family. Over the next decade, Quakers continued to move into the interior, searching for fertile farmland and economic opportunity.[5]

A sufficient number of Friends had migrated to this region by 1725 to warrant a preparative meeting at Oley, under the auspices of Gwynedd Monthly Meeting. By the 1730s, the line of settlement had extended farther north into presentday central Berks County, as members of the Houlton, Hutton, Lundy, Penrose, Starr, Wily, and Wright families moved from Bucks and Chester counties. In 1735, Gwynedd Monthly Meeting allowed the formation of Maiden Creek Preparative Meeting for these Friends. At the same time, Thomas Ellis and Ellis Hughes brought their families from North Wales Township to the Oley Valley. After the establishment of Exeter Monthly Meeting in 1737, these early Quakers provided a religious home for the English-speaking pioneers of the region.[6]

When a Quaker wished to move to a community that was within the jurisdiction of another monthly meeting, he or she first made an application to the monthly meeting they attended for a certificate of removal. The clerk then noted the request in the minutes of the meeting and identified the Friends whom the meeting had appointed to investigate the member's status. This committee normally consisted of two men or two women, depending on whether the petitioner had applied to the men's or women's meeting for a certificate. A month later, the two Friends would usually report back to the monthly meeting that the member was in good standing.

The clerk of the men's meeting then prepared a certificate, which he would sign. If the applicant were female, the clerk of the women's meeting also affixed her signature. Occasionally members attending that monthly meeting would sign as well; by the 1770s this only occurred if the member was going on a religious journey to visit other Quaker meetings.[7]

If any problems existed in the member's status within the meeting, the clerk mentioned them on the certificate. The most common notation on certificates of removal issued by Exeter Monthly Meeting was that the members had been "too remiss in attending week-day Meetings," which was noted on fifteen certificates sent by Exeter and on three received by Exeter. Economic problems, too, received attention, as in the case of Richard Moore's removal to North Carolina in 1756. At times, the comments pertaining to the status of a member were quite detailed. The certificate of Gobitha Woolaston, received by Exeter Monthly Meeting from Haverford Monthly Meeting in 1745, noted that before receiving permission to move she had first presented to her meeting "a Paper acknowledging that she had slighted & disregarded Friends' care over her; also her going out in Marriage." Rarely did the certificates of removal provide much detail concerning the spiritual welfare of the member, although certificates provided for traveling Friends did include such comments.[8]

As one of the last monthly meetings established in colonial Pennsylvania, Exeter Monthly Meeting accepted Quakers from every part of the province, throughout the middle colonies, and even from the southern colonies (see table 7.1). An overwhelming majority (over eighty percent) came from another monthly meeting in Pennsylvania, and almost ninety percent had previously held membership in another monthly meeting in the middle colonies.

Most of the Pennsylvania Quakers who transferred to Exeter Monthly Meeting came from Philadelphia and Chester counties, with less than three percent migrating from Bucks County. In fact, Sadsbury Monthly Meeting in Lancaster County alone contributed more than three times the number of Friends transferring from Bucks County. Philadelphia and Gwynedd Monthly Meetings provided the most additions from Philadelphia County, each contributing at least fifty new members. Radnor, Uwchlan, Goshen, and Chester Monthly Meetings each supplied over thirty new members from Chester County. Of those Friends who did originate outside of Pennsylvania, nine emigrated from the British Isles, and only three did not come from colonies adjacent to Pennsylvania.

It is evident that family ties played an important role in the Quaker settlement of Berks County. For example, an examination of the minutes of the men's and women's monthly meetings revealed that at least fifteen family names had more than ten additions; two clans had more than twenty

Table 7.1
Origins of Exeter Friends
[N=558]

Location	Number	Percentage
DELAWARE	11	2.0
Duck Creek	1	
Wilmington	10	
MARYLAND	35	6.3
Deer Creek	24	
Nottingham	8	
Pipe Creek	2	
Third Haven	1	
NEW JERSEY	31	5.6
Bethlehem	1	
Burlington	5	
Chesterfield	5	
Haddonfield	9	
Hardwick	11	
NEW YORK	8	1.4
Westbury	8	
NORTH CAROLINA	2	0.4
Cane Creek	1	
Eno	1	
PENNSYLVANIA	450	80.6
Bucks County		
Buckingham	1	
Richland	15	
Chester County		
Bradford	21	
Chester	33	
Darby	8	
Goshen	36	
Kennett	7	
New Garden	27	
Radnor	52	
Uwchlan	42	
Lancaster County		
Sadsbury	52	
Philadelphia County		
Abington	8	
Gwynedd	50	

continued

Table 7.1—*Continued*

Location	Number	Percentage
Horsham	8	
Philadelphia	66	
York County		
Warrington	16	
SOUTH CAROLINA	1	0.2
Bush River	1	
VIRGINIA	11	2.0
Fairfax	8	
Hopewell	3	
ENGLAND	3	0.5
Yorkshire	3	
IRELAND	6	1.1

members move to Exeter. These records, incidentally, do not reflect additions that occurred prior to 1737, when Exeter Monthly Meeting was under the control of Gwynedd Monthly Meeting. Therefore, they do not include some members of the Boone, Ellis, Hughes, Hutton, Lee, Parvin, Penrose, Starr, and Wright families, all of whom played prominent roles in the activities of the monthly meeting during the eighteenth century.[9]

Not surprisingly, during the early years of Exeter Monthly Meeting, Quakers who transferred their membership did not have a difficult time in obtaining a leadership position in the meeting if they were qualified. At least eight of the men and women who served as overseers, elders, and clerks for the men's and women's meetings obtained such positions within a year of settlement. In one case, the monthly meeting appointed both the husband and the wife overseers of Maiden Creek Preparative Meeting shortly after their arrival. By the 1750s, however, it was increasingly difficult for recent arrivals to hold leadership positions. In fact, only six of the eighty-nine leaders moved to Exeter after 1755. Four of the six had married someone who was the son or daughter of a leader, a circumstance that may have assisted in obtaining this prominent role within the meeting.

The vast majority of men and women who joined Exeter Monthly Meeting tended to reside in the area for several years, if not permanently. For example, of the 288 males who transferred their membership, 126 moved away at least once, but only thirty-nine departed within five years of settlement. Almost one-half of those who stayed less than five years returned to the same monthly meeting from which they had migrated, possibly indicating that they might have moved to Berks County either to improve their economic circumstances or to marry. Of course, they also might have found that life along the frontier did not suit them, especially a region where they were an ethnic minority.

As a backcountry Quaker community, Exeter Monthly Meeting saw a great deal of both inward and outward migration during this period. Similar to the sources of migration, the majority of Friends departing from Exeter chose to settle in another part of Pennsylvania (see table 7.2). Over one-third, however, decided to depart the colony. Of those Quakers leaving Pennsylvania, almost two-thirds moved to the southern colonies, primarily Virginia and North Carolina. This migration pattern was consistent with the settlement of German Lutheran and Reformed immigrants to the Shenandoah Valley by mid-century. Overall, members of Exeter Monthly Meeting migrated to sixteen separate monthly meetings in Pennsylvania, six in Maryland and New Jersey, three in Virginia, and two in Delaware, New York, and North Carolina.[10]

Certificates of removal from Exeter remain for 295 of the 522 removals that occurred between 1755 and 1789. The monthly meeting provided these letters of transfer for three types of Quakers migrating from Berks County: those leaving to settle in another community, those young men and women who served apprenticeships within the jurisdiction of another monthly meeting, and those marrying a member of another monthly meeting. Over ninety percent (560 of 615) of the Quakers who left Exeter Monthly Meeting did so to settle in another community.[11]

Marriage affected both migration to and removal from Exeter Monthly Meeting. During the eighteenth century, marriage was under the direction of the prospective bride's monthly meeting; if she chose to marry a man from another monthly meeting, he needed to provide a certificate of removal from his monthly meeting to indicate that he was "Clear of Debt & Marriage engagements." At least eleven men joined Exeter Monthly Meeting between 1737 and 1789 specifically to marry a member of this meeting; eighteen left to marry women who belonged to another monthly meeting.[12]

Of those Friends who moved away to serve as apprentices, six had relatives in the new monthly meeting. This process occasionally separated family members; Benjamin Pearson, Jr., and his sister Eleanor went to Goshen and Gwynedd Monthly Meetings, respectively, in 1776. In addition, Exeter Friends who had apprentices also obtained certificates of removal for them. Morris Ellis and his wife acquired a certificate for Adah Yarnall, a young girl "under their care" in 1769. The clerk noted on the certificate for Daniel Dickinson and his wife that they were taking their apprentice with them to Crooked Run, Virginia. These apprentices, however, apparently did remain in contact with their parents. Certainly one hopes that Benjamin Chandler kept in touch with his father William after relocating to Uwchlan Monthly Meeting, for his father moved to Maryland four months later.[13]

Table 7.2
Destinations of Exeter Friends
[N=615]

Location	Number	Percentage
DELAWARE	8	1.3
Duck Creek	3	
Wilmington	5	
MARYLAND	22	3.6
Deer Creek	8	
Gunpowder	1	
Indian Springs	1	
Nottingham	6	
Pipe Creek	3	
Third Haven	3	
NORTH CAROLINA	39	6.3
Cane Creek	38	
New Garden	1	
NEW JERSEY	32	5.2
Bethlehem	13	
Burlington	2	
Chesterfield	2	
Haddonfield	12	
Hardwick	1	
Salem	2	
NEW YORK	5	0.8
Westbury	5	
PENNSYLVANIA	399	64.9
Bucks County		
Falls	1	
Richland	4	
Chester County		
Bradford	32	
Chester	39	
Concord	10	
Darby	2	
Goshen	30	
Kennett	11	
New Garden	37	
Radnor	30	
Uwchlan	40	
Lancaster County		
Sadsbury	33	

continued

Table 7.2—*Continued*

Location	Number	Percentage
Philadelphia County		
Abington	5	
Gwynedd	13	
Philadelphia	68	
York County		
Warrington	44	
VIRGINIA	105	17.1
Crooked Run	12	
Fairfax	39	
Hopewell	54	
IRELAND	3	0.5

Similar to the case for additions to Exeter Monthly Meeting, when examining the removals it becomes evident that family ties played a significant role. At least seventeen families who departed from Exeter between 1737 and 1789 had more than ten members leave; five had twenty or more relocate. The two leading families were the Ellis and Starr families, which had a combined total (men and women) of thirty-six and twenty-seven removals, respectively, during this period. Both of these families were active in the affairs of Exeter Monthly Meeting, so it does not appear that a lack of participation led to the exodus. In fact, over forty percent of the men and women who served as leaders of the monthly meeting removed from the boundaries of the meeting at least once during the eighteenth century.[14]

The four surviving sons of Thomas Ellis, one of the first overseers of Exeter Preparative Meeting, demonstrated the tendency of Berks County Quakers to resettle among familiar faces. After their father's death in 1760, the families of Enos, Thomas, Morris, and Mordecai Ellis moved to Virginia. Enos Ellis, the youngest son, departed for Hopewell Monthly Meeting in mid-1763, accompanied by his wife Elizabeth and seven children. The next year, Thomas Ellis, Jr., followed his younger brother, also taking his wife Magdalene and eight children to Virginia. During the late 1760s, Morris and Sarah Ellis moved to Fairfax Monthly Meeting with their three youngest sons after Morris condemned committing a violation of the discipline; their two older sons, whom Exeter Monthly Meeting had disowned, probably accompanied them. Finally, after Jane Ellis, matriarch of the clan, died in 1772, Mordecai and Mary Ellis took their six children to Hopewell Monthly Meeting. Unfortunately, no will of Thomas Ellis has survived to determine if Mordecai, the penultimate son, had been chosen to care for his aged mother, since he was the only son to remain in Berks

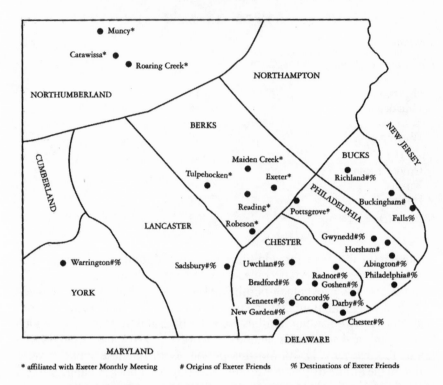

* affiliated with Exeter Monthly Meeting   # Origins of Exeter Friends   % Destinations of Exeter Friends

Map 3. Location of Quaker Meetings in Colonial Pennsylvania

County until her death. It is intriguing, however, that the three sons who had remained in good standing within the meeting settled near each other in central Virginia, while the only child of Thomas Ellis to stray from the Quaker way, Morris, relocated to another area of that colony.[15]

Once settled in the new location, Exeter Friends continued to hold leadership positions. Anthony Lee and Mordecai Ellis, both of whom served as overseers for Exeter Preparative Meeting, played the same role for Middle Creek Preparative Meeting, affiliated with Hopewell Monthly Meeting in Virginia, in the 1770s and 1780s. Ellis Ellis, second eldest son of Enos Ellis and a nephew of Mordecai, also became an overseer for Middle Creek Preparative Meeting in the 1780s. In addition, Moses and Mary Embree both became overseers of Goose Creek Preparative Meeting less than a year after moving to South River Monthly Meeting in 1787. Thus, migrants from Exeter continued to be active participants in the affairs of local meetings after their departure.[16]

The most active former resident of Exeter Monthly Meeting probably was Benjamin Parvin, brother of an Exeter clerk and son of a former assemblyman. Parvin moved to Third Haven Monthly Meeting in Maryland in 1770 to marry, and within three years the meeting had appointed him as a representative of the monthly meeting to the quarterly meeting. Between 1773 and 1783, Parvin represented Third Haven at Eastern Shore Quarterly Meeting nineteen times and served on the local committee for "the care and oversight of the Negroes, amongst us" and on the school committee. In addition, he became the clerk of the monthly meeting in 1775, and seven years later assumed the duties of overseer of Choptank Preparative Meeting. Illness, however, hindered Parvin's activity after 1783.[17]

The problems that Berks County Friends experienced in adhering to the tenets of their faith did not change following their departure from Exeter Monthly Meeting. According to excerpts from records of monthly meetings in Virginia, North Carolina, South Carolina, and Georgia, thirty-two former members of Exeter Monthly Meeting committed a violation of Quaker discipline between 1758 and 1789. Of these, twenty-one broke marriage regulations, eight committed unknown violations, and three fought in the American Revolution. Almost one-half of these violators had relatives (usually a father) who had faced disciplinary action while residing at Exeter Monthly Meeting. Apparently, then, as family ties had contributed toward removal from Berks County, the same factor influenced the behavior of Quakers at their new location.[18]

For approximately thirty of the men and women who left Exeter Monthly Meeting, the monthly meeting in Berks County was one stop on a series of migrations that eventually led to clusters of former Exeter Friends settling in the southern colonies. Jesse Vore moved to four different monthly meetings in York County and Maryland between 1780 and 1788. Four others changed locations at least three times between 1753 and 1789. One of these migrants was Jemima Green, who had temporarily relocated to Gwynedd Monthly Meeting in the late 1750s because of financial hardships suffered as a result of Native American raids. In addition, twenty-three members transferred to at least two other monthly meetings after leaving Exeter. Therefore, it appears that some of the Quakers who settled in Berks County possessed a restless body as well as spirit.[19]

The family of Moses Embree was one of the most geographically mobile. The elder Moses moved to Exeter from Radnor Monthly Meeting in Chester County in 1740 and was part of the migration to Cane Creek, North Carolina, in the 1750s. His brother John followed in 1760, and eleven years later moved to Bush River, South Carolina. Meanwhile, Moses and his family settled in Fredericksburg, South Carolina in 1768. In 1775, John and his family became some of the first Quaker residents of Wrightsborough, Georgia. In addition, a younger Moses Embree, nephew of Moses and John, also briefly lived at Cane Creek Monthly Meeting, but he primarily resided in Virginia. He moved to Hopewell in 1786 and to

South River Monthly Meeting a year later. By 1789, then, members of the Embree family were active members of Quaker meetings in four states.[20]

The settlement of former Exeter Friends especially affected several monthly meetings in Virginia, North Carolina, and Georgia. Between 1748 and 1759, thirty-seven Exeter Friends moved to Cane Creek Monthly Meeting in North Carolina; approximately 150 Quakers migrated there during this period. Among these settlers were James and Frances Taylor, who had received certificates of removal from Exeter Monthly Meeting in 1748 and were among the founding members of the new monthly meeting in 1751. Settlement at Cane Creek also appeared to be a family affair, as the group included two members of the Embree, Jones, Mooney, and Taylor families, nine Stewarts, ten Moores, and ten Elemans (including two married daughters). Two of these early migrants to Cane Creek later became some of the earliest members of Bush River Monthly Meeting in South Carolina, and two others were among the earliest settlers at Wrights-borough, Georgia. Only one of these founding members, however, had been among the leaders of Exeter Monthly Meeting; in fact, three of them had faced disciplinary action for violating the Quaker discipline.[21]

Fairfax and Hopewell Monthly Meetings in northern Virginia also were popular destinations for Exeter Friends. Between 1760 and 1787, fifty-four Exeter Friends migrated to Hopewell, while thirty-nine settled in Fairfax. Of those who moved to Virginia, fourteen later transferred their member-ship to a monthly meeting in another state. Virginia Quakers overall tended to be rather mobile, as over three-fourths of the Friends who removed from monthly meetings in that locale went to meetings outside Virginia. Appar-ently, then, moving to this area was the first stop for Exeter Friends and others as they spread Quakerism throughout the southern colonies.[22]

Exeter Friends not only left Berks County as they sought better oppor-tunity; some relocated to another township or moved into Northumberland County and introduced the principles of the Society of Friends to central Pennsylvania. Between the erection of Berks County in 1752 and 1770, in fact, almost one-eighth of the Quakers in the county moved to another township, usually one adjacent to their previous location. Derrick Cleaver, for instance, paid taxes in Amity Township in 1754 and in Douglass Township during the 1760s. From 1770 until 1789, however, Friends were only slightly more mobile. Based on the township in which their taxes were assessed, more than one-sixth of the Quakers changed residences within the county during this period.[23]

In contrast to the relative stability of Berks County Quakers, the resi-dents of Exeter, Maiden Creek, and Robeson townships were more tran-sient (see table 7.3). A sample of tax lists from these three townships between 1754 and 1785 revealed that on average slightly more than fifty percent of the taxpayers appeared on the previous list examined. The peak

Table 7.3
Number of Taxpayers Appearing on
Consecutive Sample Tax Lists, 1754–1785

Year	Number of Taxpayers	Number of Repeaters	Percentage
1754	66	—	—
1758	90	28	31%
1762	114	47	41%
1767	98	56	58%
1770	103	56	54%
1775	108	57	53%
1779	137	64	47%
1781	129	95	74%
1785	138	83	60%

	Maiden Creek Township		
	Number of Taxpayers	Number of Repeaters	Percentage
1754	37	—	—
1758	44	20	45%
1762	60	25	42%
1767	71	38	54%
1770	67	39	58%
1775	81	48	59%
1779	81	56	69%
1781	65	52	80%
1785	100	48	48%

	Robeson Township		
	Number of Taxpayers	Number of Repeaters	Percentage
1754	62	—	—
1758	66	34	52%
1762	90	45	50%
1767	104	56	54%
1770	102	59	57%
1775	114	64	56%
1779	135	65	48%
1781	139	95	68%
1785	169	89	53%

year of recurrence was 1781, as between two-thirds (Robeson) and four-fifths (Maiden Creek) had paid taxes there in 1779. Overall, Maiden Creek Township had the highest rate of constancy, since over fifty-seven percent of the taxpayers reappeared on a subsequent list. Friends comprised between one-fourth and one-third of those taxpayers that appeared on consecutive tax lists, indicating the relative stability of Quakers in the township but overrepresenting their proportion of the population.[24]

Although members of Exeter Monthly Meeting did not move that much while living in Berks County, some did relocate within the meeting, expanding into Northumberland County. The earliest European residents of central Pennsylvania, in fact, were members of the Society of Friends who had migrated north from Berks County. In 1773, Moses Roberts visited the region while serving on a jury that deliberated on the validity of a land patent. Within two years, Roberts purchased a parcel of land from Ellis Hughes, a lapsed Quaker who rejoined the Society in the late 1770s, and moved his family into the interior. William Hughes, cousin of Ellis, planned the town of Catawissa in 1786 and, the following year, granted some land to the Society of Friends for a meetinghouse. By the time Catawissa became a separate monthly meeting in 1796, Ellis's brother Job and his cousin John had also moved there, along with at least seven other families belonging to Exeter Monthly Meeting.[25]

A comparable number of Berks County Friends stopped before reaching Catawissa and instead settled near Roaring Creek. When Exeter renewed the meeting for worship at Catawissa in 1787, the monthly meeting permitted Quakers to worship alternately at Job Hughes's house in Catawissa and at the home of Richard Penrose, a former overseer of Maiden Creek and Exeter Preparative Meetings, at Roaring Creek. Other Friends who migrated there included the children and grandchildren of George Boone, Ellis Hughes, Anthony Lee, Laurence Pearson, Robert Penrose, and Moses Starr, founding fathers of Exeter Monthly Meeting in the 1730s.[26]

By the late 1780s, Exeter Friends had expanded even farther into the interior of central Pennsylvania. In 1788, enough Quakers had established farms near Muncy to warrant the creation of an indulged meeting that would be held "in a Schoolhouse near Carpenters." Joseph Carpenter, his wife Sarah, and their five children transferred to Exeter Monthly Meeting in 1778 from Hardwick Monthly Meeting in New Jersey and moved into the interior. During the 1780s, the families of Benjamin Warner and William Ellis migrated from Deer Creek Monthly Meeting in Maryland to this region. These Quaker pioneers succeeded in spreading the faith farther into the Pennsylvania backcountry, even across the Susquehanna River into present-day Lycoming County.[27]

The process of geographical migration, then, expanded Exeter Monthly Meeting's sphere of influence. As members of the Society of Friends advanced into the interior of the province and state, they carried with them their beliefs and ideals. Unlike most other monthly meetings, the boundaries of Exeter had not yet been defined, so it was the duty of the leaders of the meeting to oversee this internal expansion.

The spread of Exeter Monthly Meeting into the backcountry did not occur until after the Penn family had purchased the land from the Iroquois in 1768. This option had not been available to Exeter Friends seeking additional land during the 1750s and 1760s. As a result, when Squire Boone realized in the late 1740s that he would need to acquire more land in order to provide an adequate legacy for his growing family, remaining in Pennsylvania was not an option. In early 1750, the family of Daniel Boone left Exeter Township, following the Appalachian Mountains into the Shenandoah Valley of Virginia and southward into the North Carolina frontier.[28]

The phenomenon of inward and outward migration certainly was not unique to Exeter Monthly Meeting. Between 1718 and 1775, 238 Quaker men joined New Garden Monthly Meeting in Chester County. One hundred and twelve of these men later requested certificates to settle in another community. During this time, a total of 428 men left New Garden, and only a few ever returned. This reflects a greater disparity than for Exeter Monthly Meeting, which saw 167 men join between 1737 and 1774 and 222 leave.[29]

Richland Monthly Meeting in Bucks County, established in 1742 out of Gwynedd Monthly Meeting, was not as fluid as were Exeter or New Garden. Between 1743 and 1788, slightly more than 100 Friends moved from this meeting, compared with 615 from Exeter between 1737 and 1789. Barely half of Richland Friends remained within Pennsylvania; those Quakers who stayed in the colony and state tended to remove to Philadelphia and Chester counties, although over a dozen transferred to another monthly meeting in Bucks County. In addition, immigrants to Richland virtually equaled the number of departures, unlike Exeter or New Garden.[30]

Perhaps in response to the difficulties experienced by Exeter Friends, Philadelphia Yearly Meeting became concerned about maintaining the discipline as Friends crossed the Appalachian Mountains following the American Revolution. Like Exeter Monthly Meeting, Westland Monthly Meeting in southwestern Pennsylvania used its members' certificates of removal as a means to evaluate the moral and spiritual qualities of these westward migrants. With the increase in membership during its early years, members of Westland Monthly Meeting experienced both leadership opportunities and challenges to the discipline. Just as Exeter Monthly Meeting had served as a frontier outpost for Quakerism prior to the Revolution, Westland Monthly Meeting became a hub for additional trans-Appalachian migration during the 1790s. Unlike at Exeter, however, issues arising from the certificates of removal received by Westland contributed to a policy change by Philadelphia Yearly Meeting by the end of the eighteenth century.[31]

Upon examining the records of inward and outward migrations, several patterns become evident. A tradition of previous resettlement certainly existed; over one-third of the men's removals had previously joined another monthly meeting in the British Empire. Almost one-sixth of the men who left Exeter Monthly Meeting resided in the area less than five years, and almost one-half of these men returned to the same monthly meeting from which they had transferred their membership. Men were more likely to depart than women; women's removals outnumbered men's during only one five-year period. In contrast, almost the same number of men and women joined Exeter Monthly Meeting during this era (see tables 7.4 and 7.5). The second generation was more mobile than the first, as over two-thirds of the removals came after the first twenty years of settlement. Moreover, for the first two decades, opportunities existed for new residents to hold leadership positions in the meeting, but after that time it became increasingly more difficult for new settlers to serve as elders and overseers. Consequently, the membership of Exeter Monthly Meeting fluctuated considerably during the eighteenth century. By 1789, the composition of Exeter Monthly Meeting had changed. Many descendants of the first generation of leaders—the Boones, the Ellises, the Hugheses, the Lees, the Penroses, and the Starrs—had moved away. No longer isolated in the central and eastern sections of Berks County, Exeter Monthly Meeting had extended farther into the interior, establishing meetings for worship for Friends over one hundred miles away in Northumberland County. Several factors contributed to the mobility of these Quakers, among them Native American raids, economic hardships, family ties, the scarcity of land, and a "restless desire for new freedom from social restraints."[32] In some ways, Exeter Monthly Meeting grew to serve as a temporary religious home for these settlers, some of whom would live in the region for only a few years before moving on to another location. Usually these Quakers transferred their membership to another meeting within the province, but they also relocated to the backcountry of the southern colonies.

By examining the patterns of migration exhibited by members of Exeter Monthly Meeting, then, it becomes evident that the frontier did serve as a factor in the geographic mobility of Friends. Expansion into the interior during the eighteenth century allowed Quakers to renew themselves spiritually while searching for increased economic opportunities. In the process, members of Exeter Monthly Meeting demonstrated that the wilderness did not necessarily have to be a barrier to protect settlers from the natives; it could be an area for growth and prosperity in the secular and religious realm.

Table 7.4
Additions to Exeter Monthly Meeting
1737–1789

Years	Men	Women	Total
1737–1739	12	12	24
1740–1744	19	17	36
1745–1749	10	5	15
1750–1754	20	14	34
1755–1759	21	21	42
1760–1764	28	33	61
1765–1769	38	29	67
1770–1774	19	34	53
1775–1779	38	28	66
1780–1784	25	23	48
1785–1789	58	54	112
Totals	**288**	**270**	**558**

Table 7.5
Removals from Exeter Monthly Meeting
1737–1789

Years	Men	Women	Total
1737–1739	3	2	5
1740–1744	10	7	17
1745–1749	20	16	36
1750–1754	18	17	35
1755–1759	47	36	83
1760–1764	44	42	86
1765–1769	28	31	59
1770–1774	52	43	95
1775–1779	28	25	53
1780–1784	42	38	79
1785–1789	37	30	67
Totals	**328**	**287**	**615**

8

"To Start Instructing Young Friends at the Tenderest Age": The Concern for the Education of Youth

MEMBERS OF THE SOCIETY OF FRIENDS HAD LONG WORKED TO IMPROVE society since their arrival in Pennsylvania. Every three months, monthly meetings such as Exeter responded to a series of queries designed to address key moral issues, such as excessive drinking, sleeping in meeting, and the education of youth. Shortly after Quakers began arriving in the province in the 1680s, the yearly meeting authorized the establishment of a school system. At Exeter Monthly Meeting in the Pennsylvania backcountry, education did not receive much attention from local leaders until Philadelphia Quarterly Meeting forced Berks County Friends to establish a committee in the 1770s to examine the education of their youth. Even when Exeter Monthly Meeting leaders finally addressed this issue, however, their efforts still lagged behind those of other Quaker meetings in Pennsylvania.

For colonial Quakers, education for their children was extremely important. The purpose of this training was twofold: to read the Bible and to learn a trade. William Penn's first Frame of Government drafted in April 1682 made it the responsibility of the Governor and Provincial Council to "erect and order all public schools" so "that youth may be successively trained up in virtue and useful knowledge and arts," regardless of gender. The importance of the Bible as part of the curriculum was evident as early as 1683, when the provincial assembly passed a law that required all parents to teach their children "to read the Scriptures and to write by the time they attain twelve years of age," and levied a fine for noncompliance. Parents were encouraged to discuss the Bible with their children, helping them to gain insight into the Holy Writ so that they would be more receptive to the inner light.[1]

Philadelphia Yearly Meeting accepted the responsibility to ensure the proper education of youth. In particular, monthly meetings, especially those along the frontier, considered education to be of the utmost importance. At first, the monthly meetings financed these schools through sub-scriptions, then by charging fees to students or accepting donations. In 1722, Philadelphia Yearly Meeting counseled parents to "take due Care to bring up their Children, to some useful and necessary Employment that they may not spend their Precious Time in Idleness." Almost a quarter century later, the yearly meeting advised the monthly meetings "'to en-courage and assist each other in the settlement and support of Schools' and to employ 'such masters and mistresses as are concerned not only to instruct your children in their learning, but are likewise careful in the wisdom of God and a spirit of meekness, gradually to bring them to a knowledge of their duty to God and one another.'" Because of this concern for education, the yearly meeting expected teachers in Friends' schools to be of high moral quality and have a solid knowledge of the academic subjects they were teaching.[2]

A major goal of the colonial schoolmaster in Pennsylvania was the promotion of literacy in the language of instruction. Because of the em-phasis on Bible reading, people valued the ability to read over the ability to write. As a result, one of the first lessons learned by the pupils in colonial schools consisted of reading Bible passages, prayers, and hymns. As the child progressed, other subjects included writing (at first taught only to boys), ciphering, and spelling. Some students, particularly those in the Quaker schools, also learned languages, especially Latin, Greek, Hebrew, and French. Religious instruction, which included the singing of hymns, the recitation of prayers and the reading of the catechism, the Bible, and other religious books, occupied most of the class time.[3]

Teaching a child to read and write was not the only reason for education. A month after presenting his first Frame of Government, Penn restated the importance of education in the Laws Agreed Upon in England. According to Penn, "all children within this province of the age of twelve years shall be taught some useful trade or skill, to the end none may be idle, but the poor may work to live, and the rich, if they become poor, may not want." By acquiring marketable skills, the young Quaker lad or mistress would be able to contribute to the overall well-being of society. Without skills, the child could become a burden. Consequently, in 1695, Philadelphia Yearly Meeting for Sufferings recommended that local meetings establish schools where students "can learn languages and other sciences and also some remunerative trade, or at least skill and industry which will contribute to their support and combat many of the temptations associated with idle-ness." Because part of the Quaker ethic involved pursuing an occupation to glorify God, academic education and vocational training were crucial components of the instructional experience.[4]

In some communities, such as Philadelphia, this edict led to the forma-tion of schools. By the end of the eighteenth century, fifteen schools had been established within the boundaries of Philadelphia Quarterly Meeting. The earliest of these, begun in 1689, later became known as William Penn Charter School. Monthly meetings in Bucks, Chester, Lancaster, and York counties also sponsored educational institutions by the end of the eighteenth century. Exeter Monthly Meeting, like other frontier meetings in Pennsylvania, did not become actively involved in the establishment of schools until the late 1770s.[5]

Just because Exeter Monthly Meeting did not actively pursue the establishment of schools from its creation in 1737 did not mean that educational opportunities were not available in Berks County. Frontier settlers considered education to be important, although they probably concentrated on vocational training rather than academics. Children learned to feed and care for livestock, use firearms, and handle an axe, sickle, and flail. Mothers taught their daughters how to cook, clean, and sew, while fathers often passed along their trade to their sons. Once the settlers cleared the land and set up farmsteads, then the focus of learning expanded to include the four R's—reading, writing, arithmetic, and religion.[6]

The first mention of formally educating the young members of the meeting appeared in late 1758, when Exeter Monthly Meeting set up a youths meeting that met semiannually alternately at Exeter and Maiden Creek. These youth meetings served as an opportunity for elders to instruct the youth in religious and moral principles and to reinforce the Quaker discipline. In 1774, the monthly meeting created another youths meeting for the children who belonged to Robeson Preparative Meeting. The primary purpose of these meetings "was to start instructing young Friends at the tenderest age." Leaders of the meeting read extracts from the epistles of Philadelphia Yearly Meeting, instructing the children "on the proper behavior for Friends" both within and outside the meeting. The concept was laudable, but leaders of the quarterly and yearly meetings gradually realized that a few hours a year did not really have much of an impact on the young members of the Society.[7]

As a result, by the late 1770s, Philadelphia Quarterly Meeting requested that the various monthly meetings under its control investigate how young Quakers received schooling. In February 1778, Exeter Men's Monthly Meeting appointed Samuel Hughes, Abel Thomas, Benjamin Pearson, Mordecai Lee, James Thomas, and John Scarlet to the "Committee for the Education of Youth." Six months later, Exeter Women's Monthly Meeting appointed Eleanor Lee, Margaret Lee, Mary Hughes, Deborah Lee, Deborah Thomas, and Ann Scarlet to this committee. Over the next three and a half years, this committee sporadically reported to the monthly meeting that they had not completed this assignment. Finally, in August 1781, the committee reported that it had decided to visit the several preparative meetings within the territory of Exeter Monthly Meeting to determine the status of schools. The committee recommended that Friends should encourage education to instill into the "Tender Minds" of the children "the Principles of the Christian Religion and a Life of true Humility and Selfdenial." Perhaps to spur the committee to further action, the clerk noted in the minutes that "The Extract of a Minute from our last Quarterly meeting was received exciting Friends to Care and Diligence in promoting of Schools under pious Tutors; which Friends are desir'd to attend to." This suggestion went unheeded, and in 1782 Exeter Monthly Meeting released the committee from its obligations.[8]

The dismissal of the education committee did not signify a lack of interest in the proper education of youth. Responding to new directives from Philadelphia Quarterly Meeting, the monthly meeting appointed a new committee in February 1784, consisting of Samuel Lee, Samuel Hughes, Amos Lee, Owen Hughes, Benjamin Pearson, James Embree, John Scarlet, Edward Bonsall, and Thomas Lightfoot. Only Pearson and Scarlet remained from the earlier group, and they had previously been overseers for Maiden Creek and Robeson Preparative Meetings, respectively. This new committee, in fact, included seven men who had served as leaders of the meeting, which possibly contributed to a quicker response. Within two months of the committee's formation, in fact, its members submitted a report to the monthly meeting.[9]

According to this statement, schools existed within the neighborhoods of the indulged meetings at Maiden Creek, Reading, and Robeson. A total of ninety-three children attended the three schools; fifty of them went to the one in Reading. All of these were "pay schools," where parents would pay between 34s. and 40s. per year to educate their children. In addition, all of the teachers at these schools were Quakers who attended worship services regularly. None of these schools, though, were under the direct supervision of the monthly meeting.[10]

These "pay schools" were secular institutions mostly established for the English youth of the county during the eighteenth century. The school term was short and ran through late fall, winter, and early spring. Instructors in these schools ranged in quality from worthless to respectable academy teachers. In addition, pupils at these schools were expected to pay for their tuition and materials, usually several dollars per quarter, and, in some instances one cent a day payable at the close of the daily session.[11]

The committee on schools particularly expressed distress at the lack of a Quaker school "within the village of Exeter Preparative Meeting . . . But we are of the mind that it is necessary that one be established there." Schools, however, did exist in the Exeter area. For instance, a day school existed in 1762 near Samuel Lee's house, probably attended by Quaker children in the area. Two members of the Boone family, John and James, Jr., (uncle and cousin, respectively, of the noted pioneer Daniel Boone), taught school in Exeter Township. While John Boone failed to make much of an impression on his adventurous nephew, he did receive notice as a "man of some learning." The school that James Boone, Jr. started not only taught local students but also those from other colonies and even from England. Consequently, Quaker children could receive some sort of learning; it is probable that the lack of a formal "church-supported" system for educating the youth prompted the inquiries of the quarterly meeting during the 1770s.[12]

Of the three schools reported in the 1780s, the one at Maiden Creek gained the most renown. The schoolmaster, Thomas Pearson, was the eldest son of Benjamin Pearson, one of the members of the education committee, and a grandson of Francis Parvin. Pearson taught fifteen students year-round, and eight additional students were enrolled for the winter quarter. This school was the only one that had any symbolic links to the monthly meeting, as the patrons of the school selected "overseers" to administer it. A Friend owned the five acres on which the school was situated, which he deeded to the monthly meeting in late 1784. Over time, the institution received local notice, as many German farmers would send their children there so that they would learn to read and speak English.[13]

The Maiden Creek school also became known for its emphasis on mathematics in the curriculum. The cipher books of nine-year-old Mordecai Wright, who attended the school in early 1786, included practice exercises in compound addition, subtraction, and the multiplication of money; various systems of weights and measures; reduction; direct and indirect proportions; interest; vulgar and decimal fractions; square and cube roots; "mensuration of superficies" and of solids; and duodecimals. With this sort of instruction for a present-day fourth grader, it is not surprising that young men from Reading who wished to become surveyors would board with Quaker families to attend this institution.[14]

Friends in Robeson Township also had educational opportunities, although the Robeson school was not under the direction of Exeter Monthly Meeting. The instructor at this school, "who inclines to go to our meetings," taught twenty students. The committee remarked "Endeavors are also used to get a school established there upon a better plan," but no progress occurred in this matter before the formation of Robeson Monthly Meeting in 1789.[15]

The school in Reading was not as successful. Exeter Monthly Meeting had received a plot of land in 1768 from Thomas and Richard Penn, sons of the founder of the province, to be used for a Quaker school in Reading. Not until 1787 did Reading Friends begin construction on a school building. The earliest mention of the existence of a Friends school in the town occurred in the education committee's report in 1784, when it noted that Benjamin and Barbara Parks conducted a school in their house. Approximately fifty students attended this school. Even though the Parkses were members of the Society of Friends, the committee expressed reservations about their school because of the lack of "Overseers chosen to superintend the same." The committee did suggest "a School established there under proper Regulations & Care of the Monthly Meeting might be useful, & deserves Encouragement."[16]

Then, in February 1787, Samuel Jackson reported on behalf of the school committee that it had agreed that a subscription should occur for the erection and formal establishment of a school in the town. The following month, Exeter Monthly Meeting agreed that the committee could request funds for a school from Philadelphia Yearly Meeting. Unfortunately, the yearly meeting could not spare any funds, and Reading Friends had to construct a school with their own meager resources. Twenty-seven men signed a subscription list for the erection of this Quaker school, a log structure that they completed by the end of 1787.[17]

That October, the school committee announced the appointment of Caleb Johnson, a Reading Quaker, to serve as schoolmaster in the newly constructed schoolhouse. The committee recommended that this school "should be under the particular Care & Direction" of Exeter Monthly Meeting. A separate committee, consisting of Benjamin Pearson, Samuel Jackson, John Mears, Francis Parvin, Jr., John Lee, and James Iddings, was to supervise the school and visit it monthly. This second committee also drafted rules for the regulation of the school, which the monthly meeting read and approved. While a copy of these rules has not survived, they undoubtedly included requirements for maintaining discipline in the classroom and for moral control of the children. The Friends' school at Reading was an immediate success, as Samuel Jackson reported in February 1789 that it "appeared to be in an increasing way." The growth was short-lived, as Exeter Monthly Meeting discontinued the school in 1795 because of financial problems.[18]

Although Exeter Monthly Meeting appeared slow at providing church-sponsored education for its youth, at least the children of its members had an opportunity by the 1780s, unlike children whose parents adhered to the Church of England. Apparently the few Anglican children of Reading either attended the Quaker school or the available pay schools, for they received no formal church-sponsored education aside from catechetical training. In 1768, the Reverend Alexander Murray, the missionary for the Society for the Propagation of the Gospel in Foreign Parts to Berks County, began to catechize the younger people after the sermon, "which excites in them a Commendable Emulation, improves ye Hearers in General & stimulates ye Parents & Schoolmasters in particular to double [their] diligence in a Course of private instruction." Each class had a task assigned periodically, and they repeated catechetical exercises at the appropriate times. Murray hoped that this method would "make some lasting impressions of Christian Knowledge under their tender minds," as the older members of the parish were "so very Ignorant" that the children could not learn the material in any other way. Low membership and a Loyalist minister who fled the country during the Revolution hindered Anglican efforts to develop a parochial school for their children.[19]

The only other "English" schools envisioned during the eighteenth century actually were pioneers in bilingual education. English reformers supported the establishment of a public "charity school" in Reading, through which German immigrants would receive instruction in both German and English. This early attempt at bilingual education failed, however, mostly because the German settlers resented the notion that they were ignorant or needed charity to educate their children.[20]

The efforts of Exeter Monthly Meeting to establish schools were modest in comparison with those of other religious groups in Berks County. When the German settlers organized and formed congregations, they usually built a schoolhouse nearby. During the eighteenth century, often clergymen served as schoolmasters—or, more likely, schoolmasters doubled as preachers. The Reverend Father Theodore Schneider, priest at Goshenhoppen, opened a school for all area children regardless of their religious affiliation. Moravians who lived in the Oley Valley in eastern Berks County operated a school for children of members from the 1740s until the late 1760s.[21]

Members of Exeter Monthly Meeting who lived in or near the county seat of Reading—where Friends had authorized the establishment of an indulged meeting by the mid-1750s—faced unusual circumstances. Both the Lutheran and Reformed congregations had opened parochial schools without charge for the children of their parishioners shortly after the town's foundation in 1748. In these schools, teachers prepared individual lessons for the pupils, who then recited them to the instructor. The school term usually began at the start of winter and ended with the arrival of summer. The school day lasted six hours and opened and closed with singing and a prayer.[22]

The lack of concern for formal Quaker schools was not unique to Exeter Monthly Meeting. Warrington Monthly Meeting in York County, established ten years after Exeter, did not mention anything in its records except for the establishment of youth meetings until 1778. In that year, Warrington responded to Philadelphia Yearly Meeting's request by establishing a committee on schools. Not until 1784 did the committee report any activity in this area, with schools at York and Warrington formed that year.[23]

Sadsbury Monthly Meeting in Lancaster County, also established in 1737, did not even form a committee on schools until 1779. When the committee issued its report in June 1782, it noted that a school did exist at Sadsbury. By 1787, that school had closed, and the monthly meeting appointed a new committee to explore reopening the institution. Among the members was Gaius Dickinson, who had moved there with his family two years earlier.[24]

The failure to develop a formal educational structure prior to the 1780s did not reflect Exeter Friends' true interest in reading and learning. Typically, estate inventories did not list book titles, although the assessors did list a value for the library. Of the forty-nine surviving inventories of the estates of Exeter Friends who died prior to 1789, twenty-nine indicated that the deceased owned at least one book at the time of his or her death. Often, the appraisers only noted "Sundry old Books," without giving any sort of a description. In one case, "ye Library of Books" received the value of £1.15.0, the same amount that the appraisers gave to the decedent's pewter plates and dishes. Twelve of the Quakers possessed Bibles in varying sizes, with several "large" Bibles and one "piece of a Bible." The lack of a list of specific works is typical for the period, because seldom did the estate inventories provide an itemized record of a decedent's holdings.[25]

For eight of the estates, the appraisers did provide a catalog of the books owned by the deceased. The most commonly owned works were accounts of the lives of fellow Quakers. The journals of Thomas Chalkley, Richard Davis, William Edmundson, John Richardson, Daniel Stanton, and Thomas Story, all prominent Quaker ministers, appeared on at least two inventories. Dictionaries also were common; five estate inventories listed these types of reference books, and in a few instances they even identified the authors.[26]

Of those Quakers whose books received mention, three owned more than ten books. Jacob Lightfoot of Maiden Creek Township died in 1784, leaving behind an estate of £348.13.1½. Of this estate, £7.10.6 consisted of the fourteen books he owned, which included a Bible, a dictionary, a copy of William Sewall's *History of Quakers,* eight Quaker journals/works, "Two Books treating on physic by N Culpepper," and two volumes of "Brackens art of Farriery." Considering that Lightfoot probably was a farmer and blacksmith whose only leadership role in the monthly meeting consisted of representing Exeter at Philadelphia Quarterly Meeting, this collection could be considered rather substantial.[27]

The next largest quantity of books belonged to Francis Parvin. Parvin had served as an overseer of Maiden Creek Preparative Meeting during the early 1760s and had represented Berks County in the provincial assembly during the Seven Years' War. This dual activity in the secular and religious spheres is evident in the list of Parvin's books. His collection included four Quaker journals, "An old Book of Martyrs," "The History of Friends in Ireland," and "The way to the Sabbath of Rest." In addition, Parvin owned copies of the "Acts of Assembly & Conferences with ye Indians," "A

Guide to Justices," and "A Volume of Pennsylvania Laws." Surprisingly, he also possessed a copy of *The Archbishop of Cambray's Dissertation on Pure Love* (1750), which does not appear to be the typical reading material for a Quaker leader.[28]

By far, the most sizable collection of books belonged to Benjamin Lightfoot, a former clerk of Exeter Monthly Meeting, first sheriff of Berks County, and a prominent surveyor. The inventory of Lightfoot's estate after his death in 1777 identified sixty-four distinct titles, including multiple copies of some works. Based upon a survey of the books listed, Lightfoot's reading tastes appeared to be quite eclectic. His collection included Quaker journals, other religious treatises and tracts, law books, dictionaries, history books, books on husbandry, medical books, and works on philosophy. Among the more distinctive titles in the inventory of Lightfoot's personal estate were two volumes of "Locke on human Understanding," two copies of Robert Barclay's *Apology for the . . . People, Called in Scorn, Quakers* (1729) (one in Dutch), "Bacon's Book of Rates," and "Duchess of Marlborough's Conduct." Judging from this listing, Lightfoot probably was the most learned member of Exeter Monthly Meeting; he also possessed the largest estate, which the appraisers valued at over £2,600 at the time of his death.[29]

Although men such as Francis Parvin and Benjamin Lightfoot probably built their collections through purchases made while in Philadelphia on business, Friends could acquire books through subscriptions held by the yearly meeting. Throughout the eighteenth century, Exeter Monthly Meeting received copies of treatises and journals written by prominent Quakers, and occasionally members of the meeting contributed toward the cost of publishing these books. The monthly meeting circulated these books, along with the yearly meeting epistles, among the membership. The first works noted in the meeting minutes were the journals of John Burnyeat (1691) and of William Edmundson (1713), which were available for circulation in 1740. In 1753, the three preparative meetings distributed thirty-four copies of George Fox's journal. By the end of 1760, multiple copies of Robert Barclay's *Apology for the People called Quakers* (1729), Barclay's *Anarchy of the Ranters* (1757), David Hall's *Mite into the Treasury* (1758), the *Works of Isaac Pennington,* John Rutty's *Liberty of the Spirit and of the Flesh Distinguished* (1759), and William Dell's *Doctrine of Baptism* (1759) arrived at Exeter Monthly Meeting for Friends' use. In the 1770s, members subscribed for three dozen copies of Barclay's Catechisms and sixty of John Churchman's journal. Additions to the libraries of Exeter Friends by the mid-1780s included Anthony Benezet's *Short Account of the People Called Quakers* (1780, 1783) (in English and German), Benezet's "Case of the Oppressed Africans," Samuel Fuller's *Some Principles and Precepts of the Christian Religion* (1783), the journal of John Griffith, "a Number containing Counsel & Advice by William Penn," Penn's *Primitive Christianity Revived* (1783), *Three Treatises* by Penn, Barclay, and Joseph Pike (1783), *Select Essays from the Writings of Isaac Pennington,* and *The Original, and Present State of Man* by Joseph Phipps. Certainly the German translation of Benezet's *Short Account of the People Called Quakers* would be useful to distribute among the German-speaking settlers of Berks County to explain Quaker beliefs during a time when they faced oppression for their beliefs. Of course, the yearly meeting did not include a query on reading or circulating Quaker books, so it is difficult to ascertain the full impact of book acquisition on education. Judging from the relative availability of books, members of Exeter Monthly Meeting evidently did not oppose education beyond the minimum standards. Still, it is surprising that they did not officially establish any schools for children until the 1780s if they had this much interest in books.[30]

In the realm of education, although their efforts at establishing schools did not match those of other denominations, Quaker schools achieved some renown. Members of the meeting had eclectic reading interests, reflecting their concerns with the secular and spiritual world. The monthly meeting itself promoted reading by making the writings of prominent Friends available to Berks County Quakers and other interested parties. Despite lagging behind fellow Friends, the members of Exeter Monthly Meeting did provide a shining example of an educational system that did not merely teach young men and women to read and write, but provided practical learning so that they could function in the outside world.

9

"Said Slave Be Suitable for Liberty": The Abolition of Slavery and Exeter Monthly Meeting

THE PROMOTION OF EDUCATION DURING THE LATE 1770S AFFECTED AN-other moral issue addressed by Philadelphia Yearly Meeting—the abolition of slavery. Although Exeter Monthly Meeting lagged behind the other denominations in establishing schools, it did take a leadership role within the county in this special instance. As early as 1688, German Quakers and Mennonites in Pennsylvania led by Francis Daniel Pastorius began to voice opposition to the sale and importation of slave labor. These Friends argued that slavery was inhumane, since the institution demonstrated how human beings could be treated worse than cattle. In addition, the petitioners contended that the slave trade promoted theft and adultery, suggested the possibility of rebellion among the slaves, and argued that the practice was contrary to the Golden Rule. This protest by Germantown Quakers, most of whom were German, did not cause an immediate stir, but it did begin the questioning of the morality of slavery.[1]

Although the Germantown Protest did not lead to an immediate call for emancipation, Quakers in the Philadelphia area continued to oppose the institution. In 1693, George Keith, leader of a dissident group of Quakers, published *An Exhortation & Caution to Friends Concerning Buying or Keeping of Negroes*. Keith recommended that members of the Society of Friends free their slaves once the cost of their purchase had been repaid through their labor—in other words, view them as indentured servants instead of as property to be held for life. Three years later, Philadelphia Yearly Meeting advised Friends to refrain from importing slaves. William Southeby, one of the Friends who had demanded this ban, did not believe that this action was effective enough, so in 1712 he submitted a petition to the colonial assembly requesting emancipation for all Pennsylvania slaves. The assembly rejected his request, but it did levy a tariff on slave imports that served to inhibit the slave trade. Although the Quaker-dominated Assembly was reluctant to extinguish the slave trade, Philadelphia Yearly Meeting responded to the increasing pressure by including a ban on importing slaves when it revised the *Book of Discipline* in 1719.[2]

In spite of the prohibition, Quaker merchants continued to participate in the slave trade, often risking disownment for their actions. Beginning in 1730, Philadelphia Yearly Meeting requested that the monthly meetings in Pennsylvania and New Jersey condemn any members engaged in this activity. Not until the 1750s, however, did the yearly meeting begin to take serious action against offenders. With the increasing tension in the province because of the threat of warfare in the early 1750s, Philadelphia Quakers realized that one way to maintain some semblance of control would be to ensure that members of the monthly meetings were following the dictates of the yearly meeting.[3]

In 1754, Philadelphia Yearly Meeting began to revisit the issue of slaveholding among the Society of Friends. That year, the provincial organization declared "that slaveholding itself, and not just importation, was an un-Christian practice." One reason why Philadelphia Yearly Meeting revisited the slavery issue at this time clearly related to the reform movement occurring in Quakerism that contributed to the increased emphasis on social control and enforcing the discipline. Slave ownership was on the rise in Chester County following the importation ban adopted by the yearly meeting in 1719, as farmers and artisans employed Africans and indentured servants. With the arrival of the Seven Years' War, however, immigration from Europe slowed dramatically, and purchasing slaves to serve as a labor force became more common.[4]

When Philadelphia Yearly Meeting revised the queries to local meetings two years later, the wording for the eleventh query (later numbered ninth) read: "'Are Friends clear of importing and buying Negroes; and do they use those well which they are possessed of by Inheritance or otherwise; endeavouring to train them up in the Principles of the Christian Religion?'" Each year, when Exeter Monthly Meeting supplied written responses to this request, these men and women usually commented that those "Negroes within the Compass of the Meeting . . . are used well as to Food and Raiment, but there is some Neglect in instructing them in the Principles of the Christian Religion." Although members of Exeter Monthly Meeting might have been remiss in educating their slaves, they were "Clear of Importing or Buying Negroes," and thus at least fulfilled one goal of Philadelphia Yearly Meeting. Friends who owned slaves were subject to disciplinary action, but the yearly meeting did not require disownment at this time.[5]

Through these annual responses, it is evident that few Berks County Quakers owned slaves. According to these accounts, members of Exeter Monthly Meeting never owned more than two slaves. More often, the meeting reported that only one or no "Negroe Slaves" were the property of Exeter Friends. The greater concern was that "the necessary Care is not taken to Instruct [them] in the Principles of the Christian Religion." That

Berks County had fewer slaves than any other county in Pennsylvania also explains Exeter Monthly Meeting's lack of emphasis on manumission. In addition, there was not a strong sentiment for abolition within Berks County, so Exeter Friends might have been influenced by external factors. In spite of these reports, in 1774 Philadelphia Yearly Meeting instructed Exeter and other monthly meetings to appoint a committee to visit members who held slaves.[6]

Exeter Men's Monthly Meeting responded to this request by appointing its own Committee on Slaves. This committee reported in January 1775, that it found only "one, who is held as a Slave term of life" whose mistress was willing to free him, but it wondered "whether the said slave be suitable for liberty." This concern reflected interest in the slave's readiness for freedom, although it also might have indicated a desire to protect the slave from potential danger. Membership on this committee included Joseph Penrose, Samuel Hughes, and Gaius Dickinson. Three months later, the committee members noted that "one mulatto is set free," perhaps referring to the above-mentioned slave. Visitations continued, and the slaveholders seemed genuinely interested in releasing the blacks as soon as they had proven capable of living on their own.[7]

Philadelphia Quarterly Meeting also responded to this dictate by establishing its own Committee on Slaves. In November 1774, Samuel Embree, John Lee, and Thomas Thomas—two of whom were Exeter's delegates to the quarterly meeting—agreed to serve on this committee. Two years later, Philadelphia Men's Quarterly Meeting appointed Joseph Penrose, William Tomlinson, Merrick Starr, Mordecai Lee, and John Hutton to this body. Philadelphia Women's Quarterly Meeting included Mary Dickinson, wife of Gaius Dickinson, on its Committee on Slaves in May 1781. While there is no clear indication about the length of these appointments, it is evident that the quarterly meeting membership believed it was important to include Exeter Monthly Meeting's representatives in the group in the hopes of spurring manumission in the backcountry.[8]

In January 1775, the same month that the first notice of slave ownership appeared in the monthly meeting minutes, Anthony Benezet and a group of Philadelphia Quakers established "The Society for the Relief of Free Negroes Unlawfully Held in Bondage." The arrival of the War for Independence brought an abrupt end to the Relief Society's activities, but the organization restarted in 1787 as "The Pennsylvania Society for Promoting the Abolition of Slavery, the Relief of Free Negroes unlawfully held in Bondage, and for Improving the Condition of the Colored Race," more commonly known as the Pennsylvania Abolition Society.[9]

In 1776, Philadelphia Yearly Meeting announced expulsion for Friends who did not manumit their slaves. A problem arose when one spouse was a member and the other had been previously disowned by the meeting, and the family held slaves. In the case of Exeter Monthly Meeting, all current or past members who held slaves in 1780 ensured freedom for their slaves by the end of the decade.[10]

In Exeter Monthly Meeting, the first wave of manumissions began in 1777, but these slaves did not immediately receive their freedom. John Scarlet, Jr., an overseer and elder of Robeson Preparative Meeting, freed his two mulatto "servant Lad[s]," Abner and Barnes Streve, when they reached the age of twenty-one. Following the passage of the Gradual Abolition law, James Lewis manumitted his mulatto "servant Lad named Jesse" in 1781 when the boy reached his majority. None of these early manumissions, however, came quickly; Scarlet would be able to hold Barnes Streve as a slave until 1793 (although he manumitted him before 1790).[11]

Once the Pennsylvania Assembly passed the Act for the Gradual Abolition of Slavery in 1780, the Committee of Slaves erroneously believed that its work had ended. In June 1780, the committee reported to Exeter Men's Monthly Meeting, "some of their Number had a Conference together yesterday and apprehend they have fully performed the Business to which they were appointed." The committee did acknowledge that "it may be necessary to appoint a Friend or more belonging to each Meeting where Negroes or other Slaves are placed who may yet required Care or Assistance." Gaius Dickinson continued on the committee, along with Abel Thomas, Samuel Lee, Benjamin Pearson, Moses Embree, and Jonathan Stephens. At this time, all of the indulged meetings had at least one slaveowner among its membership at this time.[12]

Because members of Exeter Monthly Meeting were slow in complying with the wishes of the yearly meeting, Philadelphia Quarterly Meeting requested a written account "of the particular Circumstances of each Slave, within the Verge of" the meeting. In response to this directive, Mary Dickinson, Deborah Lee, Benjamin Pearson, and Moses Embree from the Committee on Slaves reported in July 1782 that members of the meeting owned ten slaves. Husbands of female members of the meeting (who might not have been members or might have already been disowned for misconduct) held three of the slaves under discussion. These women members professed opposition to slavery, yet they apparently did not object to their husbands' purchase of the servants. In all three of these instances, non-Quaker husbands promised to educate the slaves before releasing them. Two other blacks identified in the report technically were not slaves, as they had been bound by their mother ("a free Woman") for their master to teach them a skill and educate them. Another three were the slaves mentioned above, all of whose "Masters promise to give them Learning." Finally, the widow of Revolutionary War surgeon Dr. Jonathan Potts owned two slaves. All but two of these slaves held by Exeter Friends were children. Consequently, in all of the cases described in the minutes of Exeter Monthly Meeting, the masters guaranteed that the slaves would receive some education prior to manumission.[13]

Although owning slaves was not unique to Exeter Monthly Meeting among fellow Quakers or among local residents, several distinctive aspects are evident. Compared with other monthly meetings in Pennsylvania, Exeter Monthly Meeting was the slowest in manumitting its slaves. Fully two-thirds did not formally receive their freedom until after 1780; four-fifths of the slaves held by members of Philadelphia Yearly Meeting had been freed by this time. In Berks County, the percentage of Quakers to other slaveholders was lower than the percentage of Quakers to the total population, probably because of the increasing opposition of the Society of Friends to the institution. In addition, unlike members of other religious groups in the county, no Exeter Friend still possessed slaves in 1790. In contrast, fifteen of the non-Quaker slaveholders identified in the tax lists of 1779–1781 still owned slaves in 1790, and the census identified fourteen new slaveholders. Finally, Exeter Friends were different from others in the county because of their emphasis on educating the slaves before they set them free.[14]

The slow rate of manumission by Exeter Friends in comparison to other Pennsylvania Quakers perhaps reflected the overall opposition to the abolition of slavery in Berks County. Only two of five of Berks County's representatives to the 1779–1780 Assembly supported the Act for the Gradual Abolition of Slavery introduced in November 1779, and passed in March 1780. All three of the assemblymen who voted against the measure were Germans (Valentine Eckert, Gabriel Hiester, and Christian Lower), while the two supporters were a French Huguenot (Sebastian Levan) and a Welsh Anglican (Jonathan Jones). Jones appeared on the 1780 and 1781 tax lists as a slaveowner, and Eckert, Hiester, and Lower also held slaves. Hiester and Lower, in fact, still held slaves in 1790.[15]

This low percentage of support for the abolition law by Berks County legislators paralleled the pattern of the two other German-dominated counties in Pennsylvania. The majority of representatives from both Northampton and Lancaster counties, part of the "German arc" of southeastern Pennsylvania, opposed the gradual abolition act. In contrast, predominantly English or Scots-Irish areas tended to support the law, in some cases because of the Quaker influence and in others because the local economies were not conducive to slave labor. In Berks, Lancaster, and Northampton counties, however, slaves were used on both farms and in industry, since they provided some of the labor force at the growing number of iron plantations in the region. In fact, ironmasters held the largest number of slaves in early Berks County; Mark Bird of Hopewell Furnace, John Lesher of Oley Forge, John Patton of Berkshire Furnace, and George Ege of Charming Forge all possessed at least ten slaves in 1780. The Quaker slaveowners, in contrast, tended to be farmers, although John Scarlet and Judah Boone did operate gristmills.[16]

Germans opposed the Act for the Gradual Abolition of Slavery for a variety of reasons. First, the revivals of the 1740s that in some ways contributed to abolitionist sentiment in the colony and state affected the German "church people" (Lutherans and Reformed) very little, as many of them did not migrate to the colony until after the spirit of evangelicalism had diminished. Many of these recent immigrants were of laboring stock, and while they themselves might not have owned slaves, they did recognize the status associated with the institution. In addition, antislavery sentiment seemed to coincide with Revolutionary ideology, as abolitionists picked up on the failure of the Declaration of Independence to address what they perceived as one of the great injustices perpetrated by the British Empire. Meanwhile, not all Germans embraced the separation from England, as some expressed gratitude that imperial authorities had welcomed their migration to Pennsylvania. The German representatives, too, did not always reflect the wishes of their constituents in their voting habits. Consequently, religious experience, cultural and economic values, and political beliefs influenced German opposition to the abolitionist movement.[17]

Opponents of the act presented their views in a substantial rebuttal to the passage of the law. Possessing a more national outlook than the proponents of the law, they argued that by passing such a bill the assembly was inviting discontent within the nation. In addition, they contended that the law did not take into account a possible change in attitude toward slavery in the near future. Instead, it presupposed that the blacks could integrate peacefully into Pennsylvania society with little difficulty.[18]

The law, the culmination of the Quakers' fight to abolish slavery, did not have an immediate impact. The legislation only provided for the gradual emancipation of slaves; newborn children of slaves would be freed once they reached age twenty-eight. Until reaching age twenty-eight, these blacks would have the same rights as indentured servants and legally were to be considered as such. The assembly required that all slaveowners register their slaves in the county of residence; any black not registered before November 1, 1780, would be considered free. Over the next eight years, the assembly adopted additional legislation that closed some of the loopholes in the original law, particularly those pertaining to slaves held by visitors to Pennsylvania and to slaveowners who would take their pregnant female slaves out of the state so that the child would not be born under Pennsylvania law and thus could be held for life. By providing for the gradual abolition of slavery, the assembly sought to ease the transition from a slave to a free economy. In spite of the intent of the law, slaves continued to reside in Pennsylvania. Not until 1850, in fact, did the decennial census reveal the end of slavery in the Commonwealth.[19]

Tax lists for Berks County from 1779 to 1781 recorded the number of slaves owned by residents. According to these tax lists, only seven members of Exeter Monthly Meeting were among the 162 total slaveholders identified. These Quakers came from a variety of socioeconomic backgrounds. For example, Elizabeth Lightfoot, widow of Benjamin Lightfoot, owned one slave in 1780. Her husband had served Exeter Monthly Meeting as clerk during the 1750s and 1760s, and he had worked as a surveyor for the province of Pennsylvania and was a prominent merchant in Reading prior to his death. In addition, at the time of his death Lightfoot possessed an estate of over £2,600, the largest of any Exeter Friend during the eighteenth century. Yet the inventory for Lightfoot's estate did not identify any enslaved persons among his personal or real property.[20]

Another Reading slaveowner was Dr. Jonathan Potts, who during this period was a surgeon and hospital administrator with the Continental Army. Although Potts himself was not a member of Exeter Monthly Meeting, he did consider himself a Quaker, and his wife Grace had transferred from Philadelphia Monthly Meeting in 1774. His two slaves, Pompey and Esther (Hester), probably were house servants, since he owned property in downtown Reading. Potts bequeathed these slaves to his wife upon his death in 1780; he specified that they would be freed after five years if they served her faithfully. Undoubtedly they fulfilled this requirement, as Grace Potts freed them in 1783 after they reached their majority.[21]

The remainder of the Quaker slaveowners resided outside of Reading and probably used their slaves as farm hands. James Boone, a tanner and farmer in Exeter Township, owned one slave in 1780 and 1781. Boone had served as overseer for Exeter Preparative Meeting at various times between 1737 and 1757, and he was the clerk of the monthly meeting during the late 1740s. In later years, however, Boone fell on hard times spiritually; the meeting disowned him in 1780 for complying with the provisions of the Test Act. Consequently, no record of the manumission of Boone's slave appears in the meeting records. This slave, however, probably received his freedom by 1785, as neither the inventory for Boone's estate nor his will mentioned a slave.[22]

James Boone's son Judah, an Exeter Township farmer who also operated a gristmill, owned two slaves in 1779 but only one in 1780. Judah Boone had not held any leadership roles within the meeting, but he did follow in the family tradition by being expelled from the monthly meeting for swearing the oath of allegiance. His wife Hannah, however, remained in good standing. When the Committee on Slaves for Exeter Monthly Meeting visited her, the members indicated that "we have Reason to think she was consenting to the Purchase" of the slaves. After Judah's death in

Table 9.1
Berks County Slaveholders/Number of Slaves by Township

Township	1779	1780	1781	1790
Albany	0	0	0	0
Alsace	0	2/2	3/4	0
Amity	12/15	7/8	6/6	1/1
Bern	2/3	3/5	4/6	2/2
Bethel	0	1/1	1/1	0
Brecknock	0	0	0	0
Brunswick	0	0	1/2	1/1
Caernarvon	6/14	6/12	5/11	2/4
Colebrookdale	3/3	3/3	5/5	0
Cumru	2/3	6/6	6/8	0
District	1/1	1/1	1/1	0
Douglass	0	2/2	2/2	1/1
Earl	0	0	0	1/1
Exeter	7/9	5/5	4/4	2/7
Greenwich	0	0	0	0
Heidelberg	2/11	5/8	7/10	3/6
Hereford	2/2	2/2	2/2	1/1
Longswamp	0	1/1	1/1	0
Maiden Creek	2/2	5/6	6/9	0
Maxatawny	5 /6	4/7	4/6	0
Oley	18/25	10/13	10/12	2/4
Reading*	15/24	15/21	11/15	5/9
Richmond	0	3/3	3/3	3/4
Robeson	1/1	0	1/1	1/1
Rockland	0	2/2	1/1	0
Ruscombmanor	0	0	0	0
Tulpehocken	6/12	15/32	12/25	4/15
Union	7/25	5/21	3/19	2/3
Windsor	0	1/1	1/1	0
TOTALS	**91/156**	**104/162**	**100/155**	**31/60**

*Also 3/3 in 1768

1787, the appraisers of his estate valued his "Negroe girl" at £0.0.0, realizing that Hannah Boone intended to free her within a few months.[23]

Samuel Boone, James's nephew and Judah's cousin, also owned a slave according to the monthly meeting records. Unlike James and Judah, Samuel Boone's name does not appear as a slaveowner on any of the Berks County tax lists. Exeter Monthly Meeting had disowned both Samuel and his wife, Jane, during the mid-1760s for a variety of offenses, yet apparently the Committee on Slaves still considered their ownership of slaves worthy of note in its report. The committee reported, "she says she is against Slavery, & was ignorant of the Purchase, and seems desirous he may have his Liberty." Contrary to other instances investigated, this was the only case in which the committee did not believe the wife was aware of the slave's purchase.[24]

Another miller who probably used his mulatto slaves on his 428-acre farm was John Scarlet. Scarlet operated two gristmills, a sawmill, and a hemp mill between 1779 and 1781. He also was the first member of Exeter Monthly Meeting to emancipate his slaves when he granted Abner and Barnes Streve their freedom in 1777 once they reached their majority, although he continued to own them another decade because of their ages.[25]

The remaining Berks County Quakers identified as slaveowners also probably used their slaves on the farm. James Lewis owned a 175-acre farm in Cumru Township south of Reading. He also operated a ferry across the Schuylkill River and was an innkeeper. Joseph Penrose, an overseer for Maiden Creek Preparative Meeting during the 1740s and 1750s and a one-time member of the Committee on Slaves, undoubtedly used his slave to assist with chores on his 250-acre farm north of Reading. No account of Penrose's slave appeared in the minutes of Exeter Monthly Meeting, but he apparently had freed the servant before 1790.[26]

Three of the "slaves" identified in the Committee on Slaves report properly should be considered indentured servants rather than slaves. Christopher Garrett, whose wife, Mary, joined Exeter Monthly Meeting in November 1776 through a profession of faith, owned Betty until she reached age twenty-one and had promised to educate her. Rachel Bias's mother bound her to William Hughes and his wife until she reached age nineteen. Andrew Bias's mother placed him with George Hughes until he reached age twenty-one. Both William and George Hughes agreed to educate the Bias children as part of their apprenticeships.[27]

Socioeconomic circumstances, then, apparently had some impact on whether a Quaker owned slaves. Although most of these slaveowners had held leadership positions within the monthly meeting, the fact remains that only four of the fifty men who served in a leadership capacity between 1737 and 1789 owned slaves. Economic success clearly played a more significant role in determining slaveholders. Benjamin Lightfoot was one of the wealthiest men in the county at the time of his death, so he might have considered owning a slave a sign of prestige. On the other hand, there is no record of Lightfoot owning slaves, so it is possible that his widow acquired the servant after his death. James, Judah, and Samuel Boone were among the top taxpayers in Exeter Township in 1779, as were James Lewis in Cumru Township, Joseph Penrose in Maiden Creek Township, and John Scarlet in Robeson Township. In addition, Jonathan Potts ranked among the top ten percent of taxpayers in Reading, and his status as a physician in a growing backcountry community also had some merit. Finally, all of these men and women either had grown children who had left the family homestead or small children who were too young to work. As a result, these slaves provided extra labor at a time when indentured servants might have been difficult to obtain.[28]

Within Berks County, slaveholding was not unique to members of Exeter Monthly Meeting. The main source of information on slavery in early Berks County, county tax lists, cannot be considered exhaustive. Of the seven individuals mentioned above, no more than five appeared on a single list, and that was in 1780 (see table 9.2). None of the four Quakers whose manumissions appeared among the meeting records were named on all three tax lists. The total number of slaveholders identified on these lists ranged from 91 in 1779 to 104 in 1780, with a slight decline to 100 in 1781. Three members of Exeter Monthly Meeting identified as slaveholders on the tax lists were not mentioned in the minutes or in the manumission records as owners of unfree labor. Nevertheless, slave owning appeared to have been resolved by 1790. Exeter Monthly Meeting discharged the Committee on Slaves in March 1789, satisfied that Friends had complied with Philadelphia Yearly Meeting's directives from 1776. The first decennial census in 1790 affirmed this decision, as it did not identify any Exeter Friends as slaveowners.[29]

At Middletown Monthly Meeting in Bucks County, a correlation existed between leadership status and slave ownership. Those who were more active in the meeting's activities were less likely to own slaves. Abolitionism divided the meeting in other ways. Friends either supported abolition wholeheartedly, reluctantly, or not at all—and the latter chose expulsion from Quaker society rather than compliance with yearly meeting policy. Members of Middletown Monthly Meeting debated whether Philadelphia Yearly Meeting intended to curtail all slave ownership or merely desired to prohibit the importation of slaves. By spring 1763, Middletown leaders believed it was the former and created a committee to visit slaveowners within the meeting. Six of the seven men visited by the committee condemned their actions in purchasing the slaves; the meeting disowned the seventh man. Middletown leadership, however, permitted at least one of the slaveowners to retain his property even after condemning his actions in purchasing the slaves. Within a year of the passage of the Act for the Gradual Abolition of Slavery in 1780, members of Middletown Monthly Meeting had completed the process of manumission, although Quaker households might have included slaves if the meeting had previously disowned the husband for this or another offense.[30]

The movement toward abolitionism had a different impact on Friends in neighboring Lancaster County, which also had a sizable German population. Leaders of the earliest Quaker settlements at Columbia and Lancaster

Table 9.2
Quaker Slaveholders

Name	Tax Lists	Meeting Records*
James Boone	1780, 1781	
Judah Boone	1779 (2), 1780	1782 (freed 1787)
Samuel Boone		1782
Christopher Garrett		1782
George Hughes		1782 (bound by parent)
William Hughes		1782 (bound by parent)
James Lewis	1779, 1780	1782 (freed 1781)
Elizabeth Lightfoot	1780	
Joseph Penrose	1781	
Grace Potts	1779 (2)**, 1780 (2)**	1782 (2) (freed 1782)
John Scarlet	1781	1782 (2) (freed 1777)

*Record of Manumissions, Men's Minutes for 31st day, 7th month, 1782
**Identified under husband Jonathan Potts

owned slaves. Some Quaker slaveowners in Lancaster whom Sadsbury Monthly Meeting had disowned for buying and selling slaves requested reinstatement once they manumitted them in 1776. In eastern and southern Lancaster County, home of Sadsbury Monthly Meeting, Friends continued to own slaves following the yearly meeting's edict, with notations regarding slave owning still appearing in monthly meeting minutes in June 1790. Although Lancaster County Quakers appeared to be as slow at freeing their slaves as their Berks County counterparts, they clearly were more active abolitionists in the nineteenth century, as these Quakers became prominent participants in the activities of the Underground Railroad.[31]

By the early nineteenth century, frontier Quaker meetings in western New York—some of whose members had ancestors active in Exeter Monthly Meeting in the 1700s—spearheaded the antislavery policies adopted by New York Yearly Meeting. Farmington Quarterly Meeting, which had both Orthodox and Hicksite branches after 1828, applied the rhetoric of the "burned-over district" in its condemnations of slavery. Beginning in 1811, the quarterly meeting's Committee on Slavery encouraged Friends to abstain from purchasing any goods produced through slave labor. Yet abolitionists in western New York questioned the Quakers' sincerity, because they did not actively participate in the larger abolitionist movement. That some Friends in western New York did not permit abolitionists to conduct public meetings in their meetinghouses certainly caused outsiders to wonder about the Quakers' adherence to their antislavery policies. Thus, while all Friends within the jurisdiction of Farmington Monthly Meeting agreed that slavery should be abolished, they disagreed on the impact of participation in the larger reform movement. In particular, Friends worried that involvement in the national abolitionist movement might lead to conflict (and thus violate their pacifist beliefs) or perhaps encourage Friends to stray from their faith. Just as Friends in Pennsylvania responded to the Great Awakening of the 1740s with a renewed emphasis on social control, Quakers in western New York chose to focus on their faith rather than participate in political action.[32]

In conclusion, the Quaker attitude toward slavery did affect the emancipation movement in Berks County. Because Exeter Monthly Meeting was one of the last monthly meetings established by Philadelphia Quarterly Meeting during the colonial period, its members faced few of the slavery conflicts that its eastern counterparts confronted. The location of the meeting along the Pennsylvania frontier, however, played a role in the relative slowness of manumitting slaves. Family relationships were also a factor, as at least six were related to another slaveholder. None of the slaves owned by members of Exeter Monthly Meeting experienced freedom prior to Philadelphia Yearly Meeting's edict in 1776, and over two-thirds were not emancipated before 1780—the most of any monthly meeting in Pennsylvania. In particular, the fact that strong proslavery sentiment existed within the county indicates that local attitudes might have also influenced Quakers' actions. Slaveholding Exeter Friends, nevertheless, did differ from their non-Quaker counterparts in their emphasis on ensuring the education of slaves prior to manumission. Consequently, even though they lagged behind Friends, members of Exeter Monthly Meeting provided a shining example of benevolent slave owning along the Pennsylvania frontier.

10

Men and Women of High Morals:
Exeter Monthly Meeting and the Outside World

ALTHOUGH MEMBERS OF EXETER MONTHLY MEETING MIGHT HAVE PRE-
ferred to live among other Quakers, they undoubtedly accepted that they
would have to deal with non-Quakers in their everyday lives. Almost all
members of the meeting had migrated to the area from another monthly
meeting in the Middle Colonies, so they had already experienced the
diversity of the region prior to settling in Berks County.

Few surviving contemporary comments describe the secular and religious activities of Berks County Quakers outside the meeting. As members of the Society of Friends in colonial Pennsylvania, it would not have
been unrealistic for them to expect to have some political influence within
the county, perhaps even to control local politics. Meanwhile, Berks
County residents generally perceived Friends as respectable neighbors, but
it is debatable whether Quakers held their fellow non-Quaker settlers in
high regard. At the same time, Philadelphia Quarterly Meeting found the
contributions made by Exeter Friends crucial in encouraging the expansion
of Quakerism along the frontier. Finally, visitors to Berks County remarked favorably about the piety of these frontier Friends, and Quaker
meetings along the east coast welcomed the religious visits of Quaker
ministers from Berks County.

Over time, members of Exeter Monthly Meeting did adapt to the cultural pluralism of the region. In the political arena, however, they encountered some problems because of this diversity. Quakers dominated the
government of colonial Pennsylvania from its establishment in 1681 virtually until the beginning of the American Revolution, with a brief break
during the Seven Years' War. In Berks County, however, the majority of
Friends who held political offices did so in the 1750s. By the early 1760s,
the concern for defense had become so important that voters had begun to
elect members of the more militant religious groups to public office. At the
same time, Philadelphia Yearly Meeting recommended that Friends with-

draw from political life to avoid encouraging "Military Services, or [actions] which may Oppress the Consciences of their Brethren." Anglicans proceeded to assume political control of the county, and by the 1770s the German settlers had become more self-conscious politically and successfully sought election. As a result, only one Quaker, Benjamin Lightfoot, served as a government official in the mid-1770s.[1]

The first members of Exeter Monthly Meeting to receive political appointments were justices of the peace for Philadelphia County. Justices of the peace in Pennsylvania presided over the courts of quarter sessions (criminal), common pleas (civil), and orphans' court, and they did not require any legal training. George Boone, one of the earliest English settlers in the Oley Valley, held this position from 1733 until the early 1740s. His eldest son, George, Jr., the first recorder of births and deaths for the monthly meeting, succeeded his father and continued in that post until 1748. Francis Parvin of Maiden Creek Township and Anthony Lee of Oley Township joined Boone in 1745 and continued to serve as justices after the formation of Berks County in 1752. Joining Lee and Parvin in 1752 were Moses Starr, later an overseer for Maiden Creek Preparative Meeting, and James Boone, son of George and a former clerk and overseer. Within a decade of the erection of the county, however, the number of Quaker justices had declined. Only Parvin and Benjamin Lightfoot served in this capacity after 1760; more than fifty non-Quakers became judges.[2]

Quakers held other elective and appointive posts in Berks County during the eighteenth century. A listing of the men who served as county commissioners, coroners, and representatives to the provincial assembly identifies three Quakers at each of these positions during the colonial period. The first two representatives and three of the first four, in fact, were members of Exeter Monthly Meeting. In addition, the first two county sheriffs were members of the Society of Friends—Benjamin Lightfoot and William Boone. Only five Quakers held more than one office, and none served in more than two different positions over the course of his political career. In contrast, Anglican James Read dominated county government for almost a quarter century by himself, holding five separate positions concurrently from 1752 until 1774. Of course, the proprietor's supporters in the 1750s would have preferred a Quaker to serve as prothonotary, register, recorder, orphans' court clerk, and quarter sessions clerk to maintain their political influence in the interior, but they apparently could not find one in Berks County qualified to hold these posts. Because of this lack of continuity, members of Exeter Monthly Meeting never established a political elite in Berks County, as had their coreligionists in Bucks, Chester, and Philadelphia Counties.[3]

The only potential political dynasty among Berks County Quakers during the eighteenth century was among members of the Boone family.

Table 10.1
Quaker Officeholders Affiliated with Exeter Monthly Meeting

BERKS COUNTY

Justice of the Peace:	Francis Parvin	1752–1755
	Anthony Lee	1752–1755
	Moses Starr	1752–1755
	James Boone	1752–1755
	Benjamin Lightfoot	1770–1776
County Commissioner:	Jacob Lightfoot	1753–1756, 1759–1762
	John Hughes	1762–1765
	Richard Lewis	1765–1767
Sheriff:	Benjamin Lightfoot	1752–1754, 1757–1759
	William Boone	1755–1756
Coroner:	William Boone	1752–1754
	Benjamin Parvin	1755
	Samuel Jackson	1770
Collector:	John Hughes	1752–1763
Assembly:	Moses Starr	1752–1754
	Francis Parvin	1755
	James Boone	1758

PHILADELPHIA COUNTY

Justice of the Peace:	George Boone	1738–1748*
	Francis Parvin	1745–1752
	Anthony Lee	1745–1752

NORTHUMBERLAND COUNTY

Justice of the Peace:	Ellis Hughes	1772–1775

*Both George Boone, Sr., and George Boone, Jr.; son succeeded father in early 1740s

George Boone, a justice of the peace for Philadelphia County in the 1730s and 1740s, began the family tradition of service. His eldest son, George, Jr., succeeded him as judge, and his sixth son James also followed in his father's footsteps by serving as a justice of the peace for Berks County and in the provincial assembly. Meanwhile, George's grandson, George, Jr.'s eldest surviving son, and James's nephew, William Boone, was county coroner between 1752 and 1754 and followed that with a term as sheriff. Unlike his uncle and grandfather, William did not hold any leadership positions within the monthly meeting. Another Boone grandson, George Webb, whom Exeter Monthly Meeting had disowned in 1743 for exogamy, was a justice of the peace for Berks County in the 1760s and 1770s. Even so, the Boone family did not establish a political dynasty, as they all had left office by the end of the colonial period.[4]

Benjamin Lightfoot, the first sheriff for the county, was the only member of Exeter Monthly Meeting to hold office at the time of the Revolution. Lightfoot had been deputy surveyor for the province prior to moving to Reading, and he served two terms as sheriff in the 1750s. In 1770, he began his first term as a justice of the peace, to which the proprietor reappointed him in 1773. When Lightfoot began his second term as sheriff in 1757, he was also clerk of the monthly meeting, thus holding secular and religious leadership positions concurrently.[5]

Although members of Exeter Monthly Meeting did not dominate local politics, they did obtain some minor appointments from the colonial government. In 1749, Anthony Lee and Francis Parvin received authorization from the proprietor to obtain land in the county seat of Reading for a courthouse and prison. Three years later, Benjamin Lightfoot served as one of the surveyors "required to mark out the boundary lines between Philadelphia, Chester, Lancaster and Berks County," a duty he repeated in 1769 prior to the formation of Northumberland County. Shortly after the creation of the county, the assembly selected Francis Parvin, Benjamin Lightfoot, James Boone, and Joseph Penrose to examine a route for a road from Easton, the county seat of newly formed Northampton County, to Reading. Parvin even assisted in laying out the road between the two towns. In 1753, Lightfoot, John Hutton, Merrick Starr, and James Starr petitioned the assembly for another road from Reading to Easton. Finally, in 1770, Isaac Willits, Job Hughes, Thomas Wright, Joseph Penrose, and Ellis Hughes became commissioners responsible for maintaining a road from Ellis Hughes's sawmill on the Schuylkill River north of Reading to Fort Augusta near the Susquehanna River.[6]

Members of Exeter Monthly Meeting also worked to improve the environment and develop the economic potential of the region. In 1760, the assembly selected Francis Parvin, Benjamin Lightfoot, and John Hughes, along with thirteen other Berks Countians, as commissioners "to clean, scour and make [the] Schuylkill River navigable." Twelve years later, James Starr of Reading joined ten other residents in keeping the river clear for navigation. Once the Revolution began, however, Berks County Quakers refrained from participating in any governmental functions, choosing instead to obey the yearly meeting's edict against officeholding.[7]

Although frontier Quakers withdrew from the political arena, they continued to be active in the affairs of the colony's Quaker organizations. Representatives from Exeter Monthly Meeting regularly attended sessions of Philadelphia Quarterly Meeting between 1737 and 1789. When they did not make the trip to Philadelphia, illness or weather conditions prohibited them from performing this service. While at the quarterly meeting, Exeter's representatives commented on conditions within the monthly meeting, reported on the success of family visitations, and submitted contributions toward the yearly meeting's treasury. After 1743, these men and women also served as representatives to Philadelphia Yearly Meeting, held each fall in Philadelphia.[8]

At first, distance and inexperience prevented members of Exeter Monthly Meeting from holding any committee assignments within the quarterly meeting. By the 1750s, however, the monthly meeting had become sufficiently stabilized along the frontier that its members could be considered for these positions. Moses Starr, a future overseer of Maiden Creek Preparative Meeting who at the same time was serving as the assemblyman from Berks County, joined the committee on schools in 1754. Over a dozen representatives from Exeter participated on various appeals committees chosen to consider specific requests to overturn the decisions of monthly meetings in disciplinary matters between 1755 and 1786. In addition, nine Exeter Friends served on the quarterly meeting's committee on slaves. One of these Quakers was Mary Dickinson, the lone woman from Exeter selected for a committee assignment.[9]

Because of Exeter Monthly Meeting's frontier location, it was important that someone from this meeting have a place in the Meeting for Sufferings, to ensure that their brethren in Philadelphia could truly understand the sometimes tumultuous nature of life in the backcountry. When Philadelphia Yearly Meeting formed the Meeting for Sufferings in 1757, the quarterly meeting appointed Benjamin Lightfoot, clerk of the meeting, to serve on this body. Lightfoot was especially active in quarterly meeting activities, as he also served on two separate appeals committees and on a special committee selected in 1764 to speak with Governor John Penn, Anglican grandson of the founder, concerning horse races scheduled to be run in Philadelphia at the same time the yearly meeting would be held. He served on the Meeting for Sufferings until 1769, when health problems forced him to resign.[10]

Exeter Monthly Meeting had no representative at the Meeting for Sufferings between 1769 and 1775, when Samuel Lee, an overseer for Exeter Preparative Meeting, joined this body. Lee proved to be just as active as Lightfoot in quarterly meeting activities. In 1778, the quarterly meeting appointed him to the Committee on Youth. Five years later, Lee served on a committee formed to alter the yearly meeting quota. Finally, in 1786, he was one of the delegates from Philadelphia Quarterly Meeting chosen to represent the organization at the opening of Abington Quarterly Meeting.[11]

Two other Exeter Friends held at least four committee assignments for the quarterly meeting during the 1770s and 1780s. Mordecai Lee, an overseer for Maiden Creek Preparative Meeting for over two decades, served on an appeals committee in 1772, joined the slave committee in

Table 10.2
Committee Assignments of Exeter Friends
Who Attended Philadelphia Quarterly Meeting

Date Appointed	Name	Committee
4th–12mo.–1754	Moses Starr	Schools
3rd–11mo.–1755	Morris Ellis	Appeal
2nd–2mo.–1756	Francis Parvin, Jr.	Appeal
7th–11mo.–1757	Benjamin Lightfoot	Meeting for Sufferings
1st–5mo.–1758	Ellis Hughes	Revise Memorials
5th–2mo.–1759	Benjamin Lightfoot	Appeal
	Joseph Penrose	
5th–5mo.–1760	Benjamin Lightfoot	Appeal
6th–8mo.–1764	Benjamin Lightfoot	Speak with Governor concerning horse races scheduled during yearly meeting
5th–8mo.–1765	Samuel Hughes	Appeal
	Benjamin Pearson	
	James Hutton	
	John Lee	
6th–11mo.–1769	John Starr	Appeal
	Samuel Hughes	
	Thomas Thomas	
4th–5mo.–1772	Benjamin Pearson	Problems in Philadelphia Monthly Meeting
	Richard Lewis	
	James Starr	
	Samuel Embree	
2nd–8mo.–1773	John Lee	Appeal
	Mordecai Lee	
7th–11mo.–1774	Samuel Embree	Slaves
	John Lee	
	Thomas Thomas	
6th–11mo.–1775	Samuel Lee	Meeting for Sufferings
5th–8mo.–1776	Joseph Penrose	Slaves
	William Tomlinson	
	Merrick Starr	
	Mordecai Lee	
	John Hutton	
2nd–2mo.–1778	Samuel Lee	Youth
	Joseph Penrose	
7th–5mo.–1781	Mary Dickinson	Slaves
3rd–11mo.–1783	Samuel Lee	Altering Yearly Meeting quota
	Benjamin Pearson	
5th–5mo.–1784	Mordecai Lee	Visit Quarterly Meeting
	James Embree	Schools

continued

Table 10.2—*Continued*

Date Appointed	Name	Committee
2nd–5mo.–1785	Francis Parvin	Investigate formation of new quarterly meeting
	Moses Roberts	
	John Scarlet	
	Edward Bonsall	
6th–2mo.–1786	Moses Roberts	Attend opening of Abington Quarterly Meeting
	Edward Bonsall	
	Samuel Lee	
	Abel Thomas	
7th–8mo.–1786	John Hutton	Investigate problem at Haverford
	James Embree	
	Moses Roberts	
	Joseph Penrose	Appeal and reinstatement
	Abel Thomas	
	Mordecai Lee	
	Moses Roberts	

1776, visited schools within the quarterly meeting in 1784, and participated in the committee on appeal and reinstatement in 1786. Moses Roberts, a minister, accompanied Lee on the latter assignment, along with investigating in 1785 whether a new quarterly meeting was necessary, attending the opening of Abington Quarterly Meeting, and attempting to resolve a dispute at Haverford Monthly Meeting in 1786. In spite of this flurry of activity, especially in the 1780s, representatives from Exeter seldom received the choice committee assignments, lagging behind Friends from Philadelphia and Chester Counties. This, of course, is understandable given the difficulty Berks County Friends often faced in traveling the rugged country roads to Philadelphia, especially during the winter months.[12]

The failure of Exeter Friends to play a larger role within the quarterly meeting certainly did not result from a lack of piety among frontier Quakers. Even though the Society of Friends did not have an ordained clergy, those men and women whose faith led Quakers to consider them as leaders often traveled to other meetings to demonstrate their piety and to reinforce the meaning of the inner light to Friends. As a Pennsylvania Quaker meeting, Exeter Monthly Meeting welcomed visits by traveling Friends and encouraged its own ministers to make religious excursions to other meetings.[13]

The first itinerant Friend to journey to Berks County was William Reckitt, a weaver from Lincolnshire, England, and a "dedicated minister." Reckitt came to the British colonies in 1757, after an aborted attempt the

Table 10.3
Quakers Who Visited Exeter Monthly Meeting

Name	Origin	Date
William Reckitt	Lincolnshire, England	1757
John Churchman	Nottingham, Maryland	1757–1758
Grace Fisher	Philadelphia	1758
Abner Hamilton	Philadelphia	1764
Joseph Shotwell	Philadelphia	1764
William Mathews		1770
Grace Fisher	Philadelphia	1771
Susanna Lightfoot	Uwchlan	1771
Thomas Vickers	Bradford	1777
William Iddings	Bradford	1777
William Jackson	New Garden	1780
Rebecca Chambers	New Garden	1780
Elizabeth Nichols	Kennett	1780
Phebe Miller	Chester	1781
Joseph Potts	Gwynedd	1783
Job Scott	Massachusetts	1785
Thomas Titus	Westbury	1787
Richard Titus	Westbury	1787

previous year resulted in a six-month stay in a French prison. He remarked upon visiting a first-day meeting at Robeson that it was "much neglected"; then he moved on to Exeter. On fifth-day he held services in Reading "in the town-house, or court-house, where several soldiers came, and many of the town's people, who behaved very soberly; the good power of Truth coming over all, and prevailing, many minds were humbled and brought low." Reckitt expressed amazement that all in attendance had "a good time, especially . . . some of the soldiers, who were reached by the invisible power of Truth." After the meeting concluded, he and his companion went to Maiden Creek, where they stayed overnight with Moses Starr's family. The following day another meeting convened at the Maiden Creek meetinghouse, which he found to be "large, and to tolerable good satisfaction." Reckitt then journeyed back east to Great Swamp, satisfied with the conditions of Friends' meetings in the Pennsylvania backcountry.[14]

John Churchman, a prominent minister from Nottingham Monthly Meeting in Maryland, visited Exeter Monthly Meeting shortly after Reckitt had departed. Toward the end of 1757, he met with Exeter Friends at their meetinghouse and stayed with Ellis Hughes, a former overseer. Churchman, too, held services in Reading at the courthouse, "which [he] thought was pretty well considering the company, many loose people attending; but Truth seemed to come into dominion and quieted them, that

the meeting ended in a degree of awful sweetness." The minister cele-
brated the beginning of 1758 with a first-day meeting at the Maiden Creek
meetinghouse, lauding the service because it "afforded peace and comfort,
from a prospect that there were among the youth in particular, some true
branches of the Vine of life, who could not be satisfied without the living
sap from the holy Root." After returning to Reading that evening, he
traveled to Robeson the following day, and witnessed the redemption of
several Friends "who had many years made profession of the pure Truth,
and yet dwelt in that which is impure, as drinking to excess and other
evils." Similar to Reckitt's experience, Churchman considered members of
Exeter Monthly Meeting to be favored with the "mercy of the Lord our
God" before he continued to Chester County.[15]

Benjamin Lightfoot seemed particularly affected by Churchman's visit
to Reading. In October 1761, Lightfoot informed Exeter Monthly Meeting
of his desire to accompany the Nottingham minister on a religious visit to
Barbados. Later that month, Lightfoot commented to long-time friend
Israel Pemberton, Jr., that he would like to perform this service "if my
Company was agreeable to him, that my Friends were willing and that I
cou'd leave my Business reputeably . . . tho' it's almost continually in my
Mind yet I never went on any religious business when the thought of it was
so exceeding low." He hoped that embarking on this voyage would improve his health, but instead illness forced him to return the certificate
authorizing his travel, and he remained in Berks County.[16]

Although the visits of neither William Reckitt nor John Churchman
received mention in the minutes of Exeter Monthly Meeting, in later years
the clerk recorded when members of other monthly meetings came to
Exeter to visit with the families. In 1764, Abner Hamilton and Joseph
Shottwell of Philadelphia came to Exeter, and the monthly meeting found
"their Company and Service . . . acceptable and Satisfactory thereto."
Thomas Vickers and William Iddings journeyed from Bradford Monthly
Meeting in Chester County in late 1777; three former overseers accompanied them on a "Visit to all Families of Friends within the Compass" of
the monthly meeting "& also to many others not in Membership with us,
. . . to the general Satisfaction of Visitors and Visited." Vickers, in fact,
appeared so impressed with the conditions in Exeter that he moved to
Berks County in the early 1780s. During that decade, surprisingly, almost
as many women as men traveled to Exeter Monthly Meeting; most came
from monthly meetings in Chester County.[17]

In contrast with Friends who visited Exeter Monthly Meeting, little
evidence has survived relating the impressions Exeter Friends had of other
Quaker communities or of the impact Exeter Friends had on members of
other meetings. Jane Ellis returned from her trip in 1737 with certificates

Table 10.4
Berks County Quakers Who Performed Religious Visits

Women

Name	Destination	Date
Jane Ellis	Third Haven, Maryland	1737
	Hopewell, Virginia	1737
	Nantucket, Rhode Island	1751
	Portsmouth, Rhode Island	1751
	Flushing, New York	1752
	Jerseys (with Mary Evans)	1757
Mary Lightfoot	Chester	1757
	York	1757
	Westbury, New York	1772
Eleanor Lee	Plymouth (with Mary Evans)	1766
	New Providence	1766
	Richland	1769
	Warrington (with Martha Roberts)	1771
	Jerseys (with Martha Roberts)	1771
	Westbury, New York	1772
	Plymouth	1772
	Haverford	1773
	Gwynedd (with Martha Roberts)	1773
	Lancaster & Lampeter	1774
	Warrington	1774
	Jerseys (with Martha Roberts)	1776
Margaret Lee	Lancaster & Lampeter	1774
Eunice Starr	Warrington	1774
	Duck Creek, Delaware	1780
	Third Haven, Maryland	1780
	Cecil, Maryland	1780
Mary Dickinson	Concord	1774
	Lancaster	1777
	Chester	1779
	Duck Creek, Delaware	1780
	Third Haven, Maryland	1780
	Cecil, Maryland	1780
Mary Dickinson	Sadsbury	1782
	Fairfax Quarterly, Virginia	1784
	Darby	1785
Deborah Lee	Chester	1779
Hannah Jackson	Darby	1785

continued

Table 10.4—*Continued*

Men

Name	Destination	Date
Ellis Hughes	Flushing, New York	1760
Benjamin Parvin	Chester Quarterly	1765
	(with Susanna Lightfoot and Grace Fisher)	
Abel Thomas	Jerseys	1771
	Bucks County & Jerseys	1771
	Long Island	1772
	New England	1772
	Rhode Island	1773
	Western Quarter	1775
	Maryland & Virginia	1775
	Chester Quarter	1776
	West Jersey	1777
	New York & New Jersey	1778
	Warrington & Fairfax	1779
	Virginia & Carolinas	1780
	Bucks & Salem Quarter	1781
	Chester	1782
	New England	1783
	New York & New England	1785
	New York	1786
Richard Penrose	Bucks County & Jerseys	1771
Samuel Hughes	Long Island	1772
	Plymouth	1772
	Richland	1774
	Western Quarter	1775
	Warrington & Fairfax	1779
	Bucks & Salem Quarter	1781
	New York	1786
Joseph Penrose	New England	1772
Moses Roberts	Plymouth	1772
	Gwynedd (with Martha Roberts)	1773
Samuel Embree	Haverford	1773
Samuel Lee	Rhode Island	1774
James Thomas	Chester Quarter	1776
	West Jersey	1777
	New York & New Jersey	1778
Amos Lee	Virginia & Carolinas	1780
Isaac Bonsall	Warrington (with James Iddings)	1785

Accompanying Exeter Friends:
Mary Evans from Philadelphia   **Grace Fisher** from Philadelphia
Martha Roberts from Richland   **James Iddings** from Darby
Susanna Lightfoot from Uwchlan

from Hopewell Monthly Meeting in Virginia and from Baltimore Yearly Meeting, both "signifying their Unity with her Concern & Labour of Love, & that her Testimonies were Edifying & well Accepted amongst them." Mary Lightfoot, who had become a minister in 1745, joined Eleanor Lee, a former overseer and elder for Exeter Preparative Meeting, in a visit to Westbury Monthly Meeting on Long Island in 1772. While at Westbury, the two women "visited most of the Meetings belonging thereto" and provided a "Service & Labour of Love in the Ministry [that] was well accepted among them." Westbury Friends seemed quite affected by this visit, as they noted that "our Desires are that in their return they may be rewarded with True peace and Satisfaction in their own Minds."[18]

Eleanor Lee was particularly energetic at performing religious visits, making eleven journeys between 1766 and 1776 to more than a dozen monthly meetings in the Middle Colonies. In addition, Mary Dickinson, whom the meeting had acknowledged as a minister in 1776, visited at least eight monthly meetings and one quarterly meeting in Pennsylvania, Delaware, Maryland, and Virginia between 1774 and 1785, occasionally accompanied by other Exeter Friends. In 1780, both Duck Creek Monthly Meeting in Delaware and Third Haven Monthly Meeting in Maryland recognized that a visit performed by Dickinson and Eunice Starr of Maiden Creek "was acceptable to us, And we hope Serviceable among us."[19]

Men Friends, too, received favorable comments about their works. Benjamin Lightfoot noted in the meeting minutes in 1760 that Friends of Westbury Monthly Meeting had noted on Ellis Hughes's certificate "their Unity with his Ministry and Conversation." Benjamin Parvin performed a "Seasonable and Satisfactory" visit to Chester Quarterly Meeting in 1765. In addition, Friends at Plymouth Preparative Meeting in northern Philadelphia County professed their approval of the visit by Moses Roberts and Samuel Hughes in 1772.[20]

Two men Friends, Samuel Hughes and Abel Thomas, made more than six religious journeys during the 1770s. Hughes, a former overseer for Exeter Preparative Meeting, generally remained within Pennsylvania on his trips, although he did accompany Thomas to Fairfax Monthly Meeting in Virginia in 1779, to New Jersey and Delaware in 1781, and to New York in 1786. Richland Friends found his visit to their families in 1774 "very acceable" [sic], but when he traveled with Thomas, his work paled in comparison.[21]

Abel Thomas was, by far, the most active minister affiliated with Exeter Monthly Meeting during the eighteenth century. An anonymous Friend noted in 1824 that "his labours in the exercise of the gift of gospel ministry committed to him, were savoury and truly edifying, not in the words which man's wisdom teacheth, but in demonstration of the spirit and of power." Thomas began his religious journeys in 1771, when he visited New Jersey, and he toured most of the thirteen colonies over the next two decades. On his first trip to New England, accompanied by Joseph Penrose, a former overseer and elder for Maiden Creek Preparative Meeting, he "performed a religious visit which was well accepted by them." Throughout the Revolutionary War, Thomas continued his travels, even risking imprisonment on at least two occasions. Friends in attendance at Cedar Creek Quarterly Meeting in Hanover County, Virginia, in early 1781 found "that his company & services have been truly acceptable to us, his Ministry being sound, & his conversation and deportment Edifying and Exemplary." The clerk of Black Water Quarterly Meeting in Surry County, Virginia, expressed "desires for his preservation and safe return to his Family and Friends" later that year, realizing that the American Army had already captured Thomas for traveling without a pass.[22]

While on one of his religious visits to New York, Abel Thomas succeeded in restoring the faith of one adolescent, Joseph Hoag. Hoag had experienced a spiritual crisis when he was fifteen, and "rejoined my young companions, and ran into mirth at a rapid rate, carrying the anguish of my soul with me wherever I went."[23] Shortly before Hoag's eighteenth birthday, Abel Thomas visited Nine Partners Monthly Meeting in New York, where Hoag resided. Hoag felt compelled to hear Thomas speak, and it is evident that the minister's words had a tremendous effect on the lad:

> Thomas . . . was enabled to speak to my condition so clearly that I could not deny a single word. He described my progress from the first religious impressions which I was favored to experience to my then condition more correctly than I could have done it myself; clearly showing me from what I had departed, and that this departure was the occasion of the distress which I had undergone. When he took up my principles of infidelity, he placed his eye upon me, and in a wonderful manner unfolded my reasoning, laying waste all my arguments, and then warned me, in a solemn manner, to return to the Truth from which I had departed, closing in these words: 'That Jesus whom thou hast denied has revealed to me thy state and condition.'[24]

Thomas's words had shaken Hoag, forcing him to reconsider his purpose in life. After Thomas attended the New York Yearly Meeting on Long Island, he returned to Nine Partners, and then proceeded, in Hoag's words, "to denounce my final doom." Instead of damning the youngster's soul for eternity, Thomas merely cautioned against the forces of evil—and, by doing so, not only saved Hoag but even inspired him to become a Quaker minister in his own right.[25]

Joseph Hoag's account of his conversion experience is the only one that has survived as a testimony of the faithful preachings of Exeter ministers such as Abel Thomas. These religious excursions, however, did serve their purpose, as in all instances the visited meetings found the actions of Exeter men and women to be noteworthy.

To non-Quaker residents of Berks County, members of the Society of Friends were men and women of high morals whose judgment was fair and impartial. One of the few contemporary descriptions of Berks County Quakers was a list of men considered for the jury in the civil lawsuit *Wallis v. Proprietors* (1773). Samuel Wallis had obtained a patent for land in Muncy Manor in northern Berks County in 1768, but the property had not yet been acquired from the Native Americans. Officials representing the proprietor contested the legality of Wallis's title, and a selected group of county residents assembled in Reading to decide the issue.[26]

The preparer of this jury list identified thirteen men as Quakers and classified them according to their abilities and character. James Starr and Benjamin Pearson of Reading, John Harrison of Maiden Creek, and Richard Penrose of Exeter all achieved notice as men of "Common abillitys." Pearson, however, was somewhat suspect because he "will be Likely to be influenced by James Starr, if he desents from his Own Judgment." Samuel Lee, Samuel Hughes, Samuel Jackson, and George Hughes all were men "of good abillitys," while John Scarlet was "a good kind of man" and Moses Roberts "a very sensible, Juditious, Honest man." In addition, the recorder supposed that Samuel Lee "will have influence with the rest of the Jury," possibly because he was a former elder of Exeter Preparative Meeting.[27]

A couple of the members of Exeter Monthly Meeting, however, apparently lacked some desirable capacities, at least in the eyes of this clerk. Thomas Wright of Maiden Creek, currently serving as an overseer, was "a good Liver, Independent, no great Judgment, but will use what he has without byas." Benjamin Parks, in contrast, was "a man of weak abillitys; in low circumstance; apt to be influenced; Take if no better to be had." In general, the preparer of this jury list believed that Quakers would be honest men who would serve faithfully; only Parks was of questionable merit.[28]

Aside from this jury list, few contemporary comments about Berks County Quakers have survived. Anglican missionary Alexander Murray did not mince words when he commented about the state of disarray in Reading's German congregations during the 1760s, but his only remarks about Quakers related to his supposed success in converting them to Anglicanism.[29] During wartime, of course, county residents viewed Friends with derision and suspicion for their pacifist tenets. Even so, such comments were not personal, but instead would refer to the Society of Friends and other pacifist sects in general.

An examination of the minutes of Exeter Monthly Meeting reveals few references to people of other faiths. Those comments that did appear viewed non-Quakers with suspicion. One possible explanation of why

Exeter Friends did not become too involved with non-Quakers was that they considered their neighbors, especially the Germans, as uninformed. In 1777, Philadelphia Quarterly Meeting sent several books to Exeter Monthly Meeting "in order to be lent to Persons of other Societies who may discover an Inclination & Desire to read them." A listing of these books has not survived, but their purpose undoubtedly was to inform the general public about the principles and tenets of Quakerism at a time when Friends were beginning to suffer persecution for their pacifism. Additionally, in 1783, the three preparative meetings received several copies of Anthony Benezet's *Kurzer Bericht von den Leuten, die Man Quaker, nennet . . . (A Short Account of the People Called Quakers . . .)*, to be distributed among the German-speaking settlers of the region.[30]

Over the course of the eighteenth century, members of Exeter Monthly Meeting came to accept their part in the emerging cultural pluralism of the Pennsylvania backcountry. Quakers were a conspicuous minority along the frontier, yet they did not openly work to remind other settlers of their distinctiveness. Rather than trying to dominate local society as other Friends had done in the original three counties of the province, Quakers in Berks County strove to maintain their faith, even though other settlers occasionally perceived them as difficult or irresponsible.

In contrast, Quakers throughout the colony generally considered Exeter Friends pious people faithfully serving and worshipping God. When members of Exeter Monthly meeting performed religious visits, Quakers in those areas truly appreciated their efforts and occasionally professed a spiritual renewal as a result. Moreover, Berks County Friends proved to be dependable representatives to Philadelphia Quarterly Meeting, and members of this organization often chose them to attend the yearly meeting or to serve on various committees.

In conclusion, although members of Exeter Monthly Meeting lived along the frontier, they did not exist in total isolation. County residents and fellow Friends recognized the contributions these men and women were making to the evolution of the backcountry, even though they comprised less than one-tenth of the population. As the Quaker beacon on the provincial horizon, Berks County Friends had indeed displayed the experience necessary for the Society of Friends to survive and prosper in Pennsylvania after the loss of political power, which Friends in the original three counties confronted after 1776. Through these contacts with non-Quakers in the secular realm and with other Quakers in religious gatherings, members of Exeter Monthly Meeting demonstrated that Quakerism could successfully extend beyond the coast and expand into the interior.

11

Conclusion: The Contraction and Decline of Exeter Monthly Meeting

WHEN BERKS COUNTY QUAKERS HELD THE FIRST MONTHLY MEETING OF the year at Exeter meetinghouse in January 1775, all appeared to be business as usual. The Committee on Slaves, which the meeting had formed the previous year, presented a preliminary report on their investigation of slaveholding among members. Abel Thomas and Samuel Hughes informed the gathering of their desire to visit the meetings affiliated with Western Quarterly Meeting in Pennsylvania and Maryland. Four members agreed to represent Exeter at the next gathering of Philadelphia Quarterly Meeting, the regional organization. Perhaps most important, however, was the acknowledgment of an event that had occurred the previous month. Friends from Robeson Preparative Meeting in southern Berks County notified the members present that they had failed to attend the previous monthly meeting "on account that they thought it too difficult to travel through the snow."[1]

This instance, of course, was not the first time that members of Robeson Preparative Meeting had failed to travel to the monthly meeting. Robeson representatives did not attend the monthly meeting held in March 1742, barely six months after the establishment of the preparative meeting south of the Schuylkill River. Frequent nonattendance, especially during the winter months, had forced Exeter Friends to send Ellis Hughes and James Boone, two former overseers, to visit Robeson Preparative Meeting in January 1749/50, to find out why these representatives did not come. Almost a decade later, clerk Benjamin Lightfoot noted in the minutes that the problem persisted, and the monthly meeting appointed four Friends "to Visit [Robeson] at their next Preparative Meeting in order to Stir them up to more Care in that respect, or any other wherein they find Freedom to Advise them in." Nevertheless, the Schuylkill River proved to be an imposing barrier for Robeson Friends, as ice during the winter and high waters in the spring often made it difficult to cross.[2]

In June 1775, representatives from Robeson Preparative Meeting proposed a solution to the dilemma. They presented a request to hold the monthly meeting every three months at their meetinghouse. At best, this action would promote the attendance of Robeson Friends at the monthly meeting; at worst this suggestion would force Quakers from Exeter and Maiden Creek to recognize the travel difficulties. The members of the committee appointed to consider this proposal rejected it two months later, but they did acknowledge that a problem existed.[3]

Continuing difficulty in travel throughout the late 1770s and early 1780s prompted leaders of Robeson Preparative Meeting to renew their request in November 1785. This time, they proposed the establishment of a separate monthly meeting for Friends residing south of the Schuylkill. A year later, Exeter Monthly Meeting's delegates to Philadelphia Quarterly Meeting brought the matter to the regional organization's attention. The quarterly meeting appointed eight Friends, including Isaac Potts, a former worshiper at Pottsgrove Indulged Meeting, to inquire into the matter. At the next quarterly meeting, the committee informed the gathering that the request of Robeson Preparative Meeting did not have merit.[4]

This initial denial did not deter Robeson representatives from continuing to pursue their goal. Exeter Monthly Meeting appointed another committee in early 1788. This group realized that "it will be most to the Relief of Friends, & the Preservation of Unity" to allow Robeson to separate. The delegates to the quarterly meeting then renewed the request, and finally, in February 1789, Philadelphia Quarterly Meeting recognized that "the meeting at Robeson was composed of more friends than they expected." At the next quarterly meeting in May, the representatives from the assorted monthly meetings throughout Philadelphia, lower Montgomery, and Berks counties agreed to reconstitute Exeter Monthly Meeting to include "the Particular Meetings of Exeter, Maiden Creek, and Reading." Disciplinary cases still pending would be resolved by Exeter, and the two monthly meetings would contribute toward the care of indigent members. Disowned Friends who wished to rejoin the Society first had to be readmitted by Exeter, and then their membership would transfer to Robeson. The decline of Exeter Monthly Meeting as a frontier Quaker community had begun.[5]

Although Exeter Monthly Meeting was shrinking geographically in Berks County, for a brief time it continued to expand into the interior. Friends resumed moving into the backcountry once the turmoil of the Revolution had subsided. In May 1787, William Hughes of Catawissa informed Maiden Creek Preparative Meeting that he wanted to deed a plot of land to Friends to use as a burial ground "& other Uses as Friends may see Occasion." Exeter Monthly Meeting officially reestablished Catawissa Indulged Meeting that October; Friends in the region met alternately at the homes of Job Hughes at Catawissa and Richard Penrose at Roaring Creek. At the same meeting, Friends in the Muncy region of central Pennsylvania requested an indulged meeting for Quakers in that area, which the monthly meeting granted in May 1788. In July 1794, Quakers residing near Fishing Creek in Northumberland County successfully petitioned for an indulged meeting in their region. Within six years, then, Exeter Monthly Meeting had lost one preparative meeting in Berks County, but gained four indulged meetings in central Pennsylvania.[6]

The final contraction for Exeter Monthly Meeting began shortly after the approval of Fishing Creek Indulged Meeting. In August 1794, Catawissa and Roaring Creek jointly requested "the liberty of holding a Preparative Meeting," which Exeter Monthly Meeting granted that October with the approval of the quarterly meeting. Less than a year later, representatives from Catawissa Preparative Meeting asked Exeter to obtain permission for a separate monthly meeting. The committee of seven men appointed to investigate the matter reported that they "thought right to accommodate Friends thereaway" and recommended that the monthly meeting seek the approval of Philadelphia Quarterly Meeting. The regional organization also selected a committee to investigate the request, and they unanimously consented to the proposal. This new monthly meeting, officially formed in February 1796, would include Catawissa and Roaring Creek Preparative Meetings and the indulged meetings at Fishing Creek and Muncy. Exeter Monthly Meeting had passed its status as a frontier meeting on to the new settlements in Northumberland and Lycoming Counties.[7]

The concerns of Exeter Monthly Meeting now returned to Berks County, but not without some distress. Reading Friends, whose numbers had declined during the War for Independence, attempted to recover during the 1780s. By the middle of the 1790s, however, Exeter Monthly Meeting had begun to note in its responses to the queries that "our meetings for worship and discipline we believe are all kept up (except an instance of one being neglected at Reading)." Philadelphia Quarterly Meeting requested "that care might be extended to friends of Reading" and that some Quakers should be appointed "to visit them and communicate such advice as they may think needfull."[8]

The committee formed to investigate the problem at Reading discovered that neither the quarterly meeting nor the monthly meeting had ever officially established an indulged meeting, so Friends from the county seat commenced to request the continuation of their meeting.[9] Exeter's offspring at Robeson and Catawissa were thriving, while the "mother meeting" had begun its decline.

❧

The story of Exeter Monthly meeting does not end in 1789 with the creation of Robeson Monthly Meeting or with the formation of Catawissa

Monthly Meeting in 1796. The Hicksite schism of 1827–28 that divided Friends caused a split in what remained of Exeter Monthly Meeting. The indulged meetings at Exeter and at Pottstown in Montgomery County remained within the Orthodox fold, while Friends at Reading and Maiden Creek followed the teachings of Elias Hicks. The new Hicksite Exeter Monthly Meeting met alternately at the two meetinghouses until the 1880s, when declining membership in Maiden Creek led Friends to convene only at Reading. First-day services continued to be held sporadically at the Maiden Creek meetinghouse into the early twentieth century, when Friends in central Berks began to worship in private homes.[10]

The monthly meeting in Exeter Township did not fare as well as the Hicksite meetings in central Berks. Philadelphia Quarterly Meeting officially closed the monthly meeting in 1899, when the membership consisted solely of one family, descendants of Anthony Lee, the first Quaker settler in the Oley Valley. Ironically, the fledgling meeting at Reading of the 1790s was the only one to grow; in 1868 Friends in the city constructed a new stone meetinghouse on the site of the original log structure Reading Friends had built in the 1750s and torn down a decade later when they had outgrown the small building.[11]

❧

The meetinghouses in which Exeter Friends gathered each month to discuss admitting new members, transferring membership to another meeting, disciplinary problems, and other business have survived to the present. The building in Exeter Township has remained virtually unchanged from the colonial period. In 1958, the Historic American Buildings Survey remarked that the meetinghouse "is a good example of the small stone meeting house built by the Quakers in Pennsylvania in the eighteenth century." County and state historical markers commemorate the spirit of the Boone, Ellis, Hughes, Lee, and Lincoln families who settled in eastern Berks County in the early 1700s and supplied the English-speaking settlers of the frontier with a place to worship. Another tablet, embedded in the wall of the burial ground, identifies the leading families of Exeter meeting. This small plot of land, deeded by George Boone, Sr., to the meeting in 1736, is unique among burial grounds in the county. In 1817, the burial ground reached capacity; land already was at such a premium that Friends hauled an additional layer of soil four feet deep over the older portion of the cemetery and began a second level of graves.[12]

The Historical Society of Berks County also placed commemorative markers outside the meetinghouse and schoolhouse in Maiden Creek Township. These buildings, however, have changed locations since the eighteenth century. Progress necessitated the construction of a fresh-water reservoir for the city of Reading in the 1920s; part of the new lake covered the Hicksite school and meetinghouse. Local residents recognized the need to preserve the heritage of the staunch pioneers, so they arranged for the two structures to be moved a mile west and rebuilt, using the exact same materials placed in the same order, inside and out. Not all features of colonial Quaker settlement, though, were as easy to relocate. In the process, the burial ground became disturbed. Scant burial records and unmarked graves made it difficult to determine whether all bodies had been disinterred.[13]

Robeson Monthly Meeting, the first formed from Exeter, fared worse. Business meetings ended in 1872, when membership had decreased to such an extent that Caln Quarterly Meeting (to which it had become affiliated in 1800) recommended that the few surviving members discontinue their meeting. Within a decade the few remaining Quakers in southern Berks County had affiliated with other denominations, and the meetinghouse fell into disrepair. By the turn of the twentieth century, the owners used the building to store farm implements, and in 1925 it became a home for chickens, much to the dismay of the descendants of Robeson Friends.[14]

~

When Philadelphia Quarterly Meeting approved the formation of Oley Monthly Meeting in May 1737, it certainly could not have anticipated that the Quaker community along the edge of European civilization would become an outpost for Friends and serve as a "launching pad" for the spread of Quakerism along the American frontier. Members of the Society of Friends then dominated the colony's government, and settlers continued to arrive from the British Isles. Greater numbers of immigrants, however, were beginning to sail from central Europe, hoping to find religious freedom and economic opportunity in William Penn's province.

By 1789, members of Exeter Monthly Meeting had confronted many obstacles and crises in maintaining their faith in the Pennsylvania backcountry. Like other Friends in Pennsylvania, the leaders of Exeter Monthly Meeting responded to increasing external pressures by closing ranks and reinforcing the discipline, rather than adapting totally to the frontier environment and relaxing restrictions. The armed conflicts of the mid- and late-eighteenth century affected frontier Quakers by forcing them to choose between defending their property, and thus risking expulsion, or remaining pacifist, and possibly losing their lives and property.

Unlike their coreligionists in Philadelphia, Berks County Quakers did not dominate the economic life of the county, representing all levels of the economic spectrum. In addition, Exeter Friends had lost political influence within the county, replaced within a decade of the county's establishment by English Anglicans intent on controlling the government and by German immigrants intrigued by the prospect of having a voice in political affairs. In some areas, Berks County Quakers followed the patterns set by their fellow county residents. Exeter Friends were the slowest in Pennsylvania at manumitting their slaves, perhaps reflecting the opposition of German settlers in the county to the abolition movement. Both men and women were active in the religious life of the congregation. Finally, even though the frontier environment contributed to a higher percentage of Exeter Friends dying intestate, a larger proportion of women wrote wills, reflecting the influence of Germanic testation practices.

Over the course of the eighteenth century, the composition of Exeter Monthly Meeting did not change appreciably. Membership lists compiled from meeting minutes, birth and death records, and certificates of removal indicated that the meeting included 449 members in 1750 and 585 in 1775 (see Appendix 2 and Appendix 3). Several core families, among them the Boone, Hughes, Jackson, Lee, Parvin, Pearson, Penrose, Scarlet, Starr, and Thomas clans, comprised over one-half of the membership of the meeting by 1775. The 1790 census identified only 750 residents of Berks County (out of a population over 30,000) whose families had even received mention in meeting records for the eighteenth century, and over one-fourth of these men and women belonged to Robeson Monthly Meeting. Only in Maiden Creek and Robeson Townships did Quakers exceed ten percent of the population by 1790; in Reading less than four percent of the residents were affiliated with the Society of Friends.[15]

In only three townships—Exeter, Maiden Creek, and Robeson—did members of the Society of Friends ever comprise even one-fifth of the taxpayers at some time during the eighteenth century, and they never were among the majority. Most of their neighbors did not even speak the same language, as fewer than five percent of the Quakers had English-speaking settlers on adjoining tracts. The turmoil of the frontier, with the constant threat of native attacks and the unstable nature of the economy, contributed to a high degree of mobility among Quakers who moved into Berks County in search of a better life, especially after 1750.

Family ties contributed to the early growth of Exeter Monthly Meeting, and they also affected migration from Berks County. In spite of the scattered nature of Quaker settlement in the county—Friends listed in the 1790 census lived in over half of the townships—the fact remains that Friends did concentrate in several townships. Only one Quaker family lived in the German townships of northern and western Berks after 1758. Upon leaving Exeter, these Quakers spread across the eastern United States and into Canada. Men and women who worshiped at Exeter and its affiliated meetings during the eighteenth century died as members of Quaker meetings in New Jersey, Maryland, Virginia, North Carolina, South Carolina, and Georgia during the 1700s and in Ohio, Indiana, Kentucky, Tennessee, and

Iowa during the 1800s.[16] Berks County often was one stop on these Quakers' trek for spiritual and economic satisfaction.

Exeter Monthly Meeting is not famous as the religious home for prominent Friends. Only two Quakers who resided in Berks County during the eighteenth century have warranted book-length biographies. Neither of these men, however, received fame for their religious experiences, but instead for their actions in the secular world. Dr. Jonathan Potts of Reading, whom Philadelphia Monthly Meeting had disowned for violating the marriage discipline, received attention for his work as a Continental Army surgeon and hospital administrator. More prominent than Potts, however, was the sixth child of Exeter overseers Squire and Sarah Boone, the lad named Daniel who became famous in history and fiction for his exploits as a frontiersman in Kentucky.[17]

Today, Exeter meeting is but a shadow of its former self. Closed for half a century, Exeter meetinghouse reopened for services in 1949. Philadelphia Yearly Meeting reestablished the monthly meeting in 1956, with Exeter now affiliated with Caln Quarterly Meeting in northern Chester County. To this day, "worship at Exeter is characterized by much silence enriched by the presence of Christ, [its] rural setting, and a mystical air induced by a 250-year-old meetinghouse which unites simplicity and beauty." The average attendance at first-day services was seventeen in 1993 and has declined to fifteen in 2004. The meeting at Reading is somewhat larger, as over forty people attend first-day services during the winter, and there is a growing first-day school for children. During the summer months, Maiden Creek meetinghouse reopens, and many Friends affiliated with Reading worship there. No members of either of these meetings have continuous affiliation with Exeter Monthly Meeting from the eighteenth century, although the current recording clerk for Exeter Monthly Meeting is a descendant of Ellen Roberts, the child born to Moses and Jane Roberts two weeks after Northumberland County officials imprisoned him during the Revolution.[18]

Berks County no longer resembles the frontier, as Native Americans have not lived in the region for over two hundred years. Even the humble birthplace of Berks County's most famous pioneer is now a two-story stone house, as succeeding owners tore down Squire Boone's modest log cabin and built a more durable home. Yet the spirit of these frontier Quakers remains evident. For most of the eighteenth century, members of Exeter Monthly Meeting provided the last stronghold of William Penn's religion in his province, practicing the faith in a region in which they were a minority virtually from the earliest days of settlement. At the same time that they were defending their faith against outsiders, they managed to become the lone religious group providing services for most of the English-speaking population of the county. Not until Exeter Monthly

Meeting ceased to be the Quaker outpost on Pennsylvania's northwestern frontier did the adherence of Friends in this region begin to decline. The willingness of these Berks County Quakers to adapt to what could have been perceived as a hostile environment set an example for Friends as they followed the spread of European civilization across the North American continent.

Appendix 1
Leaders of Exeter Monthly Meeting
1725–1789

Oley/Exeter Preparative Meeting

Men's Overseers	Women's Overseers
Anthony Lee 27/08/30—29/10/37	Jane Hughes —29/10/37
Thomas Ellis 29/08/34—29/10/37	Deborah Boone —29/04/38
Ellis Hughes 29/10/37—27/10/39	Sarah Boone 29/10/37—26/12/40
James Boone 29/10/37—27/10/39	Mary Lee 29/04/38—26/12/40
Squire Boone 29/10/37—27/11/40	Jane Hughes 26/12/40—25/04/54
Thomas Ellis 27/10/39—29/11/40	Deborah Boone 26/12/40—31/01/43
John James 29/11/40—30/02/41	Jane Ellis 31/01/43—29/09/50
Anthony Lee 29/11/40—27/11/42	Eleanor Lee 29/09/50—29/10/61
Morris Ellis 20/02/41—27/11/42	Eleanor Harrison 25/04/54—30/11/58
Thomas Ellis 27/11/42—27/10/44	Sarah Ellis 30/11/58—26/06/69
James Boone 27/11/42—27/10/44	Ann Boone 29/10/61—30/08/80
Ellis Hughes 27/10/44—31/06/49	Margaret Lee 29/06/69—26/02/83
Thomas Lee 27/10/ 44—31/06/49	Ellen Thomas 30/08/80—*
Thomas Ellis 31/06/49—29/11/53	Jane Roberts 26/02/83—28/10/89
James Boone 31.06.49—29/11/53	
Samuel Hughes 29/11/53—28/08/55	
Thomas Lee 29/11/53—28/08/55	
James Boone 28/08/55—31/03/57	
Samuel Hughes 29/03/59—27/12/64	
John Harrison 28/08/55—25/01/59	
Mordecai Ellis 31/03/57—28/02/60	
John Lee 29/03/59—25/04/70	
Thomas Lee 28/02/60—24/04/76	
Richard Penrose 27/12/64—27/04/74	
Anthony Lee 25/04/70—28/04/73	
George Hughes 28/04/73—28/10/78	
Samuel Lee 27/04/74—*	
John Lee 28/10/78—*	

Men's Elders	Women's Elders
Anthony Lee 27/08/37—29/09/57	Eleanor Lee 29/04/56—28/10/67
Samuel Lee 29/09/57—28/02/60	Margaret Lee 28/10/67—29/08/87
Thomas Lee 28/02/60—24/04/76	Sarah Lee 29/08/87—*
Mordecai Lee 24/04/76—03/10/87	
Thomas Lee 03/10/87—*	

Maiden Creek Preparative Meeting

Men's Overseers	Women's Overseers
John Wily 31/10/34—29/01/37	Elizabeth Lundy 25/09/35—29/01/39
Robert Penrose 31/10/34—29/01/37	Margaret Penrose 25/09/35–29/01/39
Richard Lundy 29/01/37—27/01/40	Abigail Wily 29/01/39—30/05/41
Sismore Wright 29/01/37—28/12/39	Martha Houlton 29/01/39—30/05/41
Nehemiah Hutton 28/12/39—27/09/40	Deborah Starr 20/05/41—28/05/44
Laurence Pearson 27/01/40—28/02/43	Esther Pearson 30/05/41—29/03/53
Joseph Penrose 27/09/40—28/02/43	Margaret Starr 28/05/44—27/05/49
Nathaniel Houlton 28/02/43—26/05/50	Sarah Hutton 27/05/49—26/01/58
John Wily 28/02/43—27/05/49	Abigail Wily 29/03/53—26/06/55
John Eleman 27/05/49—27/08/52	Eleanor Parvin 26/06/55—27/07/58
Laurence Pearson 26/05/50—28/03/54	Phebe Starr 26/01/58—29/05/60
Samuel Embree 27/08/52—26/06/55	Sarah Penrose 27/07/58—24/09/61
William Penrose 28/03/54—26/06/55	Mary Hutton 29/05/60—29/12/63
Thomas Wright 26/06/66—29/07/56	Margaret Penrose 24/09/61–26/04/64
Joseph Penrose 26/06/55—29/07/56	Sybilla Wright 29/12/63—26/11/66
Moses Starr 29/07/56—29/09/57	Mary Hughes 26/04/64—28/01/67
William Tomlinson 29/07/56—26/10/58	Phebe Starr 26/11/66—30/11/68
Benjamin Pearson 26/10/58—26/11/61	Mary Hutton 28/01/67—26/07/69
Richard Penrose 29/09/57—27/12/59	Sarah Penrose 30/11/68—26/11/77
Mordecai Lee 27/12/59—31/12/61	Mary Hughes 26/07/69—28/08/76
Joseph Penrose 26/11/61—30/06/63	Margery Starr 28/08/76—27/07/85
Francis Parvin 31/12/61—29/03/64	Ann Wright 26/11/77—24/06/89
Richard Penrose 30/06/63—29/03/64	Eleanor Wright 27/07/85—*
John Starr 29/03/64—27/01/68	
Mordecai Lee 29/03/64—28/02/87	
Thomas Wright 27/01/68—31/12/83	
Benjamin Wright 31/12/83—29/07/89	
Owen Hughes 28/02/87—*	
Mordecai Lee 29/07/89—*	

Men's Elders	Women's Elders
Richard Lundy 27/08/37—31/10/47	Eleanor Parvin 28/07/57—27/07/58
Joseph Penrose 31/10/47—29/09/57	Sarah Penrose 27/07/58—*
John Harrison 29/09/57—*	

Robeson Preparative Meeting

Men's Overseers
John Scarlet 30/08/40—29/05/55
Moses Embree 30/08/40—22/02/53
Ephraim Jackson 22/02/53—26/10/58
Thomas Thomas 29/05/55—29/07/62
Enos Ellis 26/10/58—28/04/63
John Scarlet, Jr. 29/07/62—28/04/79
James Cadwalader 28/04/63—28/10/67
Gaius Dickinson 28/10/67—31/01/76
David Jackson 31/01/76—**
Jonathan Stephens 28/04/79—05/10/85
William Scarlet 05/10/85—**

Women's Overseers
Eleanor Scarlet 30/08/40—26/03/43
Mary Cadwalader 30/08/40—26/03/43
Rachel Long 26/03/43—30/03/45
Frances Dowdle 26/03/43—28/01/45
Mary Embree 28/01/45—30/08/53
Eleanor Scarlet 30/03/45—????
Ann Scarlet 30/08/53—29/04/78
Rebecca Thomas ????—30/12/56
Mary Jackson 30/12/56—30/08/64
Deborah Thomas 30/08/64—26/04/80
Elizabeth Jackson 29/04/78—**
Rebecca Scarlet 26/04/80—29/04/89
Catharine Scarlet 29/04/89—**

Men's Elders
John Scarlet 24/04/42—27/04/44
John Scarlet, Jr. 27/04/44—**

Women's Elders
Mary Cadwalader 24/04/42—30/04/43
Deborah Thomas 28/10/78—30/07/88
Mary Jackson 30/07/88—**
Elizabeth Jackson 30/07/88—**

*continued to hold this position after 1789
**overseers and elders for Robeson Monthly Meeting after 1789

Ministers	Date Acknowledged	Men's Clerks	Appointed
Mary Lightfoot	25/05/45	Richard Lundy	1737
Moses Roberts	27/04/68	James Boone	1746/7
James Thomas	27/04/74	John Hughes	1749
Eunice Starr	25/01/75	Benjamin Lightfoot	1756
Mary Dickinson	24/04/76	Francis Parvin, Jr.	1765
Abel Thomas		Moses Roberts	1771
Jane Ellis		Francis Parvin, Jr.	1775
Ellis Hughes		Thomas Lightfoot	1780
Thomas Ellis			

Recorder of Births and Deaths
George Boone appointed 27/08/37
Samuel Hughes appointed 12/12/50

Women's Clerks	Appointed
Esther Pearson	1737
Margaret Lee	1759
Eunice Starr	1765
Deborah Lee	1776
Ann Wright	1779
Eunice Starr	1780
Ann Wright	1782

Appendix 2
Exeter Monthly Meeting Membership List
1750

Name	Preparative Meeting
Barger, John, wife Mary, 8 children	Maiden Creek
Boone, George, wife Deborah, 2 children	Exeter
Boone, James, wife Mary, 9 children	Exeter
Boone, Jeremiah	Exeter
Boone, John	Exeter
Boone, Joseph, wife Catharine, 2 children	Exeter
Boone, Joseph, wife Elizabeth	Exeter
Boone, Josiah, wife Hannah	Exeter
Boone, Samuel	Exeter
Boone, Sarah, 8 children	Exeter
Boone, William, wife Sarah, 1 child	Exeter
Cadwalader, David, wife Mary, 2 children	Robeson
Cadwalader, David, Jr., wife Hannah	Robeson
Cadwalader, John, wife Sophia	Robeson
Cadwalader, Nathan, wife Elizabeth	Robeson
Cleaver, Derrick, wife Mary, 3 children	Exeter
Clews, William, wife Mary, 3 children	Exeter
Coles, Dinah, 3 children	Exeter
Coles, Martha, 5 children	Exeter
Dowdle, Frances	Robeson
Eleman, John, wife Mary, 7 children	Maiden Creek
Eleman, Thomas	Maiden Creek
Ellis, Enos, wife Elizabeth, 2 children	Exeter
Ellis, Mordecai, wife Mary	Exeter
Ellis, Morris, wife Sarah, 6 children	Exeter
Ellis, Thomas, wife Jane	Exeter
Ellis, Thomas, Jr., wife Magdalene, 2 children	Exeter
Embree, Elizabeth	Robeson
Embree, John	Robeson
Embree, Moses, wife Mary	Robeson
Embree, Moses, Jr.	Robeson
Embree, Rebecca	Robeson
Embree, Samuel, wife Rachel, 2 children	Robeson

Embree, Thomas	Robeson
Fincher, John, wife Jane, 7 children	Maiden Creek
George, Richard, wife Rebecca, 7 children	Maiden Creek
Harrison, Caleb, wife Eleanor	Exeter
Harrison, John, wife Mary, 3 children	Exeter
Hopkins, Matthew	Exeter
Houlton, Nathaniel, wife Martha, 4 children	Maiden Creek
Hughes, Ellis, wife Jane	Exeter
Hughes, John, wife Martha, 2 children	Exeter
Hughes, Samuel, wife Elizabeth, 2 children	Exeter
Hughes, William, wife Amy, 3 children	Exeter
Humphrey, Owen, wife Sarah, 4 children	Exeter
Hutton, James	Maiden Creek
Hutton, John	Maiden Creek
Hutton, Nehemiah, wife Sarah, 5 children	Maiden Creek
Jackson, Ephraim, wife Mary, 5 children	Robeson
Jordan, Elizabeth	Robeson
Jordan, James	Robeson
Jordan, John, Jr., wife Rachel	Robeson
Jordan, Joseph, wife Margaret, 1 child	Robeson
Jordan, Martha, 1 child	Robeson
Kirby, Joseph, wife Mary	Exeter
Lee, Anthony, wife Mary, 2 children	Exeter
Lee, John, wife Jane, 2 children	Exeter
Lee, Samuel, wife Margaret, 2 children	Exeter
Lee, Thomas, wife Eleanor, 5 children	Exeter
Long, Henry	Robeson
Long, Robert, wife Rachel, 2 children	Robeson
Longworthy, Benjamin, wife Jane	Maiden Creek
May, James, wife Margaret, 2 children	Exeter
May, Robert	Exeter
Millard, Benjamin	Exeter
Millard, Joseph, wife Jane, 5 children	Exeter
Mooney, Samuel, wife Martha	Exeter
Moore, Richard, wife Sarah, 6 children	Exeter
Musgrave, Thomas, wife Hannah, 4 children	Robeson
Parks, Benjamin, wife Barbara	Maiden Creek
Parvin, Benjamin	Maiden Creek
Parvin, Francis, wife Eleanor, 6 children	Maiden Creek
Parvin, Francis, Jr.	Maiden Creek
Parvin, Thomas	Maiden Creek
Pearson, Benjamin	Maiden Creek
Pearson, Lawrence, wife Esther, 5 children	Maiden Creek
Pearson, Margery	Maiden Creek
Pearson, Thomas, wife Elizabeth, 3 children	Maiden Creek
Penrose, Joseph, wife Sarah, 6 children	Maiden Creek

Penrose, Richard, wife Margaret, 5 children	Maiden Creek
Penrose, William, wife Ann, 4 children	Maiden Creek
Rhodes, Hannah	Exeter
Sands, Elizabeth	Exeter
Scarlet, John, wife Eleanor	Robeson
Scarlet, John, Jr., 5 children	Robeson
Smith, John, wife Sarah	Maiden Creek
Starr, Isaac, wife Margaret, 5 children	Maiden Creek
Starr, Isaac, Jr.	Maiden Creek
Starr, James	Maiden Creek
Starr, John	Maiden Creek
Starr, Merrick, wife Phebe, 4 children	Maiden Creek
Starr, Moses, wife Deborah, 3 children	Maiden Creek
Starr, Moses, Jr.	Maiden Creek
Stephens, Richard, wife Dorothy, 8 children	Maiden Creek
Thomas, Evan, wife Ann, 4 children	Robeson
Thomas, Jacob, wife Rebecca, 7 children	Robeson
Thomas, Jane	Robeson
Thomas, Peter, wife Margaret, 4 children	Robeson
Thomas, Thomas, wife Martha, 3 children	Robeson
Tomlinson, William, wife Ann, 5 children	Maiden Creek
Webb, George, wife	Exeter
Webb, John, wife Mary, 6 children	Exeter
Webb, John, Jr., wife Rachel, 2 children	Exeter
Williams, John, wife Mary, 1 child	Exeter
Willits, Henry, wife Sarah, 3 children	Maiden Creek
Willits, Jesse	Maiden Creek
Willits, John	Maiden Creek
Wily, Abigail, 2 children	Maiden Creek
Wily, Benjamin	Maiden Creek
Wily, Jane	Maiden Creek
Wily, Jane	Maiden Creek
Wily, John	Maiden Creek
Wily, John, wife Martha, 1 child	Maiden Creek
Wily, John, Jr.	Maiden Creek
Wily, Joseph, wife Abigail	Maiden Creek
Wily, Thomas, wife Rebecca, 2 children	Maiden Creek
Wily, William	Maiden Creek
Woolaston, Samuel, wife Gobitha, 5 children	Maiden Creek
Worrall, George	Robeson
Worrall, John, Jr.	Robeson
Wright, Mary, 2 children	Maiden Creek
Wright, Sizemore, wife Margaret	Maiden Creek
Wright, Thomas, wife Sibilla, 6 children	Maiden Creek
Yarnall, Joseph, wife Elizabeth, 5 children	Maiden Creek

*children are under the age of 21; unmarried children over 21 are listed separately

Appendix 3
Exeter Monthly Meeting Membership List
1775

Name	Preparative Meeting
Barger, John	Maiden Creek
Barger, Lydia, 5 children	Maiden Creek
Barger, Thomas	Maiden Creek
Boone, Hugh, wife Catharine	Exeter
Boone, Isaac, wife Sarah, 1 child	Exeter
Boone, Isaiah	Exeter
Boone, James, wife Ann	Exeter
Boone, James, Jr.	Exeter
Boone, Jeremiah	Exeter
Boone, John	Exeter
Boone, Joseph, wife Catharine	Exeter
Boone, Joshua	Exeter
Boone, Judah, wife Hannah	Exeter
Boone, Mary	Exeter
Boone, Moses	Exeter
Boone, Rachel	Exeter
Boone, Sarah, 5 children	Exeter
Boone, William, Jr.	Exeter
Cadwallader, John, wife Sophia, 2 children	Robeson
Cadwallader, Nathan, wife Elizabeth	Robeson
Cherington, Thomas, wife Rachel	Exeter
2 children of Isaac and Phebe Clendennon*	Maiden Creek
2 children of Isaac and Elizabeth Clendennon*	Maiden Creek
Clews, Mary	Maiden Creek
Coles, Deborah	Maiden Creek
Coles, Mary	Maiden Creek
Coles, Solomon, wife Esther, 4 children	Maiden Creek
Collins, William, wife Eleanor	Exeter
Dickinson, Gaius, wife Mary, 10 children	Robeson
Edwards, Ann	Robeson
Edwards, Martha	Robeson
Ellis, Deborah	Exeter
Embree, James, wife Phebe, 2 children	Robeson

Embree, John, wife Mary	Robeson
Embree, Moses, wife Mary, 1 child	Robeson
Embree, Samuel, wife Rachel	Robeson
Embree, Thomas	Robeson
Evans, Cadwalader	Robeson
Evans, Margaret	Robeson
Evans, Sarah	Robeson
George, Edward, wife Martha, 7 children	Robeson
George, Ellis, wife Lydia	Robeson
George, Evan	Robeson
George, John, wife Sarah, 4 children	Robeson
George, Rachel	Robeson
George, Richard, wife Rebecca	Robeson
Harrison, Caleb	Robeson
Harrison, John, wife Mary, 2 children	Robeson
Harrison, John, Jr.	Robeson
Harrison, Joseph	Robeson
Harrison, Richard	Robeson
Harrison, Samuel, wife Tamer	Robeson
Hughes, Edward, wife Elizabeth, 4 children	Exeter
Hughes, Ellis, wife Hannah, 6 children	Maiden Creek**
Hughes, George, wife Martha, 7 children	Exeter
Hughes, Jesse	Exeter
Hughes, Job, wife Esther, 1 child	Maiden Creek**
Hughes, John	Exeter
3 children of Jonathan and Jane Hughes*	Exeter
Hughes, Owen, wife Mary, 1 child	Maiden Creek
Hughes, Samuel	Exeter
Hughes, Samuel, wife Margaret, 7 children	Exeter
Hughes, Thomas, wife Hannah, 5 children	Maiden Creek**
Hughes, William, wife Mary, 1 child	Exeter
Humphrey, Owen, wife Sarah	Robeson
Hutton, James, wife Hannah, 7 children	Maiden Creek
Hutton, John, wife Mary, 2 children	Maiden Creek
Irwin, John, wife Sarah, 1 child	Maiden Creek
Jackson, Ann	Robeson
Jackson, Caleb, wife Ann, 1 child	Robeson
Jackson, David, wife Elizabeth, 3 children	Robeson
Jackson, Ephraim, Jr., wife Mary, 9 children	Robeson
1 child of Ephraim and Mary Jackson*	Robeson
Jackson, Hannah	Robeson
Jackson, Joseph	Robeson
Jackson, Lydia	Robeson
Jackson, Mary	Robeson
Jackson, Samuel, Jr., wife Mary, 7 children	Maiden Creek
James, Joseph, wife Lydia, 2 children	Exeter

John, Isaac, 3 children	Maiden Creek**
Jordan, William, wife Elizabeth	Exeter
Lee, Amos	Exeter
Lee, Ann	Exeter
Lee, Eleanor	Exeter
Lee, Eleanor	Exeter
Lee, Esther	Exeter
Lee, Isaac	Exeter
Lee, John, wife Ann, 3 children	Exeter
Lee, Mordecai, wife Deborah	Maiden Creek
Lee, Sarah	Exeter
Lee, Samuel, wife Margaret, 6 children	Exeter
Lee, Samuel	Exeter
Lee, Susanna	Exeter
Lee, Thomas	Exeter
Lewis, Richard, wife Sarah, 2 children	Robeson
Lightfoot, Ann	Maiden Creek
Lightfoot, Benjamin, wife Elizabeth, 1 child	Maiden Creek
Lightfoot, Jacob, wife Mary	Maiden Creek
Lightfoot, Joseph, wife Deborah, 7 children	Maiden Creek
Lightfoot, Thomas, wife Hannah, 1 child	Maiden Creek
May, Robert	Exeter
Morris, Enos	Robeson
Morris, Jane, 2 children	Robeson
Morris, Nicholas	Robeson
Morris, William, wife Ellin, 4 children	Robeson
Morris, William, Jr.	Robeson
Pancoast, Adin, wife Abigail, 3 children	Exeter
Parks, Benjamin, wife Barbara, 8 children	Maiden Creek
Parks, Samuel	Maiden Creek
Parvin, Eleanor	Maiden Creek
Parvin, Francis, Jr., wife Sarah, 6 children	Maiden Creek
Parvin, John, wife Mary	Maiden Creek
Parvin, Thomas, wife Mary, 11 children	Maiden Creek
Pearson, Elijah, wife Hannah, 4 children	Maiden Creek
Pearson, Jonathan	Maiden Creek
Pearson, Mary	Maiden Creek
Pearson, Mary, 4 children	Maiden Creek
Pearson, Sarah	Maiden Creek
Pearson, Thomas, 4 children	Maiden Creek
Penrose, Abigail	Maiden Creek
Penrose, Isaac	Maiden Creek
Penrose, Joseph, wife Sarah, 2 children	Maiden Creek
Penrose, Joseph, Jr., wife Elizabeth, 1 child	Maiden Creek
Penrose, Mary	Maiden Creek
Penrose, Richard, wife Margaret, 6 children	Exeter

Penrose, Robert, wife Rebecca	Maiden Creek
Penrose, Thomas, wife Abigail	Maiden Creek
Potts, Grace	Maiden Creek
Potts, Isaac, wife Martha	Maiden Creek
Quaintance, Joseph	Exeter
Reed, Sarah, 2 children	Exeter
Roberts, Moses, wife Jane, 5 children	Exeter
Scarlet, Benjamin, wife Rebecca, 2 children	Robeson
Scarlet, John, Jr., wife Ann	Robeson
Scarlet, John, III, wife Catharine, 1 child	Robeson
Scarlet, William, wife Susanna, 4 children	Robeson
Starr, Abraham	Maiden Creek
Starr, Esther	Maiden Creek
Starr, Isaac, Jr., wife Elizabeth	Maiden Creek
Starr, Jacob, wife Hannah	Maiden Creek
Starr, James, wife Elizabeth, 6 children	Maiden Creek
Starr, John, wife Eunice, 6 children	Maiden Creek
Starr, Merrick, wife Phebe, 3 children	Maiden Creek
Starr, Merrick, Jr.	Maiden Creek
Starr, Moses, Jr., wife Margery, 8 children	Maiden Creek
Starr, Pearson	Maiden Creek
Starr, Samuel	Maiden Creek
Starr, Thomas, wife Jane	Maiden Creek
Starr, William, wife Jane	Maiden Creek
Stephen, Jonathan, wife Mary, 7 children	Robeson
Stephen, Samuel	Robeson
Stephens, Ann	Maiden Creek
Stephens, George	Maiden Creek
Stephens, John	Maiden Creek
Stephens, Richard, wife Dorothy	Maiden Creek
Stephens, Richard, Jr.	Maiden Creek
Stephens, Robert	Maiden Creek
Stephens, Susanna	Maiden Creek
Thomas, Abel, wife Margaret, 4 children	Exeter
Thomas, Dinah	Exeter
Thomas, Elizabeth	Exeter
Thomas, Evan	Exeter
Thomas, Jacob, wife Rebecca, 1 child	Exeter
Thomas, Jacob, Jr.	Exeter
Thomas, James, wife Deborah, 3 children	Robeson
Thomas, Jonathan	Robeson
Thomas, Jonas	Robeson
Thomas, Peter, Jr., wife Margaret, 4 children	Robeson
Thomas, Peter, III, wife Deborah	Robeson
Thomas, Rebecca	Robeson
Thomas, Thomas, wife Martha	Robeson

Thomas, Thomas, Jr.	Robeson
Tomlinson, John	Maiden Creek
Tomlinson, William, wife Ann, 5 children	Maiden Creek
Tomlinson, William, Jr., wife Grace, 2 children	Maiden Creek
Vore, Gideon, wife Mary, 7 children	Robeson
Walker, Lewis, wife Anna, 3 children	Exeter
Webb, Samuel, wife Rebecca, 6 children	Exeter
Wickersham, Isaac, wife Mary, 2 children	Maiden Creek
Williams, Abner	Exeter
Williams, Adino, wife Dinah	Exeter
Willits, Richard	Maiden Creek
Wilson, John, wife Phebe, 8 children	Robeson
Wily, Benjamin	Maiden Creek
Wily, Martha	Maiden Creek
Wily, Penrose	Maiden Creek
Wily, Vincent	Maiden Creek
Woolaston, Rachel, 7 children	Maiden Creek
Wright, Benjamin, wife Ann, 4 children	Maiden Creek
Wright, Isaac, wife Eleanor, 2 children	Maiden Creek
Wright, Joseph, wife Eleanor, 1 child	Maiden Creek
Wright, Margaret	Maiden Creek
Wright, Phebe	Maiden Creek
Wright, Thomas, wife Sibilla, 2 children	Maiden Creek

*parents deceased
**settled near Catawissa in Northumberland County
Reading Friends affiliated with Maiden Creek Preparative Meeting
Children are under the age of 21; unmarried children over 21 are listed separately

Notes

CHAPTER 1. INTRODUCTION

1. "Frame of Government," in Soderlund, *William Penn,* 118–33; "*Second* Frame of Government," in Soderlund, *William Penn,* 265–73; Klein and Hoogenboom, *A History of Pennsylvania,* 16–48, 227–28; Klepp, "Encounter and Experiment," in Miller and Pencak, *Pennsylvania,* 61–65, 69–84; and Crist, "The Colonial Period," in Crist, *Penn's Example to the Nations,* 3–21. For the concept of Pennsylvania as a model, see Frantz, "Religion in the Middle Colonies," 9–22. See also Frost, "William Penn's Experiment," 577–606.

2. Trussell, *Architect of a Nation,* 2–11; Bronner, *The Quakers,* 4–13; *Book of Discipline* 27–65; and Tolles, *Meeting House and Counting House,* 4–11. See also Endy, *William Penn and Early Quakerism;* and Schwartz, "William Penn and Toleration," 284–312.

3. *Inventory of Church Archives,* 43; *Book of Discipline,* 71–72, 76; Eckert, *Guide to Records,* vii–xii; and Lapansky and Verplanck, *Quaker Aesthetics* 373, 376.

4. *Book of Discipline,* 67–73, 75–117; Eckert, *Guide to Records,* vii–ix, xi–xiii; Bauman, *Reputation of Truth,* 231–34; Doncaster, *Quaker Organisation,* 13–16, 81–83; and Lapansky and Verplanck, *Quaker Aesthetics,* 375, 377.

5. "Deborah Boone," in Heiss, *Biographical Sketches* 220; "Jane Ellis," in Heiss, *Biographical Sketches,* 309; Doncaster, *Quaker Organisation,* 10, 21–24; Eckert, *Guide to Records,* 269, 272–73; Lapansky and Verplanck, *Quaker Aesthetics,* 372, 374–77; and *Book of Discipline,* 22–24, 77, 94–96.

6. *Inventory of Church Archives,* 43–45, 108–11, 120–21, 131, 133, 160, 174–75; and Nelson, "Backcountry Pennsylvania."

7. For more information on the religious diversity of early Berks County, see Guenther, "A 'Garden for the Friends of God,'" 138–44; Hummel, "Religion on a Moving Frontier," 22–26; Pendleton, *Oley Valley Heritage,* 103–33; and Somers, "Conditions and Contributions," 12–15, 34–36, 38. See also chapter 2.

8. Minutes of Gywnedd Men's Monthly Meeting, 28th, 7 mo., 1725; 28th, 8th mo., 1735; "Exeter Monthly Meeting Book A," Minutes of Exeter Men's Monthly Meeting, 1737–1765, 27th, 6 mo., 1741; 26th, 8 mo., 1749; 27th, 12 mo., 1753; 30th, 12 mo., 1756; "Exeter Monthly Meeting Book B," Minutes of Exeter Men's Monthly Meeting, 1765–1785, 25th, 12 mo., 1771; 31st, 5 mo., 1775; and "Exeter Monthly Meeting Book C," Minutes of Exeter Men's Monthly Meeting, 1785–1808, 31st, 10 mo., 1787; 28th, 5 mo., 1788. Studies of Exeter Monthly Meeting include Cook, "Glimpses of Life in a Frontier Friends Meeting," 122–23, 126–27, 138–42; Eshelman, "The Society of Friends, and Their Meeting Houses, in Berks County," 104–9, 117–23; and Grant, "Exeter Friends Meeting 1737–1787," 62–63, 71, 74–77, 79–80.

9. "Exeter Monthly Meeting Book B," 27th, 12 mo., 1775 (source for quote). Important

studies of the Society of Friends in colonial Pennsylvania include Bauman, *Reputation of Truth;* James, *A People Among Peoples;* Marietta, *Reformation of American Quakerism;* Sharpless, "Quakers in Pennsylvania," in Jones, *The Quakers in the American Colonies,* 415–580; and Tolles, *Meeting House and Counting House.*

10. Zuckerman, "Introduction: Puritans, Cavaliers, and the Motley Middle," in Zuckerman, *Friends and Neighbors* 3–25.

11. Ibid., 7–16, 22–25. See also Frantz, "Religion in the Middle Colonies," 9–22.

12. Bauman, *Reputation of Truth;* Bronner, *William Penn's "Holy Experiment";* Fisher, *The Making of Pennsylvania;* Fiske, *The Dutch and Quaker Colonies in America,* vol. 2, 294–329; Nash, *Quakers and Politics;* Schwartz, *"A Mixed Multitude";* Sharpless, *A History of Quaker Government;* Thayer, *Pennsylvania Politics;* Tully, *Forming American Politics,* 257–309; Tully, *William Penn's Legacy;* and Wertenbaker, *The Founding of American Civilization.*

13. Lemon, *The Best Poor Man's Country,* xiii; Ridner, "'A Handsomely Improved Place'"; Franz, *Paxton;* Wolf, *Urban Village;* Becker, "American Revolution as a Community Experience"; Wood, *Conestoga Crossroads;* Henderson, *Community Development;* and Doutrich, "Evolution of an Early American Town."

14. Forbes, "'As Many Candles Lighted'"; and Grundy, "'In the World But Not of It.'"

15. Wolf, *Urban Village;* Wood, *Conestoga Crossroads;* Henderson, *Community Development;* Becker, "American Revolution as a Community Experience"; and Doutrich, "Evolution of an Early American Town."

16. Jensen, *Loosening the Bonds;* Soderlund, *Quakers & Slavery;* Smith, *Breaking the Bonds;* Wilson, *Life after Death;* Levy, *Quakers and the American Family;* Frost, *The Quaker Family.*

17. Hinderaker and Mancall, *At the Edge of Empire;* Merrell, *Into the American Woods;* Merritt, *At the Crossroads;* Pencak and Richter, *Friends and Enemies in Penn's Woods;* Richter, *Facing East from Indian Country.*

18. Montgomery, *History of Berks County,* 26–56.

19. Ibid., 929–1018, passim.

20. Ibid., 1021–76, passim.

21. Ibid., 1147–86, passim.

22. Ibid., 1082–1143, passim.

23. Ibid., 650–54; Albright, *Two Centuries of Reading,* 14–20, 25; and Harbaugh, *The Life of Rev. Michael Schlatter,* 201.

24. Acrelius, *History of New Sweden,* 226–27; Oudinot, "Andreas Rudman," 59, 62–64, 80; Pendleton, "Swedish Settlement at Old Morlatton," 129–133, 141, 143; Richards, "Swedish Settlement at Morlatton," 125–33; and *Early Swedes and St. Gabriel's Church,* 1–2, 7–9.

25. For more information on the settlement of the Oley Valley, see Bertolet, *Fragments of the Past,* 1–2; Croll, *Annals of the Oley Valley,* 7–16; Pendleton, *Oley Valley Heritage;* Stapleton, "The Huguenot Element," 386–401; and Stoudt, "Great Religious Revival," 255.

26. Dieffenbach and Irgang, "John Conrad Dieffenbach," 42–48; Lichtenthaeler, "Storm Blown Seeds of Schoharie," 3–105; Montgomery, *School History of Berks County,* 27–31; and Commissioners of Berks County, *Berks County, Pennsylvania,* 5–6.

27. Eshelman, "Anthony and Mary Lee," 114; McKenna, "Early Irish in Berks County," 20–21, 25; McKenna, "Early Welsh in Berks County," 179–86; Myers, *Immigration of Irish Quakers,* 109–372, passim; and *The Goshenhoppen Registers,* passim; and Warrantee Township Maps, Berks County, Pennsylvania. For a more detailed analysis of Quaker migration from Ireland to North America, see Lockhart, "The Quakers and Emigration," 67–92. For more information on Welsh settlement in Pennsylvania, see Browning, *Welsh Settlement of Pennsylvania;* Dodd, "Background of Welsh Quaker Migration," 111–27.

28. Eshelman, "Anthony and Mary Lee," 113–16; and Eshelman, "Quaker Marriage Certificate," 77–79.

29. Wallace, *Daniel Boone in Pennsylvania,* 1–3; and Spraker, *Boone Family,* 19–28, 590–91.

30. Minutes of Gwynedd Men's Monthly Meeting, 31st, 10 mo., 1717; 29th, 4 mo., 1725; 27th, 2 mo., 1731; Spraker, *Boone Family,* 590–591; and Eshelman, "Anthony and Mary Lee," 114.

31. "Ellis Hugh," in Heiss, *Biographical Sketches,* 234–35; "A Testimony . . . concerning Ellis Hugh," in *A Collection of Memorials . . . ,* 223–29; and Minutes of Philadelphia Men's Quarterly Meeting, 1723–1772, 7th, 12 mo., 1725/6; 3rd, 12 mo., 1728/9.

32. "Thomas Ellis," in Heiss, *Biographical Sketches,* 223; Minutes of Gywnedd Monthly Meeting, 29th, 8 mo., 1734; and "Jane Ellis," in Heiss, *Biographical Sketches,* 309.

33. Myers, *Immigration of Irish Quakers,* 109–10, 289, 328, 332, 341, 350–52, 369; Eshelman, "Descendants of Moses and Deborah Starr," 67–74; and Minutes of Gwynedd Men's Monthly Meeting, 29th, 11 mo., 1733; 27th, 3 mo.,1735; 30th, 7 mo., 1735; 28th, 8 mo., 1735; 25th, 9 mo., 1735; 29th, 1 mo., 1737.

34. Myers, *Immigration of Irish Quakers,* 289, 328–29, 332, 341, 350–51.

35. Minutes of Gwynedd Men's Monthly Meeting, 29th, 1 mo., 1737; 26th, 2 mo., 1737; 31st, 3 mo., 1737; 28th, 4 mo., 1737; 26th, 5 mo., 1737; "Exeter Monthly Meeting Book A," 25th, 6 mo., 1737; 27th, 3 mo., 1742; and Minutes of Philadelphia Men's Quarterly Meeting, 2nd, 3 mo., 1737; 1st, 6 mo., 1737.

36. "Exeter Monthly Meeting Book A," 27th, 6 mo., 1741; 1737–1754, passim; and "Women's Monthly Meeting Book A," Minutes of Exeter Women's Monthly Meeting, 1737–1789, 26th, 11 mo., 1743/4; 29th, 10 mo., 1737; 1737–1754, passim.

CHAPTER 2. A LAND OF DIVERSITY AND CONTENTION

1. "Exeter Monthly Meeting Book A," 27th day, 10th mo., 1739; 29th day, 5th mo., 1742; 26th day, 6th mo., 1742; 31st day, 10th mo., 1747; 26th day, 3rd mo., 1748; "Women's Monthly Meeting Book A," 29th day, 10th mo., 1737; 26th day, 2nd mo., 1750; Guenther, "Interpretation Manual, Daniel Boone Homestead," 1, 8–9, 29–30; McCarthy, "Daniel Boone: The Formative Years" 34–37; Seitz, *Pennsylvania's Historic Places;* 62–65; Silverman, "A Kentucky Frontiersman's Pennsylvania Roots," 30–39; Silverman, *Pennsylvania Trail of History Guide;* and Wallace, *Daniel Boone in Pennsylvania.*

2. Pastorius, "Positive Information from America," in Soderlund, *William Penn,* 355; "Kirchen-Buch," 7; Muhlenberg, *Journals* 1:68; and Mittelberger, *Journey to Pennsylvania,* 41.

3. "Governor Thomas to the Bishop of Exeter," 23 April 1748, in Perry, *Historical Collections,* 256; Letter, Johann Philips Boehm and the Philadelphia Consistory to Deputy Velingius, 28 October 1734, in Hinke, *Life and Letters of Boehm,* 239; *Minutes and Letters of the Coetus,* 10; Letter, Johann Philips Boehm and the Philadelphia Consistory to Deputy Velingius, 28 October 1734, in Hinke, *Life and Letters of Boehm,* 239; and Muhlenberg, *Journals,* 1:66–67. Boehm offered his impressions of the different sects in Letter, Johann Philips Boehm to the Classis of Amsterdam, 12 November 1730, in Hinke, *Life and Letters of Boehm,* 200–203.

4. Studies of religious diversity in colonial Pennsylvania include Crist, "The Colonial Period," 3–21; Fortenbaugh, "Pennsylvania," 88–102; Frantz, "Religious Freedom," 10–13; Frantz, "Religion in the Middle Colonies," 9–22; Frost, *A Perfect Freedom,* 1–73; Schwartz, *"A Mixed Multitude";* Schwartz, "Religious Pluralism," in Mitchell, *Ap-*

palachian Frontiers, 52–68; and Stoudt, "Early Pennsylvania Religious Movements," 9–10, 31. Most of the religious groups in eighteenth-century Berks County are identified in Howell, *Genealogical Guide,* 133–80. Surveys of religious diversity in early Berks County include Guenther, "A 'Garden for the Friends of God'," 138–44; Hummel, "Religion on a Moving Frontier," 22–26; Montgomery, *History of Berks County,* 26–56; and Somers, "Conditions and Contributions," 12–15, 34–36, 38. See also Holton, *Berks County,* 11–21; and Pendleton, *Oley Valley Heritage,* 103–33. For additional information on religious affiliation in colonial America, see Bonomi and Eisenstadt, "Church Adherence," 245–86.

5. Acrelius, *History of New Sweden,* 208–10, 226–27; Oudinot, "Andreas Rudman," 59, 62–64, 80; Pendleton, "Swedish Settlement at Old Morlatton," 129–33, 141, 143; Richards, "Swedish Settlement at Morlatton," pp. 125–33; *Early Swedes and St. Gabriel's Church,* 1–2, 7–9; and Weis, *Colonial Churches,* 63.

6. "Church Book for the Congregation at St. Gabriel's Church, Morlattan, Amity Township, Berks County," 1–3; *Early Swedes and St. Gabriel's,* 2, 4, 11; Glatfelter, *Pastors and People,* vol. 1: 248; Muhlenberg, *Journals,* 1:186–88, 196–97, 202, 222, 229, 245, 259, 319; Richards, "Swedish Settlement," 125–31; Stabb, "Lutheran Congregations" 419–32; and White, "Affiliation of Swedish Churches," 171–86.

7. Dieffenbach and Irgang, "John Conrad Dieffenbach," 42–48; Lichtenthaeler, "Storm Blown Seeds of Schoharie," 3–105; Montgomery, *History of Berks County,* 1021–76, passim; Montgomery, *School History of Berks County,* 27–31; and Commissioners of Berks County, *Berks County, Pennsylvania,* 5–6.

8. Spaeth, et al., *Documentary History,* 8–221, passim; Glatfelter, *Pastors and People,* vol. 1, 258–59, 261–64; Howell, *Genealogical Guide,* 133–76, passim; Kidd, *Lutherans in Berks County,* passim; and Weis, *Colonial Churches,* 19–105, passim. A list of these Lutheran congregations can be found in table 1. For more information on Lutherans in Pennsylvania during the colonial period, see Glatfelter, *Pastors and People,* vol. 1, 233–65; Jacobs, *History of Evangelical Lutheran Church;* Nelson, *Lutherans in North America;* Roeber, *Palatines, Liberty, and Property;* Schmauk, *History of Lutheran Church;* and Weiser, "The Lutherans," in Crist, *Penn's Example to the Nations,* 74–77.

9. Ahlstrom, *Religious History of American People,* 246; Glatfelter, *Pastors and People,* vol. 1, 233–65; "First Report of Mr. Boehm to the Synods of North and South Holland, October 28, 1734," in Hinke, *Life and Letters of Boehm,* 250; "Report of Mr. Boehm to the Classis of Amsterdam, January 14, 1739," in Hinke, *Life and Letters of Boehm,* 276–81; "Enclosure D, Certified Pledges of the Reformed Congregations Towards Ministers' Salaries, February-March 1740," in Hinke, *Life and Letters of Boehm,* 288–89; "The Classis of Amsterdam to Rev. John Philip Boehm, April 1, 1740," in Hinke, *Life and Letters of Boehm,* 298–99; "Mr. Boehm to the Classis of Amsterdam, July 25, 1741, Enclosure C, Letter of the Tulpehocken Consistory to Mr. Boehm, April 20, 1740," in Hinke, *Life and Letters of Boehm,* 342; "Tulpehocken Congregation to Mr. Boehm, March 27, 1744," in Hinke, *Life and Letters of Boehm,* 385; "Report of Mr. Boehm to the Synods of North and South Holland, July 8, 1744," in Hinke, *Life and Letters of Boehm,* 412–13, 416–17; "Mr. Boehm to a Classical Commissioner, December, 1748," in Hinke, *Life and Letters of Boehm,* 449–50; Howell, *Genealogical Guide,* 133–76, passim; and Weis, *Colonial Churches,* 19–100, passim. A list of these German Reformed congregations can be found in table 1. For more information on the German Reformed church during the colonial period, see Dubbs, "History of Reformed Church, German," in *History of Reformed Church, Dutch;* Dubbs, *Reformed Church in Pennsylvania;* Frantz, "United Church of Christ," in Crist, *Penn's Example to the Nations,* 129–34; and Good, *History of Reformed Church.*

10. *Minutes and Letters of the Coetus,* 162–430, passim.

11. *The Goshenhoppen Registers,* 1–122; Fink, "First Catholics in Reading," 92–97, 109; Howell, *Genealogical Guide,* 151, 167; Quinter, *Most Blessed Sacrament Church,* 1–

28, 33–40, 47–50, 60–65; Schrott, *Pioneer German Catholics,* 43–47, 57–60, 82–87, 94–95; and Waldenrath, "Roman Catholicism in Berks County," 93–95, 111–15. For more information on Roman Catholics in the colonies, see. Connelly, "Roman Catholic Church," in Crist, ed., *Penn's Example to the Nations,* 105–10; and Ellis, *Catholics in Colonial America.*

12. "The Charter of Pennsylvania," in Soderlund, *William Penn,* 49; "Congregation of Bangor Church to the Secretary," 23 October 1749, in Perry, *Historical Collections,* 258; The Reverend Thomas Barton to the Secretary of the SPG, 16 November 1764, in Perry, *Historical Collections,* 369–70; Howell, *Genealogical Guide,* 167; and Weis, *Colonial Churches,* 29. Barton's letters to the Revered Dr. Daniel Burton, Secretary of the SPG, published in Perry's *Historical Collections* are dated 8 November 1756 (282–83), 6 December 1760 (294), 6 July 1761 (329), 28 June 1763 (348), 16 November 1764 (369–70), 8 August 1765 (387–88), 10 November 1766 (406), and 17 December 1770 (449). Biographies of the Reverend Thomas Barton include Jeffries, "Thomas Barton," 39–64; and Russell, "Thomas Barton," 313–34. Studies of the Church of England in colonial America include Albright, *History of Protestant Episcopal Church;* Arnold, "Anglicanism in Pennsylvania," in Crist, ed., *Penn's Example to the Nations,* 22–28; and Manross, *History of American Episcopal Church.*

13. William Bird, et al., to the SPG, "The humble Representation of the Subscribers, Inhabitants of the county of Berks in the province of Pennsylvania [1760]," in Perry, *Historical Collections,* 288–89; Letter, The Reverend Alexander Murray to the Secretary of the SPG, 26 March 1772, in Perry, *Historical Collections,* 458; Letter, The Reverend Alexander Murray to the Secretary of the SPG, 25 January 1764, in Perry, *Historical Collections,* 356; and Owen, "Papers," 372–82, 537–43. Murray's letters to the Reverend Dr. Daniel Burton, Secretary of the SPG, published in Owen's collection are dated 9 April 1763 (376–78), 25 January 1764 (378–82), 25 January 1765 (537–38), 8 January 1768 (538–39), 25 September 1768 (539–41), 28 March 1771 (541), 26 March 1772 (542–43), and 26 March 1774 (543). Murray's letters published in Perry's *Historical Collections* are dated 9 April 1763 (344–46), 25 January 1764 (356–59), 25 June 1765 (383–84), 25 March 1769 (438–41, and 26 March 1772 (458–59). Biographies of the Reverend Alexander Murray include Bertolet, "Rectors of Christ Church," 16–17; Dives, "Alexander A. Murray, D.D.," 34–39; Guenther, " 'Faithful Soldier,' " 5–20; and Nolan, "Plaintive Record of a Distracted Missionary," in Nolan, *Early Narratives of Berks County,* 17–34.

14. Perry, *Historical Collections,* 344–46, 356–59, 383–84, 438–41, 458–59; Owen, "Papers," 541, 543; Keim, "Episcopal Church in Reading, Pa.," 72–74; "Church Book for the Congregation at St. Gabriel's Church," 29; and DuHamel, *Historical Annals of Christ Church,* 10–16.

15. Thayer, *Pennsylvania Politics,* 163, 172; Pendleton, " 'Dutch Buggers' "; Pennington, "Anglican Clergy of Pennsylvania," 404–5; Guenther, " 'Faithful Soldier,' " 12–15; Jeffries, "Thomas Barton," 56–61; and Glatfelter, *Pastors and People,* vol. 1, 66–67.

16. *Minutes of Philadelphia Baptist Association,* 23–138, passim; Howell, *Genealogical Guide,* 140, 173; and Weis, *Colonial Churches,* 36, 92. For more information on Baptists in Pennsylvania, see Keim, "Growth of Baptist Denomination," in Crist, ed., *Penn's Example to the Nations,* 33–36.

17. Pilmore, *Journal of Joseph Pilmore,* 135; Nicholson, "Growth of Methodism," 140–42, 162–64; and Witman, *1773 Bicentennial 1973.* Studies of Methodists in Pennsylvania include Maser, "Methodists," in Crist, ed., *Penn's Example to the Nations,* 196–203.

18. Mann, et al., *Nachrichten,* vol. 1, 347; Stoudt, "Mathias Baumann," 136–38, 142–44, 147; Weis, *Colonial Churches,* 71; and Croll, *Annals of the Oley Valley,* 17–19.

19. Letter, The Reverend John Philip Boehm to the Classis of Amsterdam, 12 November 1730, in Hinke, *Life and Letters of Boehm,* 202; Letter, The Reverend John Philip Boehm to

the Classis of Amsterdam, 14 January 1739, in Hinke, *Life and Letters of Boehm,* 278–79; Croll, *Annals of the Oley Valley,* 17; Weiss, *Der in der Americanischen Wildnusz;* and "The Newborn," 359. "The Newborn" is a parallel translation of Weiss's tract, with facing pages in English and in German.

20. Falkenstein, *German Baptist Brethren or Dunkers,* 24, 40, 63, 84–85, 91–92; Durnbaugh, *Brethren in Colonial America,* 65, 79, 179, 182–83, 222; Brumbaugh, *History of German Baptist Brethren,* 297–98, 321; Howell, *Genealogical Guide,* 133, 145, 147; and Weis, *Colonial Churches,* 24, 71, 82, 97. See also Kaylor, "Church of the Brethren," in Crist, ed., *Penn's Example to the Nations,* 45–50; and Sachse, *German Sectarians of Pennsylvania.*

21. Smith, *Mennonite Immigration,* 140–41, 147–48; MacMaster, *Land, Piety, Peoplehood,* 107, 185–86; Quinter, *Most Blessed Sacrament Church,* 24, 40; and Ruth, *Maintaining the Right Fellowship,* 98–99, 103, 140. See also Ruth, "Mennonites," in Crist, ed., *Penn's Example to the Nations,* 85–87.

22. Smith, *Mennonite Immigration,* 229–43; MacMaster, *Land, Piety, Peoplehood,* 70–72, 86–87, 125–27; Hostetler, *Amish Society,* 57–59; Stoltzfus, "Amish Backgrounds," 39; Stoltzfus, "First Amish Mennonite Communities," 237–45; and Howell, *Genealogical Guide,* 150, 153, 173. See also *Early Amish Land Grants.*

23. Brecht, *Genealogical Record,* 22, 67, 69, 71, 76; Kriebel, *Schwenkfelders in Pennsylvania,* 42; Landis, "Schwenkfelders and Their School System," 101; and MacMaster, et al., *Conscience in Crisis,* 219, 228–30, 256–59. For more information on Schwenkfelders, see Erb, "Schwenkfelders in Pennsylvania," in Crist, ed., *Penn's Example to the Nations,* 124–26. For relationships between Schwenkfelders and other denominations, see Frantz, "Schwenkfelders and Moravians," in Erb, *Schwenkfelders in America,* 101–11; Ruth, "Mennonite Reflections on Schwenkfelders," in Erb, *Schwenkfelders in America,* 163–72; and Yoder, "Schwenkfelder-Quaker Connection," in Erb, *Schwenkfelders in America,* 113–62.

24. Hamilton and Hamilton, *History of the Moravian Church;* and Schattschneider, "Moravians in Pennsylvania," in Crist, ed., *Penn's Example to the Nations,* 90–96. See also Weinlick, "Moravianism in the American Colonies," in Stoeffler, *Continental Pietism and Early American Christianity,* 123–63.

25. Hamilton, "The Confusion at Tulpehocken," 235–73; Miller, "Moravian Settlements," 330–33; Nelson, "Moravian Contribution," 3–16; Glatfelter, *Pastors and People,* vol. 1, 80–81, 141, 262–63; Howell, *Genealogical Guide,* 176; Weis, *Colonial Churches,* 71–72; Muhlenberg, *Journals,* 1:170–73; "Boehm's Book Against the Moravians, August 23, 1742," in Hinke, *Life and Letters of Boehm,* 348–72; and *Bethlehem Diary,* 46–199, passim.

26. Miller, "Moravian Settlements," 323–30; Dech, "The North Heidelberg Church," 85–86; *Bethlehem Diary,* 123, 151, 184, 210; Glatfelter, *Pastors and People,* vol. 1, 261; Howell, *Genealogical Guide,* 153; and Weis, *Colonial Churches,* 48. See also "Second Faithful Warning of Mr. Boehm, May 19, 1743," in Hinke, *Life and Letters of Boehm,* 373–84.

27. Stoudt, "Count Zinzendorf," 366–80; Miller, "Moravian Settlements," 312–23; Hamilton, "Moravian Work," 8–18; Durnbaugh, *Brethren in Colonial America,* 284; *Bethlehem Diary,* 37–191, passim; Howell, *Genealogical Guide,* 154; Weis, *Colonial Churches,* 59–60; and "Kirchen-Buch," 14. For the proceedings of the Oley Synod, see *Zuverläßige Beschreibung.*

28. Stoudt, "Count Zinzendorf," 375–78; *Minutes and Letters of the Coetus,* 32; Spaeth, *Documentary History,* 3; Stoudt, "Great Religious Revival," 269–70; and Glatfelter, *Pastors and People,* vol. 1, 117–19. See also Harbaugh, *The Life of Rev. Michael Schlatter.*

29. Hamilton, "Moravian Work," 14; Croll, *Annals of the Oley Valley,* 119–21; Gerhard, "First Preacher of Universalism," 15–19; and Stoudt, "Great Religious Revival," 268–69.

30. Burnett, "Jewish Community," 58–59, 79–80; and Neumann, "American Jewish Letters," 81–99. For more information on Jews in colonial Pennsylvania, see Ashton, *Jewish Life in Pennsylvania* 1–10; and Whiteman, "Pennsylvania Jewry," in Crist, ed., *Penn's Example to the Nations,* 61–64.

31. "Register of Property," 177–301; MacMaster, et al., *Conscience in Crisis,* 364; "Record of County Tax," Berks County, Reading, 1785–1790; Glatfelter, *Pastors and People,* vol. 1, 95, 263; Miller, "Conrad Weiser as a Monk," 169–81; Miller, *History of Reformed Church,* 15–16; Nolan, "Conrad Weiser's Inventory," 265–69; Wallace, *Conrad Weiser,* 573; and Will Book, Berks County, 1:78.

32. Casino, "Anti-Popery," 279–309; Stillé, "Religious Tests," 391; Minutes of the Provincial Council, 29th, 6th mo., 1689, *Minutes of Provincial Council,* vol. 1, 257; "An Act to Ascertain the Number of Members," in Mitchell and Flanders, *Statutes at Large,* vol. 2, 219; Connelly, "Roman Catholic Church," 106, 108–9; and Letter, Justices of Berks County to Governor Robert Hunter Morris, 23 July 1755, *Minutes of Provincial Council,* vol. 6, 503. This oath required officeholders to "make and subscribe the following declarations and profession of his Christian belief" by professing "that I do believe that in the sacrament of the Lord's Supper there is not any transubstantiation of the elements of bread and wine into the body and blood of Christ, at or after the consecration thereof by any person whatsoever; and that the invocation or adoration of the Virgin Mary or any other saint, and the sacrifice of the Mass, as they are now used in the Church of Rome, are superstitious and idolatrous." "Act to Ascertain the Number of Members," 219.

33. "List of Roman Catholicks," 144–45.

34. Muhlenberg, *Journals,* 1:151; "Hill Church Record, Pike Township," copied by J. W. Early, 1–2; Will Book, Berks County, vols. 1–3, passim; *The Goshenhoppen Registers,* 23, 26–100; Burnett, "Jewish Community," 58; and Fry, *Trinity Lutheran Church,* 21. On the relationship between ethnicity and religion, see Marty, "Ethnicity," 5–21; and Stout, "Ethnicity," 204–24. See also Tully, "Englishmen and Germans," 237–56.

35. Glatfelter, *Pastors and People,* vol. 2, 161–70; Bartholomew, "The Union Church," 1–9; MacMaster, *Land, Piety, Peoplehood,* 18; and Wentz, "Lutheran and Reformed Churches," 308–10.

36. Letter, John Philip Boehm to the Classis of Amsterdam, 29 January 1730, in Hinke, *Life and Letters of Boehm,* 185; Letter, John Philip Boehm to the Classis of Amsterdam, 16 March 1739, in Hinke, *Life and Letters of Boehm,* 265; and Muhlenberg, *Journals,* 2:375.

37. Muhlenberg, *Journals,* 1:152; and Glatfelter, *Pastors and People,* vol. 2, 138–47.

38. Mittelberger, *Journey to Pennsylvania,* 47–48.

39. Glatfelter, *Pastors and People,* vol. 1, 15–172; vol. 2, 189–205; and *Minutes and Letters of the Coetus,* 276.

40. Glatfelter, *Pastors and People,* vol. 1, 154–56; and Wagner, *Abscheid-Rede.*

41. Muhlenberg, *Journals,* 1:533; and Glatfelter, *Pastors and People,* vol. 1, 15–172.

42. "Women's Monthly Meeting Book A," 29th day, 5th mo., 1760; 26th day, 6th mo., 1760; Glatfelter, *Pastors and People,* vol. 1, 89–90; *Minutes and Letters of the Coetus,* 226, 236; and Rapp, "Philip Jacob Michael," 14–26.

43. Muhlenberg, *Journals,* 1:154, 2:749–50, 3:34; Glatfelter, *Pastors and People,* vol. 1, 19–20, 92–93, 121–122, 139–43, 152, 165–68; Fry, *Trinity Lutheran Church,* 26–28, 86–88; *Minutes and Letters of the Coetus,* 265–266; *Der Wöchentliche Pennsylvanischer Staatsbote,* 3; "Protocoll über die Verhandlungen mit B. Willy," "Minutes and Letters of the Coetus of Pennsylvania, 1747–1792," transcribed by William John Hinke, 758–60 "Women's Monthly Meeting Book A," passim; "Exeter Monthly Meeting Book A," passim; "Exeter Monthly Meeting Book B," passim; and "Exeter Monthly Meeting Book C," passim. For more information on disciplinary problems among Exeter Friends, see

Guenther, "Social Control," 150–63; and chapter 3. See also Marietta, *Reformation of American Quakerism.*

44. Glatfelter, *Pastors and People,* vol. 1, 125–29, 154–57, 258–64; *Daniel Schumacher's Baptismal Register;* Wagner, *Abscheid-Rede,* passim; *Minutes and Letters of the Coetus,* 309; and "Baptismal and Marriage Records," 147–282.

45. Weis, *Colonial Churches,* 19–107; *Inventory of Church Archives,* 43–44, 108–9, 111, 120, 131, 133, 160; Paul and Howell, *Berks County, Pennsylvania, Births,* vol. 1–3, passim; *Daniel Schumacher's Baptismal Register;* "Bern Church Records," 38–52; "Höhn's Church Records," 53–109; *The Goshenhoppen Registers,* 2–14, 26–41; "Baptismal and Marriage Records," 147–282; and *Early Lutheran Baptisms and Marriages.* Community studies that contain information on religious activity include Becker, "American Revolution as a Community Experience"; Doutrich, "Evolution of an Early American Town"; Ford, "Germans and Other Foreign Stock"; Franz, *Paxton;* Henderson, *Community Development;* Ridner, "'A Handsomely Improved Place'"; Wolf, *Urban Village;* and Wood, *Conestoga Crossroads.*

46. Frantz, "Religion in the Middle Colonies," 9–22. The debate still rages, of course, whether the Mid-Atlantic can be considered a distinctive region within the British North American colonies. See especially Wayne Bodle, "Myth of Middle Colonies Reconsidered," 527–48; and Gough, "Myth of the 'Middle Colonies," 393–419.

Chapter 3. Maintaining "Ye Establish'd Order Amongst Us"

1. Moore, "Society of Friends," in Crist, ed., *Penn's Example to the Nations,* 56; Klein and Hoogenboom, *A History of Pennsylvania,* 28–29, 229; Sharpless, "Quakers in Pennsylvania," 445–58; Barbour and Frost, "George Keith," in *Dictionary of Christianity in America,* 608–9; and Rev. George Keith to the Bishop of London, 2 April 1703, in Perry, *Historical Collections,* 17. See also Frost, *The Keithian Controversy.*

2. Sharpless, "Quakers in Pennsylvania," 535–38. For more information on the uses of queries as a form of social control, see Beeth, "'Know Thyself,'" 3–13.

3. "Exeter Monthly Meeting Book A"; "Exeter Monthly Meeting Book B"; and "Exeter Monthly Meeting Book C," 1785–1789.

4. Tolles, "Quietism Versus Enthusiasm," 26–49; Marietta, *Reformation of American Quakerism,* 3–35, 131–68; Logan, "Gilbert Tennent," in *Dictionary of Christianity in America,* 1164–65; Trinterud, *Forming of an American Tradition,* 86–195; and Philadelphia Men's Quarterly Meeting Minutes, 2nd, 8 mo., 1756. For more information on the Great Awakening in Pennsylvania, see Bonomi, "'Watchful Against the Sects,'" 273–83; Frantz, "Awakening of Religion," 266–88; Lodge, "Crisis of the Churches," 195–210; Lodge, "The Great Awakening"; Maxson, *The Great Awakening;* and Rothermund, *The Layman's Progress.*

5. "Exeter Monthly Meeting Book B," 26th, 7 mo., 1780; 28th, 7 mo., 1784; and "Exeter Monthly Meeting Book C," 30th, 7 mo., 1788.

6. "Exeter Monthly Meeting Book A"; "Exeter Monthly Meeting Book B," passim; "Exeter Monthly Meeting Book C," 1785–1789, and "Women's Monthly Meeting Book A."

7. "Exeter Monthly Meeting Book A," 17th, 11 mo., 1760; 25th, 12 mo., 1760; 29th, 1 mo., 1761.

8. Philadelphia Quarterly Meeting Minutes, 6th, 2 mo., 1758; and "Exeter Monthly Meeting Book A," 30th, 3 mo., 1758.

9. "Women's Monthly Meeting Book A," 29th, 11 mo., 1764; Exodus 20:8 RSV; "Act Against Riotous Sports," *Statutes at Large,* vol. 2, 186–87; "Act for Prevention of Vice," *Statutes and Large,* vol. 12, 313–22; and *The Weekly Advertiser,* 1. See also Jable, "Pennsylvania's Early Blue Laws," 107–21.

10. *Rules of Discipline.* For more information on the Quaker discipline, see Marietta, *Reformation of American Quakerism,* and Frost, *Quaker Family,* 48–63.

11. "Exeter Monthly Meeting Book A," 24th, 2 mo., 1757; and Frost, *Quaker Family,* 55–56.

12. Frost, *Quaker Family,* 55–56. The statistical data are derived from men's and women's minutes of Exeter Monthly Meeting between 1737 and 1789.

13. Marietta, "Attitudes of 18th-Century Friends," 21–22; "Exeter Monthly Meeting Book A," 26th, 3 mo., 1748; and "Women's Monthly Meeting Book A," 26th, 2 mo., 1750.

14. "Exeter Monthly Meeting Book B," 26th, 2 mo., 1783; 27th, 10 mo., 1784; 23rd, 2 mo., 1785; 25th, 5 mo., 1785; "Women's Monthly Meeting Book A," 29th, 6 mo., 1785; and "Exeter Monthly Meeting Book A," 26th, 8 mo., 1756; 23rd, 2 mo., 1758.

15. Minutes of Gwynedd Monthly Meeting, 26th, 5 mo., 1720; 29th, 7 mo., 1730; 30th, 8 mo., 1733; 31st, 1 mo., 1736; 27th, 2 mo., 1736.

16. "Exeter Monthly Meeting Book A," 1737–1759; and Marietta, *Reformation of American Quakerism,* 55. Marietta contended that violations increased 64.1 percent between 1755 and 1756 and more than doubled between 1756 and 1760. Chapter 4 examines the impact of the Seven Years' War on Exeter Friends.

17. "Exeter Monthly Meeting Book A;" "Exeter Monthly Meeting Book B;" "Exeter Monthly Meeting Book C," 1785–1789; and "Women's Monthly Meeting Book A."

18. "Exeter Monthly Meeting Book A," 29th, 1 mo., 1744; 28th, 9 mo., 1751; 27th, 12 mo., 1754; 28th, 3 mo., 1754; 30th, 1 mo., 1755; 27th, 12 mo., 1764; 28th, 2 mo., 1765; 1st, 4 mo., 1765; "Exeter Monthly Meeting Book B," 28th, 5 mo., 1777; 24th, 2 mo., 1779; 31st, 5 mo., 1780; 26th, 7 mo., 1780; "Exeter Monthly Meeting Book C," 1785–1789; and "Women's Monthly Meeting Book A."

19. Bauman, *Reputation of Truth,* 232–34.

20. "Exeter Monthly Meeting Book A," passim; "Exeter Monthly Meeting Book B"; "Exeter Monthly Meeting Book C"; and "Women's Monthly Meeting Book A."

21. Marietta, *Reformation of American Quakerism,* 6–7, 19–23.

22. "Exeter Monthly Meeting Book A," 31st, 7 mo., 1760; and "Exeter Monthly Meeting Book B," 27th, 7 mo., 1768. For more information on drinking in colonial America, see Kross, "Sociology of Drinking," 28–55; and Lender and Martin, *Drinking in America,* 1–40.

23. "Exeter Monthly Meeting Book A," 28th, 3 mo., 1741.

24. Ibid., 28th, 5 mo., 1743; 24th, 2 mo., 1757; 27th, 7 mo., 1757.

25. Ibid., 27th, 9 mo., 1753; 29th, 11 mo., 1753; 30th, 12 mo., 1756; 27th, 6 mo., 1754; 27th, 4 mo., 1758; 25th, 8 mo., 1763; and "Women's Monthly Meeting Book A," 27th, 8 mo., 1752.

26. *Rules of Discipline,* 130–32; and Brunhouse, *Counter-Revolution in Pennsylvania,* 40–41. Chapter 5 examines the effect of the Revolutionary War on members of Exeter Monthly Meeting.

27. "Exeter Monthly Meeting Book A," 1754–1764; 29th, 12 mo., 1763; 23rd, 2 mo., 1764; and "Exeter Monthly Meeting Book B," 1775–1784.

28. *Rules of Discipline,* 65–68; and Marietta, "Attitudes of 18th-Century Friends," 23–24.

29. Marietta, *Reformation of American Quakerism,* 10–19; "Exeter Monthly Meeting Book A"; "Exeter Monthly Meeting Book B," passim; "Exeter Monthly Meeting Book C," 1785–1789; and "Women's Monthly Meeting Book A."

30. "Exeter Monthly Meeting Book A," 28th, 7 mo., 1749; 30th, 9 mo., 1749; 27th, 4 mo., 1751; and "Women's Monthly Meeting Book A," 28th, 7 mo., 1749; 28th, 10 mo., 1749.

31. "Exeter Monthly Meeting Book A," 30th, 12 mo., 1756; 25th, 8 mo., 1757; 27th, 10 mo., 1757; 26th, 1 mo., 1758.

32. Ibid., 29th, 12 mo., 1757; 29th, 9 mo., 1757.

33. Ibid., 29th, 12 mo., 1757; 26th, 12 mo. 1758; and "Women's Monthly Meeting Book A," 26th, 1 mo., 1758; 30th, 3 mo., 1758.

34. Marietta, *Reformation of American Quakerism,* 23–26.

35. "Exeter Monthly Meeting Book A," 30th, 9 mo., 1756; 28th, 10 mo., 1756; 25th, 11 mo., 1756; 30th, 12 mo., 1756; 24th, 2 mo., 1757; 25th, 8 mo., 1757; 31st, 8 mo., 1745 (two separate cases); 28th, 9 mo., 1745. The meeting reported in November 1745 (9th month) that if Moore did not pay Samuel Woolaston "before the next Monthly Meeting he will be at liberty to recover it by Law." This certainly was an unusual penalty for a Friends' meeting to impose, because the *Rules of Discipline* stated that beginning in 1701 the meeting should disown any Friends who collected debts through lawsuits. *Rules of Discipline,* 62.

36. Ibid., 30th, 1 mo., 1749; 30th, 7 mo., 1749; 26th, 8 mo., 1749; 28th, 10 mo., 1749; 31st, 3 mo., 1750; *Rules of Discipline,* 10; and Minutes of Philadelphia Men's Quarterly Meeting, 5th, 12 mo., 1749/50; 1st, 3 mo., 1750; 7th, 2 mo., 1780. Only one other appeal overturned the decision of Exeter Monthly Meeting. In 1769, Philadelphia Quarterly Meeting repealed the disownment of Mary Cleaver, after the women's meeting refused to accept her condemnation of committing fornication with Benjamin Lightfoot and bearing an illegitimate child. Minutes of Philadelphia Men's Quarterly Meeting, 5th, 2 mo., 1769; and "Women's Monthly Meeting Book A," 30th, 9 mo., 1765; 25th, 12 mo., 1765; 18th, 4 mo., 1769.

37. Certificates of Removal (Received), Exeter Monthly Meeting, 1737–1797, 50, 61, 62.

38. Certificates of Removal (Issued), Exeter Monthly Meeting, 1755–1886, 3–137, passim. The removal process is further explored in chapter 7.

39. Marietta, *Reformation of American Quakerism,* 27; Forbes, "'As Many Candles Lighted,'" 125–38; and Forbes, "Quaker Tribalism," in *Friends and Neighbors,* 168–69.

40. Grundy, "'In the World But Not of It,'" 52–59.

41. "Early Minutes," passim.

42. Marietta, "Attitudes of 18th-Century Friends," 17–27; and Frost, *Quaker Family,* 58.

43. "Exeter Monthly Meeting Book A," passim, quote from 28th, 1 mo., 1751; "Exeter Monthly Meeting Book B"; "Exeter Monthly Meeting Book C," 1785–1789; and "Women's Monthly Meeting Book A."

44. These problems followed the pattern for other frontier Quaker communities. See Dowless, "Preserving the Quaker Way," 1–16.

Chapter 4. War and the Frontier Friends

1. Histories of Quakers and politics in colonial Pennsylvania include Bauman, *Reputation of Truth,* 1–183; Bronner, *William Penn's "Holy Experiment";* Marietta, "Quaker Self-Consciousness," in Frost and Moore, *Seeking the Light,* 79–104, Nash, *Quakers and Politics;* Tully, *Forming American Politics,* 257–309; Tully, *William Penn's Legacy;* Wellenreuther, "Political Dilemma," 135–72; and Wellenreuther, "Quest for Harmony," 537–76.

2. Secondary studies of Pennsylvania history for this period include Cochran, *Bicentennial History,* 3–45; Illick, *Colonial Pennsylvania;* Kelley, *Pennsylvania;* Klein and Hoogenboom, *A History of Pennsylvania,* 3–94; Pencak, "The Promise of Revolution," in Miller and Pencak, *Pennsylvania,* 109–15; and Schwartz, *"A Mixed Multitude."* The population figures are derived from Sutherland, *Population Distribution,* 124–34.

3. For more information on the settlement of the Pennsylvania backcountry, see Lemon, *Best Poor Man's Country,* 42–97, 118–49; and Nelson, "Backcountry Pennsylvania."

4. Gertney, "Formation of Berks County," 88–89, 101–9; and "Petition of the Inhabitants," Draper MSS 2 C 8.2–8.3 [microfilm].

5. Gertney, "Formation of Berks County," 88–89, 101–9; Albright, *Two Centuries of Reading,* 1–17; Montgomery, *History of Berks County,* 23–45; Nolan, *Foundation of Town of Reading,* 13–66; and Rupp, *History of Berks and Lebanon,* 3–22.

6. Studies of Quakers and pacifism include Brock, *Pacifism in the United States,* 81–158; Brock, *The Quaker Peace Testimony,* 87–131, 142–54; Davidson, *War Comes to Quaker Pennsylvania;* Hershberger, "Pacifism and the State," 54–74; Hirst, *Quakers in Peace and War;* Ketcham, "Conscience, War, and Politics," 416–439; Marietta, "Conscience, the Quaker Community," 3–27; Marietta, "Wealth, War and Religion," 230–36; and Tully, "Politics and Peace Testimony," 159–77.

7. Ford, "Germans and Other Foreign Stock," 47–48; Davidson, *War Comes to Quaker Pennsylvania,* 113–96; Ketcham, "Conscience, War, and Politics," 416–19; and Wallace, *Indians in Pennsylvania,* 147–51. Studies of the Seven Years' War in Pennsylvania include Kent, *French Invasion of Western Pennsylvania;* Merritt, *At the Crossroads;* Waddell and Bomberger, *French and Indian War;* and Ward, *Breaking the Backcountry.* General histories of the Seven Years' War include Anderson, *Crucible of War;* Gipson, *The British Empire,* vols. 6–8; and Jennings, *Empire of Fortune.* The best biography of Conrad Weiser is Wallace, *Conrad Weiser.* Another interpretation of Weiser's role as diplomat is Merrell, *Into the American Woods.*

8. Crauderueff, *War Taxes,* 6–11; Marietta, *Reformation of American Quakerism,* 154–55; and Thayer, *Pennsylvania Politics,* 41–46.

9. Crauderueff, *War Taxes,* 11–16; and "Epistle of Tender Love," in Woolman, *Journal and Major Essays,* 85–86.

10. Ketcham, "Conscience, War and Politics," 419–21, 428; and Stillé, "Attitude of the Quakers," 301. Studies of Quakers and Indians include Daiutolo, "Early Quaker Perception," 103–19; Kelsey, *Friends and the Indians,* 1–88; and Tolles, "Nonviolent Contact," 93–101.

11. *Votes and Proceedings,* vol. 5, 4245, 4247, 4249; *Minutes of Provincial Council,* vol. 7, 148–49; Sharpless, *History of Quaker Government,* vol. 2, 223–24; and Thayer, *Pennsylvania Politics,* 56.

12. "Act for Forming and Regulating the Militia," vol. 3, 120–37; and Philadelphia Yearly Meeting, Minutes of the Meeting for Sufferings, 1756–1775, fol. 128, cited in MacMaster, et al., *Conscience in Crisis,* 78, 161.

13. Marietta, "Conscience, the Quaker Community," 3–27; and Marietta, *Reformation of American Quakerism,* 150–86.

14. Letter, Conrad Weiser to William Allen, 30 October 1755, *Minutes of Provincial Council,* vol. 6, 659–60; Montgomery, *History of Berks County,* 134–36; and Rupp, *History of Berks and Lebanon,* 33– 79.

15. Nolan, *Foundation of Town of Reading,* 95–140; Albright, *Two Centuries of Reading,* 48–57; Ford, "Germans and Other Foreign Stock," 46–52; and Letter, John Potts, et al., to Robert Hunter Morris, 31 October 1755, *Minutes of Provincial Council,* vol. 6, 667. The forts built in Berks County are discussed in Hunter, *Forts on the Pennsyl-*

vania Frontier, 301–64; and Waddell and Bomberger, *French and Indian War,* 76–78, 84–86.

16. Ford, "Germans and Other Foreign Stock," 50; Montgomery, *History of Berks County,* 104–36; and Rupp, *History of Berks and Lebanon,* 33–79.

17. Letter, Robert Hunter Morris to Thomas Jocelyn, 15 January 1756, *Minutes of Provincial Council,* vol. 6, 774–75; and Letter, Conrad Weiser to Richard Peters, vol. 3, 575. See also MacMaster, et al., *Conscience in Crisis,* 77.

18. Letter, Conrad Weiser to William Denny, 19 October 1756, *Minutes of Provincial Council,* vol. 7, 302; and Letter, Peter Spycker to ???, 28 November 1757, 311–12.

19. *Pennsylvania Gazette,* 20 November 1755, 3; 18 November 1755, 3; 1 April 1756, 3; 11 November 1756, 3; 9 December 1756, 3; 5 May 1757, 3; 4 July 1757, 3; Montgomery, *History of Berks County,* 134–36; and Rupp, *History of Berks and Lebanon,* 33–79, 132–33.

20. "Letter of Do. Stoy to the Classical Deputies, September 30, 1757," *Minutes and Letters of the Coetus,* 163.

21. James, *A People Among Peoples,* 15, 82–83, 169–73; and Lapsansky and Verplanck, *Quaker Aesthetics,* 374.

22. "Exeter Monthly Meeting Book A," 29th, 9 mo., 1757; Minutes, PMS, 10th, 11 mo., 1757; and Owen, "Taxables in Berks County," Over the Mountains, 1754.

23. "Exeter Monthly Meeting Book A," 30th, 12 mo., 1756; 27th, 1 mo., 1757; 24th, 2 mo., 1757; 29th, 9 mo., 1757; 29th, 12 mo., 1757; 25th, 10 mo., 1764; and "The cases of sundry Friends (members of Exeter Monthly Meeting) who have left their habitations on account of the Indians," Misc. Papers, PMS.

24. "The cases of sundry Friends," Misc. Papers, PMS; Minutes, PMS, 10th, 2 mo., 1757; and "Exeter Monthly Meeting Book A," 24th, 2 mo., 1757; 24th, 3 mo., 1757 (source for last quote).

25. "Exeter Monthly Meeting Book A," 29th, 9 mo., 1757; 29th, 12 mo., 1757.

26. Ibid., 28th, 1 mo., 1751; 29th, 9 mo., 1757; and "The cases of sundry Friends," Misc. Papers, PMS.

27. "Exeter Monthly Meeting Book A," 29th, 9 mo., 1757; 28th, 10 mo., 1757; 24th, 11 mo., 1757; 27th, 10 mo., 1763; 25th, 10 mo., 1764; 30th, 5 mo., 1765; Certificates of Removal (Issued), 7; and Inventory of the estate of Richard Stephens, 22 April 1785. Stephens's estate, valued at £27.3.0, was the third smallest among Exeter Friends who died before 1790.

28. "Exeter Monthly Meeting Book A," 20th, 9 mo., 1756; 29th, 9 mo., 1757; 28th, 10 mo., 1757; 25th, 1 mo., 1759; 31st, 5 mo., 1759; 29th, 11 mo., 1759; 17th, 4 mo., 1760; 19th, 6 mo., 1760; 24th, 9 mo., 1761; 29th, 7 mo., 1762; and Minutes, PMS, 10th, 11 mo., 1757; 15th, 2 mo., 1759; 15th, 3 mo., 1759.

29. "Exeter Monthly Meeting Book A," 26th, 8 mo., 1756; 30th, 9 mo., 1756; 28th, 10 mo., 1756; 27th, 1 mo., 1757; 30th, 3 mo., 1757; 29th, 9 mo., 1757; 27th, 10 mo., 1757; 29th, 12 mo., 1757; 26th, 11 mo., 1761; 30th, 4 mo., 1766; Minutes, PMS, 10th, 11 mo., 1757; 17th, 1 mo., 1760; 19th, 6 mo., 1760; and Misc. Papers, PMS, 18.

30. "Exeter Monthly Meeting Book A," 29th, 9 mo., 1757; 30th, 3 mo., 1758; 27th, 4 mo., 1758; 31st, 8 mo., 1758; 26th, 10 mo., 1758; "The cases of sundry Friends," Misc. Papers, PMS; and Minutes, PMS, 10th, 11 mo., 1757.

31. "Exeter Monthly Meeting Book A," 28th, 12 mo., 1758; 22nd, 2 mo., 1759; and "Women's Monthly Meeting Book A," 22nd, 2 mo., 1759.

32. "Women's Monthly Meeting Book A," 29th, 3 mo., 1759; 28th, 5 mo., 1766; "Exeter Monthly Meeting Book A," 29th, 3 mo., 1759; 26th, 4 mo., 1759; 31st, 5 mo., 1759; 29th, 7 mo., 1762; and Certificates of Removal (Issued), 40.

33. "Exeter Monthly Meeting Book A," 1755–1765; "Women's Monthly Meeting Book A," 1755–1766; "Exeter Monthly Meeting Book B," 1765–1766; and Owen, "Taxables in Berks County."

34. Bronner, *The Quakers,* 37; "Exeter Monthly Meeting Book A," 28th, 10 mo., 1756; Letter, James Read to William Denny, 7 November 1756, vol. 3, 36; Letter, Jacob Morgan to William Denny, 4 November 1756, vol. 3, 30; and *Pennsylvania Gazette,* 11 November 1756, 3.

35. Letter, Jonas Seely to John Penn, 10 September 1763, *Minutes of Provincial Council,* vol. 9, 43–44; "Exeter Monthly Meeting Book A," 24th, 11 mo., 1763; Certificates of Removal (Issued), 30; Eshelman, "Genealogical Record of Members," 94–95; *Pennsylvania Gazette,* 17 January 1765, 1; and Petitions to the Orphans Court, Estate File of John Fincher.

36. *Rules of Discipline,* 130–32.

37. *Apology for People called Quakers,* passim.

38. "Exeter Monthly Meeting Book A," 1755–1764; quotes form 28th, 10 mo., 1756; 23rd, 2 mo., 1764; and "Women's Monthly Meeting Book A," 1755–1764. For more information on reform in Philadelphia Yearly Meeting, see Marietta, *Reformation of American Quakerism.*

39. Certificates of Removal (Issued), 3–33; "Exeter Monthly Meeting Book A," 1755–1764, passim; and "Women's Monthly Meeting Book A," 1755–1764. Geographic mobility of Exeter Friends will be discussed in chapter 7.

40. Letter, Edward Biddle to [William Biddle], 16 November 1755, *Minutes of Provincial Council,* vol. 6, 705; Letter, Conrad Weiser to William Allen, 30 October 1755, *Minutes of Provincial Council,* vol. 6, 659–60; and Schultze, *Journals and Papers,* vol. 1, 170–73, cited in MacMaster, et al., *Conscience in Crisis,* 76, 161.

41. Letter, Justices of Berks County to Robert Hunter Morris, 23 July 1755, *Minutes of Provincial Council,* vol. 6, 503.

CHAPTER 5. A CRISIS OF ALLEGIANCE

1. Claussen, "Impact of the Revolutionary War," 52–53; Eshelman, "Society of Friends, 104–9, 117, 119, 121, 123; and "Exeter Monthly Meeting Book B," 31st, 5 mo., 1775. For additional information on Berks County during the Revolution, see Guenther, "Berks County," in Frantz and Pencak, *Beyond Philadelphia,* 67–84. Portions of this chapter first appeared in the article, "A Crisis of Allegiance," 15–34.

2. Montgomery, *Berks County in Revolution,* 23–29; and "Berks County Resolves," vol. 14, 306–07, 322–23.

3. Montgomery, *Berks County in Revolution,* 32–33, 75–144; and Albright, *Two Centuries of Reading,* 82. Montgomery's volume includes lists of members of Berks County companies and regiments in specific battles on 75–144.

4. "Minutes of the Committee of Berks County," 649; Letter, William Reeser to Committee of Safety, 11 September 1775, vol. 4, 653; Albright, *Two Centuries of Reading,* 66; and Montgomery, *Berks County in Revolution,* 37. See also Ousterhout, *A State Divided;* and Ousterhout, "Controlling the Opposition," 3–34.

5. *Testimony of People called Quakers,* 1; and *Rules of Discipline,* 132.

6. *Ancient Testimony,* 3; *Epistle from Yearly-Meeting, Philadelphia,* 3; *Epistle from Yearly-Meeting in London;* and *Epistle from Yearly-Meeting in London.* . . . See also Olson, "Lobbying of London Quakers," 131–52.

7. *To our Friends and Brethren,* 1; *Epistle from Yearly-Meeting, Philadelphia,* 2, 3; and

From our General Spring Meeting, 2. For additional information on Quakers and other pacifist groups during the Revolution, see Currey, "Evangelical Opposition," 17–35; Durnbaugh, "Religion and Revolution," 2–9; James, "Impact of American Revolution," 360–82; Kashatus, *Conflict of Conviction;* Kashatus, "The Friends Fight for Freedom," 4–9; MacMaster, et al., *Conscience in Crisis,* chapters 3 to 7; Marietta, *Reformation of American Quakerism,* chapters 11 and 12; MacMaster, "Neither Whig nor Tory," 8–24; Marietta, "Wealth, War and Religion," 236–41; and Mekeel, *Relation of Quakers to American Revolution.* For additional information on religion in Pennsylvania during the American Revolution, see Frantz, "'Prepare Thyself,'" 28–32.

8. *Rules of Discipline,* 130–34.

9. Blanco, *Jonathan Potts* 32–34; Will of Frederick Weiser, 9 December 1773, Will Book, vol. 2, 140–46; and Will of Edward Biddle, 27 July 1779, Will Book, vol. 3, 8–9. Potts's wife Grace did submit a Paper of Condemnation expressing remorse for violating the discipline and transferred her membership to Exeter Monthly Meeting in 1774.

10. Blanco, *Jonathan Potts,* 1–82; Blanco, "Diary of Jonathan Potts," 119–30; Claussen, "Reading Doctor," 8–9; Montgomery, *Berks County in Revolution,* 263–64; and "Berks County Resolves," 322–23.

11. Blanco, *Jonathan Potts,* 83–159; Claussen, "Reading Doctor," 9–11, 22–26; and Duncan, *Medical Men,* 184.

12. Duncan, *Medical Men,* 184, 275, 300–301, 331; Claussen, "Reading Doctor," 27; and Blanco, *Jonathan Potts,* 161–212.

13. "Exeter Monthly Meeting Book B," 27th, 12 mo., 1775; 28th, 8 mo., 1776; 1777–1783, passim.

14. Ibid., 26th, 6 mo., 1776; 28th, 1 mo., 1778; 27th, 11 mo., 1776; 25th, 10 mo., 1780; 25th, 4 mo., 1781; *Rules of Discipline,* 133–34; Eshelman, "Genealogical Record"; and Montgomery, *Berks County in Revolution,* 131, 133, 165.

15. Marietta, *Reformation of American Quakerism,* 234; and Radbill, "Socioeconomic Background," 8–10, 60, 122.

16. "Exeter Monthly Meeting Book B," 25th, 7 mo., 1781; and "Women's Monthly Meeting Book A," 25th, 10 mo., 1780.

17. *State of Accounts of Jacob Morgan,* 8–49; and "Exeter Monthly Meeting Book B," 1775–1783.

18. "Proceedings of the Committee [of Observation], vol. 14, 308–9; and "Register of Property," 175–301. For more on Gaius Dickinson, see Cook, "Gaius and Mary Dickinson," 35–38.

19. Brunhouse, *Counter-Revolution in Pennsylvania,* 40–41; "Remonstrance and Protest of Prisoners," vol. 6, 509; and "Act Obliging Male White Inhabitants," vol. 9, 110–14. In 1784, Benjamin Rush unsuccessfully argued for the repeal of the Test Act, contending that the law was contrary to the principles of freedom upon which the Revolution had been fought. Benjamin Rush, *Considerations upon Present Test-Law.*

20. "Exeter Monthly Meeting Book B," 24th, 2 mo., 1779; 28th, 4 mo., 1779; 26th, 5 mo., 1779; 28th, 7 mo., 1779; 25th, 8 mo., 1779; 27th, 10 mo., 1779; 24th, 11 mo., 1779; 28th, 1 mo., 1780; 4th, 10 mo., 1780; 25th, 10 mo., 1780; 27th, 2 mo., 1781; 25th, 7 mo., 1781; 28th, 8 mo., 1782; 29th, 1 mo., 1783; 18th, 5 mo., 1783; Minutes of Philadelphia Men's Quarterly Meeting, 7th, 2 mo., 1780; and Owen, "Names of Persons who took Oath of Allegiance," vol. 268, passim. Leadership positions included clerk, overseers, elders, and representatives to Philadelphia Quarterly Meeting. At least thirty active Exeter Friends swore or affirmed the oath of allegiance; ten never faced punishment, four of them proclaimed loyalty in 1786 and 1787.

21. "Exeter Monthly Meeting Book B," 1779–1783.

22. Graydon, *Memoirs,* 325–26.

23. Misc. Papers, PMS, 15, 30, 48, 49, 83.

24. Misc. Papers, PMS, 30, 48. See also Letter, ??? to James Read, 25 March 1777, RG 27, Records of Pennsylvania's Revolutionary Governments, 1775–1790, Clemency File, 1775–1790.

25. Misc. Papers, PMS, 19. For additional information on Quakers in Northumberland County, see Eshelman, "History of Catawissa Friends' Meeting," 4–20; and Rhoads, *Catawissa Quaker Meeting*. Evidence of the tense relations can be seen in Taylor, *The Susquehannah Company Papers,* vol. 5, 67, 81–86; vol. 6, 325–26, 335, 345–46. Recent accounts of the situation in Wyoming include Martin, "The Wyoming Valley Dispute"; Miner, *History of the Wyoming Valley;* Moyer, "Wild Yankees"; Ousterhout, "Frontier Vengeance," 330–63; Russ, *Pennsylvania Present Boundaries,* 49–52; and Stefon, "The Wyoming Valley," in Frantz and Pencak, *Beyond Philadelphia,* 133–52.

26. Misc. Papers, PMS, 11; and Roberts, "Journal," 71–73. See also Roberts, "Some account of me ... ," Miscellaneous Manuscripts.

27. Roberts, "Journal," 73; Misc. Papers, PMS, 20, 21; and "Exeter Monthly Meeting Book B," 25th, 10 mo., 1780.

28. Letter, Moses Roberts to the General Assembly of Pennsylvania, 1st day, 10th month, 1780, RG 27; and Misc. Papers, PMS, 7, 13, 29. See also Letter, Moses Roberts to Jane Roberts, 23 October 1780, Vaux Papers, Correspondence; Letter, Moses Roberts to John Pemberton, 30 December 1780, Pemberton Papers, vol. 35, 68–69; Letter, Moses Roberts to John Pemberton, 15 December 1781, Pemberton Papers, vol. 36, 37.

29. *Brief Memoir Concerning Abel Thomas,* 12–42; and "Exeter Monthly Meeting Book B," 25th, 1 mo., 1775; 29th, 3 mo., 1775; 30th, 8 mo., 1775; 30th, 10 mo., 1776; 27th, 11 mo., 1776; 29th, 1 mo., 1777; 26th, 2 mo., 1777; 25th, 3 mo., 1778; 26th, 6 mo., 1778; 28th, 10 mo., 1778. See also Thomas, "Abel Thomas's account of capture in New Jersey," Society Collection.

30. "Exeter Monthly Meeting Book B," 24th, 11 mo., 1779; 23rd, 2 mo., 1780; 26th, 12 mo., 1780; 25th, 7 mo., 1781; 26th, 12 mo., 1781.

31. Ibid., 30th, 3 mo., 1780; 26th, 4 mo., 1780; 31st, 5 mo., 1780; 28th, 6 mo., 1780; 31st, 1 mo., 1781; 27th, 2 mo., 1781; 30th, 3 mo., 1781; 29th, 1 mo., 1783. See also Receipt from George Hughes & Co., 7 August 1782, for six bags of shot for John Cadwalader, Cadwalader Collection.

32. Bodle and Thibaut, *Valley Forge,* vol. 3, 77–80, 92; Metz, *Historical Furnishings Report,* 5–15; Treese, *Valley Forge,* 12–13; "Exeter Monthly Meeting Book B," 26th, 11 mo., 1777; 26th, 7 mo., 1780; Philadelphia Women's Quarterly Meeting Minutes, 4th, 5 mo., 1778; and Eshelman, "Society of Friends," 108.

33. "Exeter Monthly Meeting Book B," 1775–1783.

34. Ibid.; quote from 28th, 5 mo., 1783. Northumberland County officials had questioned the prisoners regarding Job Webb's actions while they were held in Lancaster jail; they each replied that they "knew nothing about it until after it was reported they were come back." Misc. Papers, PMS, 11.

35. "Exeter Monthly Meeting Book B," 26th, 7 mo., 1775; 29th, 11 mo., 1775; 27th, 12 mo., 1775; 31st, 1 mo., 1776; Lippincott, *Abington Friends,* 32; *Two Hundred Fifty Years of Quakerism,* 102; and Martin, *Gwynedd Monthly Meeting,* 16.

36. Grundy, "In the World But Not of It," 92–109. See also "Bucks County Quakers," 291–99.

37. *Bi-Centennial of Brick Meeting House,* 54–58.

38. Marietta, *Reformation of American Quakerism,* 240–42; and Michel, "Philadelphia Quakers," 54–109.

39. Kashatus, *Conflict of Conviction,* 101–65; and "Exeter Monthly Meeting Book B," 24th, 11 mo., 1779.

40. Misc. Papers, PMS, 7. See also Eshelman, "History of Catawissa Friends' Meeting," 12, 17.

CHAPTER 6. THE QUAKER ETHIC

1. "Some Account of the Province in Pennsylvania," in Soderlund, *William Penn,* 58–65.

2. Tolles, *Meeting House and Counting House,* 51–62; and Nash, *The Urban Crucible,* 73–74. See also Doerflinger, *A Vigorous Spirit of Enterprise;* and Tully, "Economic Opportunity," 111–28. The standard monograph on the colonial economy is McCusker and Menard, *Economy of British America.* For more information on the Quaker ethic in England, see Walvin, *The Quakers: Money and Morals.*

3. Turner, "Significance of Frontier," 199–227.

4. Pole, "Historians," 626–46.

5. "Record of County Tax, 1754," Exeter, Maiden Creek, and Robeson Townships.

6. "Record of County Tax," Exeter Township, 1754, 1758, 1762, 1770, 1775; "Proprietary Return," vol. 18, 42–45; "Register of Property," 219–23; "Return and Assessment 1781," vol. 18, 478–81; and "Assessment of Taxes," vol. 18, 740–44.

7. "Record of County Tax," Robeson Township, 1754, 1758, 1762, 1770, 1775; "Proprietary Return," 71–74; "Register of Property," 279–83; "Return and Assessment 1781," 518–21; and "Assessment of Taxes," 781–85.

8. "Record of County Tax," Maiden Creek Township, 1754, 1758, 1762, 1770, 1775; "Proprietary Return," 69–71; "Register of Property," 245–48; "Return and Assessment 1781," 504–6; and "Assessment of Taxes," 764–66.

9. Becker, "American Revolution as a Community Experience," 440, 466, 485; and "Register of Property," 219–23, 245–48, 279–83.

10. Lemon and Nash, "Distribution of Wealth," 1–24. See also Ball, "Dynamics of Population and Wealth," 621–44; and Lemon, *Best Poor Man's Country.*

11. See note 6; "Proprietary Return," 69–71; and "Record of County Tax," Robeson Township, 1758.

12. "Record of County Tax," Exeter Township, Maiden Creek Township, 1754, 1758, 1762, 1770, 1775; "Proprietary Return," vol. 18, 42–45, 69–71; "Register of Property," 219–23, 245–48, 279–83; "Return and Assessment 1781," vol. 18, 478–81, 518–21; and "Assessment of Taxes," vol. 18, 740–44, 781–85.

13. "Record of County Tax," Exeter Township, 1754; "Register of Property," 279–83; and "Return and Assessment 1781," 518–21.

14. "Record of County Tax," Maiden Creek Township, 1754, 1758, 1762, 1770, 1775; Exeter Township, 1770; and "Proprietary Return," 42–45. A list of the leaders of Exeter Monthly Meeting may be found in Appendix 1.

15. "Record of County Tax," Exeter Township, 1754, 1758, 1762, 1770, 1775; "Proprietary Return," 42–45; "Register of Property," 219–23; "Return and Assessment 1781," 478–81; and "Assessment of Taxes," 740–44.

16. "Record of County Tax," Robeson Township, 1754, 1758, 1762, 1770, 1775; "Proprietary Return," 71–74 "Register of Property," 279–83; "Return and Assessment 1781," 518–21; and "Assessment of Taxes," 781–85.

17. "Record of County Tax," Robeson Township, 1770, 1775; "Proprietary Return," 71–74; "Register of Property," 279–83; "Return and Assessment 1781," 518–21; and "Assessment of Taxes," 781–85.

18. "Record of County Tax," Robeson Township, 1762, 1770, 1775; "Proprietary Re-

turn," 42–45, 71–74; "Register of Property," 219–23, 279– 83; "Return and Assessment 1781," 478–81; "Assessment of Taxes," 740–44; and "Record of County Tax," Exeter Township, 1762, 1770, 1775.

19. "Record of County Tax," Exeter Township, Maiden Creek Township, 1754, 1758, 1762, 1770, 1775; "Proprietary Return," 42–45, 69–71; "Register of Property," 219–23, 245–48, 279–83; "Return and Assessment 1781," 478–81, 518–21; "Assessment of Taxes," 740–44, 781–85; and Becker, "American Revolution as a Community Experience," 270.

20. "Exeter Monthly Meeting Book A," 31st, 8 mo., 1745; 28th, 9 mo., 1745; 30th, 9 mo., 1756; 28th, 10 mo., 1756; and "Record of County Tax," Robeson Township, 1754.

21. "Exeter Monthly Meeting Book A," 28th, 6 mo., 1755; 31st, 7 mo., 1755.

22. Ibid., 28th, 2 mo., 1754; 28th, 3 mo., 1754; 31st, 10 mo., 1754; 26th, 12 mo., 1754; 29th, 5 mo., 1755; "Exeter Monthly Meeting Book B," 28th, 1 mo., 1767; 25th, 11 mo., 1767; and Minutes of Philadelphia Men's Quarterly Meeting, 2nd, 11 mo., 1767.

23. "Exeter Monthly Meeting Book A," 28th, 10 mo., 1762; 25th, 11 mo., 1762; 26th, 5 mo., 1763; 30th, 6 mo., 1763; "Exeter Monthly Meeting Book B," 30th, 3 mo., 1780; 26th, 4 mo., 1780; 31st, 5 mo., 1780; 28th, 6 mo., 1780; 31st, 1 mo., 1781; 27th, 2 mo., 1781; 30th, 3 mo., 1781; 29th, 1 mo., 1783; "Exeter Monthly Meeting Book C,", 27th, 5 mo., 1789; and "Women's Monthly Meeting Book A," 28th, 10 mo., 1762; 25th, 11 mo., 1762; 30th, 12 mo., 1762; 24th, 2 mo., 1763; 31st, 3 mo., 1763; 28th, 4 mo., 1763; 26th, 5 mo., 1763; 30th, 6 mo., 1763; 28th, 7 mo., 1763; 25th, 8 mo., 1763; 27th, 10 mo., 1763; 29th, 12 mo., 1763; 26th, 1 mo., 1764; 30th, 1 mo., 1765; 1st, 4 mo., 1765; 25th, 4 mo., 1765; 26th, 6 mo., 1765; 28th, 2 mo., 1781.

24. "Proprietary Return," 3–86; and "Register of Property," 177–301. For occupational diversity in Reading, see Becker, "American Revolution as a Community Experience," 108–47. For economic development in colonial Pennsylvania, see Bining, *Pennsylvania Iron Manufacture;* and Fletcher, *Pennsylvania Agriculture and Country Life.*

25. "Register of Property," 219–23; and "Return and Assessment 1781," 478–81.

26. Ibid., 279–83; and Ibid., 518–21.

27. Lightfoot, *Benjamin Lightfoot,* 9–10. See also Frankhouser, "Surveying the County Line," 110–14.

28. Daybook of Benjamin Lightfoot, 6, 7, and 20; For colonial accounting practices, see Gambino and Palmer, *Management Accounting in Colonial America.*

29. Daybook of Benjamin Lightfoot.

30. Ibid., 9, 23.

31. Letter, Benjamin Lightfoot to John Reynell, 7 April 1770, Gratz MSS, Coates-Reynell Papers, Case 7, Box 4; and Lightfoot, *Benjamin Lightfoot,* 11–21.

32. Ledger of Moses Boone, 1778–1822; Spraker, *Boone Family,* 48, 95; "Register of Property," 177–301; "Return and Assessment 1780," vol. 18, 305–430; "Return and Assessment 1781," 433–555; and "Assessment of Taxes," pp. 693–814. For more on Moses Boone's business relationships, see Guenther, "World of Moses Boone," 19–23.

33. Ledger of Moses Boone, 1–77.

34. Ibid., pp. 6, 36.

35. Grantee Index, Berks County, passim; Warrantee Township Maps, Herbein, "Berks County, Pennsylvania Warrantee Township Maps Index, Original Land Holdings," passim; and Warrantee Township Maps, Berks County, Pennsylvania (available for Bern, Breck-nock, Caernarvon, Cumru, Exeter, Lower Heidelberg, Reading, Robeson, Spring, Tilden, Union, and Upper Tulpehocken Townships).

36. Will Book, Berks County, vol. 1–3, B; "Exeter Monthly Meeting Book A," 27th, 4 mo., 1758; 31st, 8 mo., 1758; and Williams and Williams, *Index of Berks County Wills.*

37. Will Book 1:4–172, passim; 2:26–355, passim; 3:8–179, passim.

38. Inventories of the estates of James Boone (1785), Jeremiah Boone (1787), John Boone (1773), Joseph Boone (1785), Judah Boone (1787), William Boone (1772), Derrick Clever (1768), Mary Clews (1782), Thomas Davis (1786), Samuel Embree (1786), John Fincher (1763), John Harrison (1786), Jonathan Hughes (1768), James Hutton (1782), Jacob Lightfoot (1784), Joseph Lightfoot (1784), Francis Parvin (1767), Evan Thomas (1757), Joseph Webb (1781), Henry Willits (1755), Jesse Willits (1782), John Wily (1755), and Samuel Woolaston (August 1768). For more information on the use of probate records, see Main, "Probate Records," 89–99; and Shammas, "Constructing a Wealth Distribution," 297–307.

39. Will of Anthony Lee, 19 May 1755, 12 Aug 1763, Will Book 1:135–38; Will of Derrick Clever, 25 Oct 1767, Will Book 2:39; and Will of Benjamin Lightfoot, 1 Apr 1777, Will Book 2:345–46. For a comparison with Quaker estate practices in a larger community, see Thatcher, "'To Desire an Inheritance Incorruptible'."

40. Inventory of John Hughes, 13 Aug 1766; Letter of Administration for John Hughes, Administration Book 2:113; Inventory of John Boone, 24 Apr 1773; Letter of Administration for John Boone, Administration Book 3:96; Will of Joseph Barger, 18 Jul 1769, Will Book 2:112; Inventory of Joseph Barger, 17 Aug 1772; Will of Richard Stephens, 11 Sep 1781, Will Book B:112–14; Inventory of Richard Stephens, 22 Apr 1784; Inventory of Joseph Boone, 4 Jun 1776; and Letter of Administration for Joseph Boone, Administration Book 3:156.

41. Inventory of Evan Thomas, 4 Feb 1757; and "Exeter Monthly Meeting Book A," 30th, 12 mo., 1756; 28th, 5 mo., 1761.

42. Williams and Williams, *Index of Berks County Wills,* passim; Paul and Howell, *Berks County, Pennsylvania, Births;* Fritsch, "Testation Practices"; Fritsch, "Women Inside the Law"; Matthews, "'Set Thy House in Order'," 36–40; and Roeber, "German-American Concepts," 141. Women in other Pennsylvania counties also left wills. See Bethke, "Chester County Widow Wills," 36–40; and Jensen, *Loosening the Bonds,* 18–27. See also Salmon, *Women and Law of Property;* and Wilson, *Life After Death.*

43. Will Book 2:73–75, 92.

44. Ibid., 29–30, 171–72, 253; B:178–79; Will of Eleanor Parvin, 8 Jan 1776, Will Book 2:246–47; Will of William Boone, 23 May 1768, Will Book 2:100; and Will of Jeremiah Boone, 20 Feb 1787, Will Book B:196.

45. Morgan, "The Puritan Ethic," in Greene, *Reinterpretation of American Revolution,* 235–51.

46. Draper MSS, 2 B 35.

47. "Exeter Monthly Meeting Book A," 27th, 4 mo., 1758; 31st, 8 mo., 1758.

CHAPTER 7. "A RESTLESS DESIRE"

1. Turner, "Significance of Frontier," 200. Portions of this chapter first appeared in the article, Guenther, "'A Restless Desire,'" 331–60.

2. Ibid., 199–227; Klein and Hoogenboom, *The History of Pennsylvania,* 3–21; Mekeel, "The Founding Years," in Moore, *Friends in the Delaware Valley,* 15–16; and Moore, "Society of Friends in Pennsylvania," in Crist, ed., *Penn's Example to the Nations,* 54–56. Other studies of backcountry settlement in colonial America include Bailyn, *Voyagers to the West;* Elliott, *Quakers on the American Frontier;* Lemon, *Best Poor Man's Country;* Meinig, *The Shaping of America,* vol. 1: *Atlantic America;* Merritt, *At the Crossroads;* Morgan, *Wilderness at Dawn;* and Nobles, "Breaking into the Backcountry," 641–70. For this chapter, the Turner interpretation, although dated, is most applicable.

3. Mekeel, "The Founding Years," 15–16; and *Inventory of Church Archives,* 43–45, 108–11, 120–21, 131, 133, 160, 174–175.

4. For additional information on the settlement of the Pennsylvania interior, see Florin, *Advance of Frontier Settlement;* and Nelson, "Backcountry Pennsylvania."

5. Wallace, *Daniel Boone in Pennsylvania,* 1; Eshelman, "Anthony and Mary Lee," 113–16; and Eshelman, "Society of Friends," 104–5. Additional accounts of the Boone settlement in Berks County include Bakeless, *Daniel Boone,* 3–7; Bogart, *Daniel Boone,* 14–16; Faragher, *Daniel Boone,* 9–10; Hill, *Daniel Boone,* 16–18; Lofaro, *Life and Adventures of Daniel Boone,* 1–3; and Spraker, *Boone Family,* 20–22.

6. Minutes of Gwynedd Men's Monthly Meeting, 1720–1737, passim; and Eshelman, "Society of Friends," 105.

7. *Book of Discipline,* 81–82; Lapsansky and Verplanck, *Quaker Aesthetics,* 377; and Certificates of Removal (Issued), 3–137.

8. "Exeter Monthly Meeting Book A," 30th, 9 mo., 1756. For comments pertaining to problems in attending meetings or in following the Quaker discipline, see Certificates of Removal (Received), 11–12, 56, 61–62, 70; and Certificates of Removal (Issued), 3–90, passim. For more remarks pertaining to traveling Friends, see Certificates of Removal (Received), 3–96, passim; and Certificates of Removal (Issued), 14–129, passim.

9. The phenomenon of family ties playing an important role in settlement patterns has been addressed in Kross, *Evolution of an American Town: Newtown;* Rutman and Rutman, *A Place in Time;* and Snydacker, "Kinship and Community," 41–61.

10. "Exeter Monthly Meeting Book A"; "Exeter Monthly Meeting Book B"; "Exeter Monthly Meeting Book C," 1785–1789; "Women's Monthly Meeting Book A"; and Certificates of Removal (Received), 2–102. For more information on the settlement of German Lutheran and Reformed in the Shenandoah Valley, see Glatfelter, *Pastors and People,* vol. 1, 484–506. See also Bronner, "Inter-colonial Relations," 3–17; Fawcett, "Quaker Migration," 102–8.

11. Certificates of Removal (Issued), 3–137.

12. Ibid., 10, 13, 31, 45–46, 64, 88, 113–14, 129, 133; "Exeter Monthly Meeting Book A"; "Exeter Monthly Meeting Book B"; "Exeter Monthly Meeting Book C," 1785–1789; "Women's Monthly Meeting Book A"; and Certificates of Removal (Received), 36.

13. Certificates of Removal (Issued), 47, 49, 56, 84–85, 131.

14. "Exeter Monthly Meeting Book A," passim; "Exeter Monthly Meeting Book B"; "Exeter Monthly Meeting Book C," 1785–1789; and "Women's Monthly Meeting Book A."

15. "Exeter Monthly Meeting Book A," 30th, 12 mo., 1756; 25th, 8 mo., 1757; 27th, 10 mo., 1757; 26th, 1 mo., 1758; 28th, 4 mo., 1763; 29th, 11 mo., 1764; "Exeter Monthly Meeting Book B," 18th, 4 mo., 1769; 3rd, 10 mo., 1770; 29th, 1 mo., 1772; 28th, 4 mo., 1763; and Eshelman, "Genealogical Record."

16. Hinshaw, *Encyclopedia of Quaker Genealogy,* 6:309–85, 412.

17. McGhee, "Maryland Quaker (Friends) Records," 2:40, 46–47, 50, 61–62; 2 (Part 2):17–135, passim.

18. Hinshaw, *Encyclopedia of Quaker Genealogy,* 1:410, 423, 1029, 1048–49; 2:207, 247; 6:384–85, 406, 412, 414, 452, 473, 509, 586; and Davis, *Quaker Records in Georgia,* 52, 69–70, 72–74, 101, 112, 122–23.

19. "Exeter Monthly Meeting Book A," passim; "Exeter Monthly Meeting Book B"; "Exeter Monthly Meeting Book C," 1785–1789; "Women's Monthly Meeting Book A"; Walmer, *100 Years at Warrington,* 166, 168; and Hinshaw, *Encyclopedia of Quaker Genealogy,* 1: 385–86, 401, 410, 421, 538, 1029, 1048–49; 2:247; 6:385–86, 405, 437, 473, 479, 495, 586.

20. "Exeter Monthly Meeting Book A," 31st, 5 mo., 1740; 26th, 7 mo., 1753; Hinshaw, *Encyclopedia of Quaker Genealogy,* 1:388, 1029, 1048; 6:309, 385–86; and Davis, *Quaker Records in Georgia,* 48.

21. Hinshaw, *Encyclopedia of Quaker Genealogy,* 1:370–430, 1029, 1048–1049; Hitz, "Wrightsborough Quaker Town," in Davis, *Quaker Records in Georgia,* 10–14; and "Exeter Monthly Meeting Book A," 28th, 5 mo., 1748; 28th, 6 mo., 1753; 25th, 7 mo., 1754; 31st, 7 mo., 1755; 28th, 8 mo., 1755; 30th, 6 mo., 1757; 25th, 8 mo., 1757; 25th, 5 mo., 1758. Quaker settlement in North Carolina is examined in Dowless, "Quakers of Colonial North Carolina." Quaker settlement in South Carolina is discussed in McCormick, "Quakers of Colonial South Carolina." The settlement of the South Carolina backcountry is explored in Johnson, *Frontier in the Colonial South.*

22. Hinshaw, *Encyclopedia of Quaker Genealogy,* 6:384–607, passim. For additional information on Quaker settlement in Virginia, see Gragg, *Migration in Early America.* The settlement of the Virginia backcountry is also examined in Beeman, *Evolution of Southern Backcountry.* The religious diversity of the Shenandoah Valley of Virginia is described in Frantz, "Religious Development of Early German Settlers," 66–100.

23. Hollenbach, "Index," Faust, "Index," passim. The lives of Derrick Clever and his family in early Berks County are described in Owens, *A Fair and Happy Land,* 25–37.

24. "Record of County Tax," Exeter, Maiden Creek, and Robeson Townships, 1754, 1758, 1762, 1770, 1775, "Proprietary Return," 42–45, 69–74; "Register of Property," 219–23, 245–48, 279–83; "Return and Assessment," 478–81, 504–6, 518–21; and "Assessment of Taxes," 740–44, 764–66, 781–85.

25. Theiss, "Quakers to Central Pennsylvania," 67–70; Eshelman, "History of Catawissa Friends' Meeting," 4–12; Meginness, *Otzinachson,* vol. 1, 377–79; and Rhoads, *Catawissa Quaker Meeting,* 15–18, 58–59.

26. Eshelman, "Genealogical Record"; "Exeter Monthly Meeting Book C," 31st, 10 mo., 1787; and Rhoads, *History of Catawissa Quaker Meeting,* 19–23, 60–61.

27. "Exeter Monthly Meeting Book C," 28th, 5 mo., 1788; Theiss, "Quakers to Central Pennsylvania," 72–73; Rhoads, *History of Catawissa Quaker Meeting,* 27, 65–66; and Certificates of Removal (Received), 46, 48.

28. Draper MSS, 1 B 34; Yogg, *"Best Place for Health and Wealth,"* 136; and Kelley, *Pennsylvania,* 648. See also Gragg, *Migration in Early America;* and Mitchell, *Commercialism and Frontier.*

29. "Exeter Monthly Meeting Book A," passim; "Exeter Monthly Meeting Book B," 1765–1774, passim; and Forbes, "As Many Candles Lighted," 107–9.

30. "Exeter Monthly Meeting Book A," passim; "Exeter Monthly Meeting Book B"; "Exeter Monthly Meeting Book C," 1785–1789; "Women's Monthly Meeting Book A"; and Roberts, *Old Richland Families,* 60–62.

31. Specht, "Removing to a Remote Place," 45–69.

32. Wallace, *Daniel Boone in Pennsylvania,* p. 16.

CHAPTER 8. "TO START INSTRUCTING YOUNG FRIENDS"

1. James, "Quaker Meetings and Education," 88; "Frame of Government," in Soderlund, *William Penn,* 125; "Law About Education," in *Statutes at Large,* vol. 1, 84; "Law About Education of Youth," in *Statutes at Large,* vol. 1, 211–12; and "Minutes of Provincial Council and Assembly," 24 March 1683, in Soderlund, *William Penn,* 248.

2. Straub, "Quaker School Life," 449, citing Minutes, Philadelphia Yearly Meeting, 15–19 July 1722; and Brinton, *Quaker Education,* 23–29. See also Marietta, "Quaker

Family Education," 3–16; Kashatus, "What Love Can Do," 4–9; and Tully, "Literacy Levels," 301–12.

3. Livingood, *Reformed Church Schools,* 267; Maurer, *Early Lutheran Education,* 265; *Neue Unpartheyische Readinger Zeitung und Anzeigs-Nachrichten,* 1; Woody, *Early Quaker Education,* 190; Wetzel, *History of First Reformed Church,* 41; and Mann, et al., *Nachrichten,* 2:181.

4. "Frame of Government," 131; and Brinton, *Quaker Education,* 79.

5. Woody, *Early Quaker Education,* 41–166.

6. Jones, "Schools," 136–39; and Woody, *Early Quaker Education,* 192.

7. "Exeter Monthly Meeting Book A," 16th, 10 mo., 1758; "Exeter Monthly Meeting Book B," 27th, 4 mo., 1774; Brinton, *Quaker Education,* 53; and James, *People Among Peoples,* 272, 69, 70.

8. "Exeter Monthly Meeting Book B," 25th, 2 mo., 1778; 29th, 8 mo., 1781; 31st, 7 mo., 1782; and "Women's Monthly Meeting Book A," 26th, 8 mo., 1778.

9. "Exeter Monthly Meeting Book B," 25th, 2 mo., 1784; 28th, 4 mo., 1784.

10. Ibid., 28th, 4 mo., 1784.

11. Kemp, "Early Schools," 67–68; and Albright, *Two Centuries of Reading,* 47.

12. "Exeter Monthly Meeting Book A," 29th, 4 mo., 1762; "Exeter Monthly Meeting Book B," 28th, 4 mo., 1784; Spraker, *Boone Family,* 23, 47–48 (from a paper entitled "The Boone Family," by P. G. Bertolet, 25 May 1860); and McCarthy, "Daniel Boone," 35.

13. "Exeter Monthly Meeting Book B," 25th, 2 mo., 1784; 24th, 11 mo., 1784; and Jones, "Schools," 139.

14. "Cipher Book of Mordecai Wright. 1st mo., 7th. 1786," 2 vols.; and Jones, "Schools," 139.

15. "Exeter Monthly Meeting Book B," 28th, 4 mo., 1784.

16. Ibid., 25th, 2 mo., 1784; 28th, 4 mo., 1784; Ford, "Germans and Other Foreign Stock," 34; and Woody, *Early Quaker Education,* 81–82.

17. "Exeter Monthly Meeting Book C," 28th, 2 mo., 1787; 28th, 3 mo., 1787; 27th, 6 mo., 1787; and Montgomery, *History of Berks County,* 798.

18. "Exeter Monthly Meeting Book C," 31st, 10 mo., 1787; 25th, 2 mo., 1789; 28th, 1 mo., 1795; Woody, *Quaker Education,* 82; Eshelman, "Short History of Reading Friends' Meeting," 4; and Jones, "Schools," 139. For another view of Quaker education at the turn of the century, see Jensen, "Not Only Ours But Others," 3–20.

19. Letter, The Reverend Alexander Murray to the SPG, 25 September 1768, in Owen, "Papers," 540.

20. Knauss, *Social Conditions,* 75; Maurer, *Early Lutheran Education,* 213; and Wetzel, *History of First Reformed Church,* 39. For more information in the Charity School movement, see Weber, *Charity School Movement.*

21. Jones, "Schools," 136–39.

22. Kemp, "Early Schools," 66–68, 72; and Livingood, *Reformed Church Schools,* 220. For more information on education in early Reading, see Guenther, "Development of Education," 167–71, 180–85.

23. Woody, *Early Quaker Education,* 117–19.

24. Ibid., 141–42; and "Exeter Monthly Meeting Book C," 25th, 5 mo., 1785.

25. Inventories of the estates of Anthony Lee ("Sundry old Books") (1763); John Harrison ("ye Library of Books") (1786); William Tomlinson, Jr. ("piece of a Bible") (1784); John Wily (1754); John Wily (1755); Evan Thomas (1756); John Fincher (1763); Sarah Hutton (1767); Francis Parvin (1767); Samuel Woolison (1768); Samuel Wooleson, Jr. (1768); William Boone (1772); William Parvin (1772); John Boone (1773); Elizabeth Clendenon (1774); Owen Hugh (1774); Joseph Boone (1776); Eleanor Parvin (1776); Benjamin Lightfoot (1778); Jacob Lightfoot (1781); Jesse Willits (1781); James Hutton

(1782); Joseph Lightfoot (1784); Joseph Penrose, Jr. (1784); Richard Stephens (1784); James Boone (1785); Jeremiah Boone (1787); Judah Boone (1787); and Moses Roberts (1788). J. William Frost remarked that "[i]nventories of the estates of deceased Pennsylvania Friends are not helpful in showing the variety of books owned because only folio volumes and Bibles are listed." Frost, "Quaker Books," 22.

26. Inventories of the estates of John Wily (1754); Francis Parvin (1767); John Boone (1773); Benjamin Lightfoot (1778); Jacob Lightfoot (1781); Jesse Willits (1781); Joseph Lightfoot (1784); and James Boone (1785).

27. Inventory of the estate of Jacob Lightfoot, 18 August 1781; "Proprietary Return," 70; and "Exeter Monthly Meeting Book A," 28th, 4 mo., 1757.

28. Inventory of the estate of Francis Parvin, 21 September 1767; *Minutes of Provincial Council,* vol. 7, 148–49; and "Exeter Monthly Meeting Book A," 31st, 12 mo., 1761; 29th, 3 mo., 1764.

29. Inventory of the estate of Benjamin Lightfoot, 4 December 1778; "Exeter Monthly Meeting Book A," 24th, 6 mo., 1756; *Minutes of Provincial Council,* vol. 5, 597; and Lightfoot, *Benjamin Lightfoot,* 9–20.

30. "Exeter Monthly Meeting Book A," 28th, 6 mo., 1740; 26th, 4 mo., 1753; 25th, 8 mo., 1757; 31st, 8 mo., 1758; 29th, 11 mo., 1759; 30th, 10 mo., 1760; and "Exeter Monthly Meeting Book B," 29th, 11 mo., 1775; 27th, 1 mo., 1779; 26th, 7 mo., 1780; 28th, 5 mo., 1783; 27th, 8 mo., 1783; 6th, 10 mo., 1784; 29th, 12 mo., 1784. Full titles of these books may be found in Evans, *American Bibliography,* 1:400; 3:157, 196, 240, 222; 6:7, 77, 200, 214, 232, 233, 241, 270; and Smith, *A Descriptive Catalogue of Friends' Books,* 1:178–180, 244–45, 349, 407, 522, 557–58, 826, 871, 906; 2: 316, 414, 521. See also Frost, "Quaker Books," 1–2.

CHAPTER 9. "SAID SLAVE BE SUITABLE FOR LIBERTY"

1. Soderlund, *Quakers and Slavery,* 18–27; Hopkins, "The Germantown Protest," 19–29; and "The Germantown Protest," in Waddell, *Unity from Diversity,* 36–37. An early study of slavery in Pennsylvania is Turner, *Slavery in Pennsylvania.*

2. Soderlund, *Quakers and Slavery,* 18–26; "First Printed Protest," 265–70; Brown, *Negro in Pennsylvania History,* 3; and Lapsansky, *Black Presence in Pennsylvania,* 1–6. See also Brown, "Pennsylvania's Antislavery Pioneers," 59–77; and Frost, "Origins of Quaker Crusade," 42–58.

3. Soderlund, *Quakers and Slavery,* 26–28.

4. Soderlund, *Quakers and Slavery,* 27; and Soderlund, "Black Importation and Migration," 144–53.

5. Soderlund, *Quakers and Slavery,* 27 (citing Philadelphia Yearly Meeting Minutes, 20th to 26th, 9 mo., 1755), 30–31; and "Exeter Monthly Meeting Book A," 26th, 10 mo., 1758.

6. "Exeter Monthly Meeting Book A," 28th, 10 mo., 1756; 27th, 10 mo., 1757; 26th, 10 mo., 1758; 26th, 1 mo., 1764; "Exeter Monthly Meeting Book B," 29th, 7 mo., 1767; 26th, 7 mo., 1771; 27th, 7 mo., 1774; and Soderlund, *Quakers and Slavery,* 101–3. See also Jennings, "British Quakerism and Response to Slavery," 23–46.

7. "Exeter Monthly Meeting Book B," 25th, 1 mo., 1775; 26th, 4 mo., 1775; 26th, 7 mo., 1775.

8. Minutes of Philadelphia Men's Quarterly Meeting, 7th, 11 mo., 1774; 5th, 8 mo., 1776; and Minutes of Philadelphia Women's Quarterly Meeting, 7th, 5 mo., 1781.

9. Wax, "Reform and Revolution," 403–29.

10. Cook, "Glimpses of Life," 139.

11. Ibid., 25th, 6 mo., 1777; and "Record of Manumission," Exeter Monthly Meeting, 3, 5–6.

12. "Exeter Monthly Meeting Book B," 28th, 6 mo., 1780.

13. "Exeter Monthly Meeting Book B," 3rd, 4 mo., 1782; "Women's Monthly Meeting Book A," 27th, 6 mo., 1781; and "Record of Manumission," 1–6.

14. "Register of Property," 177–301, Bern, Reading, and Robeson Townships; "Return and Assessment 1780" 305–430, Amity, Bern, and Tulpehocken Townships; "Return and Assessment," 433–555, Amity, Bern, and Tulpehocken Townships; U.S. Department of Commerce and Labor, 28, 43; "Act for Gradual Abolition of Slavery," in *Unity from Diversity,* 87–88; *Journal of House of Representatives,* 325, 392, 398–99, 402, 410, 424, 435, 455; and Nash and Soderlund, *Freedom by Degrees,* 105.

15. *Journal of House of Representatives,* 325, 392, 398–99, 402, 410, 424, 435, 455; "Register of Property," passim; "Return and Assessment 1780," passim; "Return and Assessment," passim; and U.S. Department of Commerce and Labor, 26–45.

16. Nash and Soderlund, *Freedom by Degrees,* 104–8; Ireland, "Germans Against Abolition," 685–706; and Schaeffer, "Slavery in Berks County," 112. See also Johnson, "Blacks in Western Berks," 179–81, 187–89, 192; Johnson, "Slaves and Indentured Blacks," 8–14; and Johnson, "Slaves in Berks County," 159, 161, 184–89.

17. Ireland, "Germans Against Abolition," 689–706.

18. *Journal of House of Representatives,* 436.

19. Ibid., 435–36; "Act for Gradual Abolition of Slavery," 87–88; Brown, *Negro in Pennsylvania History,* 6–8; and Nash and Soderlund, *Freedom by Degrees,* 99–113.

20. "Register of Property," 177–301; "Return and Assessment 1780," 305–430; "Return and Assessment," 433–555; "Exeter Monthly Meeting Book A," 24th, 6 mo., 1756; Lightfoot, *Benjamin Lightfoot,* 9–20; and Inventory of the estate of Benjamin Lightfoot, 4 December 1778.

21. "Exeter Monthly Meeting Book B," 31st, 7 mo., 1782; "Record of Manumission," 1, 4; "Register of Property" (Reading); "Return and Assessment 1780" (Reading); Becker, "American Revolution as a Community Experience," 89, 334; Will of Frederick Weiser, 9 December 1773, Will Book 2:140–46; Will of Edward Biddle, 27 July 1779, Will Book 3:8–9; and Will of Jonathan Potts, 11 October 1781, Will Book B:20. The appraisers of Potts's estate valued Pompey, the male slave, at twice the value of Esther (Hester), the female. Inventory of the estate of Jonathan Potts, 15 October 1781.

22. "Return and Assessment 1780" (Exeter); "Return and Assessment" (Exeter); "Exeter Monthly Meeting Book A," 29th, 10 mo., 1737; 27th, 10 mo., 1739; 27th, 11 mo., 1742/3; 27th, 10 mo., 1744; 29th, 11 mo., 1746/7; 31st, 6 mo., 1749; 30th, 9 mo., 1749; 29th, 11 mo., 1753; 28th, 8 mo., 1755; 31st, 3 mo., 1757; "Exeter Monthly Meeting Book B," 28th, 4 mo., 1779; 28th, 6 mo., 1780; Brunhouse, *Counter-Revolution in Pennsylvania,* 40–41, 49; Inventory of the estate of James Boone, 14–15 September 1785; and Will of James Boone, 12 July 1785, Will Book B:126–28.

23. "Register of Property" (Exeter); "Return and Assessment 1780" (Exeter); "Exeter Monthly Meeting Book B," 28th, 4 mo., 1779; 28th, 6 mo., 1780; 31st, 7 mo., 1782 (source for quote); "Record of Manumission," 2; and Inventory of the estate of Judah Boone, 29 June 1787.

24. "Exeter Monthly Meeting Book B," 31st, 7 mo., 1782. Samuel Boone had been disowned in 1765 for gambling, quarreling, fighting, and cursing; Jane Hughes Boone was disowned in 1767 for exogamy (because her spouse had been disowned) and for having the ceremony performed by a minister. "Exeter Monthly Meeting Book A," 25th, 4 mo., 1765; "Exeter Monthly Meeting Book B," 28th, 1 mo., 1767.

25. "Register of Property" (Robeson); "Return and Assessment 1780" (Robeson); "Return and Assessment" (Robeson); "Record of Manumission," 5–6; and "Exeter Monthly Meeting Book B," 31st, 7 mo., 1782. The men's monthly meeting minutes identify Abner Streve as belonging to John Scarlet and Barne Streve to John Scarlet, Jr.

26. "Register of Property" (Cumru, Maiden Creek); "Return and Assessment 1780" (Cumru, Maiden Creek); "Return and Assessment" (Cumru, Maiden Creek); "Exeter Monthly Meeting Book A," 27th, 9 mo., 1740; 28th, 2 mo., 1743; 26th, 6 mo., 1755; 29th, 7 mo., 1756; 26th, 11 mo., 1761; 30th, 6 mo., 1763; "Exeter Monthly Meeting Book B," 31st, 7 mo., 1782; and "Record of Manumission," 3.

27. "Exeter Monthly Meeting Book B," 27th, 11 mo., 1776; 31st, 7 mo., 1782. The acquisition of indentured servants would not have been that remarkable, since members of Exeter Monthly Meeting hired at least eight indentured servants during the colonial period. See *Record of Indentures of Individuals,* 36–37, 66–67, 168–69, 220–21, 306–7, 316–17.

28. Minutes of Exeter Monthly Meeting, 1737–1789, "Register of Property" (Cumru, Exeter, Maiden Creek, Reading, Robeson); and Becker, "American Revolution as a Community Experience," 89, 420.

29. "Register of Property," passim; "Return and Assessment 1780," passim; "Return and Assessment," passim; U.S. Department of Commerce and Labor, 26–45; "Exeter Monthly Meeting Book B," 31st, 7 mo., 1782; "Exeter Monthly Meeting Book C," 25th, 3 mo., 1789; and "Record of Manumission," 1–6.

30. Grundy, "Middletown Meeting," 68–85.

31. Ebersole, "Abolition Divides Meeting House," 2–27.

32. Densmore, "Dilemma of Quaker Anti-Slavery," 80–91.

CHAPTER 10. MEN AND WOMEN OF HIGH MORALS

1. Bronner, *The Quakers,* 29–40; Montgomery, *Political Hand-Book,* 10–12, 15–17, 19–20, 23, 26–27, 29–32; Commissioners of Berks County, *Berks County Government,* 74–80; "Officers for Philadelphia County," vol. 9, 705–9; "Officers for Berks County," vol. 9, 784–87; "Exeter Monthly Meeting Book A," 28th, 7 mo., 1763; 25th, 10 mo., 1764; and Minutes of Philadelphia Men's Quarterly Meeting, 7th, 2 mo., 1763. For more information on Quakers and politics in colonial Pennsylvania, see Bronner, *William Penn's "Holy Experiment"*; Nash, *Quakers and Politics;* Thayer, *Pennsylvania Politics;* and Tully, *William Penn's Legacy.* See also Smolenski, "Friends and Strangers."

2. *Minutes of Provincial Council,* vol. 4, 312, 482, 762; vol. 5, 388; vol. 8, 562; "Officers for Berks County," vol. 9, 785–87; and *County Government and Archives,* 31–32. See also Bockelman, "Local Government," Daniels, *Town and County,* 216–37.

3. Commissioners of Berks County, *Berks County Government,* 74–80; "Officers for Berks County," 784–87; Tully, *William Penn's Legacy,* 42; Foster, "Francis Parvin," in Horle, et al., *Lawmaking and Legislators,* 808–12; Horle, "Moses Starr," in Horle, et al., *Lawmaking and Legislators,* vol. 2, 944–50; Hummel, "Emergence of Ruling Elite," 101–6, 115–20, 124; and Spyker, "Francis Parvin," 16. See also Ryerson, "Portrait of a Colonial Oligarchy," Daniels, *Power and Status,* 106–35.

4. Spraker, *Boone Family,* 21–22, 24, 31, 44, 54; "Officers of Philadelphia County," vol. 9, 705–9, 784, 786–87; *Minutes of Provincial Council,* vol. 4, 312, 482; Faragher, *Daniel Boone,* 10–11; and "Exeter Monthly Meeting Book A," 25th, 6 mo., 1743.

5. Tully, *William Penn's Legacy,* 42; *Minutes of Provincial Council,* vol. 5, 597, 662; vol. 6, 144; vol. 8, 562; vol. 9, 673–74; Montgomery, *Political Hand-Book,* 29; and

"Officers for Berks County," vol. 9, 784. According to Tully, Lightfoot's relocation to Berks County created a crisis for provincial officials: "When Richard Peters set out to find a replacement for the deceased deputy surveyor Benjamin Lightfoot, he could not find a qualified Quaker to fill the post." Tully, *William Penn's Legacy,* 42.

6. *Minutes of Provincial Council,* vol. 5, 612; vol. 9, 651; "Petition from Berks and Northampton Counties," vol. 2, 98–99; and Livengood, *Genealogical Abstracts of Laws,* 15, 20, 24, 26.

7. Livengood, *Genealogical Abstracts of Laws,* 18, 29. On Quakers and ecology during this period, see Kelley, "Friends and Nature in America," 257–72; and Kelley, "Evolution of Quaker Theology," 242–53.

8. Minutes of Philadelphia Men's Quarterly Meeting, 1737–1789.

9. Ibid., 4th, 12 mo., 1754; 3rd, 11 mo., 1755; 2nd, 2 mo., 1756; 5th, 2 mo., 1759; 5th, 5 mo., 1760; 5th, 8 mo., 1765; 6th, 11 mo., 1769; 2nd, 8 mo., 1773; 7th, 11 mo., 1774; 5th, 8 mo., 1776; and Minutes of Philadelphia Women's Quarterly Meeting, 7th, 5 mo., 1781.

10. Minutes of Philadelphia Men's Quarterly Meeting, 7th, 11 mo., 1757; 5th, 2 mo., 1759; 5th, 5 mo., 1760; 6th, 8 mo., 1764.

11. Ibid., 6th, 11 mo., 1775; 2nd, 2 mo., 1778; 3rd, 11 mo., 1783; 6th, 2 mo., 1786.

12. Ibid., 2nd, 8 mo., 1773; 5th, 8 mo., 1776; 5th, 5 mo., 1784; 2nd, 5 mo., 1785; 6th, 2 mo., 1786; 7th, 8 mo., 1786.

13. On the importance of the traveling minister to colonial Quakers, see Campbell, "Difficulties and Dangers of Travel;" and Hinshaw, "Agents for Truth," 5–20.

14. Reckitt, *Life and Labours of William Reckitt,* 109. Biographical information on Reckitt obtained from Woolman, *Journal and Major Essays,* 310.

15. Churchman, *John Churchman,* 244–45. Biographical information of Churchman obtained from Woolman, *Journal and Major Essays,* 308. See also Mazzenga, "John Churchman," 71–98.

16. "Exeter Monthly Meeting Book A," 29th, 10 mo., 1761; 29th, 4 mo., 1762; Certificates of Removal (Issued), 19; and Letter, Benjamin Lightfoot to Israel Pemberton, Jr., 25 October 1761, Pemberton Papers, vol. 15, 63.

17. "Exeter Monthly Meeting Book A," 29th, 1 mo., 1764; "Exeter Monthly Meeting Book B," 28th, 1 mo., 1778; 28th, 11 mo., 1770; 30th, 10 mo., 1771; 28th, 6 mo., 1780; 26th, 11 mo., 1783; and "Women's Monthly Meeting Book A," 27th, 7 mo., 1758; 30th, 10 mo., 1771; 28th, 6 mo., 1780; 28th, 2 mo., 1781.

18. "Women's Monthly Meeting Book A," 29th, 10 mo., 1737; 23rd, 9 mo., 1772; and Certificates of Removal (Received), 95. For more information on Quaker women ministers, see Larson, *Daughters of Light;* Spann, "Ministry of Women;" and Tomes, "The Quaker Connection," in Zuckerman, *Friends and Neighbors,* 174–95.

19. "Women's Monthly Meeting Book A," 30th, 9 mo., 1765; 30th, 4 mo., 1766; 5th, 4 mo., 1769; 29th, 4 mo., 1767; 30th, 8 mo., 1769; 24th, 4 mo., 1771; 30th, 10 mo., 1771; 29th, 4 mo., 1772; 23rd, 9 mo., 1772; 25th, 11 mo., 1772; 24th, 2 mo., 1773; 28th, 7 mo., 1773; 6th, 10 mo., 1773; 29th, 12 mo., 1773; 30th, 3 mo., 1774; 27th, 4 mo., 1774; 25th, 4 mo., 1774; 27th, 10 mo., 1774; 30th, 11 mo., 1774; 28th, 12 mo., 1774; 24th, 4 mo., 1776; 30th, 7 mo., 1777; 28th, 4 mo., 1779; 26th, 5 mo., 1779; 28th, 7 mo., 1779; 26th, 7 mo., 1780; 30th, 3 mo., 1781; 31st, 7 mo., 1782; 26th, 3 mo., 1783; 28th, 4 mo., 1784; 23rd, 2 mo., 1785.

20. "Exeter Monthly Meeting Book A," 31st, 7 mo., 1760; 30th, 5 mo., 1765; and "Exeter Monthly Meeting Book B," 24th, 2 mo., 1773.

21. "Exeter Monthly Meeting Book B," 29th, 1 mo., 1772; 28th, 10 mo., 1772; 30th, 11 mo., 1774; 25th, 1 mo., 1775; 24th, 11 mo., 1779; 26th, 12 mo., 1781; 25th, 10 mo., 1786.

22. *Brief Memoir Concerning Abel Thomas,* 9; "Exeter Monthly Meeting Book B," 27th, 1 mo., 1773; and Certificates of Removal (Received), 86.

23. *Transformation of Joseph Hoag,* 1–2, adapted from Hoag, *Journal of Joseph Hoag.*

24. Ibid., 3.

25. Ibid., 5–6.

26. Meginness, *Otzinachson,* vol. 1, 377–79; and Eshelman, "History of Catawissa Friends' Meeting," 4. For more information about Wallis's land speculation ventures in central Pennsylvania, see Mancall, *Valley of Opportunity,* 98–99, 166, 168, 170, 172, 190, 202–3, 229; and Maxey, "Honorable Proprietaries," 361–95.

27. Meginness, *Otzinachson,* 377–79.

28. Ibid., 378–79.

29. Letter, Alexander Murray to the Secretary of the SPG, 25 January 1764, in Perry, *Historical Collections,* 356.

30. "Exeter Monthly Meeting Book B," 25th, 6 mo., 1777; 28th, 5 mo., 1783.

CHAPTER 11. CONCLUSION

1. "Exeter Monthly Meeting Book B,"25th, 1 mo., 1775.

2. "Exeter Monthly Meeting Book A," 25th, 1 mo., 1742; 25th, 1 mo., 1749/50; 22nd, 2 mo., 1759; 1742–1765, passim; and "Exeter Monthly Meeting Book B," 1765–1775.

3. "Exeter Monthly Meeting Book B," 28th, 6 mo., 1775; 30th, 8 mo., 1775.

4. Ibid., 29th, 10 mo., 1777; 26th, 11 mo., 1777; 30th, 12 mo., 1778; 27th, 1 mo., 1779; 29th, 12 mo., 1779; 23rd, 2 mo., 1780; 30th, 3 mo., 1780; 28th, 1 mo., 1784; "Exeter Monthly Meeting Book C," 30th, 11 mo., 1785; and Minutes of Philadelphia Men's Quarterly Meeting, 6th, 11 mo., 1786; 5th, 2 mo., 1787.

5. "Exeter Monthly Meeting Book C," 27th, 2 mo., 1788; 27th, 5 mo., 1789; 29th, 7 mo., 1789; and Minutes of Philadelphia Men's Quarterly Meeting, 2nd, 2 mo., 1789; 4th, 5 mo., 1789.

6. "Exeter Monthly Meeting Book C," 30th, 5 mo., 1787; 3rd, 10 mo., 1787; 28th, 5 mo., 1788; 30th, 7 mo., 1794.

7. Ibid., 27th, 8 mo., 1794; 28th, 10 mo., 1794; 24th, 6 mo., 1795; 28th, 10 mo., 1795; 24th, 2 mo., 1796; 27th, 4 mo., 1796; and Minutes of Philadelphia Men's Quarterly Meeting, 2nd, 11 mo., 1796. See also Cook, "Glimpses of Life," 9–10.

8. "Exeter Monthly Meeting Book C," 28th, 1 mo., 1795; 25th, 3 mo., 1795.

9. Ibid., 30th, 3 mo., 1796; 27th, 4 mo., 1796; 25th, 5 mo., 1796.

10. Eshelman, "Society of Friends," 109, 117, 119. For more information on the Hicksite schism, see Bacon, *The Quiet Rebels,* 87–89; Barbour and Frost, *The Quakers,* 171–82; Doherty, *The Hicksite Separation;* and Ingle, *Quakers in Conflict.*

11. Eshelman, "Society of Friends," 108, 119; Eshelman, "Short History of Reading Friends' Meeting," 5–6; and Matlack, "Brief Historical Sketches," vol. 2, 466–69.

12. Eshelman, "Society of Friends," 105, 119, 121; Matlack, "Brief Historical Sketches," vol. 2, 469–70; Alexander, *Historic American Buildings Survey,* 1; and Beyer, *Guide to Markers,* 56. The meeting houses at Maiden Creek, Catawissa, Roaring Creek, and Reading have also been surveyed by HABS (Historic American Buildings Survey). *Silent Witness.* Two state historical markers have also been erected to commemorate the log meetinghouse at Catawissa, which still stands. Beyer, *Guide to Markers,* 117–18. See also Cook, "Nomination of Exeter Friends," 1–5.

13. Matlack, "Brief Historical Sketches," vol. 2, 489–91; Eshelman, "Society of Friends," 117, 121. Photographs of reconstructed buildings and historical markers taken by the author in August 1986.

14. Matlack, "Brief Historical Sketches," vol. 1, 257–61; and Eshelman, "Society of Friends," 106–7, 119, 121.

15. "Exeter Monthly Meeting Book A," 1737–1765, passim; "Exeter Monthly Meeting Book B," 1765–1785, passim; "Exeter Monthly Meeting Book C," 1785–1789; "Women's Monthly Meeting Book A"; Yearly Meeting of Friends, passim; Eshelman, "Genealogical Record;" and U.S. Department of Commerce and Labor 9, 26–45.

16. Eshelman, "Genealogical Record," passim; and Yearly Meeting of Friends.

17. Blanco, *Diary of Jonathan Potts;* Bakeless, *Daniel Boone;* Bogart, *Daniel Boone;* Faragher, *Daniel Boone;* Hill, *Daniel Boone;* Lofaro, *Life and Adventures of Daniel Boone;* Stoudt, "Daniel and Squire Boone: A Study," 27–40; Stoudt, "Daniel and Squire Boone," 108–12; and Wallace, *Daniel Boone in Pennsylvania.* Daniel Boone, of course, was also the subject of a television series on NBC from 1964 until 1970. Brooks and Marsh, *Directory to TV Shows,* 206.

18. Telephone interview with Kenneth L. Cook; Letter, Kenneth L. Cook to Karen Guenther, 17 January 2004; and "Exeter Friends Meeting, Report on Worship and Ministry for 1989." According to Cook, when Exeter renewed its position as a monthly meeting, it created a problem for the meeting at Reading, which had been called Exeter Monthly Meeting since the Hicksite schism. To resolve the confusion, this meeting changed its name to Reading Monthly Meeting. Letter, Kenneth L. Cook to Karen Guenther, 21 June 1993, page B.

Bibliography

UNPUBLISHED MATERIALS

Primary Sources

MATERIALS USED AT THE ARCHIVES OF THE MORAVIAN CHURCH, BETHLEHEM, PENNSYLVANIA.

"Kirchen Buch des Brüder Gemeinleins in Oley, 1758." (Handwritten)

MATERIALS USED AT THE BERKS COUNTY COURT HOUSE, READING, PENNSYLVANIA.

Administration Book. Volumes 1–3. Register of Wills office. (Handwritten)

Grantee Index, Berks County. Recorder of Deeds office. (Typewritten)

Inventories for the estates of John Barger, Joseph Barger, James Boone, Sr., Jeremiah Boone, John Boone (1773), John Boone (1785), Joseph Boone, Judah Boone, William Boone, Elizabeth Clendennon, Isaac Clendennon, Derrick Clever, Mary Clews, Thomas Davis, Rowland Ellis, Samuel Embree, Penal Evans, John Fincher, Jonathan Fincher, John Harrison, John Hughes, Jonathan Hughes, Owen Hughes, James Hutton, Sarah Hutton, Ephraim Jackson, Mary Jackson, Anthony Lee, Benjamin Lightfoot, Jacob Lightfoot, Joseph Lightfoot, Eleanor Parvin, Francis Parvin, William Parvin, Lawrence Pearson, Joseph Penrose, Jr., Jonathan Potts, Moses Roberts, Richard Stephens, Evan Thomas, William Tomlinson, Jr., Joseph Webb, Henry Willits, Jesse Willits, John Wily, John Wily, Jr., Rebecca Woolaston, Samuel Woolaston, Samuel Woolaston, Jr., and Mary Wright. Register of Wills office. (Handwritten)

Petitions to the Orphans Court, Estate File of John Fincher. Register of Wills office. (Handwritten)

Will Book, Berks County. Volumes 1–3, B. Register of Wills office. (Handwritten)

MATERIALS USED AT THE CLAYTON LIBRARY CENTER FOR GENEALOGICAL RESEARCH, HOUSTON PUBLIC LIBRARY, HOUSTON, TEXAS.

McGhee, Lucy Kare, comp. "Maryland Quaker (Friends) Records of Third Haven (Tred Avon), Talbot County." 3 vols. (Typewritten)

MATERIALS USED AT THE EVANGELICAL AND REFORMED HISTORICAL
SOCIETY, LANCASTER THEOLOGICAL SEMINARY, LANCASTER,
PENNSYLVANIA.

"Protocoll über die Verhandlungen mit B. Willy." "Minutes and Letters of the Coetus of
Pennsylvania, 1747–1792," 758–60. Transcribed by William John Hinke. (Handwritten)

MATERIALS USED AT THE FRIENDS HISTORICAL LIBRARY, SWARTHMORE
COLLEGE, SWARTHMORE, PENNSYLVANIA.

Certificates of Removal (Received). Exeter Monthly Meeting, 1737–1797. (Handwritten)

Exeter Monthly Meeting. Miscellaneous Papers.

"Exeter Monthly Meeting Book A." Minutes of Exeter Men's Monthly Meeting, 1737–
1765. (Handwritten)

"Exeter Monthly Meeting Book B." Minutes of Exeter Men's Monthly Meeting, 1765–
1785. (Handwritten)

"Exeter Monthly Meeting Book C." Minutes of Exeter Men's Monthly Meeting, 1785–
1808. (Handwritten)

Matlack, T. Chalkley, comp. "Brief Historical Sketches concerning Friends' Meetings of
the Past and Present with special reference to Philadelphia Yearly Meeting." 4 vols.
(Typewritten)

Minutes of Philadelphia Meeting for Sufferings. 1757–1764, 1775–1784. (Handwritten)

Minutes of Philadelphia Men's Quarterly Meeting. 1723–1789. (Handwritten)

Miscellaneous Papers. Philadelphia Yearly Meeting. Meeting for Sufferings. (Handwritten)

Roberts, Moses. "Some account of me and others being taken prisoner by Thomas Howitt
and others on the 9th Day of the 4th mo 1780." Miscellaneous Manuscripts.
(Handwritten)

"Women's Monthly Meeting Book A." Minutes of Exeter Women's Monthly Meeting,
1737–1789." (Handwritten)

Yearly Meeting of Friends for Pennsylvania, New Jersey, Delaware, and the Eastern Parts
of Maryland. "Record of Births, Deaths, Etc. of the Members of Exeter Monthly Meeting, Commencing the First day of the First Month, A.D. 1830." (Handwritten)

MATERIALS USED AT THE HISTORICAL SOCIETY OF BERKS COUNTY,
READING, PENNSYLVANIA.

"Church Book for the Congregation at St. Gabriel's Church, Morlatton, Amity Township,
Berks County." (Handwritten)

"Cipher Book of Mordecai Wright. 1st mo., 7th, 1786." 2 vols. (Handwritten)

Cook, Kenneth L. "The Nomination of Exeter Friends Meetinghouse and Burying Ground
to the National Register of Historic Places." (Typewritten)

Eshelman, John E., comp. "A Genealogical Record of Members Composing The Society of
Friends or Quakers Resident at Some Time in Berks County, Pennsylvania or Attached
to the Meetings Located in the said County." (1930) (Handwritten)

Faust, Warren D., comp. "Index to all Names Found in our Original Tax Lists for the Years
1770 Through 1789 with the Years 1776, 1777 and 1784 Missing." (Typewritten)

Herbein, Edith R., comp. "Berks County, Pennsylvania Warrantee Township Maps Index,
Original Land Holdings." (Typewritten)

"Hill Church Record, Pike Township." Copied by J. W. Early. (Handwritten)

Hollenbach, David M., comp. "Index to all Names Found on Original Bound Tax Lists of Berks County for the Years 1754, 1760, 1762, 1763, 1764, 1765, 1766, and 1768." (Typewritten)

Ledger of Moses Boone. 1778–1822. (Handwritten)

"Record of County Tax." Berks County, Pennsylvania. Bound by year, arranged by township. 1754–1790. (Handwritten)

"Records of Trinity Evangelical Lutheran Church, Reading, Berks County, Pennsylvania, 1751–1812." Copied by J. W. Early. (Handwritten)

Warrantee Township Maps, Berks County, Pennsylvania. Available for Bern, Brecknock, Caernarvon, Cumru, Exeter, Lower Heidelberg, Reading, Robeson, Spring, Tilden, Union, and Upper Tulpehocken Townships.

MATERIALS USED AT THE HISTORICAL SOCIETY OF PENNSYLVANIA, PHILADELPHIA, PENNSYLVANIA.

Cadwalader Collection. Manuscript Department. (Handwritten)

Daybook of Benjamin Lightfoot. Lightfoot Papers. Manuscript Department. (Handwritten)

Gratz MSS. Coates-Reynell Papers. Manuscript Department. (Handwritten)

Owen, B. F., comp. "Taxables in Berks County, Pa., for the Years 1754, 1755, 1758, 1760, 1765, 1770, 1774, 1780, 1785, 1790." (Handwritten)

———. "The Names of Persons who took the Oath of Allegiance in Berks County, Pennsylvania, Act of the General Assembly June 13, 1777." Collections of the Genealogical Society of Pennsylvania, vol. 26. (Handwritten)

Pemberton Papers. Vols. 15, 35, 36. Manuscript Department. (Handwritten)

Thomas, Abel. "Abel Thomas's account of capture in New Jersey." Society Collection. Manuscript Department. (Handwritten)

Vaux Papers. Correspondence. Manuscript Department. (Handwritten)

MATERIALS USED AT THE PENNSYLVANIA STATE ARCHIVES, HARRISBURG, PENNSYLVANIA.

RG 27, Records of Pennsylvania's Revolutionary Governments, 1775–1790. Clemency File, 1775–1790. (Handwritten)

MATERIALS USED AT THE QUAKER COLLECTION, HAVERFORD COLLEGE, HAVERFORD, PENNSYLVANIA.

"A Record of Manumission." Exeter Monthly Meeting. Bound in volume with Certificates of Removal (Issued). (Handwritten)

Certificates of Removal (Issued). Exeter Monthly Meeting, 1755–1786. (Handwritten)

Minutes of Gwynedd Men's Monthly Meeting. 1714–1737. (Handwritten)

Minutes of Philadelphia Women's Quarterly Meeting. 1725–1796. (Handwritten)

MATERIALS HELD AT THE STATE HISTORICAL SOCIETY OF WISCONSIN, MADISON, WISCONSIN.

Draper, Lyman Copeland. Draper Manuscript Collection. [Microfilm copy.] (Handwritten)

OTHER MATERIALS IN THE AUTHOR'S POSSESSION.

"Exeter Friends Meeting, Report on Worship and Ministry for 1989." Supplied by Kenneth
L. Cook to the author. (Typewritten)

Letter, Kenneth L. Cook to Karen Guenther, 21 June 1993. (Handwritten)

Letter, Kenneth L. Cook to Karen Guenther, 17 January 2004. (Typewritten)

Telephone interview with Kenneth L. Cook, Recording Clerk, Exeter Monthly Meeting. 15
June 1993.

Secondary Sources

Becker, Laura Leff. "The American Revolution as a Community Experience: A Case Study
of Reading, Pennsylvania." Ph.D. diss., University of Pennsylvania, 1978.

Campbell, Mary C. "The Difficulties and Dangers of Eighteenth Century Travel as Revealed in Quaker Journals." M.A. thesis, Columbia University, 1946.

Cook, Kenneth L. "Glimpses of Life in a Frontier Friends Meeting." Paper presented at the
250th anniversary of Exeter Monthly Meeting, 1987.

Doutrich, Paul E. "The Evolution of an Early American Town: Yorktown, Pennsylvania,
1740–1790." Ph.D. diss., University of Kentucky, 1985.

Dowless, Donald Vernon. "The Quakers of Colonial North Carolina, 1672–1789." Ph.D.
diss., Baylor University, 1989.

Eshelman, John E. "A Short History of Reading Friends' Meeting, Reading, Pennsylvania."
Typewritten, Reading Public Library, Reading, Pennsylvania.

Forbes, Susan Mary. "'As Many Candles Lighted': The New Garden Monthly Meeting,
1718–1774." Ph.D. diss., University of Pennsylvania, 1972.

Ford, Raymond W., Jr. "Germans and Other Foreign Stock: Their Part in the Evolution of
Reading, Pennsylvania." Ph.D. diss., University of Pennsylvania, 1963.

Fritsch, Christopher Neil. "Testation Practices in Ethnic Groups of Berks County, Pennsylvania, 1752–1775." Seminar paper, Temple University, 1989.

———. "Women Inside the Law: Female Estate Planning, Berks County, Pennsylvania,
1752–1789." Paper presented at the 1992 Pennsylvania Historical Association meeting.

Grundy, Martha Paxson. "'In the World But Not of It': Quaker Faith and the Dominant
Culture, Middletown Meeting, Bucks County, Pennsylvania, 1750–1850." Ph.D. diss.,
Case Western Reserve University, 1990.

Guenther, Karen. "Interpretation Manual, Daniel Boone Homestead." Typewritten, Daniel
Boone Homestead, Pennsylvania Historical and Museum Commission, 1986.

Lodge, Martin Ellsworth. "The Great Awakening in the Middle Colonies." Ph.D. diss.,
University of California at Berkeley, 1965.

Martin, James Kirby. "The Wyoming Valley Dispute, 1753–1788." M.A. thesis, University
of Wisconsin, 1967.

McCormick, Jo Anne. "The Quakers of Colonial South Carolina, 1670–1807." Ph.D. diss.,
University of South Carolina, 1984.

Moyer, Paul Benjamin. "Wild Yankees: Settlement, Conflict and Localism Along Pennsylvania's Northeast Frontier, 1760–1820." Ph.D. diss., College of William and Mary,
1999.

Nelson, Russell Sage. "Backcountry Pennsylvania (1709 to 1774): The Ideals of William
Penn in Practice." Ph.D. diss., University of Wisconsin, 1968.

Pendleton, Philip E. "'Dutch Buggers': The Anglican Elite of Berks County, Pennsylvania, in the American Revolution." M.A. thesis, University of North Carolina at Chapel Hill, 1981.

Radbill, Kenneth A. "Socioeconomic Background of Nonpacifist Quakers During the American Revolution." Ph.D. diss., University of Arizona, 1971.

Ridner, Judith. "'A Handsomely Improved Place': Economic, Social, and Gender-Role Development in a Backcountry Town, Carlisle, Pennsylvania, 1750–1810." Ph.D. diss., College of William and Mary, 1994.

Smolenski, John. "Friends and Strangers: Religion, Diversity, and the Ordering of Public Life in Colonial Pennsylvania, 1681–1764." Ph.D. diss., University of Pennsylvania, 2001.

Spann, Anna L. "The Ministry of Women in the Society of Friends." Ph.D. diss., Iowa University, 1945.

Thatcher, Patricia. "'To Desire an Inheritance Incorruptible': Quaker Ideas of Inheritance, Gift, and Benevolence in Philadelphia, 1690–1760." Ph.D. diss., University of Delaware, 1996.

PUBLISHED MATERIALS

Primary Sources

"An Act Against Riotous Sports, Plays and Games." In *The Statutes at Large of Pennsylvania from 1682 to 1801.* Vol. 2: 1700 to 1712, compiled by James T. Mitchell and Henry Flanders, 186–87. Harrisburg, PA: Clarence M. Busch, State Printer, 1896.

"Act for Forming and Regulating the Militia, 1757." *Pennsylvania Archives,* 1st ser., vol. 3, edited by Samuel Hazard, 120–37. Philadelphia: Joseph Severns & Co., 1853.

"Act for the Gradual Abolition of Slavery." In *Unity from Diversity: Extracts from Selected Pennsylvania Colonial Documents, 1681 to 1780, in Commemoration of the Tercentenary of the Commonwealth,* compiled and edited by Louis M. Waddell, 87–88. Harrisburg, PA: Pennsylvania Historical and Museum Commission, 1980.

"An Act for the Gradual Abolition of Slavery." In *The Statutes at Large of Pennsylvania from 1682 to 1801.* Vol. 10: 1779 to 1781, compiled by James T. Mitchell and Henry Flanders, 67–73. Harrisburg, PA: William Stanley Ray, State Printer, 1904.

"An Act for the Prevention of Vice and Immorality and Unlawful Gaming and to Restrain Disorderly Sports and Dissipation." In *The Statutes at Large of Pennsylvania from 1682 to 1801.* Vol. 12: 1785 to 1787, compiled by James T. Mitchell and Henry Flanders, 313–22. Harrisburg, PA: Harrisburg Publishing Co., 1906.

"An Act Obliging the Male White Inhabitants of This State to Give Assurances of Allegiance to the Same and for Other Purposes Therein Mentioned." In *The Statutes at Large of Pennsylvania from 1682 to 1801.* Vol. 9: 1776 to 1779, compiled by James T. Mitchell and Henry Flanders, 110–14. Harrisburg, PA: William Stanley Ray, State Printer, 1903.

"An Act to Ascertain the Number of Members of Assembly and to Regulate the Election, 12 January 1705/06." In *The Statutes at Large of Pennsylvania from 1682 to 1801.* Vol. 2: 1700 to 1712, compiled by James T. Mitchell and Henry Flanders, 212–221. Harrisburg, PA: Clarence Busch, State Printer, 1896.

Alexander, Drury B. *Historic American Buildings Survey, Exeter Friends Meeting House.* HABS No. PA–1021. Washington, D. C.: U.S. Department of the Interior, National Park Service, 1958.

The Ancient Testimony and Principles of the People Called Quakers, renewed, with Respect to the King and Government; and Touching the Commotions now prevailing in these and other Parts of America, Addressed to the People in General. Philadelphia: n.p., 1776.

"Assessment of Taxes for the County of Berks for the Year 1785." *Pennsylvania Archives,* 3rd ser., vol. 18, edited by William H. Egle, 691–814. Harrisburg, PA: William Stanley Ray, State Printer, 1898.

"Baptismal and Marriage Records, Rev. John Waldschmidt, 1752–1786." *Pennsylvania Archives,* 6th ser., vol. 6, edited by Thomas Lynch Montgomery, 147–282. Harrisburg, PA: Harrisburg Publishing Company, State Printer, 1907.

"Berks County Resolves, 1774." *Pennsylvania Archives,* 2nd ser., vol. 14, edited by John B. Linn and William H. Egle, 321–22. Harrisburg, PA: Clarence M. Busch, State Printer, 1896.

"Bern Church Records, 1739–1835." *Publications of the Genealogical Society of Pennsylvania* 5 (1912): 38–52.

The Bethlehem Diary. Vol. 1: 1742–1744. Translated and edited by Kenneth G. Hamilton. Bethlehem, PA: Archives of the Moravian Church, 1971.

The Book of Discipline of the Religious Society of Friends. Philadelphia: W. H. Jenkins, 1927.

A Brief Memoir Concerning Abel Thomas, A Minister of the Gospel of Christ in the Society of Friends, Compiled from Authentic Documents. Philadelphia: Benjamin & Thomas Kite, 1824.

"The Charter of Pennsylvania." In *William Penn and the Founding of Pennsylvania, 1680– 1684: A Documentary History,* edited by Jean R. Soderlund, 39–50. Philadelphia: University of Pennsylvania Press, 1983.

Churchman, John. *An Account of the Gospel Labours and Christian Experiences of That Faithful Minister of Christ, John Churchman.* Philadelphia: Joseph Crukshank, 1779. Reprint, Friends Book-Store, 1882.

A Collection of Memorials Concerning Divers deceased Ministers and others of the People called Quakers, in Pennsylvania, New-Jersey, and Parts adjacent, from nearly the first Settlement thereof to the year 1787, With some of the last Expressions and Exhortations of many of them. Philadelphia: Joseph Crukshank, 1787.

County Government and Archives in Pennsylvania. Edited by Sylvester K. Stevens and Donald H. Kent. Harrisburg, PA: Pennsylvania Historical and Museum Commission, 1947.

Daniel Schumacher's Baptismal Register. Translated by Frederick S. Weiser. Breinigsville, PA: Pennsylvania German Society, 1968.

Davis, Robert Scott, Jr., comp. *Quaker Records in Georgia: Wrightsborough, 1772–1793, Friendsborough, 1776–1777.* Augusta, GA: Augusta Genealogical Society, 1986.

Durnbaugh, Donald F., ed. *The Brethren in Colonial America: A Source Book on the Transplantation and Development of the Church of the Brethren in the Eighteenth Century.* Elgin, IL: Brethren Press, 1967.

Early Amish Land Grants in Berks County, Pennsylvania. Gordonville, PA: Pequea Brudershaft Library, 1990.

Early Lutheran Baptisms and Marriages in Southeastern Pennsylvania: The Records of Rev. John Casper Stoever from 1730 to 1779. Baltimore: Genealogical Publishing Co., 1982.

"Early Minutes of Philadelphia Monthly Meeting of Friends." *Publications of the Genealogical Society of Pennsylvania* 8 (1921–23): 174–89, 261–83; 9 (1924–26): 35–37, 164–72, 236–47; 10 (1927–29): 56–60, 123–32, 237–41; 11 (1930–32): 9–21, 127–

36, 230–38; 12 (1933–35): 30–38, 151–59, 260–67; 13 (1936–39): 24–36, 213–24; 14 (1942–44): 34–39, 160–69, 267–75; 15 (1945–47): 99–102.

"Election Returns, Berks County—1756–1789." *Pennsylvania Archives,* 6th ser., vol. 11, edited by Thomas Lynch Montgomery, 51–84. Harrisburg, PA: Harrisburg Publishing Co., State Printer, 1907.

An Epistle from our Yearly-Meeting, Held in Philadelphia, for Pennsylvania, New-Jersey, and the Western Parts of Maryland and Virginia, by Adjournments, from the 21st Day of the Ninth Month, to the 28th of the same, inclusive, 1776. To Our Friends and Brethren of the Several Quarterly and Monthly Meetings, in These and Adjacent Provinces. Philadelphia: n.p., 1776.

The Epistle from the Yearly-Meeting in London, Held by Adjournments, from the 27th of the Fifth Month to the 1st of the Sixth Month 1776, Inclusive. To the Quarterly and Monthly Meetings of Friends and Brethren in Great-Britain, Ireland, and Elsewhere. Philadelphia: n.p., 1776.

The Epistle from the Yearly-Meeting in London . . . . Philadelphia: Joseph Crukshank, 1779.

"The Frame of Government *and* Laws Agreed Upon in England." In *William Penn and the Founding of Pennsylvania, 1680–1684: A Documentary History,* edited by Jean R. Soderlund, 118–33. Philadelphia: University of Pennsylvania Press, 1983.

Frankhouser, Earle M. "Surveying the County Line—the Journal of Benjamin Lightfoot." *Historical Review of Berks County* 11 (1946): 110–14.

From Our General Spring Meeting of Ministers and Elders, Held in Philadelphia, for Pennsylvania and New-Jersey, by Adjournments, from the 21st of the Third-month to the 24th of the same, inclusive, 1778. To Our Friends and Brethren in Religious Professions. Philadelphia: n.p., 1778.

Frost, J. William. *The Quaker Origins of Antislavery.* Norwood, PA: Norwood Editions, 1980.

———, ed. *The Keithian Controversy in Early Pennsylvania.* Norwood, PA: Norwood Editions, 1980.

"The Germantown Protest." In *Unity from Diversity: Extracts from Selected Pennsylvania Colonial Documents, 1681 to 1780, in Commemoration of the Tercentenary of the Commonwealth,* compiled and edited by Louis M. Waddell, 36–37. Harrisburg, PA: Pennsylvania Historical and Museum Commission, 1980.

The Goshenhoppen Registers, 1741–1819. Baltimore: Genealogical Publishing Co., 1984.

Graydon, Alexander. *Memoirs of His Own Time, With Reminiscences of the Men and Events of the Revolution.* Edited by John Stockton Littell. Philadelphia: Lindsay & Blakiston, 1846.

Hinke, William J., ed. *Life and Letters of the Rev. John Philip Boehm, Founder of the Reformed Church in Pennsylvania, 1683–1749.* Philadelphia: Publication of the Sunday School Board of the Reformed Church of the United States 1916.

Hinshaw, William Wade. *Encyclopedia of Quaker Genealogy.* 6 vols. Ann Arbor, MI: Edwards Brother, 1936–1950.

Hoag, Joseph. *Journals of the Life of Joseph Hoag, Containing his remarkable Vision.* Auburn, NY: Knapp and Peck, Printers, 1861. Reprint, London: A. W. Bennett, 1862.

"Höhn's Church Records, 1745–1805." *Publications of the Genealogical Society of Pennsylvania* 5 (1912): 53–109.

Holy Bible. Revised Standard Version.

Journal of the House of Representatives of the Commonwealth of Pennsylvania . . . . 1776–1781. Philadelphia: n.p., 1782.

"Law About Education." In *The Statutes at Large of Pennsylvania from 1682 to 1700.* Vol. 1: 1682 to 1700, compiled by Robert L. Cable, 84. Harrisburg, PA: Legislative Reference Bureau, 2001.

"The Law About Education of Youth." In *The Statutes at Large of Pennsylvania from 1682 to 1700.* Vol. 1: 1682 to 1700, compiled by Robert L. Cable, 211–12. Harrisburg, PA: Legislative Reference Bureau, 2001.

Letter, Peter Spycker to ???, 28 November 1757. *Pennsylvania Magazine of History and Biography* 32 (1908): 311–12.

Letter, William Reeser to the Committee of Safety, 11 September 1775. *Pennsylvania Archives,* 1st ser., vol. 4, edited by Samuel Hazard, 653. Harrisburg, PA: Joseph Severns & Co., 1853.

Lightfoot, T. Montgomery, comp. *Benjamin Lightfoot and His Account of An Expedition to "Tankhannink" in the Year 1770.* Sunbury, PA: Northumberland County Historical Society, 1937.

"A List of all the Roman Catholicks in Pennsylvania, 1757." *Pennsylvania Archives,* 1st ser., vol. 3, edited by Samuel Hazard, 144–45. Philadelphia: Joseph Severns & Co., 1853.

Livengood, Candy Crocker, comp. *Genealogical Abstracts of the Laws of Pennsylvania and the Statutes at Large.* Westminster, MD: Family Line Publications, 1990.

MacMaster, Richard K., et al., eds. *Conscience in Crisis: Mennonites and Other Peace Churches in America, 1739–1789, Interpretations and Documents.* Scottdale, PA: Herald Press, 1979.

Mann, W. J., et al., eds. *Nachrichten von den vereinigten deutschen Evangelisch-Lutherischen Gemeinen in Nord-America, absonderlich in Pennsylvania.* 2 vols. Allentown, PA: B, Diehl & Co., 1886; Philadelphia: P. G. C. Eisenhardt, 1895.

Minutes and Letters of the Coetus of the German Reformed Congregations in Pennsylvania, 1747–1792, Together with Three Preliminary Reports of Rev. John Philip Boehm, 1734–1744. Edited by James I. Good and William J. Hinke. Philadelphia: Reformed Church Publication Board, 1903.

"Minutes of the Committee of Berks County, 1775." *Pennsylvania Archives,* 1st ser., vol. 4, edited by Samuel Hazard, 649. Harrisburg, PA: Joseph Severns & Co., 1853.

Minutes of the Philadelphia Baptist Association, from A.D. 1707, to A.D. 1807; Being First One Hundred Years of Its Existence. Edited by A. D. Gilette. Philadelphia: Philadelphia Baptist Association, 1851.

"Minutes of the Provincial Council and Assembly of Pennsylvania." In *William Penn and the Founding of Pennsylvania, 1680–1684: A Documentary History,* edited by Jean R. Soderlund, 229–62. Philadelphia: University of Pennsylvania Press, 1983.

Minutes of the Provincial Council of Pennsylvania, from the Organization to the Termination of the Proprietary Government [Colonial Records]. 16 vols. Harrisburg, PA: Theophilus Fenn, 1838–1853.

Mittleberger, Gottlieb. *Journey to Pennsylvania.* Edited and translated by Oscar Handlin and John Clive. Cambridge, MA: Harvard University Press, 1960.

Muhlenberg, Henry Melchior. *The Journals of Henry Melchior Muhlenberg.* Edited and translated by Theodore G. Tappert and John W. Doberstein. 3 vols. Philadelphia: Muhlenberg Press, 1942–1958.

"Muster Rolls and Papers Related to the Associators and Militia of the County of Berks." In *Pennsylvania in the War of the Revolution, Associated Battalions and Militia, 1775–*

1783. Vol. 2. *Pennsylvania Archives,* 2nd ser., vol. 14, edited by William H. Egle, 253–328. Harrisburg, PA: Clarence M. Busch, State Printer, 1895.

Neumann, Joshua N., ed. and trans. "Some Eighteenth Century American Jewish Letters." *Publications of the American Jewish Historical Society* 34 (1937): 81–99.

"The Newborn." *Penn Germania* 1 (May 1912): 336–84. Translation and transcription of Weiss's *Der in der Americanischen Wildnusz . . . .*

"Officers for Berks County." *Pennsylvania Archives,* 2nd ser., vol. 9, edited by John B. Linn and William H. Egle, 784–87. Harrisburg, PA: Lane S. Hart, State Printer, 1880.

"Officers of Philadelphia County." *Pennsylvania Archives,* 2nd ser., vol. 9, edited by John B. Linn and William H. Egle, 697–741. Harrisburg, PA: Lane S. Hart, State Printer, 1880.

Owen, B. F., comp. "Papers Relating to the Founding by the 'Society for the Propagation of the Gospel in Foreign Parts,' London, of the Missions at Reading and Morlatton, Berks County, Pennsylvania." *Pennsylvania Magazine of History and Biography* 25 (1901): 372–82, 537–43.

Pastorius, Francis Daniel. "Positive Information from *America* Concerning the Country of Pennsylvania by a German Who Traveled There." In *William Penn and the Founding of Pennsylvania, 1680–1684: A Documentary History,* edited by Jean R. Soderlund, 35–38. Philadelphia: University of Pennsylvania Press, 1983.

Paul, Frederic G., and Jeffrey J. Howell, comps. *Berks County, Pennsylvania, Births, 1705–1800.* Vol. 1: 1705–1760, Vol. 2: 1760–1770, Vol. 3: 1770–1780. Reading, PA: HP Publishing, 1988–1990.

———. *Berks County, Pennsylvania Marriages, 1730–1800.* Vol. 2. Reading, PA: HP Publishing, 1987.

Penn, William. *Some Account of the Province of Pennsylvania in America; Lately Granted under the Great Seal of England to William Penn, etc. Together with Privileges and Powers necessary to the well-governing thereof. Made public for the Information of such as are or may be disposed to Transport themselves or Servants into those Parts.* London: Benjamin Clark, 1681.

Perry, William Stevens, ed. *Historical Collections Relating to the American Colonial Church.* Vol. 2: *Pennsylvania.* Hartford, CT: Church Press, 1871. Reprint, New York: AMS Press, 1969.

"Petition from Berks and Northampton Counties, 1753." *Pennsylvania Archives,* 1st ser., vol. 2, edited by Samuel Hazard, 98–99. Harrisburg, PA: Joseph Severns & Co., 1853.

Pilmore, Joseph. *The Journal of Joseph Pilmore, Methodist Itinerant; For the Years August 1, 1769 to January 2, 1774.* Edited by Frederick E. Maser and Howard T. Maag. Philadelphia: Historical Society of Pennsylvania Annual Conference of the United Methodist Church, 1969.

"Proceedings of the Committee [of Observation]." *Pennsylvania Archives,* 2nd ser., vol. 14, edited by John B. Linn and William H. Egle, 322–28. Harrisburg, PA: Clarence M. Busch, State Printer, 1896.

"Proprietary Return for the County of Berks for the Year 1767." *Pennsylvania Archives,* 3rd ser., vol. 18, edited by William H. Egle, 1–86. Harrisburg, PA: William Stanley Ray, State Printer, 1888.

Reckitt, William. *Some Account of the Life and Gospel Labours of William Reckitt, Late of Lincolnshire in Great Britain.* London: James Phillips, 1776. Reprint, Philadelphia: Joseph Crukshank, 1783.

Record of Indenture of Individuals Bound Out as Apprentices, Servants, Etc. and of Germans and Other Redemptioners in the Office of the Mayor of the City of Philadelphia,

October 3, 1771, to October 5, 1773. Lancaster, PA: Pennsylvania German Society, 1907.

"Register of Property of the Inhabitants of Berks County, 1779." *Pennsylvania Archives,* 3rd ser., vol. 18, edited by William H. Egle, 175–301. Harrisburg, PA: William Stanley Ray, State Printer, 1898.

"Remonstrance and Protest of the Prisoners in Mason's Lodge, 1777." *Pennsylvania Archives,* 1st ser., vol. 6, edited by Samuel Hazard, 509. Harrisburg, PA: Joseph Severns & Co., 1853.

"Return and Assessment for the County of Berks for the Year 1780." *Pennsylvania Archives,* 3rd ser., vol. 18, edited by William H. Egle, 305–430. Harrisburg, PA: William Stanley Ray, State Printer, 1898.

"Return and Assessment for the County of Berks for the Year 1781." *Pennsylvania Archives,* 3rd ser., vol. 18, edited by William H. Egle, 431–557. Harrisburg, PA: William Stanley Ray, State Printer, 1898.

Roberts, Moses. "The Journal of Moses Roberts—Quaker Minister of Oley." *Historical Review of Berks County* 8 (1943): 70–74.

Rules of Discipline and Christian Advices of the Yearly Meeting of Friends for Pennsylvania and New Jersey. Philadelphia: Samuel Sansom, Jr., 1797.

Rush, Benjamin. *Considerations upon the Present Test-Law of Pennsylvania: Addressed to the Legislature and Freemen of the State.* Philadelphia: Hall and Sellers, 1784.

Schultze, David. *The Journals and Papers of David Schultze.* 2 vols. Translated and edited by Andrew S. Berky. Pennsburg, PA: Schwenkfelder Library, 1952.

"The *Second* Frame of Government." In *William Penn and the Founding of Pennsylvania, 1680–1684: A Documentary History,* edited by Jean R. Soderlund, 265–73. Philadelphia: University of Pennsylvania Press, 1983.

"Some Account of the Province of Pennsylvania." In *William Penn and the Founding of Pennsylvania, 1680–1684: A Documentary History,* edited by Jean R. Soderlund, 58–65. Philadelphia: University of Pennsylvania Press, 1983.

Spaeth, A., et al., eds. *Documentary History of the Evangelical Lutheran Ministerium of Pennsylvania and Adjacent States: Proceedings of the Annual Conventions from 1748 to 1821.* Philadelphia: Board of Publication of the General Council of the Evangelical Lutheran Church of North America, 1898.

State of Accounts of Jacob Morgan, Senior, Late Lieutenant of Berks County, From March 1777 to March 1780. Philadelphia: Robert Aitken, 1783.

Stoudt, John Joseph, trans. "Matthias Baumann: The New Born." *Historical Review of Berks County* 43 (1978): 136–38, 142–44, 147.

Taylor, Robert J., ed. *The Susquehannah Company Papers.* Vols. 5 and 6. Ithaca, NY: Cornell University Press, 1968.

The Testimony of the People called Quakers, given forth by a Meeting of the Representatives of said People, in Pennsylvania and New-Jersey, held at Philadelphia the twenty-fourth Day of the first Month, 1775. Philadelphia: n.p., 1775.

To our Friends and Brethren in religious Profession, in these and adjacent Provinces . . . . Let not the Fear of Suffering, Either in Person or Property, Prevail on any to Join with or Promote Any Work or Preparation for War . . . . Signed in and on Behalf of the Meeting for Sufferings, Held in Philadelphia, for Pennsylvania and New-Jersey, the 20th day of the Twelfth Month, 1776. John Pemberton, Clerk. Philadelphia: n.p., 1776.

The Transformation of Joseph Hoag. Philadelphia: Tract Association of Friends, n.d.

U.S. Department of Commerce and Labor. Bureau of the Census. *Heads of Families at the First Census of the United States Taken in the Year 1790: Pennsylvania.* Washington, D. C.: Government Printing Office, 1908.

Votes and Proceedings of the House of Representatives of the Province of Pennsylvania. Pennsylvania Archives, 8th ser. Edited by Gertrude MacKinney and Charles F. Hoban. Harrisburg, PA: 1931–1935.

Wagner, Tobias. *M. Tobias Wagners Abscheid-Rede an seine Lutherische Gemeinden in Pennsylvanien, welche er zu ünterschiedlichen Zeiten also Prediger alle 14 Tage oder 4 Wochen Bedient.* Ephrata, PA: Typis Societatis, 1759.

Walmer, Margaret B., comp. *100 Years at Warrington: York County, Pennsylvania, Quakers, Marriages, Removals, Births and Deaths.* Bowie, MD: Heritage Books, 1989.

Weiss, George Michael. *Der in der Americanischen Wildnusz Unter Menschen von verschiedenen Nationen und Religionen Hin und wieder herum gewandeldte Und verscheidentlich Angesochtene Prediger, Abgemahlet und vorgestellet in einem Gespräch mit Einem Politico und Neubegorenen Verschiedene Stuck insonderheit Die Neigeburt betreffende, Verfertiget und so Beforderung der Ehr Jesu Selbst aus eigener Erfahrung an das Licht gebracht.* Philadelphia: Andrew Bradfordt, 1729.

Woolman, John. *The Journal and Major Essays of John Woolman.* Edited by Phillips P. Moulton. New York: Oxford University Press, 1971.

Zuverlässige Beschreibung der dritten Conferenz der Evangelischen Religionen Teutsche Nation in Pennsylvania, Welche am 10, 11, und 12ten Februarii 1741/2 in Oley an Johann de Türcks Hause gehalten worden; Samt denen dieses mahl verfassten Gemein-Schlüssen. Philadelphia: B. Franklin, 1742.

Newspapers

Der Wöchentliche Pennsylvanischer Staatsbote (Philadelphia). 22 October 1776.

Neue Unpartheyische Readinger Zeitung und Anzeigs-Nachrichten (Reading). 18 June 1800.

Pennsylvania Gazette (Philadelphia). November 1755 through January 1765.

The Weekly Advertiser, of Reading, in the County of Berks. 24 March 1798.

Secondary Sources

Acrelius, Israel. *A History of New Sweden; of The Settlements on the River Delaware.* Translated by William M. Reynolds. Philadelphia: Historical Society of Pennsylvania, 1874.

Ahlstrom, Sydney E. *A Religious History of the American People.* New Haven, CT: Yale University Pres, 1972.

Albright, Raymond W. *A History of the Protestant Episcopal Church.* New York: Macmillan, 1964.

———. *Two Centuries of Reading, Pa., 1748–1948: A History of the County Seat of Berks County.* Reading, PA: Historical Society of Berks County, 1948.

Anderson, Fred. *Crucible of War: The Seven Years' War and the Fate of Empire in British North America, 1754–1766.* New York: Knopf, 2000.

Arnold, William E., III. "Anglicanism in Pennsylvania." In *Penn's Example to the Nations: 300 Years of the Holy Experiment,* edited by Robert Grant Crist, 22–32. Harrisburg: Pennsylvania Council of Churches, 1987.

Ashton, Dianne. *Jewish Life in Pennsylvania.* Pennsylvania History Studies, No. 25. University Park: Pennsylvania Historical Association, 1998.

Bacon, Margaret Hope. *The Quiet Rebels: The Story of Quakers in America.* New York: Basic Books, 1969. Reprint, Philadelphia: New Society Publishers, 1985.

Bailyn, Bernard. *Voyagers to the West: A Passage in the Peopling of America on the Eve of the Revolution.* New York: Random House, 1986.

Bakeless, John. *Daniel Boone: Master of the Wilderness.* New York: William Morrow, 1939. Reprint, Harrisburg, PA: Stackpole, 1967.

Ball, Duane Eugene. "Dynamics of Population and Wealth in Eighteenth-Century Chester County, Pennsylvania." *Journal of Interdisciplinary History* 6 (1976): 621–44.

Barbour, Hugh, and J. William Frost. "George Keith." In *Dictionary of Christianity in America,* edited by Daniel G. Reid, et al., 608–9. Downers Grove, IL: InterVarsity Press, 1990.

————. *The Quakers.* Denominations in America Series, No. 3. Westport, CT: Greenwood Press, 1988.

Bartholomew, Alfred C. "The Union Church: Prophecy or Poverty?" *Der Reggeboge* 1 (July 1967): 1–9.

Bauman, Richard. *For the Reputation of Truth: Politics, Religion, and Conflict Among the Pennsylvania Quakers, 1750–1800.* Baltimore: Johns Hopkins University Press, 1971.

Becker, Laura L. "Diversity and Its Significance in an Eighteenth-Century Pennsylvania Town." In *Friends and Neighbors: Group Life in America's First Plural Society,* edited by Michael Zuckerman, 196–221. Philadelphia: Temple University Press, 1982.

Beeman, Richard R. *The Evolution of the Southern Backcountry: A Case Study of Lunenburg County, Virginia, 1746–1832.* Philadelphia: University of Pennsylvania Press, 1984.

Beeth, Howard. "'Know Thyself': The Uses of the Queries Among Early Southern Quakers." *The Southern Friend: Journal of the North Carolina Friends Historical Society* 9 (1987): 3–13.

Bertolet, Frederick J. "The Rectors of Christ Church, 1763–1936." *Historical Review of Berks County* 1 (1936): 16–18.

Bertolet, Peter G. *Fragments of the Past: Historical Sketches of Oley and Vicinity.* Oley, PA: Woman's Club of Oley Valley, 1980.

Bethke, Robert D. "Chester County Widow Wills (1714–1800): A Folklife Source." *Pennsylvania Folklife* 18 (1968): 36–40.

Beyer, George R. *Guide to the State Historical Markers of Pennsylvania.* 6th ed. Harrisburg: Pennsylvania Historical and Museum Commission, 2000.

Bi-Centennial Anniversary of the Friends' Meeting House at Merion, Pennsylvania, 1695–1895. Philadelphia: Friends' Book Association, 1895.

Bi-Centennial of Brick Meeting-House, Calvert, Cecil County, Maryland. Lancaster, PA: Wickersham Printing Co., 1902.

Bining, Arthur Cecil. *Pennsylvania Iron Manufacture in the Eighteenth Century.* 2nd ed. Harrisburg: Pennsylvania Historical and Museum Commission, 1973.

Blanco Richard L. "The Diary of Jonathan Potts: A Quaker Medical Student in Edinburgh (1766–67)." *Transactions and Studies of the College of Physicians of Philadelphia* 44 (1977): 119–30.

————. *Physician of the American Revolution: Jonathan Potts.* New York: Garland, 1979.

Bockelman, Wayne L. "Local Government in Colonial Pennsylvania." In *Town and Country: Essays on the Structure of Local Government in the American Colonies,* edited by Bruce Daniels, 216–37. Middletown, CT: Wesleyan University Press, 1978.

Bodle, Wayne. "The Myth of the Middle Colonies Reconsidered: The Process of Regionalization in Early America." *Pennsylvania Magazine of History and Biography* 107 (1989): 527–48.

———, and Jacqueline Thibaut. *Valley Forge Historical Research Report.* Valley Forge, PA: Valley Forge National Historical Park, U.S. Department of the Interior, 1980.

Bogart, W. H. *Daniel Boone, and the Hunters of Kentucky.* Philadelphia: J. B. Lippincott, 1876.

Bonomi, Patricia U. *Under the Cope of Heaven: Religion, Society, and Politics in Colonial America.* New York: Oxford University Press, 1986.

———. "'Watchful Against the Sects': Religious Renewal in Pennsylvania's German Congregations, 1720–1750." *Pennsylvania History* 50 (1983): 273–83.

———, and Peter R. Eisenstadt. "Church Adherence in the Eighteenth-Century British American Colonies. *William and Mary Quarterly,* 3rd ser., 39 (1982): 245–86.

Brecht, Samuel Kriebel, ed. *The Genealogical Record of the Schwenkfelder Families: Seekers of Religious Liberty Who Fled from Silesia to Saxony and Thence to Pennsylvania in the Years 1731 to 1737.* New York: Rand McNally, 1923.

Brinton, Howard H. *Quaker Education in Theory and Practice.* 3rd ed. Pendle Hill Pamphlet, No. 9. Wallingford, PA: Pendle Hill Publications, 1967.

Brock, Peter. *Pacifism in the United States From the Colonial Era to the First World War.* Princeton, NJ: Princeton University Press, 1968.

———. *The Quaker Peace Testimony, 1660 to 1914.* York, UK: Sessions Book Trust, 1990.

Bronner, Edwin B. "Inter-colonial Relations among Quakers before 1750." *Quaker History* 56 (1967): 3–17.

———. *The Quakers: A Brief Account of Their Influence on Pennsylvania.* Pennsylvania History Studies, No. 2. Rev. ed. University Park: Pennsylvania Historical Association, 1986.

———. *William Penn's "Holy Experiment": The Founding of Pennsylvania, 1681–1701.* New York: Temple University Press, 1962.

Brooks, Tim, and Earle Marsh. *The Complete Directory to Prime Time Network TV Shows.* 5th ed. New York: Ballantine Books, 1992.

Brown, Ira V. *The Negro in Pennsylvania History.* Pennsylvania History Studies, No. 11. University Park: Pennsylvania Historical Association, 1970.

———. "Pennsylvania's Antislavery Pioneers, 1688–1776." *Pennsylvania History* 55 (1988): 59–77.

Browning, Charles H. *Welsh Settlement of Pennsylvania.* Philadelphia: W. J. Campbell, 1912.

Brumbaugh, Martin Grove. *A History of the German Baptist Brethren in Europe and America.* Elgin, IL: Brethren Publishing House, 1899.

Brunhouse, Robert L. *The Counter-Revolution in Pennsylvania, 1776–1790.* Harrisburg: Pennsylvania Historical and Museum Commission, 1971.

"Bucks County Quakers and the Revolution." *Pennsylvania Genealogical Magazine* 24 (1966): 291–99.

Burnett, Robert. "The Jewish Community of Colonial Reading." *Historical Review of Berks County* 36 (1972): 58–59, 79–80.

Casino, Joseph J. "Anti-Popery in Colonial Pennsylvania." *Pennsylvania Magazine of History and Biography* 105 (1981): 279–309.

Claussen, W. Edmunds. "The Impact of the Revolutionary War Upon Exeter Friends." *Historical Review of Berks County* 36 (1972): 52–53.

———. "Reading Doctor at Fort Ticonderoga." *Historical Review of Berks County* 40 (Winter 1974–75): 8–11, 22–27.

Cochran, Thomas C. *Pennsylvania: A Bicentennial History.* New York: W. W. Norton, 1978.

Commissioners of Berks County. *Berks County, Pennsylvania: Its History and Government.* 3rd ed. Kutztown, PA: Kutztown Publishing, 1980.

Connelly, Monsignor James F. "The Roman Catholic Church in Pennsylvania." In *Penn's Example to the Nations: 300 Years of the Holy Experiment,* edited by Robert Grant Crist, 105–23. Harrisburg: Pennsylvania Council of Churches, 1987.

Cook, Kenneth L. "Gaius and Mary Dickinson: A Quaker Couple in the American Revolution." *Historical Review of Berks County* 67 (Winter 2001–02): 35–38.

———. "Glimpses of Life in a Frontier Friends Meeting." *Historical Review of Berks County* 60 (1995): 122–23, 126–27, 138–42.

Crauderueff, Elaine. *War Taxes: Experiences of Philadelphia Yearly Meeting Quakers through the American Revolution.* Wallingford, PA: Pendle Hill Publications, 1989.

Crist, Robert Grant. "The Colonial Period: An Introduction." In *Penn's Example to the Nations: 300 Years of the Holy Experiment,* edited by Robert Grant Crist, 3–21. Harrisburg: Pennsylvania Council of Churches, 1987.

Croll, P. C. *Annals of the Oley Valley in Berks County, Pa.: Over Two Hundred Years of Local History of an American Canaan.* Reading, PA: Reading Eagle Press, 1926.

Currey, Cecil B. "Eighteenth-Century Evangelical Opposition to the American Revolution: The Case of the Quakers." *Fides et Historia* 1 (Fall 1971): 17–35.

Daiutolo, Robert, Jr. "The Early Quaker Perception of the Indian." *Quaker History* 72 (1983): 103–19.

Davidson, Robert L. D. *War Comes to Quaker Pennsylvania, 1682–1756.* New York: Columbia University Press, 1957.

Dech, Elmer A. "The North Heidelberg Church." *Historical Review of Berks County* 34 (1969): 85–86, 101–04.

Densmore, Christopher. "The Dilemma of Quaker Anti-Slavery: The Case of Farmington Quarterly Meeting, 1836–1860." *Quaker History* 82 (1993): 80–91.

Dieffenbach, Ray J., and George L. Irgang. "John Conrad Dieffenbach of Tulpehocken." *Pennsylvania Folklife* 40 (1990): 42–48.

Dives, Mary P. "Alexander A. Murray, D.D." *Historical Review of Berks County* 4 (1939): 34–39.

Dodd, A. H. "The Background of Welsh Quaker Migration to Pennsylvania." *Journal of the Merioneth Historical and Record Society* 3 (1958): 111–27.

Doerflinger, Thomas M. *A Vigorous Spirit of Enterprise: Merchants and Economic Development in Revolutionary Philadelphia.* Chapel Hill: University of North Carolina Press, 1986.

Doherty, Robert W. *The Hicksite Separation: A Sociological Analysis of Religious Schism in Early Nineteenth Century America.* New Brunswick, NJ: Rutgers University Press, 1967.

Doncaster, L. Hugh. *Quaker Organisation and Business Meetings.* London: Friends Home Service Committee, 1958.

Dowless, Don. "Preserving the Quaker Way: Guidance of Quaker Social Life by the Monthly Meeting in Colonial North Carolina." *The Southern Friend: Journal of the North Carolina Friends Historical Society* 11 (1989): 1–16.

Drake, Thomas E. *Quakers and Slavery in America.* New Haven, CT: Yale University Press, 1950.

Dubbs, Joseph Henry. "A History of the Reformed Church, German." In *A History of the Reformed Church, Dutch, the Reformed Church, German, and The Moravian Church in the United States.* Vol. 8, *The American Church History Series.* New York: Christian Literature Co., 1895.

———. *The Reformed Church in Pennsylvania. Proceedings of the Pennsylvania German Society* Vol. 11, Part 10. Lancaster, PA: New Era Printing Co., 1902.

DuHamel, William, ed. *Historical Annals of Christ Church (Formerly called St. Mary's) Reading, Berks County, Diocese of Bethlehem, Issued in Conjunction with their Celebration of the Centenary of the Parish.* Douglassville, PA: Church Press, 1927.

Dunaway, Wayland F. "The English Settlers in Colonial Pennsylvania." *Pennsylvania Magazine of History and Biography* 52 (1928): 317–41.

Duncan, Louis C. *Medical Men in the American Revolution, 1775–1783.* Carlisle Barracks, PA: Medical Field Service School, 1931.

Dunn, Mary Maples. "Women of Light." In *Women of America: A History,* edited by Carol Ruth Berkin and Mary Beth Norton, 115–33. Boston: Houghton Mifflin, 1979.

Durnbaugh, Donald F. "Religion and Revolution: Options in 1776." *Pennsylvania Mennonite Heritage* 1 (July 1978): 2–9.

The Early Swedes and St. Gabriel's Church, Founded 1720, Douglassville, Pennsylvania. n.p., n.d.

Ebersole, Mark C. "Abolition Divides The Meeting House: Quakers and Slavery in Early Lancaster County." *Journal of the Lancaster County Historical Society* 102 (Spring 2000): 2–27.

Eckert, Jack, comp. *Guide to the Records of Philadelphia Yearly Meeting.* Haverford and Swarthmore, PA: Records Committee of Philadelphia Yearly Meeting, 1989.

Elliott, Errol T. *Quakers on the American Frontier: A History of the Westward Migrations, Settlements, and Developments of Friends on the American Continent.* Richmond, IN: Friends United Press, 1969.

Ellis, John Tracy. *Catholics in Colonial America.* Baltimore: Helicon Press, 1965.

Endy, Melvin B, Jr. *William Penn and Early Quakerism.* Princeton, NJ: Princeton University Press, 1973.

Erb, Peter C. "Schwenkfelders in Pennsylvania." In *Penn's Example to the Nations: 300 Years of the Holy Experiment,* edited by Robert Grant Crist, 125–28. Harrisburg: Pennsylvania Council of Churches, 1987.

Eshelman, John E. "Anthony and Mary Lee: Pioneer Quakers of Oley." *Historical Review of Berks County* 17 (1952): 113–16.

———. "Descendants of Moses and Deborah Starr—Early Quaker Settlers of Maiden Creek Valley." *Historical Review of Berks County* 12 (1947): 67–74.

———. "A History of Catawissa Friends' Meeting, and Some of Its Earliest Members." *Berwick Historical Society, Publications* 1 (1940): 4–20.

———. "Quaker Marriage Certificate of 1736." *Historical Review of Berks County* 14 (1949): 77–79.

———. "The Society of Friends, and Their Meeting Houses, in Berks County." *Historical Review of Berks County* 19 (1954): 104–09, 117–23.

Eustace, Nicole. "Vehement Movements: Debates on Emotion, Self, and Society during the Seven Years' War in Pennsylvania." *Explorations in Early American Culture* 5 (2000): 79–117.

Evans, Charles. *American Bibliography.* 14 vols. Chicago: Blakely Press, 1903–1959. Reprint, New York: Peter Smith, 1941–1959.

Falkenstein, George W. *The German Baptist Brethren or Dunkers. Proceedings of the Pennsylvania German Society,* Vol. 10, Part 8. Lancaster, PA: New Era Printing Co., 1900.

Faragher, John Mack. *Daniel Boone: The Life and Legend of an American Pioneer.* New York: Henry Holt, 1992.

Fawcett, Thomas H. "Quaker Migration from Pennsylvania and New Jersey to Hopewell Monthly Meeting, 1732–1759." *Friends' Historical Association Bulletin* 26 (1937): 102–08.

Fink, Leo Gregory. "The First Catholics in Reading." *Historical Review of Berks County* 33 (1968): 92–97, 109.

"The First Printed Protest Against Slavery in America." *Pennsylvania Magazine of History and Biography* 13 (1889): 265–70.

Fischer, David Hackett. *Albion's Seed: Four British Folkways in America.* New York: Oxford University Press, 1989.

Fisher, Sydney George. *The Making of Pennsylvania: An Analysis of the Elements of the Population and the Formative Influences That Created One of the Greatest of the American States.* Philadelphia: J. B. Lippincott, 1896.

Fiske, John. *The Dutch and Quaker Colonies in America.* 2 vols. Boston: Houghton Mifflin, 1899.

Fletcher, Stevenson Whitcomb. *Pennsylvania Agriculture and Country Life, 1640–1840.* Harrisburg: Pennsylvania Historical and Museum Commission, 1971.

Florin, John. *The Advance of Frontier Settlement in Pennsylvania, 1638–1850: A Geographic Interpretation.* Papers in Geography, No. 14. University Park: Pennsylvania State University, Department of Geography, 1977.

Forbes, Susan M. "Quaker Tribalism." In *Friends and Neighbors: Group Life in America's First Plural Society,* edited by Michael Zuckerman, 145–73. Philadelphia: Temple University Press, 1982.

Fortenbaugh, Robert. "Pennsylvania: A Study in Religious Diversity." *Pennsylvania History* 4 (1937): 88–102.

Foster, Joseph S. "Francis Parvin." In *Lawmaking and Legislators in Pennsylvania: A Biographical Dictionary.* Vol. 2: *1710–1756,* edited by Craig W. Horle, et al., 808–12. Philadelphia: University of Pennsylvania Press, 1997.

Frantz, John B. "The Awakening of Religion among the German Settlers in the Middle Colonies." *William and Mary Quarterly,* 3rd ser., 33 (1976): 266–88.

———. "'Prepare Thyself . . . to Meet the Lord Thy God': Religion in Pennsylvania During the Revolution." *Pennsylvania Heritage* 2 (June 1976): 28–32.

———. "Religion in the Middle Colonies: A Model for the Nation." *Journal of Regional Culture* 2 (Fall/Winter 1982): 9–22.

———. "The Religious Development of the Early German Settlers in 'Greater Pennsylvania': The Shenandoah Valley of Virginia." *Pennsylvania History* 68 (Winter 2001): 66–100.

———. "Religious Freedom: Key to Diversity." *Pennsylvania Heritage, Tercentenary Issue* (1981): 10–18.

―――. "Schwenkfelders and Moravians in America." In *Schwenkfelders in America: Papers Presented at the Colloquium on Schwenckfeld and the Schwenkfelders,* edited by Peter C. Erb, 101–11. Pennsburg, PA: Schwenkfelder Library, 1987.

―――. "United Church of Christ." In *Penn's Example to the Nations: 300 Years of the Holy Experiment,* edited by Robert Grant Crist, 129–46. Harrisburg: Pennsylvania Council of Churches, 1987.

Franz, George W. *Paxton: A Study of Community Structure and Mobility in the Colonial Pennsylvania Backcountry.* New York: Garland, 1989.

Frost, J. William. "The Origins of the Quaker Crusade against Slavery." *Quaker History* 67 (1978): 42–58.

―――. *A Perfect Freedom: Religious Liberty in Pennsylvania.* University Park: Pennsylvania State University Press, 1990.

―――. "Quaker Books in Colonial Pennsylvania." *Quaker History* 80 (1991): 1–23.

―――. *The Quaker Family in Colonial America: A Portrait of the Society of Friends.* New York: St. Martin's Press, 1973.

―――. "William Penn's Experiment in the Wilderness: Promise and Legend." *Pennsylvania Magazine of History and Biography* 107 (1983): 577–606.

Fry, Jacob. *The History of Trinity Lutheran Church, Reading, Pa., 1751–1894.* Reading, PA, 1894.

Gambino, Anthony J., and John R. Palmer. *Management Accounting in Colonial America.* New York: National Association of Accountants, 1976.

Gerhard, Elmer Schultz. "The First Preacher of Universalism in Pennsylvania." *Historical Review of Berks County* 14 (1948): 15–19.

Gertney, Kenneth. "The Formation of Berks County." *Historical Review of Berks County* 37 (1972): 88–89, 101–09.

Gipson, Lawrence H. *The British Empire Before the American Revolution.* 15 vols. New York: Knopf, 1936–1970.

Glatfelter, Charles H. *Pastors and People: German Lutheran and Reformed Churches in the Pennsylvania Field, 1717–1793.* 2 vols. Breinigsville, PA: Pennsylvania German Society, 1980–1981.

Good, James I. *History of the Reformed Church in the United States, 1725–1792.* Reading, PA: Daniel Miller, 1899.

Gough, Robert George. "The Myth of the 'Middle Colonies': An Analysis of Regionalization in Early America." *Pennsylvania Magazine of History and Biography* 107 (1983): 393–419.

Gragg, Larry Dale. *Migration in Early America: The Virginia Quaker Experience.* Ann Arbor, MI: UMI Research Press, 1980.

Grant, Phyllis S. "Exeter Friends' Meeting, 1737–1787." *Historical Review of Berks County* 47 (1982): 62–63, 71, 74–77, 79–80.

Greenberg, Douglas. "The Middle Colonies in Recent American Historiography." *William and Mary Quarterly,* 3rd ser., 36 (1978): 509–30.

Greene, Evarts B., and Virginia D. Harrington. *American Population Before the Federal Census of 1790.* New York: Columbia University Press, 1932.

Guenther, Karen. "Berks County." In *Beyond Philadelphia: The American Revolution in the Pennsylvania Hinterland,* edited by John B. Frantz and William Pencak, 67–84. University Park: Pennsylvania State University Press, 1998.

―――. "A Crisis of Allegiance: Berks County, Pennsylvania Quakers and the War for Independence." *Quaker History* 90 (Fall 2001): 15–34.

————. "The Development of Education in Eighteenth-Century Reading, Pennsylvania." *Historical Review of Berks County* 53 (1988): 167–71, 180–85.

————. "'A Faithful Soldier of Christ': The Career of the Reverend Dr. Alexander Murray, Missionary to Berks County, Pa., 1762–1778." *Historical Magazine of the Protestant Episcopal Church* 55 (1986): 5–20.

————. "A 'Garden for the Friends of God': Religious Diversity in the Oley Valley to 1750." *Pennsylvania Folklife* 33 (1984): 138–44.

————. "'A Restless Desire': Geographic Mobility and Members of Exeter Monthly Meeting, Berks County, Pa., 1710–1789." *Pennsylvania History* 70 (2003): 331–60.

————. "Social Control and Exeter Monthly Meeting of the Religious Society of Friends, 1737–1789: A Research Note." *Pennsylvania History* 57 (1990): 150–163.

————. "The World of Moses Boone: The Economic Activity of a Berks County Tanner in the 1780s." *Historical Review of Berks County* 68 (Winter 2002–03): 19–23.

Hamilton, J. Taylor. "The Confusion at Tulpehocken." *Transactions of the Moravian Historical Society* 4 (1891–95): 235–73.

————. "The Moravian Work at Oley, Berks County, Pennsylvania." *Transactions of the Moravian Historical Society* 13 (1942): 8–18.

————, and Kenneth G. Hamilton. *History of the Moravian Church: The Renewed Unitas Fratrum, 1722–1957.* Bethlehem, PA and Winston-Salem, NC: Interprovincial Board of Christian Education, Moravian Church in America, 1967.

Handy, Robert T. "The Contribution of Pennsylvania to the Rise of Religious Liberty in America." In *Quest For Faith, Quest for Freedom: Aspects of Pennsylvania's Religious Experience,* edited by Otto Reimherr, 19–28. Selinsgrove, PA: Susquehanna University Press, 1987.

Harbaugh, Henry. *The Life of Rev. Michael Schlatter; With a Full Account of his Travels and Labors among the Germans in Pennsylvania, New Jersey, Maryland, and Virginia, Including his Services as Chaplain in the French and Indian War, and in the War of the Revolution, 1716 to 1790.* Philadelphia: Lindsay & Blakiston, 1857.

Heiss, Willard, ed. *[Quaker] Biographical Sketches of Ministers and Elders and other Concerned Members of the Yearly Meeting in Philadelphia, [1682–1800].* Indianapolis, IN, 1972.

Henderson, Rodger C. *Community Development and the Revolutionary Transition in Eighteenth-Century Lancaster, Pennsylvania.* New York: Garland, 1990.

Hershberger, Guy Franklin. "Pacifism and the State in Colonial Pennsylvania." *Church History* 8 (1939): 54–74.

Hill, George Canning. *Daniel Boone: The Pioneer of Kentucky: A Biography.* Dayton, OH: Edward Canby, 1859.

Hinderaker, Eric, and Peter C. Mancall. *At the Edge of Empire: The Backcountry in British North America.* Baltimore: Johns Hopkins University Press, 2003.

Hinshaw, Seth B. "Agents for Truth: Traveling Ministers and the Establishment of the Quaker Movement in North Carolina." *The Southern Friend: Journal of the North Carolina Friends Historical Society* 15 (1993): 5–20.

Hirst, Margaret E. *The Quakers in Peace and War: An Account of Their Peaceable Principles and Practice.* New York: George H. Doran, 1923. Reprint, New York: Garland, 1972.

Hitz, Alex M. "The Wrightsborough Quaker Town and Township in Georgia." In *Quaker Records in Georgia: Wrightsborough, 1772–1793, Friendsborough, 1776–1777,* compiled by Robert Scott Davis, Jr., 10–14. Augusta, GA: Augusta Genealogical Society, 1986.

Holton, James L. *Berks County: The Green Diamond of Pennsylvania.* Chatsworth, CA: Windsor Publications, 1993.

Hopkins, Leroy T. "The Germantown Protest: Origins of Abolitionism among the German Residents of Southeastern Pennsylvania." *Yearbook of German-American Studies* 23 (1988): 19–29.

Horle, Craig W. "Moses Starr." In *Lawmaking and Legislators in Pennsylvania: A Biographical Dictionary.* Vol. 2: *1710–1756,* edited by Craig W. Horle, et al., 944–50. Philadelphia: University of Pennsylvania Press, 1997.

Hostetler, John A. *Amish Society.* 4th ed. Baltimore: Johns Hopkins University Press, 1993.

Howell, Jeffrey J., comp. *Genealogical Guide to Berks County Churches.* Reading, PA, 1984.

Hummel, William W. "The Emergence of a Ruling Elite in Berks County." *Historical Review of Berks County* 49 (1984): 101–06, 115–20, 124.

———. "Religion on a Moving Frontier: The Berks County Area, 1700–1748." *Pennsylvania Heritage* 4 (March 1978): 22–26.

Hunter, William A. *Forts on the Pennsylvania Frontier, 1753–1758.* Harrisburg: Pennsylvania Historical and Museum Commission, 1960.

Illick, Joseph E. *Colonial Pennsylvania: A History.* New York: Charles Scribner's Sons, 1976.

Ingle, H. Larry. *Quakers in Conflict: The Hicksite Reformation.* Knoxville: University of Tennessee Press, 1986.

Inventory of Church Archives, Society of Friends in Pennsylvania. Philadelphia: Friends Historical Association, 1941.

Ireland, Owen S. "Germans Against Abolition: A Minority's View of Slavery in Revolutionary Pennsylvania." *Journal of Interdisciplinary History* 4 (1973): 685–706.

Jable, J. T. "Pennsylvania's Early Blue Laws: A Quaker Experiment in the Suppression of Sport and Amusements." *Journal of Sport History* 1 (1974): 107–21.

Jacobs, Henry Eyster. *A History of the Evangelical Lutheran Church in the United States. The American Church History Series,* Vol. 4. New York: Christian Literature Co., 1893.

James, Sydney V. "The Impact of the American Revolution on Quakers' Ideas about Their Sect." *William and Mary Quarterly,* 3rd ser., 19 (1962): 360–82.

———. *A People Among Peoples: Quaker Benevolence in Eighteenth-Century America.* Cambridge, MA: Harvard University Press, 1963.

———. "Quaker Meetings and Education in the Eighteenth Century." *Quaker History* 51 (1962): 87–102.

Jeffries, Theodore W. "Thomas Barton, Victim of the Revolution." *Journal of the Lancaster County Historical Society* 81 (1977): 39–64.

Jennings, Francis. *Empire of Fortune: Crowns, Colonies, and Tribes in the Seven Years War in America.* New York: W. W. Norton, 1988.

Jennings, Judith. "Mid-Eighteenth-Century British Quakerism and the Response to the Problem of Slavery." *Quaker History* 66 (1977): 23–40.

Jensen, Joan M. *Loosening the Bonds: Mid-Atlantic Farm Women, 1750–1850.* New Haven, CT: Yale University Press, 1986.

———. "Not Only Ours But Others: The Quaker Teaching Daughters of the Mid-Atlantic, 1790–1850." *History of Education Quarterly* 24 (Spring 1984): 3–20.

Johnson, George Lloyd, Jr. *The Frontier in the Colonial South: South Carolina Backcountry, 1736–1800.* Westport, CT: Greenwood Pres, 1997.

Johnson, Richard. "Blacks in Western Berks—1760–1930." *Historical Review of Berks County* 60 (1995): 179–81, 187–89, 192.

———. "Slaves and Indentured Blacks in Berks County Before 1800." *Historical Review of Berks County* 37 (Winter 1971–72): 8–14.

———. "Slaves in Berks County before 1850." *Historical Review of Berks County* 61 (1996): 159, 161, 184–89.

Jones, Alfred S. "Schools." *Historical Review of Berks County* 45 (1980): 136–43, 157–60.

Jones Rufus M. *The Quakers in the American Colonies.* London: Macmillan, 1911. Reprint, New York: Russell & Russell, 1962.

Kashatus, William C., III. *Conflict of Conviction: A Reappraisal of Quaker Involvement in the American Revolution.* Lanham, MD: University Press of America, 1990.

———. "The Friends Fight for Freedom." *Pennsylvania Heritage* 14 (Summer 1998): 4–9.

———. "What Love Can Do: William Penn's Holy Experiment in Education." *Pennsylvania Heritage* 15 (Spring 1989): 4–9.

Kaylor, Earl C., Jr. "Church of the Brethren." In *Penn's Example to the Nations: 300 Years of the Holy Experiment,* edited by Robert Grant Crist, 45–53. Harrisburg: Pennsylvania Council of Churches, 1987.

Keim, Henry May. "The Episcopal Church in Reading, Pa." *Pennsylvania Magazine of History and Biography* 4 (1880): 66–78.

Keim, Mary L. "Growth of the Baptist Denomination in Pennsylvania." In *Penn's Example to the Nations: 300 Years of the Holy Experiment,* edited by Robert Grant Crist, 33–40. Harrisburg: Pennsylvania Council of Churches, 1987.

Kelley, Donald Brooks. "The Evolution of Quaker Theology and the Unfolding of a Distinctive Quaker Ecological Perspective in Eighteenth-Century America." *Pennsylvania History* 52 (1985): 242–53.

———. "Friends and Nature in America: Toward an Eighteenth-Century Quaker Ecology." *Pennsylvania History* 53 (1986): 257–72.

Kelley, Joseph J., Jr. *Pennsylvania: The Colonial Years, 1681–1776.* Garden City, NY: Doubleday, 1980.

Kelsey, Rayner Wickersham. *Friends and the Indians, 1655–1917.* Philadelphia: Associated Executive Committee of Friends on Indian Affairs, 1917.

Kemp, A. F. "Early Schools in Berks County." *Historical Review of Berks County* 11 (April 1946): 66–72.

Kent, Donald H. *The French Invasion of Western Pennsylvania.* Rev. ed. Harrisburg: Pennsylvania Historical and Museum Commission, 1981.

Ketcham, Ralph L. "Conscience, War, and Politics in Pennsylvania, 1755–1757." *William and Mary Quarterly,* 3rd ser., 20 (1963): 416–39.

Kidd, H. S. *Lutherans in Berks County: Two Centuries of Continuous Organized Church Life, 1723–1923.* Kutztown, PA: William S. Rhode Publishing, 1923.

Klein, Philip S., and Ari Hoogenboom. *A History of Pennsylvania.* 2nd ed. University Park: Pennsylvania State University Press, 1980.

Klepp, Susan E. "Encounter and Experiment: The Colonial Period." In *Pennsylvania: A History of the Commonwealth,* edited by Randall M. Miller and William Pencak, 47–100. University Park: Pennsylvania State University Press; and Harrisburg: Pennsylvania Historical and Museum Commission, 2002.

Knauss, James Owen, Jr. *Social Conditions among the Pennsylvania Germans in the Eighteenth Century, as Revealed in the Newspapers Published in America. Proceedings of the Pennsylvania German Society,* Vol. 29, Part 30. Lancaster, PA: New Era Printing Co., 1922.

Kriebel, Howard Wiegner. *The Schwenkfelders in Pennsylvania: A Historical Sketch. Proceedings of the Pennsylvania German Society,* Vol. 13, Part 12. Lancaster, PA: New Era Printing Co., 1904.

Kross, Jessica. *The Evolution of an American Town: Newtown, New York, 1642–1775.* Philadelphia: Temple University Press, 1983.

———. "'If you will not drink with me, you must fight with me': The Sociology of Drinking in the Middle Colonies." *Pennsylvania History* 64 (1997): 28–55.

Landis, Elizabeth. "The Schwenkfelders and Their School System, 1764–1842." *Historical Review of Berks County* 35 (1970): 99–102, 111–16.

Lapsansky, Emma. *The Black Presence in Pennsylvania: "Making It Home."* Pennsylvania History Studies, No. 21. 2nd ed. University Park: Pennsylvania Historical Association, 2001.

Lapsansky, Emma Jones, and Anne A. Verplanck, eds. *Quaker Aesthetics: Reflections on a Quaker Elite in American Design and Consumption.* Philadelphia: University of Pennsylvania Press, 2003.

Larson, Rebecca. *Daughters of Light: Quaker Women Preaching and Prophesying in the Colonies and Abroad, 1700–1775.* Chapel Hill: University of North Carolina Press, 1999.

Lemon, James T. *The Best Poor Man's Country: A Geographical Study of Early Southeastern Pennsylvania.* New York: W. W. Norton, 1972.

———, and Gary B. Nash. "The Distribution of Wealth in Eighteenth-Century America: A Century of Change in Chester County, Pennsylvania, 1693–1802." *Journal of Social History* 1 (1968): 1–24.

Lender, Mark Edward, and James Kirby Martin. *Drinking in America: A History.* Rev. ed. New York: Free Press, 1987.

Levy, Barry. *Quakers and the American Family: British Settlement in the Delaware Valley, 1650–1765.* New York: Oxford University Press, 1988.

Lichtenthaeler, Frank E. "Storm Blown Seeds of Schoharie." *Pennsylvania German Folklife Society* 9 (1941): 3–105.

Lippincott, Horace Mather. *Abington Friends Meeting and School, 1682–1949.* Philadelphia: n.p., 1949.

Livingood, Frederick George. *Eighteenth Century Reformed Church Schools. Proceedings of the Pennsylvania German Society,* Vol. 38, Part 35. Norristown, PA: Norristown Press, 1930.

Lockhart, Audrey. "The Quakers and Emigration from Ireland to the North American Colonies." *Quaker History* 77 (1988): 67–92.

Lodge, Martin E. "The Crisis of the Churches in the Middle Colonies, 1720–1750." *Pennsylvania Magazine of History and Biography* 95 (1971): 195–210.

Lofaro, Michael A. *The Life and Adventures of Daniel Boone.* Lexington: University Press of Kentucky, 1978.

Logan, Samuel T., Jr. "Gilbert Tennent." In *Dictionary of Christianity in America,* edited by Daniel G. Reid, et al., 1164–65. Downers Grove, IL: InterVarsity Press, 1990.

MacMaster, Richard K. *Land, Piety, Peoplehood: The Establishment of Mennonite Communities in America, 1683–1790.* Scottdale, PA: Herald Press, 1985.

———. "Neither Whig nor Tory: The Peace Churches in the American Revolution." *Fides et Historia* 9 (1977): 8–24.

Main, Gloria L. "Probate Records as a Source for Early American History." *William and Mary Quarterly,* 3rd ser., 32 (1975): 89–99.

Mancall, Peter C. *Valley of Opportunity: Economic Culture Along the Upper Susquehanna, 1700–1800.* Ithaca, NY: Cornell University Press, 1991.

Manross, William W. *A History of the American Episcopal Church, 1600–1915.* New York: Morehouse-Gorham, 1950.

Marietta, Jack D. "Attitudes of 18th-C[entury] American Friends toward Sin and Evil." *Quaker Religious Thought* 22 (1987): 17–30.

———. "Conscience, the Quaker Community, and the French and Indian War." *Pennsylvania Magazine of History and Biography* 95 (1971): 3–27.

———. "The Growth of Quaker Self-Consciousness in Pennsylvania, 1720–1748." In *Seeking the Light: Essays in Quaker History in Honor of Edwin B. Bronner,* edited by J. William Frost and John M. Moore, 79–104. Swarthmore, PA: Friends Historical Association, 1986.

———. "A Note on Quaker Membership." *Quaker History* 59 (1970): 40–43.

———. "Quaker Family Education in Historical Perspective." *Quaker History* 63 (1974): 3–16.

———. *The Reformation of American Quakerism, 1748–1783.* Philadelphia: University of Pennsylvania Press, 1984.

———. "Wealth, War and Religion: The Perfecting of Quaker Asceticism, 1740–1783." *Church History* 43 (1974): 230–41.

Martin, A. L. *Gwynedd Monthly Meeting of the Religious Society of Friends, 1699–1949.* Lansdale, PA: A. L. Martin, 1950.

Marty, Martin E. "Ethnicity: The Skeleton of Religion in America." *Church History* 41 (1972): 5–21.

Maser, Frederick E. "Methodists." In *Penn's Example to the Nations: 300 Years of the Holy Experiment,* edited by Robert Grant Crist, 196–218. Harrisburg: Pennsylvania Council of Churches, 1987.

Matthews, Sara. "'Set Thy House in Order': Inheritance Patterns of the Colonial Germans." *Pennsylvania Folklife* 33 (1983): 36–40.

Maurer, Charles Lewis. *Early Lutheran Education in Pennsylvania. Proceedings of the Pennsylvania German Society,* Vol. 40. Norristown, PA: Norristown Press, 1932.

Maxey, David W. "The Honorable Proprietaries v. Samuel Wallis: 'A Matter of Great Consequence' in the Province of Pennsylvania." *Pennsylvania History* 70 (Autumn 2003): 361–395.

Maxson, Charles Hartshorn. *The Great Awakening in the Middle Colonies.* Chicago: University of Chicago Press, 1920. Reprint, Gloucester, MA: Peter Smith, 1958.

Mazzenga, Maria. "John Churchman and Quaker Reform in Colonial Pennsylvania: A Search for Spiritual Purity." *Quaker History* 83 (1994): 71–98.

McCarthy, Koren P. "Daniel Boone: The Formative Years." *Pennsylvania Heritage* 11 (Winter 1985): 34–37.

McCusker, John J., and Russell R. Menard. *The Economy of British America, 1607–1789.* Chapel Hill: University of North Carolina Press, 1985.

McKenna, John J., Jr. "Early Irish in Berks County." *Historical Review of Berks County* 17 (1951): 20–21, 25–29.

———. "Early Welsh in Berks County." *Historical Review of Berks County* 15 (1950): 179–86.

Mead, Frank S., Samuel S. Hill, and Craig D. Atwood. *Handbook of Denominations in the United States.* 11th ed. Nashville, TN: Abingdon Press, 2001.

Meginness, John F. *Otzinachson: A History of the West Branch Valley of the Susquehanna.* 2 vols. Philadelphia: H. B. Ashmead, 1857. Reprint, Williamsport, PA: Gazette and Bulletin Publishing House, 1889.

Meinig, D. W. *The Shaping of America: A Geographical Perspective on 500 Years of History.* Vol. 1: *Atlantic America, 1492–1800.* New Haven, CT: Yale University Press, 1986.

Mekeel, Arthur J. "The Founding Years, 1681–1789." In *Friends in the Delaware Valley: Philadelphia Yearly Meeting, 1681–1981,* edited by John M. Moore, 14–53. Haverford, PA: Friends Historical Association, 1981.

————. *The Relation of the Quakers to the American Revolution.* Washington, D. C.: University Press of America, 1979.

Merrell, James H. *Into the American Woods: Negotiators on the Pennsylvania Frontier.* New York: W. W. Norton, 1999.

Merritt, Jane T. *At the Crossroads: Indians and Empires on a Mid-Atlantic Frontier, 1700–1763.* Chapel Hill: University of North Carolina Press, 2003.

Metz, Katherine B. *Historical Furnishings Report, Washington's Headquarters, Valley Forge National Historical Park.* Harpers Ferry, WV: Harpers Ferry Center, National Park Service, U.S. Department of the Interior, 1989.

Michel, Jack. "The Philadelphia Quakers and the American Revolution: Reform in the Philadelphia Monthly Meeting." *Working Papers from the Regional Economic Historical Research Center* 3, no. 4 (1980): 54–109.

Miller, Daniel. "Conrad Weiser as a Monk." *Transactions of the Historical Society of Berks County* 3 (1910–16): 169–81.

————. "The Early Moravian Settlements in Berks County." *Transactions of the Historical Society of Berks County* 2 (1905–10): 309–14.

————. *History of the Reformed Church in Reading, Pa.* Reading, PA: Daniel Miller, 1905.

Miller, Randall M., and William Pencak. *Pennsylvania: A History of the Commonwealth.* University Park: Pennsylvania State University Press; and Harrisburg: Pennsylvania Historical and Museum Commission, 2002.

Miner, Charles A. *History of the Wyoming Valley.* Philadelphia: Crissy, 1845.

Mitchell, Robert D. *Commercialism and Frontier: Perspectives on the Early Shenandoah Valley.* Charlottesville: University Press of Virginia, 1977.

Montgomery, Morton L. *History of Berks County in Pennsylvania.* Philadelphia: Everts, Peck & Richards, 1886.

————. *History of Berks County, Pennsylvania, in the Revolution, from 1774 to 1783.* Reading, PA: Charles F. Haage, 1894.

————. *Political Hand-Book of Berks County, Pennsylvania, 1752–1883.* Reading, PA: Press of B. F. Owen, 1883.

————. *School History of Berks County in Pennsylvania.* Philadelphia: J. B. Rodgers Printing Co., 1889.

Moore, John M. "The Society of Friends in Pennsylvania." In *Penn's Example to the Nations: 300 Years of the Holy Experiment,* edited by Robert Grant Crist, 55–60. Harrisburg: Pennsylvania Council of Churches, 1987.

Morgan, Edmund S. "The Puritan Ethnic and the Coming of the American Revolution." In *The Reinterpretation of the American Revolution, 1763–1789,* edited by Jack P. Greene, 235–51. New York: Harper & Row, 1968.

Morgan, Ted. *Wilderness at Dawn: The Settling of the North American Continent.* New York: Simon & Schuster, 1993.

Myers, Albert Cook. *Immigration of the Irish Quakers into Pennsylvania, 1682–1750, with Their Early History in Ireland.* Swarthmore, PA: 1902.

Nash, Gary B. *Quakers and Politics: Pennsylvania, 1681–1726.* Rev. ed. Boston: Northeastern University Press, 1993.

————. *The Urban Crucible: Social Change, Political Consciousness, and the Origins of the American Revolution.* Cambridge, MA: Harvard University Press, 1979.

————, and Jean R. Soderlund. *Freedom by Degrees: Emancipation in Pennsylvania and Its Aftermath.* New York: Oxford University Press, 1991.

Nelson, E. Clifford. *The Lutherans in North America.* Philadelphia: Fortress Press, 1975.

Nelson, Vernon H. "The Moravian Contribution to the Tulpehocken Region." *Der Reggeboge* 7 (July 1973): 3–16.

Nicholson, Gary L. "The Growth of Methodism Behind the Frontier: Old Forest Chapel and the Upper Valley of the Conestoga Creek." *Historical Review of Berks County* 41 (1976): 140–42, 162–64.

Nobles, Gregory H. "Breaking into the Backcountry: New Approaches to the Early American Frontier, 1750–1800." *William and Mary Quarterly,* 3rd ser., 46 (1989): 641–70.

Nolan, J. Bennett. "Conrad Weiser's Inventory." *Pennsylvania Magazine of History and Biography* 56 (1932): 265–69.

————. *The Foundation of the Town of Reading in Pennsylvania.* Reading, PA: Edward Pengelly & Bro., 1929.

————. "The Plaintive Record of a Distracted Missionary." In *Early Narratives of Berks County,* 17–34. Reading, PA: Historical Society of Berks County, 1927.

Österberg, Bertil O. *Colonial America on Film and Television: A Filmography.* Jefferson, NC: McFarland & Co., 2001.

Offutt, William M., Jr. *"Of Good Laws" and "Good Men": Law and Society in the Delaware Valley, 1680–1770.* Urbana: University of Illinois Press, 1995.

Olson, Alison. "The Lobbying of London Quakers for Pennsylvania Friends." *Pennsylvania Magazine of History and Biography* 117 (1993): 131–52.

Oudinot, Ronald W. "The Life and Influence of Andreas Rudman." *Historical Review of Berks County* 44 (1979): 59, 62–64, 80.

Ousterhout, Anne M. "Controlling the Opposition in Pennsylvania During the American Revolution." *Pennsylvania Magazine of History and Biography* 105 (1981): 3–34.

————. "Frontier Vengeance: Connecticut Yankees vs. Pennamites in the Wyoming Valley." *Pennsylvania History* 62 (1995): 330–63.

————. *A State Divided: Opposition in Pennsylvania to the American Revolution.* Westport, CT: Greenwood Press, 1987.

Owens, William A. *A Fair and Happy Land.* New York: Charles Scribner's Sons, 1975.

Pencak, William. "The Promise of Revolution, 1750–1800." In *Pennsylvania: A History of the Commonwealth,* edited by Randall M. Miller and William Pencak, 101–152. University Park: Pennsylvania State University Press; and Harrisburg: Pennsylvania Historical and Museum Commission, 2002.

————, and Daniel Richter, eds. *Friends and Enemies in Penn's Woods: Colonists, Indians, and the Racial Construction of Pennsylvania.* University Park: Pennsylvania State University Press, 2004.

Pendleton, Philip E. *Oley Valley Heritage: The Colonial Years, 1700–1775.* Birdsboro, PA: Pennsylvania German Society and Oley, PA: Oley Valley Heritage Association, 1994.

————. "The Origin of the Swedish Settlement at Old Morlatton." *Historical Review of Berks County* 53 (1988): 129–33, 141, 143.

Pennington, Edgar Legaré. "The Anglican Clergy of Pennsylvania in the American Revolution." *Pennsylvania Magazine of History and Biography* 63 (1939): 401–31.

Pole, J. R. "Historians and the Problem of Early American Democracy." *American Historical Review* 67 (1962): 626–46.

Quinter, Edward, comp. *Most Blessed Sacrament Church, Bally, Pennsylvania, originally known as St. Paul's Chapel of Goshenhoppen, Berks County, Pennsylvania.* n.p., 1976.

Rapp, David H. "Philip Jacob Michael: Ecclesiastical Vagabond or 'Echt Reformirte' Pastor." *Pennsylvania Folklife* 28 (1979): 14–26.

Rhoads, Willard R. *History of the Catawissa Quaker Meeting at Catawissa, Columbia County, Pa., and the Roaring Creek Quaker Meeting near Numidia, Columbia County, Pa., Including the Quaker Activities Leading to Their Establishment.* Numidia, PA, 1963.

Richards, Louis. "Swedish Settlement at Morlatton." *Transactions of the Historical Society of Berks County* 3 (1910–16): 125–33.

Richter, Daniel K. *Facing East from Indian Country: A Native History of Early America.* Cambridge, MA: Harvard University Press, 2001.

Roberts, Ellwood. *Old Richland Families.* Norristown, PA: Morgan R. Wills, 1898.

Roeber, A. G. "The Origins and Transfer of German-American Concepts of Property and Inheritance." *Perspectives in American History,* n.s., 3 (1987): 115–71.

————. *Palatines, Liberty, and Property: German Lutherans in Colonial British America.* Baltimore: Johns Hopkins University Press, 1993.

Rothermund, Dietmar. *The Layman's Progress: Religious and Political Experience in Colonial Pennsylvania, 1740–1770.* Philadelphia: University of Pennsylvania Press, 1961.

Rupp, I. Daniel. *History of the Counties of Berks and Lebanon . . . .* Lancaster, PA: Gilbert Hills, Proprietor, 1844.

Russ, William A., Jr. *How Pennsylvania Acquired Its Present Boundaries.* Pennsylvania History Studies, No. 8. University Park: Pennsylvania Historical Association, 1966.

Russell, Marvin F. "Thomas Barton and Pennsylvania's Colonial Frontier." *Pennsylvania History* 46 (1979): 313–34.

Ruth, John L. *Maintaining the Right Fellowship: A Narrative Account of Life in the Oldest Mennonite Community in North America.* Scottdale, PA: Herald Press, 1984.

————. "Mennonite Reflections on Schwenkfelders." In *Schwenkfelders in America: Papers Presented at the Colloquium on Schwenckfeld and the Schwenkfelders,* edited by Peter C. Erb, 163–172. Pennsburg, PA: Schwenkfelder Library, 1987.

————. "Mennonites." In *Penn's Example to the Nations: 300 Years of the Holy Experiment,* edited by Robert Grant Crist, 85–89. Harrisburg: Pennsylvania Council of Churches, 1987.

Rutman, Darrett B., and Anita H. Rutman. *A Place in Time: Middlesex County, Virginia, 1640–1750.* New York: W. W. Norton, 1984.

Ryerson, Richard A. "Portrait of a Colonial Oligarchy: The Quaker Elite in the Pennsylvania Assembly, 1729–1776." In *Power and Status: Essays on Officeholding in Colonial America,* edited by Bruce C. Daniels, 106–35. Middletown, CT: Wesleyan University Press, 1986.

Sachse, Julius F. *The German Sectarians of Pennsylvania, 1708–1800.* 2 vols. Philadelphia: 1899–1900.

Salmon, Marylynn. *Women and the Law of Property in Early America.* Chapel Hill: University of North Carolina Press, 1986.

Schaeffer, Paul N. "Slavery in Berks County." *Historical Review of Berks County* 6 (1941): 110–15.

Schattschneider, David A. "The Moravians in Pennsylvania." In *Penn's Example to the Nations: 300 Years of the Holy Experiment,* edited by Robert Grant Crist, 90–96. Harrisburg: Pennsylvania Council of Churches, 1987.

Schmauk, Theodore Emanuel. *A History of the Lutheran Church in Pennsylvania (1683– 1820). Proceedings of the Pennsylvania German Society,* Vol. 11, Part 9, Vol. 12, Part 9. Lancaster, PA: New Era Printing Co., 1902–1903.

Schrott, Lambert. *Pioneer German Catholics in the American Colonies (1734–1784).* United States Catholic Historical Society, Monograph Series 13. New York: United States Catholic Historical Society, 1933.

Schwartz, Sally. *"A Mixed Multitude": The Struggle for Toleration in Colonial Pennsylvania.* New York: New York University Press, 1987.

———. "Religious Pluralism in Colonial Pennsylvania." In *Appalachian Frontiers: Settlement, Society, and Development in the Preindustrial Era,* edited by Robert D. Mitchell, 52–68. Lexington: University Press of Kentucky, 1991.

———. "William Penn and Toleration: Foundations of Colonial Pennsylvania." *Pennsylvania History* 50 (1983): 284–312.

Seitz, Ruth Hoover. *Pennsylvania's Historic Places.* Intercourse, PA: Good Books, 1989.

Shammas, Carole. "Constructing a Wealth Distribution from Probate Records." *Journal of Interdisciplinary History* 9 (1978): 297–307.

Sharpless, Isaac. "Book V: The Quakers in Pennsylvania." In Rufus M. Jones, *The Quakers in the American Colonies,* 415–580. London: Macmillan, 1911.

———. *A History of Quaker Government in Pennsylvania.* 2 vols. Philadelphia: T. S. Leach & Co., 1899–1900.

Silent Witness: Quaker Meetinghouses in the Delaware Valley, 1695 to the Present. Philadelphia: Philadelphia Yearly Meeting of the Religious Society of Friends, 2002.

Silverman, Sharon Hernes. "A Kentucky Frontiersman's Pennsylvania Roots: The Daniel Boone Homestead." *Pennsylvania Heritage* 24 (Summer 1998): 30–30.

———. *Pennsylvania Trail of History Guide: Daniel Boone Homestead.* Mechanicsburg, PA: Stackpole Books, 2000.

Smith, C. Henry. *The Mennonite Immigration to Pennsylvania in the Eighteenth Century. Proceedings of the Pennsylvania German Society,* Vol. 35, Part 33. Norristown, PA: Norristown Press, 1929.

Smith, Joseph. *A Descriptive Catalogue of Friends' Books, or Books Written by Members of the Society of Friends, Commonly Called Quakers, From Their First Rise to the Present Time, Interspersed with Critical Remarks, and Including All Writings by Authors Before Joining and by Those After Having Left the Society, Whether Adverse or Not, as far as known.* 2 vols. London: Joseph Smith, 1867. Reprint, New York: Kraus, 1970.

Smith, Merril. *Breaking the Bonds: Marital Discord in Pennsylvania, 1730–1830.* New York: New York University Press, 1991.

Snydacker, Daniel. "Kinship and Community in Rural Pennsylvania, 1749–1820." *Journal of Interdisciplinary History* 13 (1982): 41–61.

Soderlund, Jean R. "Black Importation and Migration into Southeastern Pennsylvania, 1682–1810." *Proceedings of the American Philosophical Society* 133 (1989): 144–53.

————. *Quakers and Slavery: A Divided Spirit.* Princeton, NJ: Princeton University Press, 1985.

————. "Women's Authority in Pennsylvania and New Jersey Quaker Meetings, 1681–1760." *William and Mary Quarterly,* 3rd ser., 44 (1987): 722–49.

Somers, Susan. "Conditions and Contributions of Berks County Religions to America During the Eighteenth Century." *Historical Review of Berks County* 40 (Winter 1974–75): 12–15, 34–36, 38.

Specht, Neva Jean. "Removing to a Remote Place: Quaker Certificates of Removal and their Significance in Trans-Appalachian Migration." *Quaker History* 91 (Spring 2002): 45–69.

Spraker, Hazel Atterbury, comp. *The Boone Family: A Genealogical History of the Descendants of George and Mary Boone Who Came to America in 1717.* Rutland, VT: Tuttle Company, Publishers, 1922. Reprint, Baltimore: Genealogical Publishing Co., 1982.

Spyker, Suzanne. "Francis Parvin." *Historical Review of Berks County* 24 (Winter 1958–59): 16.

Stabb, John Albin. "Why Did the Colonial Swedish Lutheran Congregations Become Episcopalian?" *Anglican and Episcopal History* 61 (1992): 419–32.

Stapleton, Amon. "The Huguenot Element in the Settlement of Berks County." *Transactions of the Historical Society of Berks County* 2 (1905–10): 386–401.

Stefon, Frederick J. "The Wyoming Valley." In *Beyond Philadelphia: The American Revolution in the Pennsylvania Hinterland,* edited by John B. Frantz and William Pencak, 133–52. University Park: Pennsylvania State University Press, 1998.

Stillé, Charles J. "The Attitude of the Quakers in the Provincial Wars." *Pennsylvania Magazine of History and Biography* 10 (1886): 283–315.

————. "Religious Tests in Colonial Pennsylvania." *Pennsylvania Magazine of History and Biography* 9 (1885): 365–406.

Stoltzfus, Grant M. "Amish Backgrounds in Berks County." *Historical Review of Berks County* 16 (1951): 38–42.

————. "History of the First Amish Mennonite Communities in America." *Mennonite Quarterly Review* 28 (1954): 237–45.

Stoudt, John Baer. "Great Religious Revival Which Occurred in the Oley Valley 175 Years Ago." *Transactions of the Historical Society of Berks County* 3 (1910–16): 255–70.

Stoudt, John Joseph. "Count Zinzendorf and the Pennsylvania Congregation of God in the Spirit: The First American Oecumenical Movement." *Church History* 9 (1940): 366–80.

————. "Daniel and Squire Boone." *Historical Review of Berks County* 1 (1936): 108–12.

————. "Daniel and Squire Boone: A Study in Historical Symbolism." *Pennsylvania History* 3 (1936): 27–40.

————. "Early Pennsylvania Religious Movements." *American-German Review* 8 (April 1942): 9–10, 31.

Stout, Harry S. "Ethnicity: The Vital Center of Religion in America." *Ethnicity* 2 (1975): 204–24.

Straub, Jean S. "Quaker School Life in Philadelphia Before 1800." *Pennsylvania Magazine of History and Biography* 89 (1965): 447–58.

Sutherland, Stella H. *Population Distribution in Colonial America.* New York: Columbia University Press, 1936.

Thayer, Theodore. *Pennsylvania Politics and the Growth of Democracy, 1740–1776.* Harrisburg: Pennsylvania Historical and Museum Commission, 1953.

Theiss, Lewis Edwin. "How the Quakers Came to Central Pennsylvania." *Northumberland County Historical Society, Proceedings* 21 (1957): 67–70.

Tolles, Frederick B. *Meeting House and Counting House: The Quaker Merchants of Colonial Philadelphia*. Chapel Hill: University of North Carolina Press, 1948.

———. "Nonviolent Contact: The Quaker and the Indians." *American Philosophical Society, Proceedings* 107 (1963): 93–101.

———. *Quakers and the Atlantic Culture*. New York: Macmillan, 1960.

———. "Quietism Versus Enthusiasm: The Philadelphia Quakers and the Great Awakening." *Pennsylvania Magazine of History and Biography* 69 (1945): 26–49.

Tomes, Nancy. "The Quaker Connection: Visiting Patterns among Women in the Philadelphia Society of Friends, 1750–1800." In *Friends and Neighbors: Group Life in America's First Plural Society*, edited by Michael Zuckerman, 174–95. Philadelphia: Temple University Press, 1982.

Treese, Lorett. *Valley Forge: Making and Remaking a National Symbol*. University Park: Pennsylvania State University Press, 1995.

Trinterud, Leonard J. *The Forming of an American Tradition: A Re-examination of Colonial Presbyterianism*. Philadelphia: Westminster Press, 1949.

Trussell, John B. B., Jr. *William Penn: Architect of a Nation*. Harrisburg: Pennsylvania Historical and Museum Commission, 1983.

Tully, Alan. "Economic Opportunity in Mid-Eighteenth Century Rural Pennsylvania." *Social History/Histoire Sociale* 9 (1976): 111–28.

———. "Englishmen and Germans: National-Group Contact in Colonial Pennsylvania." *Pennsylvania History* 45 (1978): 237–56.

———. "Ethnicity, Religion, and Politics in Early America." *Pennsylvania Magazine of History and Biography* 107 (1983): 491–536.

———. *Forming American Politics: Ideals, Interests, and Institutions in Colonial New York and Pennsylvania*. Baltimore: Johns Hopkins University Press, 1994.

———. "Literacy Levels and Educational Development in Rural Pennsylvania, 1729–1775." *Pennsylvania History* 39 (1972): 301–12.

———. "Politics and Peace Testimony in Mid-Eighteenth Century Pennsylvania." *Canadian Review of American Studies* 13 (1982): 159–77.

———. *William Penn's Legacy: Politics and Social Structure in Provincial Pennsylvania, 1726–1755*. Baltimore: Johns Hopkins University Press, 1977.

Turner, Edward Raymond. *Slavery in Pennsylvania*. Baltimore: Lord Baltimore Press, 1911.

Turner, Frederick Jackson. "The Significance of the Frontier in American History." *Annual Report of the American Historical Association for the Year 1893*, 199–227. Washington, D. C.: Government Printing Office, 1894.

Two Hundred Fifty Years of Quakerism at Birmingham, 1690–1940. West Chester, PA: Birmingham Friends, 1940.

Two-Hundredth Anniversary of the Founding of London Grove Meeting by the Society of Friends at London Grove, Pennsylvania, tenth month, third, 1914. Philadelphia: Innes and Sons, 1914.

Waddell, Louis M. "Berks County: Diamond of the Schuylkill Valley." *Pennsylvania Heritage* 17 (Fall 1991): 4–11.

———, and Bruce D. Bomberger. *The French and Indian War in Pennsylvania, 1753–1763: Fortification and Struggle During the War for Empire*. Harrisburg: Pennsylvania Historical and Museum Commission, 1996.

Waldenrath, Alexander. "Goshenhoppen (Bally), Early Center of Roman Catholicism in Berks County." *Historical Review of Berks County* 39 (1974): 93–95, 111–15.

Wallace, Paul A. W. *Conrad Weiser, Friend of Colonist and Mohawk.* Philadelphia: University of Pennsylvania Press, 1945.

———. *Daniel Boone in Pennsylvania.* Rev. ed. Harrisburg: Pennsylvania Historical and Museum Commission, 2002.

———. *Indians in Pennsylvania.* Rev. ed. Harrisburg: Pennsylvania Historical and Museum Commission, 1981.

Walvin, James. *The Quakers: Money and Morals.* London: John Murray, 1997.

Ward, Matthew C. *Breaking the Backcountry: The Seven Years' War in Virginia and Pennsylvania, 1754–1765.* Pittsburgh, PA: University of Pittsburgh Press, 2003.

Wax, Darold D. "Reform and Revolution: The Movement Against Slavery and the Slave Trade in Revolutionary Pennsylvania." *Western Pennsylvania Historical Magazine* 57 (1974): 403–29.

Weber, Samuel Edwin. *The Charity School Movement in Colonial Pennsylvania.* Philadelphia: Press of George F. Lasher, 1905.

Weinlick, John R. "Moravianism in the American Colonies." In *Continental Pietism and Early American Christianity,* edited by F. Ernest Stoeffler, 123–63. Grand Rapids, MI: William B. Eerdmans Publishing, 1976.

Weis, Frederick Lewis. *The Colonial Churches and the Colonial Clergy of the Middle and Southern Colonies, 1607–1776.* Lancaster, MA: Society of the Descendants of the Colonial Clergy, 1938.

Weiser, Frederick S. "The Lutherans." In *Penn's Example to the Nations: 300 Years of the Holy Experiment,* edited by Robert Grant Crist, 74–84. Harrisburg: Pennsylvania Council of Churches, 1987.

Wellenreuther, Hermann. "The Political Dilemma of the Quakers in Pennsylvania, 1681– 1748." *Pennsylvania Magazine of History and Biography* 94 (1970): 135–72.

———. "The Quest for Harmony in a Turbulent World: The Principle of 'Love and Unity' in Colonial Pennsylvania Politics." *Pennsylvania Magazine of History and Biography* 107 (1983): 537–76.

Wentz, Abdel Ross. "Relations Between the Lutheran and Reformed Churches in the Eighteenth and Nineteenth Centuries." *Lutheran Church Quarterly* 6 (1933): 300–27.

Wertenbaker, Thomas Jefferson. *The Founding of American Civilization: The Middle Colonies.* New York: Charles Scribner's Sons, 1938. Reprint, New York: Cooper Square Publishers, 1963.

Wetzel, Daniel J. *Two Hundredth Anniversary History of the First Reformed Church.* Reading, PA, 1953.

White, Joyce L. "The Affiliation of Seven Swedish Lutheran Churches with the Episcopal Church." *Historical Magazine of the Protestant Episcopal Church* 46 (1977): 171–86.

Whiteman, Maxwell. "Pennsylvania Jewry." In *Penn's Example to the Nations: 300 Years of the Holy Experiment,* edited by Robert Grant Crist, 61–73. Harrisburg: Pennsylvania Council of Churches, 1987.

Williams, Richard T., and Mildred C. Williams, comps. *Index of Berks County, Pennsylvania Wills and Administration Records, 1752–1850.* Danboro, PA, 1973.

Wilson, Lisa. *Life After Death: Widows in Pennsylvania, 1750–1850.* Philadelphia: Temple University Press, 1992.

Witman, Anna Houck. *1773 Bicentennial 1973, St. Paul's United Methodist Church, Geigertown, Pennsylvania.* n.p., 1973.

Wolf, Stephanie Grauman. *Urban Village: Population, Community, and Family Structure in Germantown, Pennsylvania, 1683–1800*. Princeton, NJ: Princeton University Press, 1976.

Wood, Jerome H., Jr. *Conestoga Crossroads: Lancaster, Pennsylvania, 1730–1790*. Harrisburg: Pennsylvania Historical and Museum Commission, 1979.

Woody, Thomas. *Early Quaker Education in Pennsylvania*. New York: Teachers College, Columbia University, 1920.

Wulf, Karin A. *Not All Wives: Women of Colonial Philadelphia*. Ithaca, NY: Cornell University Press, 2000.

Yoder, Don. "The Schwenkfelder-Quaker Connection: Two Centuries of Inter-denominational Friendship." In *Schwenkfelders in America: Papers Presented at the Colloquium on Schwenckfeld and the Schwenkfelders*, edited by Peter C. Erb, 113–62. Pennsburg, PA: Schwenkfelder Library, 1987.

Yogg, Michael R. *"The Best Place for Health and Wealth": A Demographic and Economic Analysis of the Quakers of Pre-Industrial Bucks County, Pennsylvania*. New York: Garland, 1988.

Zuckerman, Michael. "Introduction: Puritans, Cavaliers, and the Motley Middle." In *Friends and Neighbors: Group Life in America's First Plural Society*, edited by Michael Zuckerman, 3–25. Philadelphia: Temple University Press, 1982.

Index